Crime Control and Justice in America

Searching for Facts and Answers

Paul W. Keve

The Last Quarter Century:
A Guide to the Issues and
the Literature, no. 3
Edited by John H. Whaley, Jr.

American Library Association
Chicago and London 1995

Cover design by Richmond Jones

Composed by Precision Typographers
in Times Roman and Melior on a
Miles 33 typesetting system

Printed on 50-pound Springfield, a
pH-neutral stock, and bound in
10-point C1S cover stock
by Braun-Brumfield, Inc.

The p███ ████ ██ ██ ██blication me███ ██ ███ ████████ements of American
National Standard for ███████████ ████es—Permanence of Paper for Printed Library
Materials, ANSI Z39.48-1984. ∞

Library of Congress Cataloging-in-Publication Data

Keve, Paul W.
    Crime control and justice in America : searching for facts and
answers / Paul W. Keve.
        p.   cm. — (The Last quarter century : a guide to the issues
and the literature ; no. 3)
    Includes index.
    ISBN 0-8389-0644-3
    1. Criminal justice, Administration of—United States.
    2. Criminal justice, Administration of—United States—Bibliography.
    3. Crime—United States.   4. Crime—United States—Bibliography.
    I. Series : Last quarter century ; no. 3.
    HV9950.K48   1995
    364.973—dc20   94-45360

Printed in the United States of America.

99 98 97 96 95   5 4 3 2 1

Contents

Foreword

D aily we are bombarded with statistical information and blood-curdling rhetoric about the continuing problem of crime on our streets and, increasingly, in our boardrooms. Paul W. Keve explains and explores the complex issue of crime in our modern urban and industrial society. Drawing upon his many years in both correctional administration and in the classroom, he shows us how the criminal justice system works and why, in some instances, it doesn't.

As he makes clear, the components of the criminal justice system—police, courts, and correctional institutions—interrelate; decisions made by one always have some impact on the other, and often with unforeseen consequences.

Crime Control and Justice in America is the third title in the series "The Last Quarter Century: A Guide to the Issues and the Literature." Like the other books in the series, it provides a synthesis of recent scholarship, supported by an annotated bibliography for each chapter, and a general resource guide for researching the library. Most of the citations in the bibliographies are to books and articles published within the last decade. The resource guide will lead students and other researchers to library sources that update their knowledge of topics covered in the book. Briefly annotated citations to reference tools and journals will guide the reader to sources found in most academic and many public libraries.

John H. Whaley, Jr.
Series Editor

Preface

The process of defining and administering criminal justice policy is exceedingly complex and continually evolving. Both practical and philosophical adjustments emerge from the confrontation between newly progressive social theories and the more elemental public instinct for protection from crime and the punishment of offenders. No single book can fully cover the subject in its bewildering complexity, but it can introduce students to the basic premises that generally underlie the public debates on this area of policy. Criminal justice, as here addressed, covers the criminal justice system components of law enforcement, courts, and corrections; in addition, related public initiatives such as crime prevention and services to crime victims will be covered. Whereas all these topics have rich and interesting historical backgrounds, history will not be a part of this writing, except when brief historical reference is needed for a better understanding of present conditions or controversies.

Of special significance in any study of this area of public policy is the perspective of the so-called criminal justice *system*. Whereas it can be argued that in fact the criminal justice system is not a system, but a collection of separately operating services, it does nonetheless have much of the character of a system. This is more important than policymakers sometimes realize. As policymakers make material changes in one component of the criminal justice system, they often find it necessary to revise policy in other components to undo the damage done by the unilateral action. Courts are independent from police, as police are independent from corrections, and each of these components operates with its own different parts and agencies, quite independent of each other. But all the system parts are vitally interrelated in the sense that new policy adopted in one may have unexpected and substantive effects in another. In this book, though the various chapters are devoted to the separate components of the criminal justice system, their interacting relationships are essential.

In addition to the appraisal of criminal justice as a system rather than separate parts, this account seeks to give a perspective on one aspect of criminal justice which, though intangible, is of special importance to the long-term interests of a great democracy. It lies in the fact that the principles basic to the criminal laws, and the integrity of a country's obedience to those principles, help to define citizenship and civil rights. The acid test for the freedoms promised in the Bill of Rights comes when these freedoms must be accorded to persons who are "unpopular," whether for inherent prejudicial reasons (race, religion, ethnic identity, etc.), or because of activities considered outrageous by the public.

When the justice system must deal with a defendant accused of some notorious criminal act that has incited public anger, basic civil rights are too easily a casualty in the handling of such a case. But if despite public outrage, the system holds firm in the protection of such an individual's rights, this reinforces society's dedication to the rule of law, and reassures citizens that should they themselves ever become subjects of prosecution, their interests and rights will always be protected.

One aspect of criminal justice that is suggested incidentally by these chapters is its close kinship with political science. Because the essential concerns of political office seekers are likely to be incompatible with the best correctional measures to some degree, it is possible that significant progress in the control of crime and correction of offenders will eventually result not only from improved treatment programs, but also from discovery of ways to make these programs more compatible with democratic political processes.

The general plan of this book is to present in the first eight chapters an account of the components of the criminal justice system and the social and political conditions affecting them. The final chapter reviews the interrelationship of these same components and significant new directions they are taking. A bibliography of relevant source materials is supplied with the endnotes of each chapter, with major items annotated. It is assumed that the student will use this book as a starting point for further study of the criminal justice system; to assist this research, the appendix presents a compendium of pertinent resources, including organizations and agencies as well as conventional library sources, computerized library catalogs, and electronic databases.

The content of this work has derived mainly from my own experience of over a half century in the general field of criminal justice. In addition to administrative service with corrections agencies in three states, my experience has included teaching, occasional projects in survey and consultative work, staff training, and research or program development for many agencies throughout the country and abroad. To update and supplement the knowledge of criminal justice functions thus gained, the preparation of this work has entailed inquiries of many professionals who are experts in their respective corners of the criminal justice field. I have thanked them individually as they shared with me their wisdom, and again I say to them collectively that their help has been indispensable and sincerely appreciated.

CHAPTER 1

The Search for Understanding
of Crime

I n 1766 an aide to Catherine the Great, Empress of all the Russias, wrote on her behalf to a twenty-eight-year-old scholar in Milan, Italy, inviting him to come to Moscow and help in the daunting task of reforming Russian criminal laws. Though flattered and tempted by the invitation, the shy young Cesare Beccaria chose not to leave his comfortable home for the uncertainties of service in Russia. He had recently become famous throughout Europe for his seminal book, *On Crimes and Punishment,* which presented such a logical, fresh view on needed reforms of the criminal law that many of its principles are yet today fundamental to our practice of fairness and due process in the prosecution of criminal defendants.[1]

Beccaria's perceptive ideas help to introduce the issues to be examined in this chapter, including theories of the causes of crime and the ways that society's response to the criminal has reflected its understanding of those causes. An improved knowledge of the causal factors should affect public policy not only regarding crime control measures, but also may revise some definitions of crime. The intricate and ever-changing social factors that continually shape society's perception of what is criminal will be a focus of this opening discussion.

In the nearly two-and-a-half centuries since Beccaria, new knowledge and new practices have proliferated at an accelerating pace in a highly technological society. In such a dynamic context public policy must be constantly reexamined and adapted to the changing technology and new insights regarding deviant behavior. Policy must adjust to new definitions of crime and changing attitudes about punishment, and through it all must make steady progress in achieving fairness for accused offenders at the same time that maximum protection from crime is sought for all citizens.

1

Seeking Rational Understanding of Crime

Early criminal codes in the western world developed as patchworks of old habits, religious dogma, superstitions, and prejudices, unrestricted by any precise or clear definitions. Beccaria presumed that criminal offenders acted in rational ways, committing their crimes for the sake of calculated personal advantage. Punishment, consequently, should be just severe enough to offset the advantage gained by the crime. The specific reforms he proposed, radical at the time, included such points as:

> The criminal laws should be clear and precise and no one should be prosecuted for a crime that is not defined and published as such in law.
> Presumption of innocence should be assumed at each stage of prosecution.
> The defendant should be judged by his or her peers.
> Every aspect of the prosecution must be open to public observation, with no secret indictments or trials, as this is the only way to protect fairness of the system.
> Punishments must be defined in law, limited, and proportionate to the crime.
> The use of torture must be abolished.
> Capital punishment must be abolished. (Maestro 1973, 22–27)

In advocating these reforms Beccaria was hoping partly for enhanced deterrence of crime, but also was acting on his feeling that basic humanity in the law was a virtue in itself. He saw that the lack of logic and system in the criminal law was causing many people to be victimized through torture, wrongful convictions, and excessively harsh penalties. "If in defining the rights of man and of truth I should help to rescue from the agonies of death one victim of tyranny and ignorance, both equally fatal, the blessings and tears of that single innocent man will console me for the contempt of mankind." But it also appealed to his sense of logic to argue that rational criminal laws would be better understood by the people, and, "the greater the number of those who understand them and have in their hands the sacred code of the laws, the fewer will be the crimes committed." (Beccaria as quoted by Maestro 1973, 21–22)

The first major challenge to Beccaria's theory of crime causation and control came a little more than a century later when Cesare Lombroso, an Italian doctor, concluded from his research that crime had organic causes. His assertion that criminal offenders had anatomical characteristics that could be explained as being atavistic, or inherited throwbacks to more primitive ancestors, influenced the thinking of criminologists for many years.[2] Although his 1876 book, *Criminal Man,* contradicted Beccaria's view of the causes of criminal behavior, it did not weaken respect for Beccaria's legal principles.

Lombroso's findings remained influential until gradually repudiated by researchers early in the twentieth century. Notwithstanding the substantial departures from the theories of both these pioneers, it is striking how their ideas presaged modern thinking. Beccaria's legal theories have matured in the legal concepts of due process, whereas Lombroso's search for organic causes of crime is echoed today in the research into possible genetic factors affecting individual cases of criminal conduct.

In distinguishing the two philosophical schools of thought, the theories shaped by Beccaria became known as the "Classical School," while Lombroso's findings led to a philosophical approach known as "Positivism." (Rennie 1978, 67–78)

The Modern Concern about Causation

It could be supposed that policymakers look for a rational understanding of the factors that cause crime so that crime control policy will be based upon this soundly reasoned knowledge. Logically, if we can understand what causes people to commit criminal acts then we can design processes of prosecution and corrective punishment best calculated to suppress crime effectively. To some degree this process will work, but it is made difficult and uncertain by the bewildering complexity of the human personality and the impossibility of identifying and controlling the myriad social forces affecting it.

The human tendency to react to crime on an emotional, subjective basis rather than a logical, rational one further complicates policy on crime and criminals. Attitudes toward capital punishment sharply illustrate the irrational character of public opinion. A 1973 nationwide Harris poll showed that more than half of the respondents said that they would support the death penalty even if shown proof that it had no deterrent value. (Bedau 1982, 74) Thus, the subjective feelings of voters carry more weight than scientific knowledge in defining policy on crime control.

Nevertheless, behavioral and social scientists search avidly for causes of crime and, if definitive explanations prove elusive, at least there is continuing progress toward useful understandings of the important factors. These can be grouped as (1) those developmental and personality problems that lead to the deviant behavior of an individual juvenile or adult offender; or (2) those broad social conditions that foster the criminal tendencies of various classes of people. As one expert

puts it, "In trying to understand nonconforming behavior, we can look
inward at the individual's mind and emotions, and we can look outward
at the society in which he or she lives." (Sykes 1978, 36) Another
says, "Scientific explanations of criminal behavior may be stated either
in terms of the processes which are operating at the moment of the
occurrence of crime, or in terms of the processes operating in the earlier
history of the criminal." (Sutherland and Cressey 1974, 74)

Causation: Theories and Theorists

An understanding of the dynamics of personality factors in the individual criminal case is likely to require insights from organic medicine
and the behavioral sciences, with the focus of study often being dysfunctional family relationships. Research by a British psychiatrist, Dr. John
Bowlby, demonstrated that children deprived of loving maternal care
for a prolonged period are likely to grow up without the capacity to
feel a normal sensitivity toward other people. As they become adults,
their lack of concern for others and their withdrawn, self-centered personalities increase the likelihood of criminal behavior. (Bowlby 1952,
32) Other researchers have carried this study further to confirm the
findings that family problems, especially defects in the mother-child
relationship, are criminogenic factors.[3]

Though findings of pathology are commonly found in individual
cases, it is also apparent that many individual offenders are essentially
normal personalities, but reacting to "abnormal" social environments.
One criminologist points out the general expert opinion that "while a
small proportion of criminal behavior is due to psychiatric disturbance,
there is in general very little difference between criminals and noncrimi-
nals. Those who break the law, it is argued, tend to show a distribution of
psychological abnormality similar to that of their law-abiding fellows."
(Sykes 1978, 37) In accord with such findings, it is evident that individual factors and the broad sociological factors overlap and must be considered together. Too many times an individual offender is found to be
essentially a normal personality adapting to an antisocial environment.

With regard to the broad social conditions, three sociologists, Emile
Durkheim, Robert K. Merton, and Edwin H. Sutherland, have constructed theories important to the modern understanding of crime causation. Durkheim's theory of anomie argues that if the group loses its
cohesiveness the individual members are less restrained and some will
be more likely to resort to criminal activity. (Durkheim 1938) Merton
points to the factor of unfulfilled expectations, the frustration of an
individual who, lacking the necessary skills, is unable to acquire the
material goods that his cultural group seems to value and expect. The

individual may resort to criminal activity as the only way to achieve the living standards of the group. (Merton 1968, 220–223) Sutherland has added the theory of "differential association," explaining how one person may receive from the people important to him or to her a preponderance of messages favoring a law-abiding style of life, while another person in a more delinquent social group may receive a preponderance of influences that reward a more criminal lifestyle. (Sutherland and Cressey 1974, 75)

A Revived Interest in Biology of Crime Causation

Scientific study, which in the early twentieth century had repudiated Lombroso's theory of inherited organic causes of crime, came full cycle late in the century as a new generation of scientists, with sophisticated new techniques, found strong hints that certain biological conditions might indeed be causal factors, or at least could predispose a person to criminal conduct. But today, though improved investigative tools are available, there are complicating elements that Lombroso could not have imagined in the research about the links between biology and crime. This has become a controversial area of study, engendering strong emotional reactions to its racial and political implications, and leaving a frustrating dilemma for policymakers.

The biology of crime causation is an area of research that promises to continue as long as modern science seems to be finding antisocial behavior rooted in either inherited or traumatic physical conditions. The infant at birth, for example, is highly vulnerable to conditions causing damage to the central nervous system (CNS), damage that can eventually emerge as any of various types of disability. One expert asserts that there is "accumulating evidence that violence and some types of criminality are associated with disorders of the central nervous system." The same author explains that "Considerable research points to associations among prenatal and perinatal complications and CNS dysfunction. Generally, early brain damage, primarily due to hypoxia (a severe lack of oxygen) may be related to later neuropsychiatric disturbances." (Denno 1990, 8) Lead poisoning, another source of damage to the nervous system, is more common than usually suspected. Because the poisoning process is unseen and subtle it leaves a family unaware of its presence until the damage is done. Whereas it does not directly cause delinquent behavior, it can induce developmental problems that exacerbate any antisocial tendencies the child might have.

Whereas the potential effects on the personality of these types of trauma have long been known to the medical field, more recently, scientists have discovered that inherited genetic makeup may also be a possible explanation for criminal proclivities in some individuals. During the early 1970s, while the country was experiencing much social unrest, and minority groups were discovering newfound militancy, scientists were at the same time rapidly advancing their understanding of human genetics. These two developments were on a collision course that would add memorably to the social stress of the time.

In the 1950s, medical scientists discovered the structure of DNA, which contains the genetic "code" that transmits physical characteristics being passed from one generation to the next. During the same period, scientists were also pursuing related research into the techniques of genetic engineering to combat disease or to improve species of either animal or vegetable life.

Those concerned with the civil liberties of disadvantaged classes were quick to see a likely sinister misuse of the new techniques. If genetic science could offer the prospect of a method to identify in advance those who were likely to be threats to public peace, there could come with it the prospect of unfair preventive controls. DNA "holds an individual's unique genetic code or profile. This genetic code contains the past history and thus dictates the future of an individual's racial and geneological makeup and influences an individual's medical and psychological makeup." (Shapiro 1990, 456) Herein lies an opportunity for the dominant social group to practice what has come to be known as racial or ethnic cleansing. As with so many technical discoveries that are implemented before the ethical implications are clear, this rapidly advancing science has incited intense controversy about the motivations of its researchers, and about the possible application of the new scientific techniques for unethical purposes.

Genetic engineering caught extra public attention and controversy for its application to crime-solving. In 1985 a British medical researcher unexpectedly found that this area of scientific inquiry could be a service to criminology by providing a new way of identifying criminals. By taking a sample of tissue or bodily fluid from an identified person and comparing that person's DNA structure with organic human residue from a crime scene, the two samples can be proved to be—or not to be—from the same person (so the genetic scientists claim). This technique has proved to be so popular that one journal reported in 1992 that "DNA fingerprinting has been admitted in evidence in more than 2000 court cases since 1988."[4]

Aside from this generally accepted technique of identification, the prospect of genetic tampering, while welcomed by some, appears ominously threatening to others. An altruistic but politically naive view presents the enticing prospect that some criminal careers might be forestalled by using genetic engineering to detect a person's predisposition to future violence and then by appling preventive controls. But this kind of scientific advance encounters the determined resistance of those who are sensitive to issues of human rights. "Proposals for the prediction of violence or other forms of undesired behavior, because they are inevitably linked with control, amount to medically legitimized preventive detention. As such, they should call up in each of us the most profound concern lest we allow our society insidiously to become a therapeutic police state." (Coleman 1985, 142)

Nevertheless there is an inevitable public response to the prospect of controlling violent behavior through some process of genetic surgery. The degree of popular interest in the subject is seen in its extensive coverage in the media. As *Time* magazine reported, "Fresh interest in the field reflects a recognition that violence has become one of the country's worst public health threats. . . . Homicide is the second most frequent cause of death among Americans between the ages of 15 and 24 (after accidents) and the most common among young black men and women. More than 2 million people are beaten, knifed, shot or otherwise assaulted each year, 23,000 of them fatally."[5]

Genetic Science in a Social Context

Though scientists seem ready and eager to probe the genetic factors that may be contributing to the tendency toward violence, political sensitivity in this area is called for, since in the past, the science of eugenics has served the ends of tyranny. The reality of this as a stumbling block to unwary policymakers was made evident when the National Institutes of Health (NIH), as part of its Human Genome Project, organized and funded a conference to be held in 1992 on the subject: Genetic Factors in Crime: Findings, Uses and Implications. It seemed an obvious topic for the NIH, which exists to oversee government spending on medical research. Many scientists, pleased about the conference, saw it as a needed opportunity to share knowledge on the subject and to stimulate further research. But others objected, and shortly before the conference was to be held the objections became so strident that the NIH withdrew the funds and allowed the conference to be canceled.[6]

Some of the prospective participants heatedly protested the suppression of proper scientific inquiry, while others, particularly members of minority groups, noted that the conference planners apparently were presupposing that some feature of the genetic structuring of an individual may predispose the person to crime. This, they thought, sounded too much like racial eugenics, and was too reminiscent of Nazi concepts of race purification, and even of white racial superiority as touted not long ago in parts of the United States.[7]

The reality of such abuses is more stark than most Americans realize. During the 1920s a strong interest developed in the use of sterilization of "undesirable" people as a means of preventing feeble-mindedness, illegitimate pregnancies, and welfare families. Virginia was especially aggressive in pursuing this solution, but "within that decade thirty state governments had passed sterilization laws, many of them based on Virginia's model. . . . A total of 8000 people were involuntarily sterilized in Virginia during those years [up to 1972] and nationally more than 60,000 people underwent the same procedure." Meanwhile, the same measures were being adopted by the Nazis in Germany, where an estimated two million people were sterilized between 1933 and 1945. "Hitler's actions were applauded by American eugenicists." (Smith 1993, 6)

The new scientific interest in eugenics, set against the history of its misuse, serves to illustrate the modern dilemma for policy planners who seek a rational path to an understanding of crime and a consequent approach to crime control. In fact, it is just that expected approach that becomes the stumbling block; inherent in the objections is the awareness that when behavioral scientists find an apparent causal factor, it will promptly become the basis for procedures to correct or control the criminal. This in turn reveals how many people mistrust theories of crime causation that focus on the individual rather than on broad sociological factors. "By dwelling on the individual offender, contend the critics, scientists divert attention from the social injustice, the poverty, and the many other problems responsible for violence." (Nelkin and Swazey 1985, 354)

Notably ironic is the coincidence that strong objections to biological explorations of crime causation are coming at the same time that significant advances are being made in scientific understanding of aberrant behavior and ways to modify it. A virtual reversal of criminal justice philosophy has in recent years turned the courts and corrections practitioners away from attempts to rehabilitate, as will be discussed in chapter 3. Instead of using new knowledge of behavior for rehabilitative purposes, public policy has in large measure turned again toward a preference for punishment of the criminal. One criminologist, optimistic about the prospects for new applications of biological psychiatry, sees much reason to hope that criminal activity could yield to medical intervention were it not for the philosophical shift. "We have given up the treatment model at a time when the behavioral sciences are about to make a major contribution to our knowledge of human behavior," he asserts. (Jeffery 1985, 45) Nevertheless, the reality is that increasing knowledge of genetics and biochemistry comes at the same time that the U.S. population has also gained a new realization of its history of racial oppression, and a corresponding realization that residual unfairness persists in many everyday practices that handicap minority persons in unsuspected subtle ways. It is certain that in such a context any policies that hold, or even just seem to hold, potential for denigration of a class of people will raise deeply felt objections.

Evolving Definitions of Crime

The average citizen may suppose simplistically that crime is crime; even if it cannot be defined, a person will always know it when he or she sees it. So why must crime be defined?

In fact, the definitions of some crimes have changed considerably from time to time, and often public policymakers have had difficulty in reaching consensus in their efforts to define crime. Of course certain basic offenses are recognized as inherently criminal in virtually any society or any generation. These are usually referred to as acts which are "wrongs in themselves," distinguishing them from acts that are crimes because they are defined as such in the statutes. Inherent wrongs would include any unprovoked action, such as assault and battery, which physically hurts another person, any theft of another person's property, and the taking of another person's life. But even with these, the fine points of their definitions change from time to time. In defining murder, for instance, public policy varies considerably from state to state and recognizes different gradations of guilt according to motivation, provocation, amount of deliberate planning as compared with the impulsive act, the degree of cruelty involved, and the degree of provocation by the victim. Punishments for homicide are graded accordingly, as they are for assaults and thefts, but definitions of theft are more complex in response to varied public attitudes about property values and personal safety. Legislators face continual demands from the public fearful of crime for fine adjustments in the criminal laws.

Defining and Counting Crimes: A Frustrating Process

One of the crimes usually thought of as a "crime in itself" is rape, an act that stands as a despicable crime in all societies and in all times. But here too, application of the law is flexible, bending to adjust to the sensibilities and prejudices of the affected public at the time and place. An insensitive law enforcement agency, skeptical of a complainant's innocence, may treat the matter lightly, as in fact has been the case for much of law enforcement history. Actually, the crime of rape often causes almost unresolvable frustrations for both victims and police. The problem starts with the fact that usually this crime is committed without witnesses, leaving it exceedingly difficult to sort through the emotional, conflicting testimony of the principals. Basic to the validity of a rape charge is forced sexual intercourse despite the victim's nonconsent and resistance, but the quality of the resistance often comes into dispute. Conventional, middle-class society has long been unrealistic in expecting the rape victim to oppose the attacker with heroic physical force if the victim is to be safe from the accusation of having cooperated, or perhaps having even invited the attack.

Fortunately, prevailing social attitudes about rape have changed as new understanding has developed regarding the subtle dynamics involved. As sexism in general has become a provocative issue, sensitivity to the rights of women has become a new concern in police techniques. Accordingly, recent years have brought a much more serious response to the crime of rape, both at the point of prosecution and in the efforts to provide victim services and corrective treatment of sex offenders in prisons.

A particularly significant indicator of the prejudices that have to be confronted in defining this crime is found in the outcome of a rape case prosecuted in Austin, Texas, in 1992. In this crime, a young woman about to be forcibly raped, seeing that resistance would be futile, pleaded with her attacker to use a condom to prevent transmission of any infection. The grand jury interpreted this as the woman's consent, and so refused to indict. But it became quickly apparent that the jury's view reflected outworn attitudes, out-of-step with current sensitivities; its decision gained nationwide attention and provoked intense resentment. Consequently, the case was resubmitted, and an indictment and finally a conviction were obtained, with the rapist sentenced to forty years in prison.[8]

One persistent handicap to any comprehensive crime control effort is the difficulty of documenting the kinds and amounts of crime taking place. Policy planners need to know exactly the crimes being committed, their location, their frequency, and the demographic data regarding both offenders and victims. "The movement of the nation's crime rate has both theoretical and practical significance. The police use it as a measure of their success in fighting crime and as a leverage for the allocation of resources. . . . the press and politicians point to crime statistics and rate changes as evidence of the success or failure of governmental policies in combating crime." (Steffensmeier and Harer 1991, 332) This utilization of crime rate data lends itself handily to political purposes because it is easily susceptible to manipulation; what should be a straightforward statistical process is in fact notoriously unreliable.

The *Uniform Crime Reports,* produced annually by the Federal Bureau of Investigation (FBI), serves students and researchers as a principal source of national crime statistics, but despite its unquestioned competence in assembling data and compiling statistical tables, the FBI well knows that it cannot control or guarantee the work of the several thousand clerks in local police and sheriffs' offices who gather and submit the raw data in the first place. Nor can there be any control of the many local factors that distort the comparisons between states or cities. Changes in local crime rates will often seem self-evident, while actually being more apparent than real. In its usual disclaimer the FBI reminds the reader that "one city may report more crime than a comparable one, not because there is more crime, but rather because its law enforcement agency through proactive efforts, such as 'sting operations' identifies more offenders. Attitudes of the citizens toward crime and their crime reporting practices, especially concerning more minor offenses, have an impact on volume of crimes known to the police." Further, the FBI notes some of the many factors that affect crime rates, including seldom credited ones such as climate, public transportation and highway systems, population stability, and degree of urbanization. "The Crime Index Rate was highest in metropolitan areas and lowest in rural counties." (*Uniform Crime Reports* 1991, v. 6)

Crime Rate Statistics Can Deceive

The public easily misses the point that increases in the crime rate do not necessarily mean that society is becoming more criminal. An increase may be only the effect of natural demographic changes; an increase in the proportion of the population from the late teens to the thirties will guarantee a rise in the count of crimes. An example is found in the claim made by President Ronald Reagan during his second term that the nation's crime rate had dropped for two years due to his administration's policies. This finding was contrary, however, to the findings of researchers who refigured the rates with reference to the pertinent demographic factors. It was true that the *Uniform Crime Reports* showed a 4 percent drop in the crime rate in the period the president spoke of, but during that time there had been an appreciable change in the proportions of various age groups in the population, with a reduced number of crime-prone young adults and a greater proportion of elderly. After adjusting for this factor, the crime rate actually showed a modest rise. (Steffensmeier and Harer 1991, 343)

Another factor, increased urbanization, causes a more impersonal quality of life, which also contributes to criminal activity, a fact to keep in mind when comparing rates between jurisdictions. The District of Columbia tends to be quite high in its crime rate as compared with the states, but the District consists entirely of a congested urban area, whereas any state contains both urban and rural areas, which average out to give the state a lower overall crime rate figure. For example, although the District's crime rate is appreciably higher than that of the state of Texas, it has about the same rate as the city of Dallas.

Despite all the pronouncements from politicians and bureaucrats, experience has shown that, more often than not, the true overall crime rate tends to be quite stable over a long time period. There will be minor and predictable variations according to times of the day, days of the week, and seasons of the year, and crime rates will even be temporarily affected by such events as a heavy snowfall. (Again, from the *Uniform Crime Reports*: 1991 crime rates were highest in August, lowest in February.) But overall, the rate does not otherwise change materially under normal conditions. Particularly at local levels there may be changes in recorded crime rates, which careful scrutiny shows to be due to bureaucratic or administrative developments rather than changed amounts of criminal activity. A local increase in arrests might only reveal the effect of the emphasis given by a new police chief, the work of a recently enlarged or differently deployed police force, or the influence of a new judge or prosecuting attorney. It might only reflect an improved method of assembling statistics, or be caused by revisions in definitions of the crimes or police actions being counted. An apparent increase in prostitution may only be the result of shifting police strength to that problem in response to a sudden public concern.

As long as the general public is unaware of the complex factors behind the raw crime statistics, politicians will make use of the data to serve their best interests, especially at the national level, where the administration is usually under pressure to be "tough on crime." The government's problem is that any real amelioration of the crime problem is possible only on a long-term basis, whereas the party in power needs to show results in less than four years.

With all the other variables to contend with in measuring crime, there is the curious fact that sometimes an increased rate in a certain crime category may actually have a healthy implication. As an important example, during the 1930s any state that had an increase in arrests for the crime of lynching would have been making commendable progress, because this would not have denoted a greater incidence of lynchings, but a new determination in public policy to recognize and deal with a brutal aspect of racial prejudice that had been tolerated too much and too long. In the 1920s and 1930s states began enacting laws to outlaw and punish lynching after two centuries of officially looking the other way. Today there is an encouraging new appreciation of the need to suppress other forms of hate, but policymakers find that criminal law can be an awkward instrument for controlling this social problem.

Minority Groups and Hate Crimes

Whereas lynching was the ultimate in violent racial prejudice, race-related bias continues in the prosecution of crimes, and only in the last decade has a resolute and general effort been made to control the racist factors. This has brought criminal law into a well-intentioned but controversial attempt to punish attitudes as well as acts.

As a bitter heritage of the history of slavery, black men charged with attacks on white women have felt the fullest severity of the law;

white men charged with attacks on black women have been punished lightly, if charged at all. A graphic example has been the experience of the state of Virginia (and typical of the South in general) where, in 1908, the electric chair was adopted, replacing hanging. At that time, and until mid-century, rape was subject to capital punishment in Virginia. During that period the state executed fifty-three black men for rape, but not one white man.[9]

A recent case before the U.S. Supreme Court has underscored the potency of some intangible social factors in defining these serious crimes. In several states violent assaults resulting in grievous bodily harm or death in recent years have been subject to enhanced punishments when it can be shown that vicious prejudice motivated the crime. These laws target the so-called "hate crimes" aimed at groups such as Jews, gays, blacks, Asians, or perhaps ideological fringe groups espousing religious or political causes.

In one sense it can be seen as a hopeful sign of a maturing society when public policy makes this attempt to enforce toleration for all races, ethnic groups, and nationalities. But as the courts have found, the criminal law is a crude and blunt instrument. Although the extra penalty for hate crimes is meant as a decent response to unreasoning prejudice, its opponents have argued that it restricts free speech. In 1989 the Wisconsin hate crime law was challenged after a young black man was given an extra penalty following his conviction in the beating of a white man for no other reason than racial hatred. On appeal, the trial court decision and the Wisconsin law were upheld. In a unanimous vote, the Supreme Court ruled that crime motivated by bigotry may be given an enhanced penalty.[10]

An encouraging indicator of the country's improving sensitivity to this form of criminal bias is a new focus by the FBI on hate crimes. A special FBI report alerted the public to the severity of this type of crime and revealed its dimensions and character as indicated by the statistics for 1993. During that year, nearly eight thousand separate hate crimes were reported to the FBI. It was clear, however, that the actual number had been much higher because the nearly seven thousand law enforcement agencies submitting the figures covered only 56 percent of the population. Among the known offenders, 51 percent were white and 35 percent were black. The motivating bias was in four major categories, with race being the most frequent at 62 percent. Religious bias accounted for 18 percent, sexual orientation caused 12 percent, and ethnicity caused 8 percent. The offenses ranged from vandalism to murder.[11]

Legal Translations of Morality

Legal definitions of crimes continually change, to a large extent reflecting society's current values. "The criminal law has evolved with

morality. It expresses moral beliefs, it codifies them, and it attempts to
enforce them.'' (Nettler 1974, 36) Historically, many criminal laws have
attempted to enforce morals in what might be called the religious sense,
a notable example being the experience, in 1895, of famous British playwright Oscar Wilde, prosecuted for homosexual activity and sentenced
to two years in prison. During that same period some U.S. citizens also
went to prison for violating laws which served only to enforce the moral
standards of the time.[12] Some publishers went to prison for the ''crime''
of publishing books which were then considered criminally ''indecent,''
but which today would be considered quite ordinary in a society which
has substantially revised its definitions of morality.

This process of modifying the definitions of crime to fit changing
social attitudes and conditions is continuous, subtle, and complex. In
some cases it has simply been a move away from the old practice of
trying to legislate private moral values. The prohibition of homosexual
behavior has generally been removed from criminal law as social attitudes and court decisions have come to the view that an activity privately
conducted between consenting adults should not be illegal.

On a more pragmatic level, changing conditions in the business
world will at times require new laws and regulations to enforce evolving
concepts of business morality. Lawmakers face the necessity to restrain
men of power (the business tycoons) from engaging in practices that
unfairly exploit smaller investors or consumers. Thus, in recent years
prominent businessmen have served prison terms for crimes that would
have been quite mysterious to the public of a century ago. These crimes,
including violation of antitrust, environmental protection, price fixing,
or banking laws, even require a new kind of law enforcement capability.
Being mostly beyond the competence of the ordinary policeman, they
can be detected and proved only by ''police'' in the form of accountants,
attorneys, or other specialized professionals. When an extensive criminal enterprise involves complex financial manipulations on an international basis, a typical police agency will not have the capacity to mount
an adequate investigation. While some of the larger police organizations
have this investigative capability, a shortage of such expertise has encouraged the growth of private services. Prosecutorial agencies that
want to probe complicated bookkeeping swindles can now hire corporations specializing as ''forensic investigators.'' Unhampered by jurisdic-
tional boundaries, their accountants can audit bank records and financial
statements to find any evidence of fraud and then testify effectively for
the prosecution.

The Interests of Those in Power

Although the laws that criminalize certain business practices may
be defined by some as reflecting society's moral values, others argue

that these legislated crimes are only reflecting the self-serving, usually economic, interests of the classes in power, and maintaining their desired model of an ordered society. As one early example, the landed gentry in fourteenth-century England saw their peasant workers leaving the estates to search for work in the cities; when they were unsuccessful, the peasants would often end up as beggars or petty thieves. In an attempt to force them back to their work on the estates, the government invented the vagrancy laws, which provided harsh punishments for unemployed persons on the city streets.

One sociologist, William Chambliss, has developed this theme in detail, noting "the critical role played by social conflict in the generation of criminal law." That is, there are always conflicting interests among social classes, and in the resolution of these conflicts the stronger class defines the norm and enforces it with use of criminal law.[13] "Of course, not all groups or social classes are equally potent and those which control the economic resources of the society will influence the shape of the law more profoundly and more permanently than will any other group or class." (Chambliss 1974, 8)

One illustration offered on this point is the Comprehensive Drug Abuse, Prevention and Control Act of 1970. In the course of preparing this legislation it became apparent, writes Chambliss, that "legislators would not endorse legislation inimical to the interests of the pharmaceutical industry." Certain drugs, subject to popular disapproval, were sure to be prohibited, but other drugs, such as amphetamines, were the source of enormous profits to the pharmaceutical companies and were spared. Though expert testimony was presented to portray the dangers to health of drugs such as Librium and Valium, citing them as being much more disabling than marijuana, legislators declined to prohibit them out of "a willingness or a desire to ignore evidence that would have forced the passage of a law inimical to the interests of the drug industry." (Chambliss 1974, 18–19, 29)

Whatever one's opinion of this pragmatic view, it must be considered as significant when studying white collar crime or organized crime. Often it will be seen that organized crime is a response to the perceived needs of the underclass, which is denied easy access to goods or services it wants because the governing class has curbed that access. "The huge efforts to apply the criminal law against the use of intoxicants, narcotics, and the hallucinogenic chemicals is, of course, criminogenic." (Nettler 1974, 257) In many such ways society's efforts to regulate itself produce new forms of criminal activity. Policymakers have to anticipate that any law that prohibits sales of or imposes significant taxes on a desired commodity will directly cause an illicit market served by a supply system which, once organized, tends to extend its predatory tactics more widely.

Even something as seemingly innocuous as tobacco marketing can become a law enforcement problem when high taxes are involved.

During the 1980s, Canadian provinces raised taxes on cigarettes an average of 18 percent, causing such a substantial differential between U.S. and Canadian taxes that smuggled cigarettes from the United States could be sold in Canada for about half the cost of the tax-paid legal product. During 1991, federal and provincial Canadian governments lost about $1 billion in tobacco tax revenues, while the smuggling and marketing of contraband tobacco "incited violence at the retail store and wholesale level. Robberies are occurring more frequently by individuals who resell tobacco products on the street for profit. Law enforcement officers, borderguards and tobacco company employees have been threatened and are often powerless in the face of the native and organized crime groups."[14]

A more familiar and more universal example of the difficult enforcement of morals is the prohibition of commercial sex. When the "respectable" class expresses its moral repugnance for prostitution with laws to prohibit and punish the practice, organized crime has an opportunity to provide the service in circumvention of law. Or when government enacts laws regulating banking, money transactions, or investment practices, it leads to endless varieties of white collar crime as entrepreneurs who are more clever than conscientious find ways to evade the legal restrictions.

In summary, although today the understandings both of individual pathology and the sociological factors fostering crime can be appreciated and incorporated into penological policy, this could not have been possible without the earlier introduction of rational ways of thinking about human behavior. Pioneers attempting radical new approaches to criminal justice erred in many of their conclusions about criminal behavior, but their provocative, reasoned pronouncements stimulated the intellectual curiosity indispensable for better understanding of crime and criminal behavior.

Today, that improved knowledge is applied in the complex process of adapting public policy to crime definition and control, and by realizing that whereas criminal law is a necessary response to the existence of crime, it also can generate crimes. The reasons are as broad and diverse as the myriad elements of the whole society. "If we are to explain crime, we must first explain the social forces that cause some acts to be defined as criminal while other acts are not." (Chambliss 1974, 39)

The behavior of both groups and individuals "is generated in a dense system of causes, a system in which the roots of action are numerous, intertwined, and not uniformly entangled. . . . The despair of would-be societal engineers is this fact, that in the social web one cannot 'do just one thing.' One cannot change a law, enforce it, ignore it, or enact any reform of our collective enterprise without starting a chain of effects, many of which are bound to be unforeseen and some of which are bound to be undesirable.'' (Nettler 1974, 250)

As this discussion has suggested, a society's search for proper definitions of crime is dynamic and perpetual, and the direction the country takes in this quest tells much about its maturity and stability. The quality of the policing that a country provides for itself also reflects importantly its maturity, its commitment to civil rights, and the nature of its fears about crime. These considerations are crucial to the quality of the criminal justice processes, as will be seen next in a discussion of police policy and practice.

Notes

1. Published in 1764, the Italian title of the book was *Dei delitti e delli pene.* A discussion of both the book and its author's life is provided by Maestro 1973 (below).
2. Elio Monochesi. ''Cesare Lombroso'' in Hermann Mannheim, ed. *Pioneers in Criminology.* Montclair, N.J.: Patterson Smith, 1972, 36–43.
3. See, for example, Elsie R. Broussard. ''Neonatal Prediction and Outcome at 10/11 Years.'' *Child Psychiatry and Human Development* 7:2 (Winter 1976): 85–93; and Rene A. Spitz. *The First Year of Life: A Psychoanalytical Study of Normal and Deviant Development of Object Relations.* New York: International Universities Press, 1965.
4. *Scientific American* 266:3 (March 1992), 26.
5. *Time* 141:16 (April 19, 1993), 50.
6. *New York Times* (Sept. 5, 1992), L1.
7. Ibid.
8. *New York Times* (Oct. 25, 1992), L30. *Time* 141:21 (May 24, 1993), 24.
9. Execution record, Penitentiary papers, Department of Corrections; Archives and Records Division, Library of Virginia, Richmond.
10. Wisconsin v. Mitchell, 113 S. Ct. 2194 (1993).
11. U.S. Department of Justice. FBI. Criminal Justice Information Services. *Uniform Crime Reports: Hate Crime—1993,* 1.
12. See, for example, Heywood Broun and Margaret Leech. *Anthony Comstock: Roundsman of the Lord.* New York: Literary Guild of America, 1927. Also, Milton Rugoff. *Prudery and Passion.* New York: G. P. Putnam's Sons, 1971.
13. The late H. L. Mencken, famous newspaper columnist, reflected the same viewpoint with his customary barbed wit in commenting on the Prohibition amendment, which he lamented: ''Big business was in favor of Prohibition, believing that a sober workman would make a better slave than one with a few drinks.'' *Baltimore Evening Sun,* Aug. 4, 1924, as quoted in *The*

Impossible H. L. Mencken, ed. Marion Elizabeth Rodgers, 285. New York: Anchor Books, 1991.

14. *Contraband Tobacco Estimate, June 30, 1992;* an unpublished corporate report by Lindquist Avey Macdonald Baskerville, Inc., Toronto, Canada, i–iii.

Bibliography

Seeking Rational Understanding of Crime

Akers, Ronald L. *Criminological Theories: Introduction and Evaluation.* Los Angeles: Roxbury, 1994.

    A systematic, concise comparative summary of the principal theories of criminal behavior. It also discusses ways to evaluate the theories and provides an extensive bibliography.

Bedau, Hugo Adam. *The Death Penalty in America.* New York: Oxford University Press, 1982.

Bowlby, John. *Maternal Care and Mental Health.* Geneva: World Health Organization, 1952.

Cohn, Albert, Alfred Lindesmith, and Karl Schussler. *The Sutherland Papers.* Bloomington: Indiana University Press, 1956.

Coleman, Lee S. "Perspectives on the Medical Research of Violence," a chapter (unnumbered) in Marsh 1985 (below).

Deming, Richard. *Man and Society: Criminal Law at Work.* New York: Hawthorn Books, 1970.

Denno, Deborah W. *Biology and Violence: From Birth to Adulthood.* New York: Cambridge University Press, 1990.

    A good overview of the research findings on biological causes of violent behavior, but mainly this is a report of the findings of one mammoth research project on childhood and adolescent development as related to violence.

Durkheim, Emile. *The Rules of Sociological Method.* Chicago: University of Chicago Press, 1938.

Gaylord, Mark S. and John F. Galliher. *The Criminology of Edwin Sutherland.* New Brunswick, N.J.: Transaction, 1988.

    Essentially a biography of distinguished sociologist Sutherland. Beyond the portion dealing with his childhood years, it focuses narrowly on his professional life and growth, with discussions of the influences affecting his philosophy and general career development.

Glaser, Daniel, ed. *Handbook of Criminology.* Chicago: Rand McNally College Publishing Co., 1974.

    Glaser, one of the country's most respected criminologists, has assembled here 31 chapters on a wide range of criminal justice topics. The contributors are themselves noted authorities, giving this book a wealth of solid information and viewpoints.

Jeffery, C. R. "Criminology as an Interdisciplinary Behavioral Science," a chapter (unnumbered) in Marsh 1985 (below).

Maestro, Marcello. *Cesare Beccaria and the Origins of Penal Reform.* Philadelphia: Temple University Press, 1973.

    Though not an exhaustive biography of Beccaria, this readable book thoroughly covers the period of his life in which he made his considerable contributions to the criminal law and the philosophy of punishment as public policy. Its usefulness is enlarged by discussion of the contributions of other influential contemporary thinkers and the subsequent effects of their writings on public policy.

Marsh, Frank H. and Janet Katz, eds. *Biology, Crime and Ethics: A Study of Biological Explanations for Criminal Behavior.* Cincinnati: W. H. Anderson, 1985.

    More than thirty authors are contributors to this anthology, starting with Darwin and Lombroso, and bringing the subject down to the present state of knowledge about biology and crime, including public policy issues.

Matza, David. *Delinquency and Drift.* New Brunswick, N.J.: Transaction, 1990.

    An erudite and highly academic discussion of the author's theories about the sociology of delinquent conduct.

Merton, Robert K. *Social Theory and Social Structure.* New York: Free Press, 1968.

Nelkin, Dorothy and Judith P. Swazey. "Science and Social Control: Controversies over Research on Violence." A chapter (unnumbered) in Marsh 1985 (above).

Newman, Graeme. *The Punishment Response.* New York: J. B. Lippincott, 1978.

    Although many authors have written about the brutal history of public punishment, this is not just another compendium of such methods. It includes them, but goes beyond them into the cultural and political context in which these practices flourished. It notes the important persons who influenced the occasional shifts in policy, and brings the subject down to the present with discussion of modern schools of thought. All material is thoroughly documented.

Radzinowicz, Leon. *Ideology and Crime: A Study of Crime in Its Social and Historical Context.* London: Heinemann Educational Books, 1966.

    A widely respected criminologist's lectures delivered at the Columbia University Law School. The author addresses the development of society's understanding and its successive theories of crime and the proper response to it, rather than any practical aspect of the criminal justice system. To this extent the book is an erudite contribution to this complex subject.

Rennie, Ysabel. *The Search for Criminal Man: A Conceptual History of the Dangerous Offender.* Lexington, Mass.: Lexington Books, 1978.

    In a thoughtful and competent review of the societal response to dangerous offenders, the author discusses the historical development of studies and theories about criminality, including the work of Beccaria and Lombroso. Also discussed are the social context in which various theories formed, the modern concepts of dangerous behavior, and the appropriate response to it.

Shapiro, E. Donald and Michelle L. Weinberg. "DNA Data Banking: The Dangerous Erosion of Privacy." *Cleveland State Law Review* 38:3 (1990), 455–486.

Smith, J. David. *The Eugenic Assault on America: Scenes in Red, White and Black.* Fairfax, Va.: George Mason University Press, 1993.

Sutherland, Edwin H. and Donald R. Cressey. *Criminology.* New York: J. B. Lippincott, 1974.

Sykes, Gresham M. *Criminology.* New York: Harcourt, Brace, Jovanovich, 1978.

Evolving Definitions of Crime

Chambliss, William J. "The State, the Law, and the Definition of Behavior as Criminal or Delinquent." Chapter 1 in Glaser 1974 (above).

A thorough, scholarly, in-depth discussion of the formulation of criminal laws in light of the ways in which social factors and the understanding of human behavior explain the process of formulating criminal laws. The chapter also provides an extensive bibliography.

Nettler, Gwynn. *Explaining Crime.* New York: McGraw-Hill, 1974.

A systematic presentation of the various definitions of crime, including the many specific types of crime. Nettler also competently appraises the principal theories of causes.

Steffensmeier, Darrell and Miles D. Harer. "Did Crime Rise or Fall during the Reagan Presidency? The Effects of an 'Aging' U.S. Population on the Nation's Crime Rates." *Journal of Research in Crime and Delinquency* 25:3 (Aug. 1991), 330–359.

CHAPTER 2

Organizing the Public Response to Crime

To a considerable extent, a study of police organizations and their functioning reveals essential information about either the integrity or the corruption of the government, the society's general attitude toward crime, and the kind and degree of crime it has. Starting with policing in a simpler time, with few criminal laws, this account will look closely at the professionalism of police services, and their confrontation with modern white collar and organized crimes that challenge the most sophisticated police techniques.

In some respects the advances in policing techniques denote a recognition that crime—its causes, prevention, and correction—is far more complex than previous generations appreciated. Behavioral scientists now know that no one factor causes a person to become criminal, but that the behavior always results from a combination of elements that are difficult to identify, predict, or counteract. Law enforcement agencies, therefore, need to be inventive and flexible beyond anything that earlier constabularies dreamed of, and at the same time will severely test the adaptability of the judicial process and the punishment systems.

Today's society has inherited a criminal justice approach that is too simplistic in relation to what we now know about social forces and human behavior. Our courts still must proceed on the simplistic assumption that an alleged offender can be found altogether guilty, or altogether innocent, when in fact we know that the reality is rarely so absolute. Our prisons still take in a mass of offenders who are vastly varied in kinds and degrees of criminality, then treat them all essentially the same. Inevitably, some offenders for whom a different handling is needed are damaged. As will be seen in succeeding chapters, the public's response to crime needs to include a rich variety of options if the system is to have maximum effect on all types of offenders. This adaptability is beginning to develop, but is always impeded by natural public resistance to untried departures from the traditional. This is an area in which the makers of public policy must continually strive to be innovative. A close look at recent developments in policing is a useful introduction to this aspect of modern criminal justice policy.

Professionalism for the Police

Until the nineteenth century, both Britain and the United States relied upon harsh and highly visible punishments to deter crime, instead of organizing a police force. For many crimes, English criminal law subjected offenders to severe penalties, including heavy use of capital punishment or transportation to penal colonies. As long as crime control relied solely on this threat of severe punishment there seemed little need to develop police services beyond a local and essentially volunteer type of operation.[1] Each British village elected a constable who carried out his wide-ranging functions with casual informality. He was to apprehend felons, maintain the stocks, whipping post, and other such equipment for public punishments, and in general prevent breaches of the peace. In performing these duties he could act on his own initiative to search property or make arrests, and he could commandeer the services of fellow citizens for assistance in any of these activities. (Kent 1986, 25, 27, 31)

The local police principle, having come with the colonists to America, became well entrenched here, and though the United States now has many police organizations of massive size, the pattern of local organization is still basic. This is due largely to an attitude rooted in the colonial experience and the U.S. Revolution, when the United States, after having won freedom from an arbitrary government, rejected the idea of any authoritative central police agency that might become an instrument of repression. Consequently, the original concept of local control persists, as seen in the thousands of local police forces, often overlapping and sometimes duplicating services.[2] Nor is it just a matter of separate police departments in adjoining towns or counties; often several different police agencies serve within the same municipality. A given area may be policed by municipal, county, state, federal, private, and university police forces, each with its own authority and responsibilities.

The independence of separate police agencies frequently causes competition among jurisdictions that should be closely cooperating. An altogether human desire to get the credit for solving a case sometimes impedes investigations when two nearby agencies purposefully neglect to share information on a matter which should be of mutual concern.

Nor is this trait confined just to local agencies; it becomes more dramatic and ominous when practiced at the national level. In 1947 Congress created the Central Intelligence Agency (CIA) to gather and analyze information in the country's interest abroad; Congress prohibited the CIA from exercising any police power within the United States. By the 1970s, however, the CIA reportedly had amassed confidential information on about ten thousand American citizens and in effect competed with the FBI in this covert activity.[3] The director of the FBI at that time, J. Edgar Hoover, always determined to protect his own "turf," acutely distrusted the CIA and resisted cooperating with its directors. (Powers 1987, 271, 273, 450, 451)

At the same time that this unhealthy competition developed, the professionalization of police services was seriously delayed; small government units could not afford to provide sophisticated training to their police departments, which were sometimes only two or three officers strong. Political patronage has also hindered progress. In earlier days when police organizations were new and no body of knowledge about police techniques had yet been developed, no standards of professional qualifications guided the selection and promotion of personnel. This left the services open to control by political parties, and the practice of patronage appointments became so entrenched that police officials were quite commonly replaced or demoted whenever the city or county government had a change of the party in power. The practice reached an absurd extreme in Indianapolis from 1883 to 1891 when the city actually had two competing police departments, one Republican and one Democrat.[4]

Although police professionalism first appeared in the 1920s, the grip of political patronage on police departments persisted in many localities until the 1950s or later. Of itself, the patronage practice was not necessarily deleterious, but it defeated the desirable stability of the service, it invariably frustrated any interest in or accomplishment of professionalism, and it made the departments more vulnerable to corrupting influences. Although the police did not realize it at the time, it also had a depressing effect on their salaries. After patronage practices ended and the quality of service was upgraded, police could begin to demand salaries at levels commensurate with other professional fields. During the early twentieth century, two parallel developments undermined patronage and fundamentally altered U.S. law enforcement: the professionalism of local and state police agencies, and the creation and expansion of the FBI. (Theoharis 1990, 221)

The Beginnings of Training and Special Education

The long delayed move toward professional police service had its most ardent champion in August Vollmer, the chief of the Berkeley,

California, police force in the 1920s. Vollmer, noted for advocating college education for police, exerted wide influence not only because of the quality he built into the Berkeley police department, but also because he gained a national audience for his ideas through his effective writings. In 1931 he became the first professor of police administration at the University of California, and subsequently helped establish the country's first college-level training program for police, at San Jose State College.[5] By mid-century an impressive number of converts among police favored academic training, though this was, and still is to some extent, resisted by the macho police preference for the school of practical experience.[6]

Vollmer's pioneering efforts stirred police interest in training, a trend reinforced by the growing prestige of the FBI and its training academy. By the late 1920s, J. Edgar Hoover, director of the FBI, had organized a training program for FBI agents whose consequent professional efficiency impressed other police and led to their interest in having similar preparation. In response, the FBI opened a separate National Academy in 1935 for selected command level sheriffs and police from around the country. (Powers 1987, 151–152; Joseph 1978, 14) Graduates of the Academy enjoyed the high prestige of their certificates, and the general effect was to encourage a new respect for training.

Surprisingly, formal, basic training for police did not become standard until after World War II. Although Vollmer is best remembered for his advocacy of college education for police, he also influenced the eventual development of basic training programs. O. W. Wilson, another leader in professionalism, with the backing of Vollmer, was appointed chief of police in Wichita, Kansas, where he started an in-service training program followed by a successful push for the start of statewide training. Some years later Wilson became chief of the Chicago police department and continued to organize training programs. The idea gradually caught on and in the 1950s both New York and California enacted legislation requiring both in-service and pre-service training for police. (Deakin 1988, 213, 272)

The Law Enforcement Education Program (LEEP), a program under President Lyndon Johnson's Law Enforcement Administration Act (1968), gave the demand for training a substantial boost through tuition grants and low-cost loans for both police and corrections personnel who sought college educations. In its first six years, more than $230 million was expended for criminal justice education at more than one thousand colleges in the country.[7]

Although the LEEP program had the presumed good effect of stimulating respect for education in a field that had tended to scorn such "book-learning" for much of its existence, the results of the rapidly expanded college offerings disappointed its proponents. Funded by generous federal grants, colleges hastily organized criminal justice programs well before qualified faculty could be developed. Far too often local police officers, although lacking the proper academic credentials, moonlighted as instructors, proving that an excellent practitioner does not necessarily have the ability to teach effectively. Unfortunately, many of the police officer instructors taught only their own narrowly focused areas of experience without giving the broad and basic knowledge that would make for true quality education. (Eskridge 1989, 18–19)

Forensic Specialization

Eventually, police agencies have realized that in addition to basic training, police recruits need increasingly specialized skills. City and county governments have had to recognize that it is not enough for their police to arrest an alleged offender; it is also necessary for them to investigate the crime with sufficient meticulous care that the case can be successfully prosecuted. The untrained police officer is too likely to overlook significant evidence, interview witnesses ineffectively, or fail to prepare reports in the exacting way necessary to survive challenges in court. This is far more important today than in earlier years of policing, as courts have more precisely defined civil rights and concepts of due process. The availability of new, highly technical equipment and procedures has also brought a body of knowledge to be included in police training. In this respect an adjunct to police investigative work is the modern forensic laboratory, headed by a specialized pathologist trained in evidence analysis and the presentation of evidence in court. The forensic pathologist position typically calls for a medical degree plus four years of specialized training and certification. (Moenssens and Imbau 1978, 219–220) To help make the forensic work effective, the police officer should be trained to gather the evidence needed by the pathologist.

The forensic specialization uniquely illustrates the highly professional quality that modern police work requires. It calls not only for a high degree of technical skill, but also for an impeccable integrity in order to give unquestioned weight to the officer's testimony. The police officer's job "requires that his sincerity in conducting analyses and examinations be beyond reproach. In addition to his moral obligation, he realizes that if he evinces a credibility gap, his entire agency will be suspect, his job in jeopardy, and the defense encouraged to independently negate his findings." (Moenssens and Imbau 1978, 9)

The revolution in telecommunications is forcing the regular police officer to have a basic grasp of computer technology, for it is both an aid to police work and a new area of criminal activity. One expert notes that in "the 1990s we will see an explosion in the number of mobile

digital terminals installed in patrol vehicles. These . . . will evolve
into small computers that will offer word processing to expedite report
writing, mapping programs that display area maps with crime statistics.
. . . A future example could be a first-aid program that would ask the
officer at the scene what the general problem was (bleeding, poison,
head trauma, etc.) then follow up with logical secondary questions
(where is wound, what type of poison, how many taken, etc.) and
quickly provide the officer with suggested procedures.''[8]

A New Appreciation for Psychological Factors

Modern policing not only employs advanced technical equipment
and procedures, but also requires understanding of human and social
psychology. The average police officer's day includes a surprising
amount of noncriminal activity, making informal counseling at once a
substantial part of police work and also a factor in the quality of police
public relations. ''Recent surveys in the New York City Police Department showed that 90% of calls for police could not possibly result in
an arrest. Since that is the case, then obviously some other action is
required of the police officer who responds to these calls. In most cases,
these are disputes to be settled, ruffled nerves calmed, and angry voices
to be stilled.''[9]

Arrests for crimes would also be safer and more conducive to subsequent prosecution if handled with appreciation of psychological factors.
Sexual offenses, for instance, call for a sensitivity not usual with yesterday's police force. This is true with rape cases and child abuse cases,
which are especially difficult. As one authority points out, ''The sad
truth is that law enforcement officers trained in conventional methods
but lacking specialized training are ill-equipped to conduct a proper
investigation of a child abuse case.'' The special training needed for
child abuse cases is crucial to successful prosecution since, ''Not surprisingly, sex crimes against children have been seen by many prosecutors as the most difficult cases in which to secure convictions.''[10]

By the 1990s the idea of specialized training was well established
as a desirable, and even necessary, feature of good police work, but
this did not necessarily mean that college education was altogether accepted as prerequisite to the work. Policy on this point has been complicated by the issue of minority hiring, since it can easily be argued that
the requirement of two or more years of college for applicants would
screen out a disproportionate number of blacks and Hispanics. Whereas
this consideration has prevented many police departments from requiring college education, an enduring interest in working toward that goal
remains because ''the college-educated officer is more likely to perform

his job well, have superior field performance, have good attendance patterns, relate well to the community, be a good decision maker and use discretion wisely.''[11]

As one student of law enforcement noted, shifting ideological priorities typically plague local police departments as they periodically endure the political changes in their governments. He observed that ''the tides of change would be less disruptive of a force made up of more broadly-educated persons more philosophically attuned to political and social adjustment.''[12] The move toward more education (as distinguished from just training) for law enforcement personnel continues to grow, very gradually, very slowly, but inexorably.

Law Enforcement and Minority Groups

Events in the 1950s and into the turbulent 1970s began to reveal an attitudinal defect in both FBI and general police practice. Too often police practices reflected the racism so generally inherent in the white power structure. Institutionalizing his own biases, J. Edgar Hoover inculcated his agency with the dominance of the white, Anglo-Saxon, Protestant, male culture. As long as he directed the FBI he stoutly resisted hiring any blacks in regular special agent assignments. With racist attitudes among the agents tolerated if not encouraged, the FBI acted on the assumption that any public militancy on the part of blacks in support of civil rights was probably Communist inspired. (Powers 1987, 323–324, 367)

Without excusing Hoover for his discriminatory practices, it has to be noted that he was not out of step with his time—at least with regard to the time in which he began his career. This is a point that has a vital relationship to the formulation of public policy, because if the political process that tackles public policy issues is to be effective, it ordinarily must be in accord with, and not much ahead of, general public attitudes. For most of his career Hoover accurately observed the public sentiments that related to crime control. He built his enormous prestige by his adroit articulation of the popular issues—such as the threats from Communism. But by the 1950s, having nourished his deeply ingrained attitudes through more than three decades of a highly successful career, Hoover could not adapt to the substantial change developing in public attitudes toward racism, sexism, and civil rights.

For most of the country's history, prejudicial attitudes toward blacks have been chronic but kept from being overtly disruptive by entrenched social habits and practices. Since the mid-1950s, however, several parallel developments respecting minorities in the United States have sensitized the public to issues of prejudice while profoundly affecting the workings of the criminal justice system. During the 1950s militant challenges to racial segregation and other forms of discrimination awakened public awareness of the disparate rates of arrests and convictions for different races and ethnic groups. In the years since, it has been relatively easy to document the differential arrest rates, but more difficult to analyze the reasons. The 1985 FBI *Uniform Crime Report* shows that the U.S. white population, with 80 percent of the total, contributed to about 72 percent of total arrests; blacks were 12 percent of the general population but accounted for 26 percent of the arrests. Hispanics, at less than 7 percent of the population, accounted for 12 percent of the arrests. Similar discrepancies characterized the populations of correctional institutions.

Historically these discrepancies have been used to support prejudicial assertions about racial inferiority, but the current and more objective position taken by social scientists is that "biological research is inadequate to explain racial/ethnic and class variations in crime rates. There is no evidence to suggest that the high crime rate among minorities is a matter of biological differences, particularly when one considers that race and ethnicity represent socially defined groupings rather than biologically based classifications." (Flowers 1988, 62) Experts produce numerous conjectures in attempting to explain disparate crime rates. But all agree that, "the concept of equal treatment under the law has generally proved to be more of a theoretical assumption than a reality. Minorities have been shown to be discriminated against in every phase of the court process." (Flowers 1988, 155)

Cultural, Generational, and Political Minorities

Stress and hostility between police and minorities peaked during the late 1960s and early 1970s with the confluence of several nationally disturbing events. The minorities involved were not just racial; equally provocative and significant were the cultural minorities. The long-running Vietnam War focused the anger of disaffected young people, and also of blacks, who made up a disproportionate number of U.S. troops. Against the background of this intensely unpopular war, the college-age generation produced a large number of dissidents who rejected the values of their parents' generation and fought against all the elements of "the establishment." The criminal justice system was an easy target, and both police and prisons felt the resentment.

As the mood of dissension grew in the college-age generation, protest marches became a regular means of demonstrating rebellious feelings. At first police generally treated these routinely, but as the war persisted and demonstrators became more frustrated, the marches became more provocative, with the police themselves often becoming the objects of protest. Police reacted with less restraint. A general escalation of violence resulted, culminating in especially disturbing outbreaks during the violent year of 1968.

In April of that year many cities suffered riots after the assassination of Martin Luther King, Jr. Robert Kennedy was assassinated the following June, and that summer a particularly vicious riot made memorable the Democratic National Convention in Chicago. By that time, peace marches had exasperated city governments, police, and much of the more conventional citizenry. Chicago's government was in no mood to tolerate militant demonstrators. But the young protesters, contemptuous of hostile officialdom, continued their aggressive demonstrations. In return, the police lost restraint and professionalism as they attacked marchers and even uninvolved bystanders in what afterward was described as a "police riot." Dramatically and tragically, the riot highlighted the general tension between police and minorities, either racial or political. (Armstrong and Cinnamon 1976, 135–138)

There is nothing new in police having to confront hostile mobs. A century ago there was as much if not more such violence, but the nature of the issues has changed, as has the age and character of the rioters. Where once it was industrial problems such as union organizing that sparked unrest, today's rioters often are young people addressing social conditions, civil rights issues, or promoting political movements. Their sense of mission will give them what seems an uncompromising arrogance, infuriating to their opponents and particularly to the police, most of whom come to their work imbued with conventional values at odds with the likely radicalism of aggressive demonstrators.

Fortunately, the maturing professionalism of police organizations has brought new training programs which address the subject of cultural differences among racial and ethnic groups. In a limited sense this is thought of as sensitivity to the rights and feelings of others—a matter of teaching officers how to reduce, or at least control, the racial prejudice they are likely to bring to the job. But training in social skills must go well beyond this to include education in diverse cultural values and the kinds of differences that can easily cause an escalation of antagonism when police must deal with an ethnic group whose cultural values and expectations are strange to them. "The criminal justice community needs to weave cross-cultural awareness into all aspects of law enforcement training. . . . Cross-cultural issues are interrelated; they cannot be disconnected."[13] In an ordinary encounter a police officer may act with what he or she supposes to be altogether sensible, objective, and professional behavior toward another person of a different cultural or ethnic group, not knowing that he or she is using terms that are objectionable to that person. The police officer may not understand that eye contact, posture, and concepts of time and personal space all raise subtle barriers. The officer may think he or she is getting answers to questions but not realize that the officer's failure to understand cultural differences is causing the answers to be guarded and evasive, if not overtly provocative.

All such aspects of cultural differences are subjects of a curriculum of cross-cultural training now offered at the federal government's training center for personnel of law enforcement agencies at Glynco, Georgia, and which sets a respected example for other training academies. The training also includes "survival Spanish" and study of the system of Hispanic surnames.[14]

It takes only a glimpse of the demographic facts regarding the U.S. population to understand why such training is so urgently needed. Whereas the public and the police have been accustomed to thinking of a white, native-born majority, this is rapidly changing. FBI literature warns the police that "by 2010 more than one-third of all American children will be black, Hispanic or Asian."[15] Following the wars in Korea, Vietnam, and other trouble spots of the world, the United States has experienced heavy immigration, subjecting the country's attitudes toward national minorities to severe stress. Though the United States has long cherished its role as a haven for refugees from religious or political repression, the public's generosity in this respect has proven to be quickly expended when the refugees are too culturally different, too numerous, and even more so if they are too successful as entrepreneurs in competition with native workers and businesses. Sooner or later, the resulting animosities challenge the sensitivity and skill of the police at the same time that police conduct toward immigrants is important to everyone's welfare. "Many of today's new arrivals come from places where the police are feared, not respected, and the last thing they would be likely to do is ask an officer for help or share any information." That brings police both a problem and an opportunity. "The police, therefore, have a tremendous responsibility because those first impressions matter, not just in terms of how new arrivals will see the police but how they view the entire society."[16]

Most state governments now require police training programs, citing the range of subjects to be taught and the number of hours required in each. They typically specify cross-cultural studies, but proponents have discovered that it is easier to mandate them than to deliver a high-quality program. A training academy can put a social skills course in its curriculum, but its real value depends on the availability of an instructor who is truly a specialist in this area.

Women in Greater Numbers—on Both Sides of the Law

Another "minority" that has gained new prominence in the criminal justice field has been the female population. Women have been accepted into police and corrections work to a degree that would have seemed incredible three decades ago. Of course women have worked in police departments since the previous century, but until recently most were confined to "social worker" types of roles such as handling female offenders or children. But after the Law Enforcement Assistance Act (LEAA) prohibited sex discrimination in any criminal justice services it funded, the employment barriers for women eroded. Women today are usually hired, trained, and assigned on nearly the same basis as men. "Between 1968 and 1984, the number of women on patrol increased from approximately a dozen to thousands." (Feinman 1986, 90) Some notable court suits, successfully challenging policies or practices excluding women from criminal justice jobs, have accelerated the change.[17]

Not surprisingly, male police officers initially tended to be highly skeptical, and often downright hostile, toward female officers. However, findings from several substantial evaluation studies conducted to compare female police performance relative to male performance have clearly favored the women. In all instances it appears that the sexes are different in their areas of excellence: men are better on the firing range, women are better at calming distraught people, and in various other activities one sex or the other will excel. But when all is balanced out and all the studies are reviewed, the sexes are found essentially equal in general performance quality: "It has been clearly demonstrated by both the actual experience and the various research experiments that American policewomen can effectively perform general patrol duties and handle violent or potentially violent situations." (Horne 1980, 100–104)

The experience has been similar in the corrections field, where women began to appear in traditionally male jobs in the early 1970s. Prison systems that until recently would have abhorred the idea of employing women as correctional officers in men's prisons have learned that women can do most such jobs—even in maximum security units—as well as men. Also, it is often found that with the vast expansion in prison systems it would hardly be possible to staff them all without hiring both men and women. Women are also becoming wardens of men's prisons in increasing numbers. A Federal Bureau of Prisons publication reported in 1994 that "forty-five States use women to staff at least one male maximum-security prison or unit." The Federal Bureau itself began using female correctional officers to a limited extent in its prisons in the 1970s; then "in January 1992, the gender-neutral policy was extended to all positions." (Rison 1994, 19)

Unfortunately, increasing numbers of women are also becoming prisoners. Remarkably, the number of women in prison, which had remained quite constant at a little more than six thousand year after year since the 1940s, rose sharply in the mid-1970s and peaked at more than forty thousand in 1990. During that fifty-year period, while the male prisoner population had risen about 417 percent, the female population increased by 636 percent.[18] Arrest statistics reveal a similar increase. The FBI reported that from 1960 to 1983 arrests of males had somewhat less than trebled, but arrests of women quadrupled. (Feinman 1986, 20)

It is tempting to speculate, as many observers have, that among possible reasons for the increasing numbers of women in prison may be the conjunction of the drug culture and the increased female population in a high-risk age range. An equally likely explanation is that the general changes in the status of women have made judges feel less protective of them and more willing to give them prison sentences. Though such assumptions remain logical, the various experts who have researched the question find that the causal factors are complex and difficult to prove. A reasonably certain conclusion is that whereas crimes by women have increased in *number,* the pattern in the *types* of crime committed by women has not materially changed; women still are being arrested mostly for the traditionally female crimes—principally, varieties of larceny. As compared with males, ''a much larger proportion of the total arrest gains made by females is accounted for by larceny than is the case for males.''[19]

Increased drug use as a factor is probably valid, as 46 percent of female inmates in state prisons reported being under the influence of either alcohol or drugs at the time of their offenses.[20] Otherwise, as one researcher has concluded, the increased convictions and imprisonment of women are probably related to the generally sharpened concern for exacting standards of decision making and concern for equal application of the law in respect to race and class differences, all of which are a part of the improved professionalism of criminal justice agencies. And finally, ''more equal treatment of male and female defendants may be occurring irrespective of whether there are changes in cultural attitudes toward women and perhaps in spite of enduring attitudes of paternalism toward women on the part of many criminal justice agents.''[21]

The Police Confront White Collar Crime: Organized Crime

Where once police training had been seen principally as instruction in practical street methods (physical controls, firearm usage, report writing, etc.), police officers now need training in investigating the less overt, more subtle or sophisticated types of crime. These include organized crime, which, though crafty, calculated, and often vicious, is also furtive, calling for special talents and skills to investigate it successfully. White collar crime, though usually lacking the brutal nature of the organized variety, is similarly subtle, committed quietly by apparently respectable people, and so is nearly invisible to much of the public. With either type of crime, the investigating police may find themselves stalking their adversaries not so much with guns as with auditors and "informers."

Increasingly, the criminal manipulation of computer systems is becoming dominant among white collar crimes, and is a major reason why the dollar value of white collar crime is far beyond what most people would suspect. Statistics from a decade ago showed that the average bank robbery netted the robber less than $10,000, while the average computer crime had reached $430,000, a figure that continues to increase. Ironically, though this area of criminal enterprise is highest in dollars stolen, it was for some time the least targeted by police. Computer crime tends to be diffuse in its impact on most of its victims; much of it hits the individual victim only lightly and not even visibly, its effect usually being delayed and distant from the criminal act. Often the victims do not complain, and law enforcement agencies are more likely to be preoccupied with crimes committed by people in lower socioeconomic classes who, in the popular view, are more threatening.

Nevertheless, computer fraud and other forms of white collar crime permeate all levels of society, taking from the public untold millions of dollars. No student of the subject is willing to put a firm figure on the losses, but all students of the problem know that the price we pay is exorbitant. Sutherland (who invented the term *white collar crime*) observed that "the financial cost of white collar crime is probably several times as great as the financial cost of all the crimes which are customarily regarded as the 'crime problem.' " (Sutherland 1983, 9) Another author, admitting it to be gross guesswork, found the opinions of various experts to be "that about 30 percent of business failures were the result of employee dishonesty. . . . about 15 percent of the price paid for goods and services goes to cover the costs of dishonesty." (Wagner 1979, 74)

The "Respectable" Person's Crime of Choice

White collar crime ranges widely from the theft by an employee of a few sheets of his employer's stationery, to the multimillion dollar thefts from the public by corporations through illegal business ventures. And while many corporations are guilty of "sharp business practices" that, though legal, are dishonest, the corporations themselves are victims too, with insurance fraud and contrived damage claims as frequent examples.

A major area of corporate crime is misrepresentation in advertising. ''Garments are advertised and sold as silk or wool when they are entirely or almost entirely cotton. . . . Caskets are advertised as rustproof which are not rustproof. . . . Electric pads are advertised with switches for high, medium, and low, when in fact they do not give three different degrees of temperature.'' (Sutherland 1983, 131)

Even the large and generally respected companies that manufacture familiar and respected household products have persistently and flagrantly violated the law. One extensive government-funded research project, which studied a large sample of publicly owned corporations, reported that ''sixty percent of the 582 corporations studied were found to have been charged with at least one violation by the federal agencies. One company had 62 cases initiated against it. Between 1975 and 1976, the 582 companies recorded 1,860 violations. They averaged 3.2 violations each.'' The Department of Justice estimated that reported and unreported violations by corporations caused taxpayers to lose from $10 to $20 billion each year. (Larson 1984, 154, 162)

Whereas many corporate crimes are calculated and deliberate, the complexity of business ventures and federal regulations make it easily possible to slip unwittingly into practices that become criminal. As an illustration of this, in mid-1992 Sears Roebuck & Company was charged with defrauding hundreds of their auto repair customers. The California Consumer Affairs Bureau had investigated Sears' practices for more than a year, finding that often employees falsely advised customers that their cars needed extensive repairs, and in this or other ways substantially inflated the repair bills. It was clear that actual fraud had been practiced by many of the sales personnel in repair shops, and that the impetus for this had come from corporate headquarters. This impetus, however, had started as a legal effort to increase sales and to deal with an ominous volume of losses threatening the company's financial stability. To stimulate their selling, salespeople had been given reduced wages and increased commissions along with heavy pressure to sell. There was no reason to charge management with having instituted the fraudulent practices, but with the salespeople feeling so much pressure that their jobs seemed in jeopardy, this was a context that almost inevitably generated criminal activity by rank-and-file workers who were not otherwise criminally inclined.[22]

Many forms of white collar crime violate federal laws and so various federal administrative or regulatory agencies investigate them. Because of their size, such departments as the Postal Service, the Food and Drug Administration, or the Interstate Commerce Commission must have special expertise for uncovering sophisticated and elusive violations of laws. The U.S. Secret Service also has extensive technical competence in this area and is available to help state or local investigative agencies develop their own specialized units.

The immense growth of computerized information systems that freely cross state and national boundaries, thus providing tantalizing new opportunities for quietly predatory invasions of corporate information, has spurred the need for federal involvement. However, law enforcement agencies at state and local levels are finding that the investigation and prosecution of computer crimes demands that they cooperate. Although an individual crime may be committed locally, computers are linked widely, often globally, and this calls for both local and national law enforcement agencies to collaborate. After the U.S. Congress enacted the Computer Fraud and Abuse Act of 1987, most states quickly followed with their own supplementary laws. As a result, local police, sheriffs, and prosecutors increasingly have developed investigative units with this technical expertise. Among the examples cited by one federal report is Maricopa County, Arizona, where the sheriff's office, with seventeen hundred employees, has a computer crimes unit that works as needed with federal agencies, and also with specialized investigators in the offices of both the county prosecutor and the state attorney general.

An instructive example of the demands made by this type of investigative work was an Ohio case in 1977 involving Revco, one of the country's largest drugstore chains. The company "was found guilty of a computer-generated double-billing scheme that resulted in the loss of over a half million dollars in Medicaid funds to the Ohio Department of Public Welfare. . . . Where once both offender and victim were individuals, in this instance both roles were played by complex organizations, and the definition of who was offender and who was victim was not so clear." The long-running and extensive investigation pursued in preparing the case for prosecution required, in addition to local police investigators, the combined resources of the investigative unit of the State Welfare Department, the State Pharmacy Board, the Ohio State Highway Patrol, and the Ecomomic Crimes Unit of the Franklin County Prosecutor's Office. (Vaughn 1983, xii)

Local law enforcement agencies need computer systems for their own administrative functions, and these may include police bulletin boards for rapid contacts with computers of other agencies over a wide area. Police in some instances have then found their own computers being invaded, but this in turn can become an opportunity to track and apprehend the offender.[23]

Computer specialists in law enforcement have to learn of several categories of criminal technique and the accompanying vocabulary. Each crime type is highly technical; an adequate description would entail copious details about variations that can proliferate in proportion to the imagination and innovative skill of the perpetrator.

Some types of fraud result from the work of "hackers" who ordinarily are young students experimenting with their home computers without initially intending any criminal activity. In a typical case the teenager seeks to contact distant computer bulletin boards to connect with other computer devotees, but then finds the telephone line charges too costly. This leads to illicit manipulation of the system to gain telephone access numbers that will allow him or her to make "free" calls. So an activity that starts as an innocuous hobby may finally result in the crime of defrauding the telephone company of the value of the long distance contacts.[24]

More serious is the person, frequently an opportunistic corporation employee, who deliberately uses computers for criminal purposes. This person finds ways to use the company's computer to contact other computers anywhere in the world. The person may accomplish sizable thefts by entering false data to divert company assets, reroute inventories, enter fictitious names on payrolls, or alter billing records. With the proper equipment, now utterly commonplace, an adept person can commit a huge theft in less than a second, perhaps against a corporate victim in some distant part of the world. Child pornographers, drug dealers, and other illegal operators use computer bulletin boards, while organized crime employs computers for activities such as fencing, money laundering, and prostitution.[25]

Organized Crime: More Sinister, Just as Elusive

The occasional dispute regarding the existence or nonexistence of organized crime is mainly fueled by the difficulty of gaining agreement on its definition. In any event, enough evidence exists to merit serious attention to its causes and sinister effects. The fact that its structure is difficult to chart or that its exact extent is uncertain should not cause doubt that it is a real presence. Organized crime offers a particularly sophisticated challenge to law enforcement agencies, lending urgency to the professionalization of police.

A characteristic of organized crime that both defines it and accounts for its persistence is that its illegal services are wanted and solicited by those who become its customers. With rare exceptions, average citizens do not encourage, but rather abhor, crimes such as robbery, embezzlement, arson, rape, or murder. The perpetrators of such crimes can expect little or no sympathy from the general public. But some members of the public want certain goods or services they see as not inherently bad even though illegal. They will, accordingly, tolerate, if not actively encourage, the criminal enterprise that supplies the desired goods or services. As one expert has put it, "the ordinary criminal is wholly predatory, while the man participating in crime on a rational, systematic basis offers a return to the respectable members of society." (Cressey 1969, 72)

Desirable goods or products in short supply, heavily taxed, or proscribed by law are likely to become the commerce of organized crime. Perhaps the best known example of this was the illicit production and sale of liquor during the prohibition of alcoholic beverages in the United States in the 1920s and early 1930s. With a large segment of the population wanting these beverages and willing to pay well for them, underworld gangs made enormous profits by organizing a supply system. Because they already operated outside the law, the gangs had little hesitation about using brutal methods to suppress competition. The result was rampant gangsterism in the 1920s.

In later years illicit drugs have achieved a status in criminal commerce similar to that previously occupied by liquor. Fencing stolen goods of all kinds is another natural activity for organized criminal groups. In addition to supplying various illicit products, organized crime offers services such as the many forms of gambling, loan-sharking, and the maintenance of brothels or other support systems for prostitution.

The Uncertain Evidence of Organization

Estes Kefauver, a U.S. senator who conducted a highly publicized inquiry into organized crime in 1950, asserted that there was indeed an extensive criminal organization then known as the Mafia. (Kefauver 1951) In its 1967 report on organized crime, the President's Commission on Law Enforcement and Administration of Justice said that "organized crime in the United States consists of 24 groups operating as criminal cartels in large cities across the Nation. Their membership is exclusively men of Italian descent, they are in frequent communication with each other, and their smooth functioning is insured by a national body of overseers." This organization, until then known as the Mafia, was said to be changing its name to Cosa Nostra. (President's Commission on Law Enforcement and Administration of Justice 1967, 6)

Donald R. Cressey, an eminent criminologist who had provided data on the subject to the Kefauver committee, confidently described an organized Mafia. "In the United States, criminals have managed to put together an organization which is at once a nationwide illicit cartel and a nationwide confederation." He described the organization's "families" as having formal management structures just as any legitimate corporation, and noted also that all were Italians. (Cressey 1969, x–xi, 1)

Despite this testimony, an equally astute scholar of the subject later pointed out that neither Kefauver nor Cressey had presented actual evidence that the overall organization existed. (Hawkins and Zimring 1984, 158–159) An odd example of the type of rationale that fuels the debate is Kefauver's observation that witnesses before his investigating committee tended to deny the fact of the Mafia: "Some of the witnesses called before us, who we had good reason to believe could tell us about the Mafia, sought to dismiss it as a sort of fairy tale or legend that children hear in Sicily where the Mafia originated." (Kefauver 1951, 19)

Kefauver's committee had heard testimony about numerous crimes that seemed cumulatively to point to the shadowy presence of a guiding criminal organization, but critics have skeptically noted that the chairman tended to read these denials of an existing Mafia as being instead a confirmation of its existence and proof of its secret and furtive character. (Hawkins and Zimring 1984, 159) Nevertheless, the Kefauver hearings strongly affected public consciousness. For much of the citizenry it brought the first awareness of the size of the problem and the existence of the Mafia.

During the several years when organized crime was gaining public attention, and despite the intense public interest generated by the Kefauver hearings, there was very little reaction from the FBI. In retrospect this raises intriguing questions about why J. Edgar Hoover, ordinarily quick to take advantage of such highly visible issues, downplayed the threat, and dismissed the likely existence of organized crime. Some of the attempts to explain Hoover's position on the subject have been imaginative, even titillating, but a sober appraisal suggests that we may never know for sure.[26]

The Political Selection of Targets

Whether at the local or federal level, law enforcement agencies necessarily respond to the political context in which they function, with the result that targets for intensive policing may be selected for political purposes. Some project of the moment being pursued at city hall might need to be bolstered by having the public get news of certain kinds of arrests being made, and so the policing emphasis is directed accordingly. It may be an altogether benign and even constructive strategy, or it may be quite corrupt, as when police are persuaded to avoid certain areas of "protected" vice.

As an example of the politics of personality at the federal level, the FBI record on organized crime usefully highlights the way that purity of purpose can be frustrated by political expediency or private motivations.

Partly it was a matter of Hoover's wish to leave this type of crime control to local police, as he was always reluctant to get into activities in which successful outcomes would not be clearly evident. He had built his own and his agency's prestige with publicity on its high percentage of convictions and high figures of stolen property recovered. The Hoover ego resisted any activity that would not support and enhance his personal repute. "The targeting of a formidable adversary such as organized crime would dilute those statistics and undermine the FBI image of infallibility."[27] A further persuasive insight is given by a Hoover biographer. "Hoover was also reluctant to recognize the existence of organized crime because any effective campaign against it would require a 'task force' strategy using personnel drawn from all available branches of government. Under these circumstances it would be impossible for him to preserve the FBI's autonomy or to have complete control over the operations of his agents. . . . Preserving (and expanding) FBI independence of action, even at the cost of limiting the Bureau's growth and responsibilities, was an absolute must for Hoover." (Powers 1987, 333)

Eventually the reality of organized crime was made clearly explicit by an unusual event. In November 1957 a state police officer unexpectably stumbled on a conference of sixty or more top Mafia members at the home of one member in Apalachin, New York. Nationwide publicity about the event raised questions about why the FBI had been unaware of any such gathering. After that the existence of criminal organizations could hardly be denied.

In 1963 an imprisoned top member of a crime family, Joe Valachi, testified extensively before a Senate committee, attracting new attention to the organized crime issue. During the previous year Valachi had killed a fellow prisoner, presumably as a means of protecting himself from a Mafia-directed attempt on his life. Finding himself under continuing threat of death, he defied the code of silence to testify in detail about individuals and their activities in organized crime. It was, he explained, his retaliation against them for attacking him. Presumably it was this Valachi testimony that first acquainted the public with the name "Cosa Nostra." The testimony revealed the inner workings of the crime families, and reputedly gave law enforcement officials the best picture they had ever had of the Cosa Nostra organization. But was it valid? Even though some of the experts following the hearings were satisfied with Valachi's accuracy and enthusiastic about his usefulness, others remained skeptical. Some argued that he had revealed nothing new, and suspected that he padded his testimony generously with information others had fed him. (Abadinsky 1981, 243)

Whatever the accuracy of Valachi's information, it effectively forced FBI attention to the problem, it captured public interest, and governmental expenditures for law enforcement increased appreciably over the next decade. In 1967 President Lyndon Johnson set up the ambitious Commission on Law Enforcement and Administration of Justice as a part of his "war on crime," and in the next few years the FBI added about one thousand new agents for increased action against organized crime. In 1968 Congress passed the Omnibus Crime Control and Safe Streets Act; in 1970 it passed the Racketeer-Influenced Corrupt Organization Act, known as RICO, the law that became the most potent federal weapon in fighting organized crime.

The Insidious Character of Organized Crime

Whether there is truly a formal national Mafia or Cosa Nostra organization, clearly some form of organized crime exists. The controversy about this question reflects the fluid nature of criminal groups, which adapt continually to market conditions, law enforcement pressures, the talents and inclinations of the criminal organization leaders of the moment, and a variety of other transitory factors. The organizational presence behind the criminal activity remains hidden because although the general law-abiding public is the target, most members of the public not only never see the organization criminals, but also are usually unaware of being victims. For the average citizen the effect of organized crime, in one example, is to pay a penny or two more for some product because it is delivered by a trucking firm that must pay a crime group for the trucking contract. Or a citizen might patronize some supposedly legitimate business that is a front for a criminal organization that is milking the profits of the business. Or he or she patronizes a business which, unknown to customers, is having to inflate its prices to cover the cost of paying criminal groups for the right to operate. Of course a citizen may support a criminal enterprise more directly by purchasing drugs or using prostitution or gambling services; but even here he or she is not likely to encounter the criminal organization behind the services.

The political arena tends to be quite vulnerable to criminal infiltration and here too the uninvolved citizen has little reason to know of its presence. The problem is rooted in the particular nature of democracy, with its insatiable need for political influence, power, and the money to campaign for and remain in office. It is not necessary to prove that there is a Mafia or any other national organization in order to show that there may be at least a local cartel, functioning informally, but contributing significantly to the campaign of a legislator, a city council member, a judge, or other public functionary who, having been "bought," cannot then avoid giving whatever "under-the-table" favors are demanded in return.

In 1988 William S. Sessions, then director of the FBI, told a Senate committee of his concern that La Cosa Nostra had become a highly structured group of crime families, coordinated by an overall commission, and adept at compromising governmental operations. "Although much of the power of La Cosa Nostra still comes from the profits generated by gambling and by loan sharking, extortion and drug trafficking, their real power base lies in the corruption of the public officials and the influence they control and exert over labor unions." (U.S. Congress, Senate, Permanent Subcommittee on Investigations 1988, 14)

Although the complex interactions between crime figures and politicians, police, sports, gambling operators, and others are nearly invisible to all but a few, it is an accepted principle that wherever prostitution or other illicit commerce persists, protection is being bought from police and other officials. In fact, payments to one level of the political hierarchy are not enough; one organized crime veteran made the point that successful criminal infiltration depends on corrupting all governmental levels. His technique was "to pay the top people as much as necessary and to pay lesser amounts to as many others as possible in order to implicate them and prevent them from blowing the whistle. Some officials got regular weekly payoffs while relatively unimportant patrolmen on the beat were bought with nothing more than a Christmas turkey." (Dorman 1972, 15)

An insidious aspect of such corruption is that it has a discreet quality; it is little noticed by the average citizen, or sometimes citizens just prefer to ignore a condition which they feel helpless to change. A veteran Chicago newspaper reporter, writing about the career of Mayor Richard J. Daley, observed that "in many ways the citizens preferred a dishonest police department. The traffic bribe saved a trip to court. The tavern payoff was in return for favors granted. . . . That's the way the Police Department was in 1955 when Daley became mayor, and it was the same, and maybe worse, in 1960. He grew up in politics and the police force was part of the Machine." (Royko 1971, 113)

An Opportunity for Ethnic Groups

Although the Kefauver committee heard that all the organized crime figures were Italian, this view is unsupportable. It remains true, however, that certain immigrant groups have dominated organized crime, and the literature has increasingly noted the infusion of a range of other ethnic groups. Senator Sam Nunn, chairing a Senate committee in 1980, remarked that "organized crime never has known any ethnic bounds, and its activities run the gamut from the gutter to the board rooms of legitimate businesses and labor unions in this country." (U.S. Congress, Senate, Hearings before the Permanent Subcommittee on Investigations of the Committee on Governmental Affairs 1980, 11)

The history of prejudice against many ethnic groups has meant that at times the legitimate avenues of work and upward mobility have been denied to their members, leading them as an alternative to build careers in illicit activities. ''Those groups that became most heavily involved in organized crime migrated from regions in which they had developed deep suspicions of governmental authority—whether the Irish fleeing British rule in Ireland, Jews escaping from Eastern Europe, Italians migrating from southern Italy or Sicily, or blacks leaving the American South.'' (Hawkins and Zimring 1984, 144–145) One expert notes that blacks early concentrated on various forms of gambling. ''The numbers racket was, of course, invented and controlled by the blacks after World War I.'' He adds, however, that later, when whites began to take over the numbers games, blacks shifted from gambling to narcotics.[28]

Even during the height of Prohibition, when Italians were prominent in the gangs of the time, Chicago had nearly as many Irish engaged in organized criminal activities.

Urban politics, with the profitable contracts to be let for all kinds of public services, provided an opportunity for those neighborhood figures who could get elected to city offices. It led to infiltration of construction and trucking industries, taxi-dance halls, sports, labor unions, and the entertainment industry. (Hawkins and Zimring 1984, 135–136) The complex relationships among criminal organizations and the worlds of entertainment and politics can be glimpsed through an incident during the Kennedy administration when singer Frank Sinatra, friend of several crime figures, introduced to John F. Kennedy a woman who afterward became particularly close to the president. The FBI noted the developing relationship, leading J. Edgar Hoover to warn the president that the woman had links to the Mafia and that she had the potential to compromise the White House seriously. (Powers 1987, 360)

Organized Crime under Attack

After years of increasing governmental efforts to cripple the organized crime families it has been noted, not at all surprisingly, that when one family or crime boss is defeated others soon move in to fill the gap. Today there is much less talk of the crime figures all being Italian, and indeed there is recognition that the incursion of Asian immigrants in the last decade has brought those nationalities into the crime picture. Nor are the new recruits always ethnic or national in their identities; a development of recent years has been the emergence of criminal motorcycle gangs. Between eight hundred and nine hundred of these gangs are thought to exist, engaging mainly in importation and sale of illicit drugs. (President's Commission on Organized Crime, *The Impact: Organized Crime Today* 1986, 58)

Unfortunately, the punishment system, which should be discouraging organized crime, is often found to have the opposite effect. Prisons by their nature tend to encourage the formation of crime groups, leading culturally similar prisoners to band together for protection from other prisoners. As these prison-bred organizations grow and as members are released, they tend to carry the organization outside. Some states contending with prisoner gangs have tried to break them by scattering members among several institutions, only to find that in this way they have proliferated the gangs. Since the late 1970s the Federal Bureau of Prisons has found itself with five major gangs, racially or ethnically based, and violently competitive. In general, prisons cannot prevent the formation of the gangs; the usual strategy is to develop control measures which include diligent efforts to identify gang members and to house them separately to prevent any violent interactions. (Trout 1992; Buentello 1992)

Federal prosecutors are aggressively fighting criminal organizations and claiming successes. They denote four assets they have in pursuing the effort: (a) the relatively recent full utilization of electronic surveillance to penetrate criminal communications; (b) the Witness Security Program; (c) use of the RICO act along with other new federal tactics, including the merging of the efforts of the FBI and the Drug Enforcement Administration; and (d) increased cooperation between U.S. and Italian law enforcement agencies. (President's Commission on Organized Crime, *The Impact: Organized Crime Today* 1986, 48)

The witness protection program incorporated into the RICO act became an especially potent tool for prosecutors because it enabled them to obtain testimony from persons who were otherwise too fearful to talk. The RICO act enables the government to arrange and finance a new identity and new protected location for anyone who has reason to fear retaliation for his or her testimony. The program also extends to witnesses who already are federal prisoners. Normally witnesses who are prisoners would be extremely vulnerable to fatal attacks while in prison, but the federal government has built at several of its facilities special separate buildings where such prisoners can be confined under unique conditions which effectively protect them from any would-be attacker. As of the end of 1992 these units had received nearly five hundred such prisoners, no one of whom had suffered any retaliatory attack while so protected.

In 1988, speaking appreciatively of these enhanced crime weapons, the FBI director was happy to note that since 1981 the FBI had obtained convictions of nineteen organized crime bosses and sixty others from twenty Cosa Nostra families. At the same time the director of the New

York Organized Crime Task Force asserted that the old code of silence among Mafia members was no longer holding. Family members were showing a new willingness to testify against others, making far more convictions possible. He credited this trend to the new ability to offer witnesses effective protection, as well as a new generation of younger gang members who were interested mainly in immediate economic rewards rather than loyalty to old crime family traditions. (U.S. Congress, Senate, Permanent Subcommittee on Investigations 1988, 15, 151)

A glimpse of the international character of organized crime, its ruthless defiance of its opponents, as well as the recent progress in its prosecution, was afforded on the occasion of a new FBI director being appointed in September 1993. The selection for the post of Louis Freeh, a relatively unknown federal prosecutor and former FBI agent, brought to light the story of his successful collaboration with the top Italian prosecutor to obtain convictions of key figures in the U.S. and Sicilian Mafias. Together, Freeh and his Italian counterpart, Giovanni Falcone, had managed a joint strike force that "led to the most celebrated Mafia trials in many years: the 'Pizza Connection' cases in New York involving more than two dozen defendants, and the 'Maxie Trial' in Palermo, in which 364 defendants were ultimately tried en masse for crimes arising from Mafia membership."[29]

The Italian-American strike force, organized at the FBI's training academy in Quantico, Virginia, in 1981, had been aided by the witness protection program, which had given a protected identity to an important Mafia insider, Tommaso Buscetta, in exchange for his detailed testimony describing criminal activities in the United States and political corruption in Italy. The resultant prosecution was such a fundamental threat to the Mafia organization that a vicious retaliation was expected and guarded against—but not successfully; in May 1992, while driving in Palermo, Sicily, the Italian prosecutor, Falcone, his wife, and three bodyguards were all killed instantly by a bomb.

Despite such brutal defiance of the justice system, the Mafia was appreciably weakened by the successful prosecution and conviction of most of the defendants in the Maxie Trial in Italy. Similarly, in the United States as the 1990s began there seemed some justification for cautious optimism, although anyone familiar with the organized crime problem could recognize that the extraction of one or even many crime family members from the rackets would no doubt just leave space for others to move in. And the new generation might look very different. In the spring of 1992 John Gotti, head of the Gambino crime family, was in federal court in New York City defending himself from charges of murder and racketeering. The trial ended in his conviction and sentence to life in prison. But while John Gotti, age 51, was on trial, in another courtroom in the same courthouse a less known defendant was also being tried on racketeering charges. He was Chen I. Chung, age 23, leader of an aggressive new gang with links to Asian sources of drugs. As Gotti was taken to federal prison the new generation was ready to take his place.[30]

As this chapter has indicated, recent substantial advances in the professionalization and technical competence of law enforcement have paralleled, if not countered, equal advances in the sophistication of organized criminal enterprises. A heartening aspect of the trend in police science is an increased sensitivity to racial and ethnic minorities, with both police and corrections belatedly making affirmative efforts to hire proportionately from all such groups, as well as including race relations topics in their training programs. Improved technical training for all criminal justice professionals is essential if society is to keep up with the continually renewed challenge presented by organized crime groups that are likely to be as technically sophisticated as they are ruthless.

Notes

1. Kelling, George L. and David Fogel. "Police Patrol: Some Future Directions." In Cohn, Alvin W., ed., *The Future of Policing*. Beverly Hills, Calif.: Sage Publications, 1978.
2. Charles Reith. *The Blind Eye of History: A Study of the Origins of the Present Police Era*. Montclair, N.J.: Patterson Smith, 1975 reprint, 83. First published in 1952.
3. *New York Times* (Dec. 27, 1974), L1.
4. The information on the two Indianapolis police departments was furnished to the author by letter of August 14, 1992, from the Indiana Historical Society.
5. Nathan Douthit. "August Vollmer, Berkeley's First Chief of Police and the Emergence of Police Professionalism." *California Historical Quarterly* 54 (Summer 1975), 116.
6. The point is well-discussed by Lawrence W. Sherman. "College Education for Police: The Reform That Failed." *Police Studies* 1:4 (Dec. 1978), 32–37.
7. Michael Serrill. "LEAA: A Question of Impact." *Corrections Magazine* 2:4 (June 1976), 7.
8. Richard Rubin. "Computer Trends in Law Enforcement." *The Police Chief* 58:4 (April 1991), 22–24.
9. Samuel G. Janus, et al. "The Police Officer as Street Psychiatrist." *Police Studies* 2:3 (Fall 1979), 27.
10. James M. Peters. "Specialists a Definite Advantage in Child Abuse Cases." *The Police Chief* 58:2 (Feb. 1991), 21, 22.
11. Susan Braunstein. "Building a More Ethical Police Department." *The Police Chief* 59:1 (Jan. 1992), 31.
12. Gerald W. Lynch. "Educating the Police: The Debate Continues." *Police Studies* 2:1 (Spring 1979), 4.

13. Gary Weaver. "Law Enforcement in a Culturally Diverse Society." *FBI Law Enforcement Bulletin* (Sept. 1992), 6.

14. *The Police Chief* 57:1 (Jan. 1990), 46; and *FBI Law Enforcement Bulletin* (Sept. 1992), 16–17.

15. Robert C. Trojanowicz and David L. Carter. "The Changing Face of America." *FBI Law Enforcement Bulletin* (Jan. 1990), 6.

16. Ibid., 8.

17. For example, see Dothard v. Rawlinson, 97 S.C. 2720; or Manley v. Mobile County, Alabama, 441 F.Supp. 1351 (1977); or Anthony v. Massachusetts, 415 F.Supp. 485 (1976).

18. U.S. Bureau of Justice Statistics. *Sourcebook of Criminal Justice Statistics—1991*, Figures 6.1, 6.2; Table 6.71.

19. Darrell J. Steffensmeier. "Sex Differences in Patterns of Adult Crime 1965–77: A Review and Assessment." *Social Forces* 58:4 (June 1980), 1094.

20. U.S. Bureau of Justice Statistics. *Sourcebook of Criminal Justice Statistics—1991*, Table 6.88.

21. Darrell J. Steffensmeier. "Assessing the Impact of the Women's Movement on Sex-Based Differences in the Handling of Adult Criminal Defendants." *Crime and Delinquency* 26:3 (July 1980), 356.

22. *Business Week* 3272 (June 29, 1992), 38; and 3277 (Aug. 3, 1992), 24.

23. National Institute of Justice. *Issues and Practices: Organizing for Computer Crime Investigation and Prosecution* (July 1989), 15–16, 17, 39.

24. Ibid., 40.

25. Ibid., 12.

26. See Tony G. Poveda. *Lawlessness and Reform: The FBI in Transition.* Pacific Grove, Calif.: Brooks/Cole, 1990, 109.

27. Ibid.

28. Frederick T. Martins. "African-American Organized Crime, an Ignored Phenomenon." *Federal Probation* 54:4 (Dec. 1990), 43.

29. Steve Coll. "The American Connection." *Washington Post Magazine* (Oct. 31, 1993), 11.

30. *New York Times* (April 1, 1992), L1.

Bibliography

Professionalism for the Police

Armstrong, Terry R. and Kenneth M. Cinnamon, eds. *Power and Authority in Law Enforcement.* Springfield, Ill.: Charles C. Thomas, 1976.

An anthology of articles discussing the various aspects of political power and the ways they affect police. Articles extensively cover the nature of prejudice, its sources, and how it distorts police functioning.

Cohn, Alvin W., ed. *The Future of Policing.* Beverly Hills, Calif.: Sage Publications, 1978.

Another anthology presenting articles by law enforcment specialists, including police practitioners who discuss their various specialties. Included are competent discussions of private security, patrol operations, female police, and various police management issues.

Cose, Ellis. *A Nation of Strangers: Prejudice, Politics, and the Populating of America.* New York: William Morrow, 1992.

A thorough history of American prejudice toward racial, national, and ethnic groups from earliest colonial times to the present. Cose reviews the political factors historically involved in animosities toward religious categories, either Catholic or Protestant, as well as recent attitudes toward Mexicans, Cubans, and Haitians.

Deakin, Thomas J. *Police Professionalism: The Renaissance of American Law Enforcement.* Springfield, Ill.: Charles C. Thomas, 1988.

Eskridge, Chris. "College and the Police: A Review of the Issues." Chapter 2 in *Police and Policy: Contemporary Issues,* ed. Dennis Jay Kenney. New York: Praeger, 1989.

Farmer, David John. *Crime Control: The Use and Misuse of Police Resources.* New York: Plenum, 1984.

An astute look at crime prevention as related to police methods, operational philosophy, political complications, and the practical realities of police management. Gives a useful analysis of a wide variety of actual policing experiments or experiences of instructional value. Includes an unusually comprehensive bibliography of sources on police practice.

Feinman, Clarice. *Women in the Criminal Justice System.* New York: Praeger, 1986.

A review of trends in societal attitudes toward women; discusses categories of female involvement in criminal justice, trends in female criminality, and the experience with women in police work, corrections, and law.

Flowers, Ronald B. *Minorities and Criminality.* New York: Greenwood, 1988.

A carefully documented discussion of minority groups in relation to crime patterns in the United States. It gives attention to victimization of minorities, theories of race and criminality, and differential treatment of minorities by law enforcement.

Garmire, Bernard L., ed. *Local Government Police Management.* Washington, D.C.: International City Management Association, 1982.

As a general reference work on police management, this large manual is a competent and useful resource. It contains the writings of a number of police executives; it covers both philosophical and practical managerial aspects of police work; and it serves as a guide to the best current standards.

Headley, Bernard D. "Crime, Justice, and Powerless Racial Groups." *Social Justice* 16:4 (Winter 1989), 1–8.

Horne, Peter. *Women in Law Enforcement.* Springfield, Ill.: Charles C. Thomas, 1980.

Joseph, Kenneth E. "Academe and the FBI Academy: Partners in the Quest for Police Professionalism." *Police Studies* 1:1 (March 1978), 13–18.

Kelling, George L. and David Fogel. "Police Patrol: Some Future Directions," in Cohn 1978 (above).

Kent, Joan R. *The English Village Constable 1580–1642: A Social and Administrative Study.* Oxford: Clarendon Press, 1986.

Larson, Calvin J. *Crime, Justice and Society.* Bayside, N.J.: General Hall, 1984.

Moenssens, Andre A. and Fred E. Imbau. *Scientific Police Investigation.* Mineola, N.Y.: Foundation Press, 1978.

An immense and comprehensive presentation of factual information about all aspects of forensic science in crime investigation. It presents in practical, objective detail the range of procedures for scientific analysis and solving of crimes. It includes discussion of all the types of laboratory tests, the handling of psychiatric evidence, and the legal, psychological, and strategic knowledge essential for successful testimony by expert witnesses.

Powers, Richard Gid. *Secrecy and Power: The Life of J. Edgar Hoover.* New York: Free Press, 1987.

A thoroughly researched, documented, and revealing biography that not only discusses the personality and personal history of Hoover, but also provides much detail of the relevant history of the United States in the twentieth century. It gives a wealth of information about the character, philosophy, and operations of the FBI during Hoover's time.

Rison, Richard H. "Women as High-Security Officers." *Federal Prisons Journal* 3:3 (Winter 1994), 19–23.

A well-reasoned analysis of the pros and cons of hiring women into high-risk prison jobs, written by a federal warden who experienced the changing attitudes. The article gives practical, factual data on the subject by an author who is supportive of women's entry into this field.

Skolnick, Jerome H. *Justice without Trial: Law Enforcement in Democratic Society.* New York: John Wiley, 1966.

Theoharis, Athan G. "The FBI and the Politics of Surveillance, 1908–1985." *Criminal Justice Review* 15:2 (Autumn 1990), 221–230.

Theoharis, Athan G. and John Stuart Cox. *The Boss: J. Edgar Hoover and the Great American Inquisition.* Philadelphia: Temple University Press, 1988.

A biography of Hoover as director of the FBI, with emphasis on the ways in which Hoover exercised power with disregard to constitutional guarantees.

The Police Confront White Collar Crime: Organized Crime

Abadinsky, Howard. *Organized Crime.* Boston: Allyn & Bacon, 1981.

A thorough examination of the complex and elusive subject of organized crime. The author studies the difficult efforts to define organized crime; he gives numerous examples and describes ways in which well-known corporations have sometimes built their positions of wealth and power by essentially criminal methods, often corrupting the federal government into supporting their corporate goals. The book discusses the many types of corruption fostered by organized crime, the types of goods and services from which it profits, and the measures that governments use to frustrate and prosecute it. Well documented, with a comprehensive bibliography.

Anderson, Annelise Graebner. *The Business of Organized Crime: A Cosa Nostra Family.* Stanford, Calif.: Hoover Institution Press, 1979.

Bequai, August. *Organized Crime: The Fifth Estate.* Lexington, Mass.: Lexington Books, 1979.

Block, Alan A., ed. *The Business of Crime: A Documentary Study of Organized Crime in the American Economy.* Boulder, Colo.: Westview Press, 1991.

    Accounts of a selected number of prosecutions against organized crime, with extensive quotations. Though useful for the case studies, the book is limited by not attempting instruction regarding a broad view of the organized crime problem.

Block, Alan A. and William J. Chambliss. *Organizing Crime.* New York: Elsevier, 1981.

    This thorough and well-documented text examines the history of the illicit drug trade in the United States and several other countries in some depth, featuring the relevant underworld leaders and their methods. The authors discuss racketeering influences in U.S. businesses and labor unions as well as the means by which the U.S. government has attempted, through legislation and police action, to combat organized crime.

Buentello, Salvador. "Combating Gangs in Texas." *Corrections Today* 54:5 (July 1992), 58–60.

Cressey, Donald R. *Theft of the Nation.* New York: Harper & Row, 1969.

    The extended version of a report that this noted criminologist prepared for the President's Commission on Law Enforcement and Administration of Justice regarding the character of organized crime, especially of the Sicilian Mafia. Cressey examines the "families" in detail, presenting a useful history of their spread and development. He gives names and relationships of all the significant bosses, and details the techniques used by the organizations in infiltrating businesses, corrupting officials, and searching out new sources of revenue.

Currie, Elliott. *Confronting Crime.* New York: Pantheon Books, 1985.

    Among the theorists of crime causation and crime control, there are varied approaches to the issues, and varied conclusions and biases. The contribution of this author is not so much to present still another defined theory as to give cogent analysis of the current offerings of important observers of criminal justice issues. Currie gives a tightly reasoned, thorough, and rational discussion of the popular thinkers and their arguments. His own arguments are detailed, persuasive, and instructive as he offers critiques of well-known criminologists and their research. In addition to causal theories he discusses the doubtful utility of incarceration, and reviews ideas for improved penal methods.

Doleschal, Eugene, Anne Newton, and William Hickey. *A Guide to the Literature on Organized Crime: An Annotated Bibliography Covering the Years 1967–81.* Hackensack, N.J.: National Council on Crime and Delinquency, 1981.

Dombrink, John. "Organized Crime: Gangsters and Godfathers." Chapter 3 in Joseph E. Scott and Travis Hirschi, *Controversial Issues in Crime and Justice.* Beverly Hills, Calif.: Sage Publications, 1988.

Dorman, Michael. *Payoff: The Role of Organized Crime in American Politics.* New York: David McKay, 1972.

    A general discussion of one criminologist's perspective on the types of organized crime, interspersed with accounts of specific case examples of well-publicized crimes or investigations.

Gardiner, John A. *The Politics of Corruption: Organized Crime in an American City.* New York: Russell Sage Foundation, 1970.

Without giving the true name of the city he studies, the author addresses the organized crime problem in one specific urban locality, and covers in thorough and explicit detail the economic, demographic, and political context for the city's corruption.

Gardiner, John A. and David J. Olson, eds. *Theft of the City: Readings in Corruption in Urban America.* Bloomington: Indiana University Press, 1974.

Haller, Mark H. "Organized Crime in Urban Society: Chicago in the Twentieth Century." Chapter 8 in Hawkins and Zimring 1984 (below).

Hawkins, Gordon. "God and the Mafia." Chapter 9 in Hawkins and Zimring 1984 (below).

Hawkins, Gordon and Franklin E. Zimring, eds. *The Pursuit of Criminal Justice.* Chicago: University of Chicago Press, 1984.

Two of the country's most astute criminologists present essays from a dozen experts on current crime problems. Topics covered include organized crime, prison violence, deterrence, sentencing, the death penalty, and others.

Kefauver, Estes. *Crime in America.* New York: Doubleday, 1951.

The author was a U.S. senator from Tennessee who chaired a committee investigating the nature of the country's crime problem, and especially organized crime. The hearings were highly publicized at the time, and this book is Kefauver's subsequent account of the findings. It is useful as a picture of public perceptions of the time, but otherwise is not a reliable or scholarly treatment of the subject.

Larson, Calvin J. *Crime, Justice and Society.* Bayside, N.J.: General Hall, 1984.

National Advisory Commission on Criminal Justice Standards and Goals. *Report of the Task Force on Organized Crime.* Washington, D.C.: GPO, 1976.

President's Commission on Law Enforcement and Administration of Justice. *Task Force Report: Organized Crime.* Washington, D.C.: GPO, 1967.

President's Commission on Organized Crime. Record of Hearing I. *Federal Law Enforcement Perspective.* Washington, D.C.: GPO, 1983.

This item is the first in a series of eight reports, the others of which are similarly referenced and separately designated as follows:

Organized Crime and Money Laundering, Hearing II, March 1984.
Organized Crime of Asian Origin, Hearing III, Oct. 1984.
Organized Crime and Cocaine Trafficking, Hearing IV. Nov. 1984.
Organized Crime and Heroin Trafficking, Hearing V, Feb. 1985.
Organized Crime and Labor-Management Racketeering in the United States, Hearing VI, April 1985.
Organized Crime and Gambling, Hearing VII, June 1985.
The Impact: Organized Crime Today. Report to the President and Attorney General, April 1986.

Royko, Mike. *Boss: Richard J. Daley of Chicago.* New York: New American Library, 1971.

A veteran newspaper reporter covers the administration of Mayor Daley with relentless pursuit of the underlying political and personal factors which explain the shady workings of Chicago city government of that time.

Schlegel, Kip and David Weisburd, eds. *White-Collar Crime Reconsidered.* Boston: Northeastern University Press, 1992.

An anthology of competent essays on various aspects of white collar crime authored by more than twenty experts from varied academic and administrative criminal justice careers. The chapters address many viewpoints about corporate crime, and include details of significant case examples.

Sutherland, Edwin H. *White Collar Crime.* New Haven, Conn.: Yale University Press, 1983.

Sutherland, the notable sociologist who coined the term "white collar crime," presents here his influential picture of the way that corporate and other white collar crime quietly persists and defrauds the public of exorbitant amounts. Distinguished by his famous theory of differential association, this readable book is a unique contribution to the literature on white collar crime.

Sykes, Gresham. *Criminology.* New York: Harcourt, Brace, Jovanovich, 1978.

Trout, Craig H. "Taking a New Look at an Old Problem." *Corrections Today* 54:5 (July 1992), 62–66.

A detailed discription of the principal gangs in prisons (mainly in the federal system), their organizational characteristics, their criminality, and the prison management experience in their control.

U.S. Congress. Senate. Hearings before the Committee on the Judiciary. *Organized Crime in America.* 98th Cong., 1st sess. (Jan.–March 1983) Washington, D.C.: GPO, 1983.

U.S. Congress. Senate. Hearings before the Permanent Subcommittee on Investigations of the Committee on Governmental Affairs. *Organized Crime and Use of Violence.* 96th Cong., 2nd sess. (April–May 1980) Washington, D.C.: GPO, 1980.

U.S. Congress. Senate. Permanent Subcommittee on Investigations, Committee on Governmental Affairs. *Organized Crime 25 Years after Valachi.* 100th Cong., 2nd sess. (April 1988) Washington, D.C.: GPO, 1990.

Vaughn, Diane. *Controlling Unlawful Organizational Behavior: Social Structure and Corporate Misconduct.* Chicago: University of Chicago Press, 1983.

Wagner, Charles R. *The CPA and Computer Fraud.* Lexington, Mass.: Lexington Books, 1979.

CHAPTER 3

Prevention and Control
of Crime

O f the many purposes of the criminal justice system, the prevention of crime is probably both the most important and the most elusive. In addressing this topic it will be important to look at the commonly recognized categories of preventive efforts, the theories behind them, and both the promise and the disappointments they bring. Prevention must be discussed in terms of police patrol, "target hardening" (improvement of locks, alarms, lighting, etc.), environmental design of housing areas, and even correctional efforts with convicted offenders. And as always, the political issues confronting policymakers deserve careful attention.

While it is difficult either to define or achieve prevention, the proof of its accomplishment is still more difficult. There is no certain way to prove the number of crimes *not* committed, and even if it were possible there would still be doubts about whether any reduction in crime was due to prevention programs or to other factors. Nevertheless, the need for preventive measures is urgent given the public's fear of crime and the pressure that fear puts on governmental policymakers to take action for crime control.

Two different types of crime prevention can be recognized: one is concerned with deterrence in the individual or special case, and the other is composed of broadly designed deterrence measures aimed at a community or the wider society in general. (Coffey 1975, 54) The latter approach may be subdivided further into two efforts, one being promotion of measures that enhance satisfying lifestyles for everyone and thus reduce the social conditions that foster crime. The other is the more mechanical approach of "hardening the target," utilizing measures and devices that block access to crime targets or help in identifying and capturing the offender. It is here that the most effective preventive efforts can be claimed. With the use of high-quality locks, burglar alarms, and roving patrols, the safety of a particular site or building can be well ensured. Similarly, a residential neighborhood or apartment complex affluent enough to maintain a controlled and limited access point with 24-hour watchman service will ordinarily remain crime free.

While such measures do well in preventing crime in and around the target sites, this does not mean that crime in the larger context is reduced. Community planners must assume that successful hardening of specific targets may be only displacing, and not actually preventing, crime, even though this is not provable. Target hardening is necessary and important, but a community needs also to supplement this effort with more general crime prevention measures.

Prevention through "General Deterrence"

Historically, the most enduring public measure for deterrence of crime has been the use, or the threat, of punishment. Though actual experiences of governments have shown punishment to have an uncertain and unprovable effect, the reliance on it is tenacious; punishment has an immediate, direct action quality that appeals to the human need for simple solutions. Equally potent, though much less admitted and virtually never mentioned, is the human need for revenge. As a rule it can be said that in its subjective reaction to a specific, close-at-hand crime, the public demands the stringent punishment response as its preferred means of deterrence. The more objective social improvement measures are recognized only when considering the broad, impersonal problem of crime in general.

It is often argued that certain and immediate punishment would have a more deterrent effect than more severe punishment. This is a reasonable and persuasive view, but nearly impossible to confirm by any objective research. Also, the limited resources our society can afford promise little hope of increasing either the certainty of apprehension of criminals or the speed of prosecution. (Greenwood 1982, viii) The odd result is that the criminal justice system, unable to apprehend and convict more than a fraction of the criminal offenders, imposes extra prison time on those few it does manage to catch and convict instead of spreading the punishment in more moderate doses to the many who deserve it.

Reduction of the Causes of Crime

There would seem to be a simple and basic logic in the idea of preventing crime by removing what are perceived to be its causes. But this idea immediately presents the question of just what are the causes of crime. Theories abound. "What many of these theories have in common is an acceptance of the view that most criminal behavior is learned in a particular social context and that it is not different in nature from other behavior; . . . although many different factors have been shown to be associated to a greater or lesser degree with crime, it has not proved possible to organize and integrate them in a causal theory of criminal behavior. . . . the truth is there are no more causes of crime than there are causes of human behavior. Or, perhaps put more accurately, the causes of human behavior are the causes of crime." (Morris and Hawkins 1970, 47)

The popular mind assigns poverty a major role among causes of crime, and occasional governmental efforts to reduce poverty have been advocated as likely to help reduce crime. Experience has shown, how-ever, that poverty by itself cannot be proved to cause crime, nor have crime rates ever been reduced by such efforts. This is one more example of the natural human impulse to solve complex problems with simple solutions. As one observer points out, "Poverty is not a simple variable but is the product of the interaction of several variables: unemployment, undereducation, family structure, income, poor housing, and so forth. These variables interact with each other." For such reasons, antipoverty programs have failed to reduce crime rates. (Jeffery 1977, 147)

Though experience has amply shown that the federal government is not an effective instrument for reforming broad social conditions, politi-cal parties in their quest for supremacy cannot resist making attempts at social engineering. Suppression of crime is perhaps the prime example. With the inexorable rise in crime rates since the 1960s, and the consequent public fear of crime, presidential and gubernatorial campaigns have been marked by contentious rhetoric about who is tougher on crime.

In 1964 and 1965, despite the distraction of the Vietnam War, Presi-dent Johnson, with a passionate desire to make a profound impact on American society, launched his plan for the "Great Society." It com-prised various legislative initiatives for progressive social programs, including a voting rights act, aid to public education, and improvement of benefits under Social Security. Such measures would reduce poverty, it was hoped, and attack the basic causes of crime. To address the crime problem more specifically, Johnson proposed his Omnibus Crime Con-trol and Safe Streets Act, intended to give massive support to police and corrections agencies. This act established the controversial but highly influential Law Enforcement Assistance Administration (LEAA).

A Federal Initiative and Its Political Context

At the time the LEAA was created, social upheavals both spurred the adoption of this remedial legislation and led to eventual disillusion with it. Anti-Vietnam War protesters demonstrated loudly against the government. Minority groups, frustrated with the slow pace of social reform, took to the streets. In 1968, after both Martin Luther King, Jr., and Robert Kennedy were assassinated, the legislation creating LEAA, which heretofore had been stalled, was revived and soon passed with generous funding. The money was channeled to state planning agencies for allocation on the assumption by Congress that state and local governments knew best what they needed for improvement of their criminal justice agencies. Success, even for such a massive effort, is elusive and limited. An in-depth report by *Corrections Magazine* on the program's first eight years showed a truly remarkable impact in respect to refinement and repair of the criminal justice systems—but no apparent reduction of crime. During that time, among the many types of expenditures, the allocated funds had enabled forty thousand corrections personnel to take college courses; legal services to be developed throughout the country to serve prisoners; many prisons and jails to be upgraded and modernized; pretrial diversion projects (see chapter 6) to be instituted; and a variety of community-based alternative programs to be started. And these only hint at the volume and variety of activities in effect by 1976 when the annual LEAA budget had reached $800 million. (Serrill 1976, 3,4)

LEAA was a type of social engineering which provides a grim illustration of a dilemma for public policymakers. In order to get legislation of this sort enacted it often is necessary to oversell it. The danger is that the program is then discredited when achievement falls short of its promotional rhetoric. In most respects the concept embodied in the LEAA was sound; the country's criminal justice agencies very much needed the infusion of cash to modernize every aspect of their operations. But while the public looks increasingly to government to prevent crime, government is neither efficient nor effective at doing this. As one authority has expressed it, "Government is good at spending money to purchase material goods; the development of the inter-state highway system is one example of a relatively successful government policy. When the problem to be dealt with is diffuse or multifaceted or embedded in the fabric of social organization, public sector intervention is as likely to complicate matters as to ameliorate them." (Feeley and Sarat 1980, 14)

Confusing this basic administrative problem is, of course, the political element. When President Johnson was offering his Great Society legislation and at the same time campaigning for the 1964 election, his Republican opponent, Barry Goldwater, was touting his own, more punitive, version of how to be tough on crime. "He believed crime resulted from a decline in morals and in discipline, from the Supreme Court down to the individual family, and since no social welfare program could improve deficiencies in morals, the remedy was more police power, tougher laws, and a less permissive court system.'' (Cronin, Cronin, and Milakovich 1981, 24)

After Johnson won the 1964 election, crime continued to be a searing public concern through succeeding administrations. In the 1988 presidential campaign, George Bush found it effective to accuse his opponent, Michael Dukakis, of being soft on crime. The same theme had also been effective in England, where Margaret Thatcher used it in her campaign against the Labour Party in 1979. (Stenson and Cowell 1991, 5–6)

Although the LEAA had a popular and robust existence for several years, subsequent administrations reduced it, and by the late 1970s it was essentially eliminated, with its few remaining projects moved into other pockets of the Department of Justice, particularly in the Bureau of Justice Assistance. Complaints that money was often wasted while it failed to reduce crime forced its demise. However, the director of one state corrections department showed more balanced insight in a useful comment about the practical dynamics of public policy: ''The Congress will see a need in an area and they will appropriate huge sums of money and drop them down [to the states and localities] immediately. Nobody is prepared for [the money]. The organization doesn't exist to take care of it. The plans aren't there, evaluation components aren't there, and mistakes are made. Money is badly spent. . . . Then you get to the point where programs begin to be halfway reasonable, and you get constructive change. By then someone has decided it's no damn good, and so they abolish it and start another one all over again.'' (Kent Stoneman as quoted in Serrill 1976, 3)

It is a valid comment, but the seemingly illogical impatience with funded programs usually is not due so much to unskilled or unintelligent bureaucrats, but instead reflects the need for a democratic government, with its limited term in office, to reduce crime quickly. To make any appreciable reduction in the entrenched causes of crime in our society will probably require, under the best of circumstances, at least a generation. But the political party in power does not have that much time. Politically, the usual administration needs to show results within its four-year hold on office. The continuing demand from a victimized society for vigorous governmental crime prevention measures at the same time that public policy submits to the reality that a certain amount of crime must be tolerated as cost-effective further complicates the issue. No citizenry can afford the tax bill that a total crime prevention policy would require.

The Preventive Function of Policing

The average citizen no doubt looks to the police as the primary agency for crime prevention. On those infrequent occasions when a public employee strike or other unusual situation temporarily removes the police from activity, crime in the streets sharply increases. Accordingly, it can be assumed that just the existence of the police and their general everyday functioning in all their various duties serves to accomplish a preventive effect. But at the same time, there are continual questions and controversies about programs or methods the police may pursue for the more specific purpose of crime prevention.

One of the most thoroughly tested and highly touted experiments in preventive police methods was a one-year project with the Kansas City, Missouri, police department from 1974 to 1975. The project dealt with the issue of general police effectiveness, particularly the value of reduced response time. It also included a "preventive patrol experiment" in which selected police beats were given much higher numbers of marked police cars to test whether increased visibility of police would bring any reduction of crime problems. The results did not clearly support the value of the intensive patrol. Although some types of crime are reduced in this way, extra patrolling could not be proved to be cost effective. (Farmer 1984, 43–47)

Actual reduction in the numbers of crimes is not the only outcome to be sought, however. One expert notes that "Minority citizens in inner cities continue to be frustrated by police who whisk in and out of their neighborhoods with little sensitivity to community norms and values. Regardless of where one asks, minorities want both the familiarity and accountability that characterize foot patrol." He concludes that "the overwhelming public response to community and problem-solving policing has been positive, regardless of where it has been instituted." (Kelling 1988, 4)

Neighborhood Policing/Problem-Solving Policing

The positive public response to police foot patrols and problem-solving policing has caused the current emphasis on "community policing," a strategy to bring police into closer contact with neighborhoods. Along with this strategy has come a new awareness that effectiveness of police organizations has long been hampered by a built-in concern for procedural efficiency over substantive accomplishment. A smoothly operating organization is a satisfying one, and gives the police the good feeling that they are doing well even though little or nothing is being done to solve the problems they confront. For instance, as one astute critic, Herman Goldstein, points out, a police department may take pride in its record for rapid response to calls, but make no effort to improve its handling of the problems causing those calls. (Goldstein 1979, 237)

This issue represents a dilemma for the police, with their natural resistance to the implication that they should be social workers on call.

So many of the problems coming to police attention are virtually unsolvable that it is much more rewarding to have their job performance judged in terms of efficiency in organizational procedures. ''Thus, focusing on the substantive, community problems that the police must handle is a much more radical step than it initially appears to be, for it requires the police to go beyond taking satisfaction in the smooth operation of their organization; it requires that they extend their concern to dealing effectively with the problems that justify creating a police agency in the first instance.'' (Goldstein 1990, 35)

Goldstein's view is that police can and should get more involved in crime prevention measures as a goal of problem solving. Among the definitive elements of problem-solving policing he recommends the following:

> Through research, identify the very few individuals or families contributing the bulk of the calls for police service and initiate services that will ameliorate the special problems they present.
>
> Adopt a more proactive practice of referring problems to other governmental or private resources, and strengthen this with follow-through monitoring of services given.
>
> Develop affirmative coordination of services with other criminal justice agencies.
>
> Identify, report on, and urge correction of gaps or problems in services of other municipal agencies.
>
> Develop mediation services to apply in many of the situations that call for police attention. (Goldstein 1990, chapter 8)

Though the concept of problem-oriented policing fits well with the related practice of community policing, the latter concept is better understood by the public and has gained much more popular recognition. Ironically, to a considerable extent it represents a return to earlier days when the cop on foot patrol was a familiar acquaintance to the families and businesses on his beat. If any one factor can be identified as the principal reason for abandoning that original version of neighborhood policing, it would be the arrival of the radio. During the 1920s August Vollmer, police chief in Berkeley, California, had pioneered the use of automobiles for police patrol, and soon afterward the radio was ready to be adapted for use in police cars.[1] The idea took hold rapidly, and by 1933, when Baltimore installed its radio system, ninety-two cities in the country had radio-equipped fleets.[2] Combining cars and radios to give the police mobility and constant communication for quick response was considered a great advance. But by insulating the police in their cruising automobiles, the police lost the advantage of intimate acquaintance with neighborhood people. Several decades later, municipal governments became seriously concerned about recapturing that aspect of the earlier police work.

Whereas community policing gradually gained favor with many police departments during the 1980s, general public awareness and appreciation for the idea was given an extra boost as a result of a disastrous riot in Los Angeles in early 1992. The disturbance stemmed from an episode in March 1991 when Los Angeles police were observed and videotaped as they beat a young black motorist they had stopped. Tried for assault in May 1992, the officers involved were acquitted, sparking violent disturbances that riveted the attention of the nation. Many of the commentaries on the event stressed the failure of the police to stay in touch with the average citizens and their concerns. Coincidentally, at about that same time the Los Angeles police chief retired and was replaced by the Philadelphia police chief. Though it was cheering news for many that the new chief was black, the more significant and more encouraging news was that he strongly believed in the principle of community policing. In Philadelphia he had managed to bring police into a close, cooperative, mutually respectful relationship with community residents.[3]

Meanwhile, the U.S. Department of Justice encouraged more use of community policing, calling attention to model programs in operation, and conducting evaluative research on several programs. The Department pointed out that a police officer gains more information about pertinent neighborhood problems when engaged directly with people in the community than when in the anonymous patrol car, and that police accountability to the public is improved when police operations are more visible.[4]

The concept and practice of community policing vary as needed from one site to another; they may include having police attend and participate in community meetings, making more use of foot patrols, having neighborhood-assigned police officers develop personal acquaintances with storekeepers and others on their beats, redrawing police beats to fit with natural neighborhood boundaries, and opening visible and accessible police offices in strategic neighborhood areas. As currently being advocated and tried, community policing is new enough to be of unproven effectiveness. But the hopeful view is that ''Moving the officer from a position of anonymity in the patrol car to direct engagement with a community gives the officer more immediate information about problems unique to a neighborhood and insights into their solutions. Freeing the officer from the emergency response system permits him or her to engage more directly in proactive crime prevention.''[5]

As with any new and different procedure, there are trade-offs, with critics noting various problems:

While it is fine for the police officer to become a friendly acquaintance of merchants and residents on his beat, these friendly relationships are likely to cloud his judgment and resolve when he
or she has reason to make an arrest.

Community policing requires a certain amount of decentralization
in police department operation, and police managers worry that
this will decrease the authoritative control that a police department needs to maintain.

Since central authoritative control and avoidance of intimacy between police and citizens has been thought necessary for reducing
corruption, police managers worry that allowing officers to develop friendships and exercise their own judgment in their neighborhood work increases the likelihood of corruption.

To some degree community policing may squander police resources
because police on foot in the neighborhood are unavailable for
rapid response to emergency calls.

Research seems to indicate that community policing does not reduce
crime. (Kelling 1988, 5–7)

Despite such criticisms, community policing continues to be popular, and for a very human reason. The public's intense fear of crime
is in itself a problem and a matter of real concern to the police. A
reduction in that level of fear is of value to the police, and experience
seems to show that community policing calms public fears even if the
statistics do not prove any reduction in crime rates.

Special Skills for Special Problems

Community policing is one part of a larger concern for bringing to
police work a new sensitivity toward varied types of citizens—particularly important has been an improved understanding of female victims.
No aspect of police work has been more in need of increased sensitivity
than that of dealing with sex offenses, particularly rape. Sex crime
units, staffed with officers specially trained in interviewing rape victims
sympathetically, can hope to clear more rape cases as victims feel more
willing to report these crimes if they can expect to be treated with
dignity.[6]

The need for new social and technical skills means that modern
police departments must have increased budgets for sophisticated equipment and for specialized training. One challenge to modern police is the
increasing threat of terrorism, which has spurred interest in developing
SWAT (special weapons and tactics) teams to handle hostile high-risk
situations involving terrorists or other armed attackers. A "concept
developed as a result of the turmoil of the 1960s and early 1970s," the

SWAT team can be highly effective if properly trained and used, but its equipment, training, and deployment are very expensive and are not a cost-effective strategy for any but the larger police departments. (Holden 1986, 166) Also important, and expensive, is the specialty of hostage negotiation, requiring unique training done in a realistically simulated situation, preferably with professional actors in the roles of the hostage takers.[7]

Some of the new and expensive technology purports to save more than its cost through more efficient processing of cases. A computerized process known as "automated fingerprint identification" is able to process a single and even partial fingerprint, identifying its key characteristics and quickly scanning the records of all likely fingerprints to find a match, saving hours of manual labor. Another process, "computerized imaging system," stores pictures and descriptions of offenders in a way that gives immediate access to them for the purpose of a computerized line-up. This process replaces the usual need for a line-up of several actual people for a victim or witness to inspect; instead, it quickly produces on a screen a series of faces selected by a computer for similar appearances.[8]

A very different police activity, and one clearly related to prevention, is the sponsorship of the Police Athletic League, or PAL. A voluntary program used by some police departments, it was created a half century ago as a means of bringing police into close, friendly acquaintance with children from disadvantaged neighborhoods, and attempting to give them a positive rather than hostile feeling about police. The actual nature of each program and the energy with which it is pursued will vary from one locality to another depending on the leadership. A favorite format is the use of summer camp activities, with police officers volunteering to serve as counselors or athletic leaders.[9]

Crime Reduction by "Target Hardening"

For the average citizen concerned about safety, the idea of "target hardening" is the most obvious immediate recourse. The phrase covers any measures taken to intervene directly between the criminal and the prospective victim, most obviously locks on doors, but also a wide range of devices and procedures. Modern technology has produced a versatile choice of equipment to frustrate burglaries. Door locks come in a variety of styles, including an electronic lock that can be programmed to restrict access to certain persons at certain specified times. Burglar alarms are available in many modes; for example, some are silent and offer direct communication with the local police. This type of alarm has a proven usefulness in that burglars caught in the act by such an alarm are more certainly and quickly convicted than when caught in other ways. The varieties of alarms offer numerous adaptations for different uses in residence or industrial applications. (O'Block 1981, 275–292)

Among other crime defense measures are the use of lighting, sometimes using automatic equipment to turn lights on to simulate occupancy. The use of dogs has a sustained popularity, ranging from pet dogs who do nothing but bark at every sign of a person approaching the house, to the use of dogs with special training for a variety of detection or attack functions. More personal devices include belt-worn alarms, portable mace for warding off attacks, or the possession of hand guns. Unlike the other devices, however, possession of hand guns has a very controversial quality, with many people seeing the general possession of hand guns as both ineffective and dangerous, while a large and articulate portion of the population fiercely defends the right and the sense of the ordinary citizen to possess guns as he wishes (see chapter 9).

Not literally a target hardening measure, but closely related, is the effort to educate people in simple precautions that avoid or discourage attacks. These include the maintenance of a home's appearance of occupancy during the family's vacation absence, the care a lone woman should take in approaching her car in a parking lot where she could be vulnerable to attack, and the ways to avoid becoming a target for rapists.

Prevention through Environmental Engineering

It has long been known that a small, cohesive community where neighbors know each other has appreciably less crime than a large urban area where a condition of anomie develops because of the impersonal living style. An especially tragic example of the breakdown of neighborly concern captured national attention in 1964 when a young New York City woman, Kitty Genovese, was murdered at her apartment entrance while her immediate neighbors watched without interfering. Kitty, a young single woman working a night shift, drove home as usual at 3:00 A.M., but in walking from her car to her apartment, she saw an unknown man in her way. She turned and started toward a police call box, but the man intervened and stabbed her. Her screams alerted several apartment occupants who turned on lights, but did little more than to look to see what was happening. Twice the attacker was scared off temporarily, and twice he returned to the attack before the injured woman could get to her apartment door. For nearly half an hour Kitty called for help while trying desperately to hide and evade the man.

Finally, when Kitty was lying dead at the entrance and after the attacker had fled, one of the neighbors called the police, who arrived within two minutes. The police bluntly told the apartment residents that if they had been called promptly, their two-minute response time could have saved Kitty's life. Subsequent investigation revealed that there had been thirty-seven witnesses to Kitty's ordeal—thirty-seven people nearby who had heard the calls for help during the half hour, but preferred not to get involved![10]

With all of the attention this example of urban anomie earned, many city planners were still not fully aware of the lessons the episode offered. It was a time when cities were reaching for federal funding for public housing, and the new Department of Housing and Urban Development was the agency setting the pattern for them to follow. But the concept of reducing urban crime by building a neighborhood quality into housing projects had not yet taken hold. Without this concept in place, some housing projects were built with characteristics that actually encouraged crime. Unfortunately, the perceived demands of public policy were in favor of economy—in favor of designs that visibly avoided appearance of any concessions to pleasure or comfort of public housing residents.

A particularly egregious project in this regard was built near downtown St. Louis, Missouri, in 1955. Pruitt-Igoe was supposedly a model housing project, with forty-three slab-shaped, high-rise apartment buildings. Though at first a source of civic pride and great hopes, all too soon it became a crime-ridden place where discouraged tenants lived virtually under siege. More and more tenants moved out when they could, and new tenants seldom took their places. Later, the problem could easily be traced to a public policy sensible on the surface, but disastrous in operation. "Pruitt-Igoe was one of the nation's largest and (in the beginning) most trumpeted public housing projects," reported a news item at the time; but it had become the "nation's Number One slum. Pruitt-Igoe was 57 acres of physical and social devastation in the center of St. Louis."[11]

In justice to the planners of Pruitt-Igoe it must be recognized that the principles of crime prevention through architectural design were not well developed then. In this respect Pruitt-Igoe became the country's most potent lesson for urban planners. Planners now recognize that to design a mass housing project for safe living it is essential to provide a neighborhood quality by grouping the living units in manageable clusters where tenants will have a chance to know each other, and, by the same token, are able to recognize any outsider who may intrude in the designated space. To this end the common area around a cluster needs to be off the street and in a defined area where any person who enters can be identified easily as a tenant, a person on legitimate business (delivery person, etc.), or otherwise as an outsider who must be treated cautiously. Playgrounds must be close to the residence buildings and easy for parents to watch and supervise. There must be toilets at ground level near the playgrounds. It is essential for elevator lobbies to be open to view and well lighted, and for the elevators to open at all levels onto open hallways without hidden corners.

Pruitt-Igoe planners, under the expectation that public housing should be (or at least appear to be) spartan, found various ways to save money, not realizing that their success with the cheaper construction would eventually culminate in remedial costs that would far exceed the initial savings. Elevators in the eleven-story buildings stopped only at the fourth, seventh, and tenth floors. The elevator entrances were often around a corner from the main hall areas where they could not be easily seen, making it easy for a lone woman to be captured and raped. Playgrounds were too far from the buildings and as open to the streets as to the resident buildings, making them vulnerable to intruders. With no toilets available to children on the playgrounds, an impatient child would sometimes use the elevator as a convenient substitute instead of returning to his or her apartment. Mothers fearful of letting children use the playgrounds kept them in the apartments all day, with consequent increased wear and tear on the building as well as on the family members.

As another economy, buildings that should have been grouped for a sense of neighborhood and for the attractiveness of irregular appearance were lined up in regular rows to take economic advantage of the location of already existing utility lines. After only fifteen years of use, having become a magnet for criminal activity, Pruitt-Igoe was rapidly deteriorating, with much of its space empty and almost no new tenants moving in. It became evident that the only solution would be its removal, so by the mid-1970s most of the buildings were emptied and demolished. (McCue 1973, 45)

With this and similar experiences elsewhere, planners have learned the importance of both architecture and ground-level layouts in designing out the crime potential in housing projects. The most important basic principle for planners to consider is the creation of limited-size neighborhoods where families can get to know, or at least recognize, each other, and will consequently be able to identify intruders. Private streets and cul-de-sacs rather than major through streets are called for; good lighting for common areas and placement of entrances where easily observable also help materially in keeping down crime. (Poyner 1983, 15, 25, 42)

Crime Reduction or Crime Displacement?

Measures aimed at crime prevention are at the same time among the most sensible of public endeavors as well as among the most difficult to accomplish. One frustration is the difficulty of proving the effectiveness of preventive measures; there is no sure way of counting the number of crimes not committed. Sometimes there is a deceptive illusion of crime having been reduced when it has only been displaced.〕One reputed example of this has been the rise of a relatively new crime, ''carjacking,'' the direct attack on a car driver who is forced out of his or her vehicle, which then is driven away. It is a type of car theft that is thought to be prompted in large measure by the success of the steering post locks in reducing thefts of parked automobiles.

Similarly, target hardening of a residential site has been observed to displace crime to some other residential areas, with one of the attempted solutions for this outcome being the organization of tenants or residents into self-help groups for neighborhood crime prevention. These groups have the potential of being effective, but they also are potentially disappointing and transitory. Low-income resident groups can gain power through concerted action, but these organizations tend to be crisis-oriented and are not likely to last much beyond the situation that first brings them into being. Also, the bureaucrats with whom they must deal tend to see them as hostile and accordingly resist cooperating with them. In more affluent neighborhoods, the ''crime watch'' type of neighborhood organization is sensible and effective when well organized and with good leadership, but usually these too do not survive any period of peaceful conditions when there is no perceived threat of crime. (Trojanowicz, Trojanowicz, and Moss 1975, 123–124)

The key to successful volunteer projects for crime prevention is the availability of skilled and enthusiastic leadership, along with continuing activity that keeps the volunteers feeling needed and effective. Volunteers who come to organization meetings in which nothing of significance is addressed or accomplished will not long continue to give their time. They will stay with the project only if the leadership is energetic in keeping a meaningful quality of activity in motion. As one governmental commission viewed the matter, if interest can be sustained in this way, ''volunteers frequently can provide more personal attention and care to a particular problem or individual than can a harried professional. Citizen involvement also can plug many holes in the delivery of needed community services that otherwise would be unavailable because of lack of funds, personnel, or other resources.'' (National Advisory Commission on Criminal Justice Standards and Goals 1973, 46)

Crime prevention strategies encompass much more than the field of criminal justice. Equally involved are churches, every kind of social agency, schools, civic clubs, insurance companies, industrial companies, and sometimes such apparently unrelated organizations as labor unions and other social action groups. Accordingly, preventive efforts by criminal justice agencies need to reach out to other types of organizations or groups for mutually coordinated planning. And finally, when all the preventive effects attempted through measures of "general deterrence" are insufficient to prevent specific individuals from committing crime, there must then be efforts at "special deterrence" focused on that individual to prevent him or her from committing new offenses in the future.

Prevention through "Special Deterrence"

When an offender is caught and convicted, the disposition of the case presumably calls for measures that will effectively deter the offender from any more criminal activity. When crime prevention is focused in this way on an individual case it is referred to as "special deterrence," distinguishing it from "general deterrence," which is concerned with the more comprehensive crime problem. (Morris and Hawkins 1970, 255)

Legislators who must enact laws that address the deterrent response to crime are well acquainted with the conflicting messages that come from the public on the issue. On one level is the belief that true deterrence lies in the rehabilitative or treatment programs that attempt to correct those personal deficiencies that have led to the person's crime. This is the optimistic and logical view that is inherent in the word we have now adopted for our punishment system—corrections. On another level is the appealing premise that a more dependable form of deterrence is the threat of punishment. Although the efficacy of punishment as a deterrent measure is difficult to prove, the public instinct to rely on it is so strong that even when it seems not to work, even while crime rates continue to rise, the likely public reaction is that punishments must be made still more severe.

The reasons are not difficult to identify. For one thing, it is human nature to wish for simple solutions, and resorting to punishment is a relatively simplistic response. If we could assume that punishment would in fact be effective, it would be the cheapest, quickest, and most satisfying procedure of any. Satisfying—because a characteristic of the human personality is the innocent person's emotional gratification in seeing someone punished for a misdeed that the law-abiding person has avoided. Research has shown that the average person has remarkable potential for becoming a brutally severe punisher if thrust into a structured situation where punishing is expected and allowed.

A noted experiment conducted at Stanford University in 1971 gave a disturbing picture of this tendency. Twenty male student volunteers were selected for their ordinary, healthy personalities. Half were randomly assigned to take the roles of prisoners in a simulated prison setting, while the others were assigned to be guards. The experiment nearly got out of control when the ''guards'' quickly became overly punitive, while the ''prisoners'' accepted too readily their dehumanized status. ''In less than a week the behavior of the male subjects. . . could be characterized as pathological and antisocial.'' (Haney and Zimbardo 1977, 206) The experience seemed to validate an observation of one student of the subject who commented, ''We are all punishers. . . . Parents, teachers, foremen, managers, and so on are called upon to punish those under them at some time or another. . . . Punishment is therefore very close to most of our hearts, and we find it very difficult to separate our thinking from our emotional attachment to it.'' (Newman 1978, 254–255)

The Contrary Effects of Punishment

Punishment means different things to different people, and particularly it has a different meaning for middle-class, successful people who become legislators (determiners of public policy) than it has for the types of people most likely to be criminal offenders. This factor is always present when public policy is set regarding punishment as a crime deterrent. The average legislator has experienced a relatively benign and constructive kind of punishment in childhood and has a view of it as being reasonable and effective. Since he or she would personally dread serving a prison sentence it is naturally supposed that any offender would feel a similar fear of prison. With this uncritical assumption that the threat of imprisonment will have a deterrent effect for everyone, the political candidate assures all constituents that crime must be deterred by resort to tougher sentencing.

Unfortunately, this simplistic approach, so gratifying to the legislator and the voters, fails because punishment has a quite different meaning to those who are most likely to go to prison. The person brutally punished throughout childhood may easily come to accept it as a normal and even essential part of interaction with others. Punishment may denote success in achieving attention from otherwise unresponsive parents and in proving a self-image; it may even enhance the person's status with peers outside the family. Tragically, this behavior is often seen in spouse abuse cases, for the woman who has been abusively punished as a child may tolerate beatings from her husband because in her experience this is evidence of caring.

Childhood experiences among offenders have often shown that the kinds of activities that earned them punishment from their families have also earned them rewards from their peers on the street. And the reward of peer approval is more potent for them than parental punishments. These effects leave the legislator unaware that sometimes the punishments so confidently prescribed in law will actually encourage, rather than discourage, a prohibited behavior. At the very least, experience tends to show that the threat of prison, while impressive to the minds of law-abiding folk, is of little deterrent value to those who go to prison. As one criminologist notes, "the earlier and more often an offender commits crimes and has been habituated to criminal associates, the less he or she will be either deterred or further criminalized by an additional increment of incarceration." (Glaser 1983, 209)

For many decades public policy has reflected this unresolvable contrast between the public's instinctive belief in what works, and the scientific studies of what actually does or does not work. The public's political representatives understandably enact policy responsive first to the emotional demands of constituents, reconciling this with more objective considerations only as the political considerations can be made to fit.

Overview of Prevention Measures

The political processes typical of a democracy encourage a hope that crime can be prevented, or at least reduced, by a more forceful use of police, prosecution, and correctional services. Even though managers of prison systems often point out the fallacy of expecting prisons to solve the crime problem, the public continues to hope. Ordinarily it is not politically popular to recognize that careful research fails to prove that the public gets increased protection from crime by increasing the terms of imprisonment. An extensive research project conducted by the Rand Corporation for the Department of Justice confirmed the uncertainty of the effects of penal sanctions more than it could confirm any dependable deterrent effect of punishments. The researchers, citing the great difficulty of controlling for variables and contending with methodological problems, could not find support for the average citizen's hope that increased imprisonment must be a solution to crime. "Therefore, the only sentencing guidance provided by empirical deterrence studies (as opposed to various deterrence theories) is that increasing the probability of arrest, the conviction rate, or the incarceration rate appears to reduce crime more than do comparable changes in sentence length." (Greenwood 1982, viii)

If that observation is valid it points up a nagging political and economic problem. Increasing the speed and certainty of the process of arrest through conviction is the preferred goal, but this is the more difficult and expensive part of the effort to accomplish. Accordingly, the political process tends to cause successive lengthening of prison sentences. The citizen naturally listens more to his or her own subjective instinct than to the objective findings of researchers.

As important as the police are in the prevention of crime, their role in crime prevention is an area in which the identification of effective policies and practices is more a matter of educated conjecture than objective proof. The federal LEAA program committed massive amounts of money to improving police agencies, upgrading personnel training, refining policing techniques, and funding the acquisition of better equipment. Statistics do not prove any resultant effect on crime rates, but a valid belief is that any such measures that improve the professionalism of the police make a positive contribution to a better society. The police, being the most visible of the law enforcement components, do much to determine public respect—or disrespect—for governmental authority, and so a police force of obvious integrity and competence is basic to the encouragement of law-abiding attitudes.

Though prevention of crime in the broad social context is difficult to accomplish and nearly impossible to document, crime prevention in relation to a specific target area can be accomplished, as experience has shown. Environmental engineering for this purpose has been substantially improved in recent years, though it still cannot be known with certainty to what extent the prevention of crime at a specific site leads only to displacement of crime to other targets. If displacement does occur, the overall crime rate is not reduced.

In summary, governmental policymakers continually feel pressured by their political constituents to prevent crime by favoring laws that threaten harsh punishments so that "criminals will think twice" before committing crimes. This approach is perpetually popular, not because it works, but because it is emotionally satisfying to the public for its direct and simple quality. As an example of "special deterrence," this approach attempts to discourage specific crimes and specific criminals, although there is always the expressed hope of "general deterrence" being accomplished as other would-be offenders learn of the penalty and get the message.

Government's experience with "general deterrence" measures, which attempt to reduce crime by amelioration of crime-causing social conditions, is usually disappointing, even when useful to some degree. A major reason is in the diverse and bureaucratic nature of governmental activities, with initiatives carried out by many different agencies for many purposes, which are not obviously or primarily crime control. The Department of Housing and Urban Development, for example, may include among its specifications for housing construction some requirements that are incidentally for crime prevention purposes. And though these specifications may help to reduce the crime level in a housing development, they do not register on public awareness as crime control measures because (a) they are only a small part of an overall program administered by an agency that is not a part of the criminal justice apparatus, and (b) the possible effectiveness of such initiatives ordinarily is not researched, not proven, nor brought to public attention.

Even though diverse governmental efforts at improving the general quality of life may be more useful in reducing crime than making criminal sentences more severe, the effects are too subtle to be appreciated and heeded by the public in its punitive mood. The attack on crime must include improvement of training programs for all criminal justice personnel, and improvement and expansion of resources to deal with convicted offenders, whether prisons or alternative sanctions. Politically, it remains necessary to pursue the high-profile punitive measures that will persuade the public that government is seriously fighting crime. But at the same time, for the sake of more basic, long-term reduction of crime, a responsible government must also maintain continual efforts to promote a social milieu in which persons of all racial, ethnic, and socioeconomic groupings can believe their society to be fair and their opportunities to be open. When these fundamental qualities are not present, the potential value of the more direct punitive measures is undermined.

Notes

1. Nathan Douthit. "August Vollmer, Berkeley's First Chief of Police and the Emergence of Police Professionalism." *California Historical Quarterly* 54 (Summer 1975), 116.
2. *American City* (Jan. 1933), 19; and (May 1933), 64.
3. *U.S. News and World Report* (April 27, 1992), 21; *Time* (May 11, 1992), 37.
4. *National Institute of Justice Journal* (Aug. 1992), 3.
5. Ibid.
6. Suzanne Charle. "Sex Crimes Units Are Raising Conviction Rates, Consciousness, Costs . . . and Questions." *Police Magazine* 3:2 (March 1980), 52–62.
7. Steven Geiger, et al. "Training Hostage Negotiation." *The Police Chief* 57:11 (Nov. 1990), 54.
8. Judith Blair Schmitt. "Computerized ID Systems." *The Police Chief* 59:2 (Feb. 1992), 33–35.
9. Dave Austin and Jane Braaten. "Turning Lives Around." *The Police Chief* 58:5 (May 1991), 36.

10. *New York Times* (March 14, 1964), 26:4; and (May 3, 1964), VI:24.
11. *National Review* 22:45 (1970), 1335–1336.

Bibliography

Prevention through "General Deterrence"

Coffey, Alan R. *The Prevention of Crime and Delinquency.* Englewood Cliffs, N.J.: Prentice-Hall, 1975.
Cronin, Thomas E., Tania Z. Cronin, and Michael E. Milakovich. *U.S. v. Crime in the Streets.* Bloomington: Indiana University Press, 1981.
> A reasoned, in-depth discussion of national politics affecting crime control policy for the two decades beginning with the early 1960s. The authors address the factors that influenced such legislation as the Safe Streets Act and LEAA, the opposing Republican policies, the Vietnam War, and the civil rights movement.

"Community Policing." *National Institute of Justice Journal,* no. 225 (August 1992).
Farmer, David John. *Crime Control: The Use and Misuse of Police Resources.* New York: Plenum, 1984.
Feeley, Malcolm M. and Austin D. Sarat. *The Policy Dilemma: Federal Crime Policy and the Law Enforcement Administration.* Minneapolis: University of Minnesota Press, 1980.
> An informative discussion of the ways in which political situations lead to or defeat efforts to establish effective public policy in response to the need to control crime. The book gives a useful picture of how and why government tries to engage in crime control through such initiatives as the Safe Streets Act, and how its efforts fall short of the desired results.

Goldstein, Herman. "Improving Policing: A Problem-Oriented Approach." *Crime and Delinquency* 25:2 (April 1979), 236–258.
Goldstein, Herman. *Problem-Oriented Policing.* Philadelphia: Temple University Press, 1990.
> The author introduced his concept of problem-oriented policing in the journal article of 1979 (above), then later expanded on it substantially in his 1990 book. Both items have deservedly gained respectful attention in the police profession for the seminal, perceptive, and persuasive quality of the presentations. These are among the most readable, thoughtful, and constructive of any modern writings on police work.

Greenwood, Peter W. *Selective Incapacitation.* Santa Monica, Calif.: Rand Corporation for the National Institute of Justice, 1982.
Holden, Richard N. *Modern Police Management.* Englewood Cliffs, N.J.: Prentice-Hall, 1986.
Jeffery, C. Ray. *Crime Prevention through Environmental Design.* Beverly Hills, Calif.: Sage Publications, 1977.

Kelling, George L. "Police and Communities: The Quiet Revolution." *Perspectives on Policing* (June 1988).

A compact, significant report that provides a clear, explicit review of the pros and cons of community policing.

McCue, George. "$57,000,000 Later." *Architectural Forum* (May 1973), 42–45. See also *National Review* 22 (Dec. 15, 1970), 1335.

Architectural and general views of the Pruitt-Igoe debacle.

Moenssens, Andre A. and Fred E. Imbau. *Scientific Evidence in Criminal Cases.* Mineola, N.Y.: Foundation Press, 1978. (See the annotated entry for this work in the chapter 2 bibliography)

Morris, Norval and Gordon Hawkins. *The Honest Politician's Guide to Crime Control.* Chicago: University of Chicago Press, 1970.

Two of the most erudite and perceptive observers of criminal justice programs and issues offer a searching appraisal of police practices, use of bail, handling of juveniles, character of organized crime, diagnosis and treatment of offenders, and other relevant issues. They are particularly concerned with the application of objective logic and rigorous principles of fairness to the criminal justice systems. The authors do not hesitate to take clear positions on controversial issues; they take a stand, and give explicit rationale, on such matters as gun control, police administration, and capital punishment.

National Advisory Commission on Criminal Justice Standards and Goals. *A National Strategy to Reduce Crime.* Washington, D.C.: GPO, 1973.

Newman, Oscar. *Community of Interest.* Garden City, N.Y.: Anchor, 1980.

Newman, Oscar. *Defensible Space.* New York: Macmillan, 1972.

One of the best known and highly regarded works on the ways in which residential architecture and neighborhood factors function to promote or to reduce crime. In a well-organized, rational presentation, copiously illustrated, the author discusses the details of how to design living environments to minimize their vulnerability to crime.

O'Block, Robert L. *Security and Crime Prevention.* St. Louis: C. V. Mosby, 1981.

An unusually comprehensive, thorough, and competent discussion in textbook form of all aspects of crime prevention. Scholarly in its analysis of prevention theories and measures, it also adopts a practical approach to such matters as residential burglar-proofing, then ranges through types of crimes and preventive measures to problems of political corruption.

Poyner, Barry. *Design against Crime: Beyond Defensible Space.* London: Butterworths, 1983.

Rubin, Richard. "Computer Trends in Law Enforcement." *The Police Chief* 58:4 (April 1991), 23–24.

Serrill, Michael. "LEAA: A Question of Impact." *Corrections Magazine* 2:4 (June 1976).

Stenson, Kevin and David Cowell, eds. *The Politics of Crime Control.* London: Sage Publications, 1991.

A collection of articles by various experts on political aspects of public policy—though not all the chapters are relevant to the general American experience. It includes a pertinent debate between the contrasting conservative and liberal views of James Q. Wilson and Elliott Currie. Their discussion of crime prevention ideology provides a substantive and rational perspective on this divisive subject.

Trojanowicz, Robert C., John M. Trojanowicz, and Forrest M. Moss. *Community Based Crime Prevention.* Pacific Palisades, Calif.: Goodyear, 1975.

Prevention through "Special Deterrence"

Glaser, Daniel. "Supervising Offenders outside of Prison." Chapter 12 in Wilson, James Q., ed. *Crime and Public Policy.* San Francisco: Institute for Contemporary Studies, 1983.

Greenwood, Peter W., 1982 (above).

Haney, Craig and Philip G. Zimbardo. "The Socialization into Criminality." Chapter 17 in Tapp, June L. and Felice J. Levine, eds. *Law, Justice and the Individual in Society: Psychological and Legal Issues.* New York: Holt, Rinehart & Winston, 1977.

Newman, Graeme. *The Punishment Response.* New York: J. B. Lippincott, 1978.

Much of this work deals with the history of punishments for crime, but it is usefully analytical in presenting the psychological aspects and the evolution of punishment methods as attitudes gradually changed on the subject. The author is scholarly and workmanlike in ranging over the many aspects of criminal punishment, and he reviews carefully the relevant research in recent years into questions of punishment effectiveness.

CHAPTER 4

Sentencing as an Instrument for Crime Control

W hen preventive endeavors have not succeeded in stopping a crime, when the criminal has been caught, charged, and convicted, the court must decide the appropriate sentence, taking into consideration questions of fairness, deterrence, and public protection. This is an area of great concern in the ongoing effort to achieve both fairness and useful effect in the fight against crime. Here then must be examined the pros and cons of discretionary latitude to be given to judges, the design of sentencing guidelines, and the varieties of dispositions to be offered courts for the punishment or correction of offenders. Depending on the crime and its mitigating or aggravating circumstances, and depending on the laws of the particular jurisdiction, the penalties range from the suspended sentence with no follow-through measures ordered, through release on probation with various special conditions imposed, through prison terms of varied lengths, to the imposition of the death penalty. It can be expected that these options will be refined, and additional options developed in the future, whereas the search for wise principles to guide in choosing among them will be an enduring challenge.

Purpose and Nature of the Sentencing Process

In any consideration of sentencing for crime, certain philosophical concepts are commonly cited as basic reasons or justifications for punishment. Without attempting to examine these concepts in detail, it is important at this point to define them briefly, as they will continually surface in the course of this discussion of the various approaches to sentencing.

The Justifications for Punishing

Retribution is the oldest and perhaps the most generally offered reason for punishing criminals. Sometimes equated with revenge, retribution is justified as more socially controlled and more purposeful than revenge. Retribution requires that the offender be punished because that is what he or she deserves (''just deserts''), and by imposing the punishment in proportion to the severity of the crime, society in each retributive instance confirms and legitimizes the standards of lawful conduct expected of all its members.

Deterrence is seen as a practical justification for punishment, and the one upon which the public pins much of its hopes. There is no doubt that punishments imposed through the criminal justice system act as a deterrent to some undetermined extent; there is no doubt that the punishment system needs for this reason to be sustained. But there is no proof and no agreement on the precise details of the proper application and effect of punishment. Uncertainty and controversy persist regarding the degree to which any particular punishment is a deterrent, or why various types of punishments deter different people in different ways.

Incapacitation is another practical concept, applying mainly to the offender who is thought to be a threat to public safety and unamenable to corrective influence. A prison term serves to incapacitate such a person, storing the person where he or she will not be a danger to society at least for the term of confinement.

Rehabilitation, the most controversial of the sentencing concepts, will be discussed in subsequent chapters. Suffice it to say that whereas rehabilitation is the most humane of the reasons for imprisonment or other correctional sanctions, it has lately fallen out of favor. This is due partly to the public's general demand for more punitive measures, and partly to the widely recognized findings by Robert Martinson (see pp. 79–80) that rehabilitative measures seem to be ineffective.

Although the above categories of punishment rationale can be separately defined, any review of the history and current practice of sentencing for crime shows them to be mixed and generally confused in the public mind, as well as in criminal laws. When the average citizen calls for criminals to be punished it is likely that the reasons for the call are not thoughtfully differentiated but are vaguely composed of several concepts. In such a context it is understandable that courts have felt considerable latitude in the use of varying degrees of discretion when selecting an appropriate sentence in each case.

Generally the public supports the right of a court to have latitude to sentence offenders individually according to the varied degrees of their culpability. And yet the history of sentencing has shown a tendency toward gradual and continuing reduction of that discretion. As noted in chapter 1, Beccaria's treatise pointed out the gross abuses inherent in a court system that permitted judges unbridled discretion, unrestrained by any limiting definitions in the statutes. Today, even though statutes are far more explicit, there still is occasional uneasiness about the latitude allowed the courts in disposing of criminal cases, and in recent years this has resulted in some new approaches to sentencing procedures.

To understand fully the trends in sentencing reform there must be recognition of the great diversity of laws in the United States. Unlike most other countries, the U.S. justice system does not operate under one uniform criminal code, but instead functions under the separate and differing laws of fifty states, the District of Columbia, and the federal government. Consequently, it is difficult, and often impossible, to generalize about either the philosophy or the specific provisions of sentencing laws in the United States. Whereas philosophical trends tend to be common across the country, specific applications in statutes differ from state to state, depending on demographic, historical, cultural, and other factors peculiar to the individual state.

One reliable generalization would be that, notwithstanding the public's tendency to curb the discretionary latitude judges have in sentencing, there remains in the system a virtually ineradicable discretion that affects the severity of punishment from case to case. Even at the point of arrest, the police respond to various pressures that affect their decisions to arrest or not; prosecutors have discretion in deciding whether to prosecute, the level of offense to charge, and what penalty to recommend. Subsequently, probation officers and prison staffs influence the closing of probation cases or encourage favorable parole decisions. Usually when legislators try to curb judicial discretion, it is done to assure the public that tougher sentences for crime will be guaranteed, that "lenient" judges will not be able to let offenders off easy. But the public is not likely to understand that sentencing is only one element in the process of imposing punishment and that the major controlling factor will often be the unavailability of the needed resources. If the number of prison beds is insufficient, the whole system will self-adjust to reduce the flow of cases to prison. If alternatives to outright incarceration are available to the courts, sentencing practices will make use of them.

Nevertheless, though decisions by judges are only one part of the process of imposing punishment, the judge and the judge's responsibility remain of interest and significance in any examination of the exercise of discretion in punishment for crime.

The Ambivalent Views of Discretion

Judges have an altogether human inclination to pronounce sentences that reflect their own subjective reactions to the infinitely varied life situations before them. For example, in a 1967 California case, a young woman, Mercedes Dominguez, was placed on probation following her conviction for aiding in a robbery. The judge, noting that this young unmarried woman had two children, ordered that as a condition of probation she was not to get pregnant again while unmarried. Although she had been cooperative and law-abiding while on probation, Ms. Dominguez eventually became pregnant again and was duly returned to court where her probation was revoked. Subsequently, however, the appellate court recognized the revocation, as a reflection of the trial judge's personal prejudice, to be an unwarranted use of discretion. The court reversed the revocation of probation with this cogent observation: "A condition of probation which has no relationship to the crime of which the offender was convicted, relates to conduct which is not in itself criminal, and forbids conduct which is not reasonably related to future criminality, does not serve the statutory ends of probation and is invalid."[1]

This is the sort of case that points up a frustrating problem for those that design criminal laws—the need to allow the exercise of discretion in imposing varied punishments to fit different defendants and different degrees of criminality, but at the same time to discourage the sort of discretion which represents only the subjective biases of individual judges.

There has been a reasonable logic behind the right accorded to criminal courts to use wide discretion in sentencing criminals. Referred to as "individualized justice," this right has been stoutly defended by judges as necessary in shaping sentences to the varied degrees of guilt and the variety of people and situations involved in crimes. Sensible as this is, however, one could argue that while each criminal case is different, judges are different too, and their own individual, personal differences (biases) affect case dispositions more than do the legitimate demands of varied case situations. As one incensed judge expressed it, "Left at large, wandering in deserts of uncharted discretion, the judges suit their own value systems insofar as they think about the problem at all." (Frankel 1973, 7–8) Studies have shown wide-ranging, illogical variations in sentencing, explainable only as reflecting subjective attitudes of the different judges. (Starr 1986, 299–300) As a result, since the early 1960s there has been a growing awareness that exercise of discretion can all too easily be abused even by the most well-meaning court. "Where did it all start?" one expert asks in regard to the growing opposition to judicial discretion. Answering his own question—"The key actors, in my scenario, are prisoners, professors, and politicians— in that order. The precipitating events were the prisoners' rights movement and the Attica prison riot (or uprising, depending on your politics). The climate was one of rights consciousness as well as declining faith in the use of state power to coerce cures or to exercise total control." (Tonry and Zimring 1983, 102)

The disparate, widely varied sentences that seem to have no basis for their differences except differing personal attitudes of the sentencing judges became the focus of a strong sentencing reform movement in the early 1970s. In seeking to define the problem of sentencing variations that are too prejudicial and subjective, one government body explains that "disparity exists when defendants with *similar criminal records* found guilty of *similar criminal conduct* receive *dissimilar sentences.*" (United States Sentencing Commission, *The Federal Sentencing Guidelines* 1991, 31) This problem has been the target of many attempts in both state and federal laws to control discretion in the interest of fairness to criminal defendants.

The criminal justice system does not need the extra trouble it suffers when prisoners compare their punishments and grow resentful of grossly unfair disparities. The 1971 Attica prison riot was not the only time that prisoner resentment about unfairness has erupted disastrously.

Most criminologists agree that the Attica riot prompted much reappraisal of the whole punishment system. Academic criminologists built on that event to fashion new sentencing concepts. One influential polemic published shortly before Attica had already declared that, "Instead of promoting rehabilitation, the individualized system promotes inhumanity, discrimination, hypocrisy, and a sense of injustice." The members of the committee which produced this view supported their argument with the observation that "members of the dominant classes, and the political incumbents" do not permit such discretionary powers to the courts in matters that pertain to *their* interests. The authors point to "the area of property inheritance tax or business law or any area, for that matter, in which the affairs of the more powerful and rich segments are being regulated. In these areas the specificity of the law is extreme. Little margin is left for discretion." (American Friends Service Committee 1971, 125, 135)

U.S. District Court Judge Marvin Frankel made much the same point in his book on the subject, saying "how deeply we prize certainty and predictability in the workings of the law. We want to be able to plan our businesses and family decisions by knowing in advance just how painful the tax will be, what the zoning laws promise, how long an employment contract will endure. It may be imagined that knowing the actual length of a prison term might serve similar, though much more searing, needs.'' (Frankel 1973, 97)

Another authority adds the comment that ''this sort of discretion, which so directly affects individual liberty, would be viewed with great suspicion if vested in another branch of government. The notion of a government official, whose acts are circumscribed by few legal constraints, and who answers only to his or her own conscience is inconsistent with the very principle of accountability.'' (Starr 1986, 301)

No matter how valid the contention that the exercise of discretion leads to unfairness, it proves to be impossible to eliminate discretion from the criminal justice system. Often there is only the illusion of its elimination, as instead discretion is only shifted among the various decision stages, as has already been mentioned. The factor most powerfully frustrating any moves to eliminate discretion in the system is the usually overwhelming volume of cases to be processed. The prosecutor may be on record as opposed to the idea of plea bargaining, in which criminal defendants are given the chance to plead guilty to less serious charges than first filed. But if instead of plea bargaining, all cases were to be prosecuted at their most serious level, the resultant demand for jury trials would choke the court system intolerably. From arrest through final disposition of a criminal case, the system is forced to exercise discretion in adjusting to the reality of limited resources. Nevertheless, much consideration has been given lately to proposals for limiting judicial discretion in the sentencing for crime.

The Control of Sentencing Discretion

Among the seminal works appearing in the 1970s advocating and defining reformed sentencing laws was the Twentieth Century Fund report developed by a task force of twelve distinguished practitioners from various criminal justice careers as a guide for legislators. The task force presented the idea of the ''presumptive sentence,'' the sentence *presumed* to be fair and appropriate for a given crime category unless the court were to find aggravating or mitigating circumstances that would justify a higher or lower sentence. (Twentieth Century Fund Task Force on Criminal Sentencing 1976) Subsequently revised laws of several states directly reflect this book's influence,

By the 1970s sentencing reform caught the interest of various state legislatures due to the confluence of several new currents of thought. A notable element was the publication in 1974 of a report by Dr. Robert

Martinson of research he and associates had done on the effectiveness of correctional treatment methods. After evaluating reports of 231 projects, they decided that either the research methods were defective or that treatment programs simply were not working. ''This is not to say that we found no instances of success or partial success; it is only to say that these instances have been isolated, producing no clear pattern to indicate the efficacy of any particular method of treatment.''[2] This cautious statement was quickly overinterpreted to mean that treatment programs in all instances were ineffective, a view that profoundly affected the criminal justice field in general. It hurried the move toward sentencing reform by its implication that offenders should not be incarcerated for ''treatment,'' but only for punishment. The trend was further affected by the growing concern that exercise of discretion by judges has too much potential for unfairness.[3]

The long-standing rationale for judicial discretion in sentencing had been the assumption that offenders can be ''rehabilitated,'' and that the length of any prisoner's incarceration should depend upon the eventual decision by a parole board that the prisoner had made sufficient progress in reforming himself. However, the disillusionment regarding rehabilitation that followed Martinson's research convinced both liberals and conservatives that sentencing for crime should be on the more honest basis of punishment rather than being an elusive, unprovable quest for rehabilitation. During the 1970s the influential writings on the subject ''called for determinacy in sentencing, believing that criminal codes prescribing set sanctions for each offense would purge the system of discretion. . . . Because prison terms would be set in law and known at the time of sentencing, parole boards would be abolished. In this scheme, offenders would receive equal treatment before the law, they would receive punishment commensurate with the seriousness of their crimes.'' (Cullen and Gendreau 1989, 29)

Although determinacy in sentencing is a welcome prospect, the idea is unrealistically optimistic. As one expert put it, ''reformers rush to correct this disparity, then that one, then another, all with no awareness of the complexity of the criminal justice system and thus of the problem. Any serious consideration of sentencing reform in the United States is plagued by the fantastic variety of combinations and forms found in our state and local jurisdictions.''[4]

As an example of the challenge it offers to the policymakers, the New York legislature considered the creation of a sentencing commission, but its inherent reluctance to delegate any of its authority to such a body ultimately defeated the proposal. An Advisory Commission appointed by the governor in 1981 recommended a combination of determinate and indeterminate sentences. Thinking that short sentences would preclude rehabilitation, the Commission advised determinate sentences only for imprisonments of five years or less. Longer sentences would be left indeterminate because future release decisions should be left, they argued, to the parole board, which would then have updated information on the prisoner's progress. (Griset 1991, 91) After five years of study and debate, the legislature was still so divided on the issue that in 1986 Governor Mario Cuomo decided not to reintroduce the bill on the subject.

Although the design for divided categories urged by the New York Advisory Commission differed appreciably from that of any other state, the idea of short-term sentences being separable followed much of the current thinking. Penal philosophy generally accepts the several possible purposes of imprisonment to be rehabilitation, incapacitation, retribution, or deterrence, with most sentences representing a combination of two or more of these purposes. But if rehabilitation is the only goal, corrections experts can easily argue that, rather than using prison, supervised probation offers more and better opportunities to give this kind of help in the community. A year or two of imprisonment offers little hope of effective corrective treatment. "The object of brief imprisonment, for example, must be deterrence and vindication of the norm—the community's affirmation of the seriousness of its determination not to permit the proscribed behavior. Imprisonment of thirty days, or even six months, provides no opportunity for rehabilitation, particularly under the wretched conditions that characterize the typical short-term jail." (Schwartz 1983, 73)

Except for the New York attempt, the effort to accomplish determinacy has not included the separating out of short-term sentences. A notable example of rather drastic sentencing reform occurred in California, where the law had provided the ultimate in indeterminacy since the creation of the state's Adult Authority in 1944. California sentencing procedure had been essentially a matter of committing an offender to prison for the full term allowed by the statute, such as, for example, five years to life for robbery. Within that broad range the parole board determined a release date based, supposedly, on evidence of the prisoner's reform. This presented the prisoner with an onerous prospect of nearly unbearable uncertainty; in some cases a person could enter prison without knowing whether he or she would be there a year or for life. In 1977 the state abolished this indeterminacy; in its place the law grouped all felonies (except capital crimes) into four categories by levels of seriousness and provided to the criminal courts an exacting choice of three possible prison terms for each category. The middle of these three terms, the presumptive sentence, was required to be used unless mitigating or aggravating factors could justify either of the other two choices.[5] Though the California action substantially changed sentencing procedure, it did not include use of sentencing guidelines.

Among state governments, Minnesota in 1978 was the first to create a Sentencing Guidelines Commission, a statutory body carrying delegated authority to design, implement, and monitor use of a determinate sentencing structure. As in the later federal law, the Minnesota Commission designed a grid that prescribes a presumptive sentence in each case as derived from two determinates, offense severity and the defendant's prior criminal record. Another state, Pennsylvania, created guidelines for sentencing while retaining parole in 1982. Florida adopted presumptive sentencing guidelines in 1983, and the state of Washington implemented its version of the reform in 1984. (Knapp and Hauptly 1989, 5–6; Griset 1991, 39)

During the remainder of that decade, while still other states planned their versions of such legislation, the federal Congress labored to devise its own reform statute. The product was the Sentencing Reform Act of 1984. The exceptionally complex and controversial nature of this effort can be seen in the fact that the Act was passed only after seven years of congressional debate, and then was still not fully operational until finally validated by the U.S. Supreme Court in 1989. The Act reflected the general repudiation of rehabilitation as a valid basis of setting prison terms, and moved toward a concept of proportioned punishment. It established a permanent federal sentencing commission, which initially had the task of designing guidelines for federal judges to follow in sentencing criminal defendants. The guideline instrument employs a grid, one axis of which lists offenses according to level of seriousness, while the other axis lists six categories of criminal history for classifying the defendant. The intersecting lines of the grid will then reveal the "presumptive" sentence that should be pronounced. Actually, the sentence is given as a narrow range of possibilities within which the judge may choose, allowing a modest amount of latitude. If the judge feels impelled to go outside of the range to be either more lenient or more severe, the judge may do so, but is required to supply in writing a convincing rationale for this decision.

Sentencing Reform: The Effects on the Criminal Justice Systems

Many corrections professionals worry that determinate sentences will cause already crowded prisons to suffer still greater prisoner populations. This could be especially true if the sentencing reform would eliminate parole. As a matter of political reality, the public is somewhat appeased in hearing of a defendant being given a sentence of perhaps five to thirty years; the mention of thirty years has a satisfying sound to a punitively minded observer, and later, when the offender is paroled after perhaps six or seven years, this will likely get little notice. When the political climate demands legislative action to get "tough on crime," legislators have been able to achieve the appearance of greater severity by raising the maximums on indeterminate sentences. They know that prisons cannot tolerate much actual increase in prison time, so they must avoid writing tougher laws that would truly overload the system. By raising the permissible maximums there will be more appearance than substance, since it is rare for anyone actually to serve the full possible sentence. (Schwartz 1983, 78)

The dilemma for a sentencing commission designing a set of determinate prison terms is that in all fairness the new prescribed sentence lengths should be related not to the former maximums, but to the record of average time actually being served by committed offenders. The public, however, can be expected to react with indignation in hearing about prison sentences that seem to be much less time than what was familiar under the previous sentencing laws. Accordingly, a sentencing commission may be pressured to set the sentences higher than the actual time customarily served under the indeterminate plan, and this, of course, will result in a substantial prison population increase.

Again, public policy has to adapt to the subjective but strong perceptions of the citizenry and find a solution that will do what has to be done, but without burdening the system to the breaking point. That solution has seemed to be to allow a politically necessary increase in the prescribed prison time, but then to offset this with increased allowances of time off for good behavior ("good time"). The author of the "justice model," with its so-called flat time sentences, proposed that "the length on the flat time sentence be mitigated only by good time credit." For this purpose the proposed allowance was to be a generous one day off the sentence for every day served. Thus, an offender could be given a sentence of public-pleasing punitiveness, for example, ten years flat time, but then be released after five years if his or her behavior had not caused any forfeit of good time. (Fogel 1975, 247)

Policymakers are well aware of the problem and sometimes shape sentencing policy to partially counteract the prison crowding effect. In creating its sentencing commission, the Minnesota legislature was concerned that sentencing reform "has contributed to recent increases in prison crowding, first by causing the sentencing to prison of many offenders who previously would have received probation, and second by removing the 'safety valve' of early release on parole in the event of overcrowding. This problem was avoided in Minnesota, where the legislature specifically instructed the sentencing commission to take prison capacity into account when it developed the guidelines. . . . A similar provision is contained in newly enacted Federal legislation."[6]

Enough time has elapsed since inception of sentencing reforms to permit some appraisal of the intended effects, but it proves to be quite difficult to assess results reliably, even in such a factually objective area as counting prison populations. Responding to a congressional requirement that it evaluate and report on the effects of its work, the U.S. Sentencing Commission reported that after implementation of the Sentencing Reform Act, imprisonments significantly increased. "Mean sentence lengths across all offenses during this time period nearly doubled, increasing from 24 months in July 1984 to 46 months in June 1990." At the same time, however, the drug culture had become more serious, new laws had been enacted with increased penalties for drug offenders, and more law enforcement and prosecutorial personnel had been funded to fight this type of crime; all this constituted a factor that could not be charged to the reformed sentencing structure. The report reasonably commented that, "Due to considerable changes that occurred not only in legislation and sentencing policy but also in the volume, seriousness, and composition of the criminal behavior they seek to regulate, any causal influences are too confounded and close in proximity to be separately assessed and evaluated." (United States Sentencing Commission, *Federal Sentencing Guidelines* 1991, 60, 63)

Notwithstanding the confusing variables that have affected imprisonment trends since sentencing reform, observers generally agree that sentencing guidelines have certainly caused prison populations to rise substantially. One federal prison warden has noted a drastic rise in the federal prisoner count due to longer terms being served. "For example, Bureau of Prisons statistics show that the average time served for a robbery offense under the old law was 44.8 months, compared to 78.0 months under the new law." (Luttrell 1991, 56) Another writer notes that in most states the legislatures, in drafting sentencing reforms, "instruct their sentencing commissions to consider correctional costs in developing their guideline proposals and to recognize the scarcity of their correctional resources." But he notes "Florida's failure to assess adequately the impact of their sentencing guidelines on correctional resources prevented the full implementation of sentencing guidelines." (Knapp and Hauptly 1989, 14) A U.S. senator has noted that various knowledgeable sources "have detailed problems with the guidelines, including the sentiment that the guidelines are excessively time consuming, rigid and technical in their application, and overly harsh in their effect. . . . As well, Chief Justice Rehnquist has cited a 'dramatic increase' in criminal appeals since the guidelines were imposed." (Hatch 1993, 191)

Since disparity of sentencing has been a principal concern behind the use of guidelines, this too has been an important focus of evaluative studies. The federal Sentencing Commission presents extensive figures, compiled by offense categories, which in most cases document satisfactorily reduced disparity. As the report states in respect to one category, for instance, "the data strongly suggest that in all matched categories similar offenders convicted of similar bank robberies receive dramatically more similar sentences under the guidelines than did comparable offenders pre-guidelines." (United States Sentencing Commission, *Federal Sentencing Guidelines* 1991, 43) Minnesota, concerned about racial and other disparities, claims that its guidelines have made sentencing more fair.

The Effect on the Use of Parole

Inevitably the move toward determinate sentencing has affected parole practice, although different jurisdictions have had quite different concepts regarding the best way to adapt parole to the new sentencing laws. The federal parole system first tried the same principle as in presumptive sentencing, by designing an actuarial device called "Salient factor scoring." This instrument used a formula for combining characteristics of the prisoner's offense with characteristics of his personal history to produce a future "presumptive" parole date. (Gottfredson, Wilkins, and Hoffman 1978, 55) Three years in planning, this instrument went into use in late 1974. The federal sentencing reform intended to abolish federal parole as of 1992, but this proved a difficult, unpopular move, and the Congress, by an act passed in 1990, extended the life of the U.S. Parole Commission to November 1997.

Maine has made the most extreme modification of parole practice. The state legislature in 1976 rejected parole entirely, asserting that it could not be supported by any capability to predict future behavior. However, though the legislature's published rationale did not say so, the abolishment was largely a reaction against the parole board's perceived leniency in releasing too many dangerous prisoners. The new Maine law defined five classes of crimes, set a maximum term for each, and then allowed a judge to sentence a defendant to any fixed term short of that maximum. Accordingly, this did not attack the issue of disparity as judges still enjoyed a generous degree of discretion. Prisoners sentenced under this statute would serve their determinate sentences minus "good time" and then be released without parole supervision. Unlike any other state, Maine provided a procedure for review and modification of sentences; the Department of Mental Health and Corrections was authorized to study incoming prisoners and if a sentence seemed inappropriate to a particular case, the Department could petition the sentencing court to approve a reduction of sentence.[7]

California, in its adoption of determinacy, had kept its parole system, but with some substantive changes. The parole board, newly cast as the Community Release Board, would set conditions for parolees and act on cases recommended by parole officers for revocation. By law, released prisoners were to be under parole supervision for specific periods of a year or more depending on the original sentence. For violations they could be returned to prison for six months (lifers, for 18 months), though this was later increased to three years.

The Net Effect of Sentencing Policy Changes

To make a new sentencing law effective, additional resources must accompany it. Without resources, any sentencing changes will at best have little of the intended effect, and at worst may cause disruptive effects that then require further legislation. But rational legislative forethought is difficult to accomplish in the usual political context. Consequently, the quest for restraining judicial discretion in the interest of guaranteeing uniform sentences has been frustrating and has produced less provable benefit than any of its advocates would have expected. Prosecutors have retained their share of discretion, exercising it partly and very effectively through the plea bargaining process. "Plea bargaining, which has been left unregulated in virtually every determinate sentencing model, permits unregulated discretion to be exercised and may increase the power of the prosecutor." (Goodstein and Hepburn 1985, 38) The system's limited resources force the system to make adjustments. Limited prosecutorial services, limited probation service, and limited prison beds force the other parts of the system to make adjustments to keep the entire operation from becoming choked and stalled.

One observer of the problem has argued that if legislatures are really determined to reduce discretion substantially they should attack it in a balanced manner. "How, then, does one control prosecutorial discretion, particularly that associated with plea negotiations, when judicial discretion, which might otherwise be used to compensate for prosecutorial discretion, has been so severely restricted? If the discretion available to each of the primary decision-makers in the system—prosecutors and judges—were equally restricted by the legislature, then the balance within the criminal justice system would remain intact." (Steury 1989, 109)

Expansion of Sentencing Options

Before this century, judges had few options when sentencing convicted offenders. In most cases a prison sentence was the obvious and almost only choice, with the court having little discretion other than to decide how much prison time to assign. The development of probation services late in the nineteenth century was well accepted in view of the obvious need to find more humane alternatives for many minor offenders, particularly for juveniles who until then were commonly committed to the same prisons as adults. Juvenile court spread rapidly after its introduction in 1899. Similarly, during the next decade, the idea of parole as a release procedure for adult prisoners took hold and was soon adopted in most of the states. Gradually, variations on these options developed to the point that by mid-century most courts could use a variety of sentencing alternatives.

How and why the public mood changes is a question too subtle to analyze fully, but clearly the twentieth century, which opened with a decade in which liberalized policies toward offenders thrived, is now, in its closing decade, characterized by a harshly punitive mood. Political campaigns typically feature bombast about getting tough on crime, usually meaning more and longer prison sentences, fewer paroles, and more extensive and expeditious use of the death penalty. The intensity of the mood is indicated by the public's toleration of the enormous cost of building more prisons in the belief that this will reduce violent crime.

Difficult as it is with this punitive mood prevailing to foster the use of sentencing alternatives, the effort persists simply because it must. The punitive attitude, which demands more use of prisons, also drives the search for alternatives because the increased number of prisoners must somehow be accommodated. The entire criminal justice system must make internal adjustments to the pressures caused by the overload of cases, whereas the complex interaction between courts and the melange of law enforcement and other private and governmental agencies defines the concept of a criminal justice system.

Although the components of the criminal justice system (police, prosecutors, courts, corrections) function independently, the operation of each component directly affects, and is affected by, the functioning of the others. The effect may be virtually mechanical, as when increased police activity loads more cases into the courts or prisons, or when courts and prosecutors must make adjustments in their case handling in response to the limitations of prison space.

A key element in this interaction among components is the sentencing process. Ideally, the courts, in sentencing criminal defendants, could provide a flexible process of adapting the system to the availability of resources, and stimulating development of a wide range of sanctions that would serve the needs of the endlessly varied criminal cases. But courts can be only as innovative as public opinion, the law, and the limited availability of dispositional options will permit. Occasionally, legislative initiatives appear that are politically astute in designing penal alternatives that are palatable to the public while relieving undue strain on the justice system's resources. These initiatives offer instructive glimpses of what innovative planning can accomplish, while at the same time illustrating the impermanence of even the best social planning. One of these was a significant program for reducing institutional expansion in the face of increasing criminal populations in California.

Designing Policy to Enforce Sentencing Options: A California Experience

In 1965, with demand for adult and juvenile correctional institution beds expected to double within a decade, California planners proposed a bold plan for shifting sentences from incarceration to community-based programs. Generally, these were conceived to have substantially reduced probation caseloads with enhanced local therapeutic, educational, or recreational resources to augment the more intensive probation supervision. Studies of the correctional populations convinced planners that as many as 25 percent of incoming offenders could safely have been left in the communities on probation, especially if the probation service could be made more intensive. (Smith 1971, 7, 15) But counties do not willingly make an unorthodox change in practice that is likely to cost them more and alienate conservative constituencies. County officials could not ignore the fact that it was cheaper—for the counties—to send their offenders off to the state than to keep them in the county under close supervision.

Designing a politically astute strategy, the planners proposed that those counties accomplishing reductions in their commitments of adults or juveniles to state correctional institutions would receive cash payments from the state. The plan, as enacted by the legislature, provided that the counties reducing their commitments below a baseline rate derived from their commitment record for the preceding five years would receive subsidies according to a formula that linked payments to the percentage of the reduction. Each county would have to decide voluntarily to join the plan, and would be required to spend its received subsidy payments for state-approved intensive probation programs.

Legislators considering the proposal knew that the burgeoning commitment rate required expensive new correctional institutions. The subsidies would cost millions each year, but were to be paid only upon proven reduction of commitments. Advocates of the plan, predicting significant savings, won their point; the plan was enacted and in its first several years seemed to fulfill the expectations. Juvenile commitments dropped from 6,174 in 1965 to 3,746 in 1970, and adult commitments fell even more. Payments to the counties reached nearly $60 million in the period from 1966 to 1972, but cumulative savings from canceled construction, closing institutions, and delaying the opening of two new four hundred-bed institutions saved about $186 million. (Smith 1986, 49, 68)

Despite its apparent success, by 1983 the program had died. One of the more subtle causes was fading memory of the severity of the construction crisis that gave birth to the subsidy program. Also, state agency leadership changed, bringing a new director who had little feeling for the significance of the subsidy program and who consequently did little to fight growing opposition to it. In many respects the program was undermined by its own success; the presence of empty institution beds took the edge off the counties' motivation to retain for local handling those offenders who they felt should go to state facilities.

A more ostensible reason for the program's demise was the opposition from the police, and to some extent from the public schools. School officials tended to blame their growing problems with student behaviors on the young offenders who, they argued, should have been sent to the state. Faced with rising crime and feeling the sting of public criticism, law enforcement officials naturally looked for opportunity to shift the blame elsewhere. (Smith 1986, 104) The chief of police in Los Angeles, running for election to the state Senate, brought colorful attention to his campaign by referring to the subsidy payments as "blood money." He led a movement among police agencies to convince the public and the legislature that the subsidy program contributed to the increased crime rate. (The police chief, Ed Davis, won the election.) Presumably, the police were also annoyed that the subsidy payments went to probation agencies, and not to the police departments.

Under such pressure legislative resolve weakened. In 1977 the process of emasculating the subsidy program began. A cap was put on the amounts that could be paid to counties. Two years later the performance requirement was discontinued, allowing counties to receive their payments without having to prove any reduction in commitments. This, of course, undermined the real genius of the program. Various other legislative modifications followed in the next several years, and finally in 1983 a system of block grants to the counties, with no required performance standards, replaced the subsidy program.

A Michigan Experience

Whereas California sought to reduce prison populations by subsidizing sentencing options, Michigan tried another approach with its 1980 Emergency Powers Act. The Act provided that the state Department of Corrections should determine the proper capacity of the prison system. Any time that the population exceeded that limit for a period of thirty days, the Department would certify this fact to the governor. The governor then would respond with an executive order reducing the minimum terms of all prisoners by ninety days. This would immediately make more prisoners eligible for parole.

The procedure worked well enough to remain in use for about four years, and helped to control prison population growth, though in actual practice the results diminished gradually. For this type of procedure, the first application is the most effective; in subsequent applications decreasing numbers of prisoners will be eligible for earlier release. The plan finally died in 1984 when the governor ceased using it because of public reaction to a murder committed by a released prisoner.

In the long history of programs designed as alternatives to incarceration, this was one more example of the political necessity of retreating in the face of public opposition. Prisoners may and do commit murders in prisons with no resultant public demand for less use of the prison. But a similar murder by an ex-prisoner in a community program brings heated public reaction. Political leaders may be able to sustain the program by some well-publicized new restrictions on its use, but often its termination will be the only feasible political response.

The Michigan plan for control of prison populations, unlike the California plan, did not include any special programming to give intensive treatment or supervision of inmates released early. However, the field of corrections during the last decade has been showing new inventiveness in offering courts a variety of options for sentencing offenders to punishments other than prison. These options will be discussed in more detail in chapter 8; in this chapter we will discuss the controversial mandatory and selective sentencing concepts, and the sentencing options available in capital murder cases.

Sentencing Choices: Mandatory or Selective

So often this year's solution is next year's new problem, as it is with policies on the mandatory minimum type of sentence, a concept that has gained wide popularity in the last decade, though not on the basis of proven deterrent effect. Mandatory minimum sentences are another of the stringently punitive initiatives arising from public anger and frustration, showing how public policy so often responds to emotional perceptions rather than to rational and objective appraisals of what will be effective.

Mandatory minimum sentences, though proving to be self-defeating, are favored for any type of crime that is frequent, frightening, and apparently undeterred by other measures. Varying from state to state, they may be applied to such offenses as drunk driving, drug dealing, and any crime in which a gun is involved. Congress has established mandatory minimum sentences for many federal crimes, most for offenses involving weapons and drugs. The high-minded purpose behind these laws, in addition to the intended deterrent effect of the *certainty* of punishment, has been to ensure that penalties are imposed both severely and uniformly on all offenders, thus curbing the tendency of judges to be lenient with influential defendants while being harsh to others. In addition, these laws make sure that for any given offense, all convicted persons will get identical sentences. Notwithstanding the intent, however, the expected benefits have proved illusory, and substantial opposition to these penalties has emerged.

With all that has been said above about how subjective bias inappropriately affects judges' sentencing, it is equally true that judges need latitude to adapt sentences to the infinitely varied human events that come before them. Theoretically, it may seem eminently fair to give identical prison sentences to two persons convicted of the same offense. When two cases examined in detail, however, are found to present very different degrees of culpability, the identical sentences result in gross injustice. In attacking drug dealing, for example, legislators usually mean to reach the serious drug trafficker, whereas more often the person caught will be much more ordinary. One writer notes, for instance, the kind of case typified by the secretary with no criminal record who was necessarily given a five-year mandatory sentence because her "drug-dealing son hid 120 grams of crack in her attic." (Wallace 1993, 162)

Adding to this source of injustice inherent in mandatory sentences is the need to provide exceptions that will assist in prosecution. The federal law allows prosecutors to ask for a sentence below the otherwise mandatory minimum for any defendant who cooperates by giving evidence against other offenders. Thus, discretion, which has been denied to the judge, is in this way granted to the prosecutors, giving them considerable power to defeat the mandatory provisions, and unfortunately in a way that also defeats a major goal of this sentencing law. Ironically, the higher-up drug dealer who best knows the drug distribution system and so has the most to offer in cooperating with the prosecutor is also the one who is best able to avoid the full penalty. (Wallace 1993, 160)

Directed by Congress to evaluate the effects of mandatory minimum sentences, the U.S. Sentencing Commission concluded that the law defeats its own purpose. The stiff sentences faced by defendants in these cases lead most of them to trial, causing the system to be clogged, thus requiring prosecutors to do more plea bargaining. Not only does this result in a sizable proportion of eligible defendants escaping mandatory minimum sentencing, but also "since the charging and plea negotiation processes are neither open to public review nor generally reviewable by the courts, the honesty and truth in sentencing intended by the guidelines system is compromised.'' (U.S. Sentencing Commission, *Special Report* 1991, ii)

The Commission also reports a problem of racism with this type of sentencing, for the mandatory minimums have brought higher proportions of black and Hispanic offenders into prisons. ''The trend toward a greater influence of race is particularly disturbing as it coincides with mandatory minimum sentencing statutes, which one would expect to be *more* color-blind than a system that did not narrow judicial discretion.''[8] The report also notes the overwhelming disaffection with this law on the part of federal judges who find the penalties ''grossly excessive,'' while being keenly aware of the injustice of giving identical sentences to defendants who are far from identical in any way. ''It thus appears that an unintended effect of mandatory minimums is *unwarranted* sentencing uniformity.'' (U.S. Sentencing Commission, *Special Report* 1991, ii, 93)

Although the mandatory sentence does not necessarily result from the adoption of a determinate sentencing system, there is a relationship between the two, as it is easier to create mandatory sentences when to do so is little more than simply declaring a determinate sentence to be the minimum allowed for offenders convicted of some designated offense. Usually advocated for the sake of their presumed deterrent quality, mandatory sentences also appeal to those who argue that certainty of the sentence in exact proportion to seriousness of the crime is essential as a matter of fairness. One observer, a professor of philosophy, asserts that the determinate sentence is morally preferable to the indeterminate sentence because it is more deterrent, more humane, and it preserves a person's right to predict the legal consequences of his or her acts.[9] Other scholars, taking a more practical approach, argue that determinate sentencing ''goes too far in eliminating all flexibility. By requiring every single defendant convicted under the same statute to serve the identical sentence, it threatens to create a system so automatic that it may operate in practice like a poorly programmed robot.'' (Twentieth Century Fund Task Force on Criminal Sentencing 1976, 17)

However questionable the concept's philosophical merit, its current popularity is undeniable. ''Forty-six states have established mandatory sentencing laws. . . . In Alabama, there is a two-year minimum sentence for drug sales; five years are added to this sentence if the sale is made within three miles of a school or a housing project. An additional five years is imposed if the sale is made within three miles of both.''[10]

Similar provisions are present in federal sentencing laws, with rather complicated gradations for different levels of drug offenses. A person charged, as a first offense, with distribution of 100 grams of heroin or 100 kilograms of marijuana will be subject to a mandatory five years. (Other drugs and weights are also itemized.) For some of the larger amounts, or for repeated offenses, the mandatory time may be ten years. Twenty years will be mandatory in cases when drug sales result in bodily harm or death. These sentences are minimums; judges can and often do pronounce longer sentences.[11] From 1984 to 1990 drug offenders increased from 20 percent of the federal prison population to 32 percent, with the proportion of mandatory minimum sentences going up from 12 percent of total sentences in 1984 to 20 percent in 1990. Convictions for possession or sale of cocaine represented more than half of this increase.

In studying the effects of such laws, a federal research project showed mixed results. While touted as a means of thwarting judicial discretion and guaranteeing prison time without discrimination for all convicted offenders, too often the discretion just shifts to some other component of the judicial system. As the research report revealed, "almost half of the offenders who would appear to be eligible for a minimum term received a lesser sentence. This highlights that considerable discretion remains in the system, much of which rests with the prosecutor. Prosecutors decide how to charge, what plea bargains are acceptable, and whether to move the court to impose a sentence below any applicable minimum because of a defendant's 'substantial cooperation.' " (Meierhoefer 1992, 9)

Critics argue that mandatory sentencing, while adding to prison crowding, actually puts more violent offenders back on the streets. When a prison reaches its court-defined saturation point, some way must be found to give early release to some inmates in order to make space for newly committed offenders. Persons with mandatory sentences, even though nonviolent, cannot be released early, so these nonviolent drug offenders continue to occupy the scarce prison beds while more dangerous prisoners are released to make space. In consequence, without gaining any more protection from crime, the taxpayers are required to build still more expensive prison space. With the start of the 1990s, the serious dimensions of the problem became apparent to corrections administrators, and gradually their pronouncements on the subject began to register on the general public, with uncertain effect. Significantly, one of the conservative members of Congress published his concern about the excessive use of mandatory sentences: "Today, over one hundred separate mandatory minimum penalty provisions are operative in sixty criminal statutes." This same member of Congress was concerned about the evidence that the purpose of mandatory sentences is defeated because sentencing disparity is being accomplished in other ways, usually by prosecutors. (Hatch 1993, 193)

Mandatory sentencing also seems to have failed as a deterrent, prompting interest in the concept of "selective incapacitation" for a more precisely deterrent effect as well as more efficient use of prison space. As defined in a report on the subject by the Rand Corporation, this is "a strategy that attempts to use objective actuarial evidence to improve the ability of the current system to identify and confine offenders who represent the most serious risk to the community." (Greenwood 1982, vii) The Rand experts developed an instrument that would enable a court to identify those offenders who are high risk and likely to engage in violent crime again if at liberty. The obvious motivation for having such a device is the possibility of giving a long prison sentence (incapacitation) to a potentially dangerous person while not imprisoning one who is not a threat to public safety. Thus, the public would be kept safer, and prison beds, as a scarce resource, would be used more efficiently. This concept is so attractive that many attempts have been made to implement it, but serious impediments have so far frustrated its accomplishment.

Because the only way to predict violent behavior is by studying past behavior, the Rand project developed a list of past experiences to look for in an individual's history as presumed indicators of violence potential. In familiar actuarial style, the cataloging of these factors would produce a score, and any score above a certain weight would make the case eligible for a sentence selected for long-term incapacitation. (Greenwood 1982, xv) The unyielding problem, however, is that no process has yet proved reliable in predicting violence. Too many offenders would therefore be given long terms in prison when in fact they would not have been repeat offenders. Such outcomes are usually spoken of as "false positives," the imposition of prison terms for too many offenders in the interest of containing the ones among them who actually would have been dangerous.[12]

Another disturbing problem is that whenever a person is given an extra long term of confinement because of his or her perceived risk to society, this is too much akin to preventive detention. "The most fundamental criticism deals with the injustice of imprisoning persons essentially for crimes they have not yet committed." The criminal justice system might be willing to venture into this practice only if the prediction of future crime could be more nearly guaranteed. "To date, however, the various efforts to predict future crime have not been very successful. If these predictions cannot be improved, there is no adequate justification for the selective incapacitation of some convicted offenders." (Kittrie and Zenoff 1981, 24)

The Sentence of Death

Since recorded history, the right of a society to execute citizens who commit heinous crimes has been an unchallenged practice in most cultures. In the millennial perspective, one might say that only since yesterday has public policy actually prohibited the sentence of death. To some extent, of course, the acceptability of the death penalty has been philosophical or ideational, but there has also often been a simple practical factor. In earlier societies, life imprisonment, which is now a possible alternative, was clearly not feasible. A society that existed as a simple nomadic culture would not have had prisons, even for occasional minor offenders. Even a society such as the early American colonies, with only a few crude jails, had no facilities capable of secure, long-term custody. Imprisonment of that type is expensive and could not be instituted until there was a more settled and affluent society. As a natural consequence, persons with no financial resources to make them subject to a fine could be punished only with corporal penalties such as whipping for minor offenses, and death for serious crimes.

But even after prisons became common and able to hold intractable offenders with reasonable security, the momentum of the long-entrenched history of capital punishment carried the practice into recent times. In the Untited States the execution count reached its highest point during the mid-1930s when it stayed close to two hundred per year. By the 1950s, the execution count was well on its way down and in the 1960s it dropped precipitously; an execution in 1967 was the last before the so-called moratorium brought a stop to executions while the issue was under review by the Supreme Court.

The Supreme Court and the Death Penalty Reappraised

In Furman v. Georgia, the Supreme Court in 1972 found the capital punishment statutes, as then designed, to be in violation of the Eighth and Fourteenth Amendments, although the decision allowed states to rewrite their laws to meet constitutional requirements. The Court had not prohibited capital punishment, but had only ruled that it had been administered in an unacceptably arbitrary and capricious way. State legislatures responded; within two years after the Furman decision more than half the states had enacted new laws that began to populate the death rows again. In January 1977, the wildly publicized execution of Gary Gilmore in Utah signaled the effective end of the moratorium.[13]

For the next several years, even though the rate of sentencing to death rose sharply, the sentences were seldom carried out. Seven years after Gilmore's death by firing squad, only ten more persons had been executed. From 1984 to 1991, the rate of executions increased to a still modest average of 18 per year, which seemed to indicate that a high proportion of death row inmates could never be executed. By 1993, the execution rate started a sharp new climb, although it barely dented the backlog of more than twenty-five hundred men and women then on death rows. The system was facing the implacable problem that even if the execution rate were to increase drastically to 100 per year, it would still take over twenty-five years to work through the backlog, without addressing any of the new cases. Meanwhile, however, many inmates were leaving death rows for reasons other than execution. From January 1973 to January 1993, 199 executions took place, but during that same period, death row populations also experienced 36 suicides, 58 commutations, and 65 deaths by murder or natural causes.[14]

Public Ambivalence toward the Penalty

As important and interesting as such facts are, a proper understanding of the United States' attitudes and practice regarding the death penalty requires a more narrowly focused study of state and regional practices. It is misleading to think of this issue as having a nationwide uniform character when in fact substantial differences exist among different areas of the country. The heaviest use of the death penalty has been mainly in the South, where nine states across the Southeast from Texas to Virginia conducted more than 80 percent of the executions in the sixteen years following the moratorium. Outside that group, no other state had executed more than four people during that time, and in large areas of the country the death penalty was essentially unused. The District of Columbia and fourteen states authorized no capital punishment at all; two other states had the penalty on the statute books but had no one under such a sentence. From the ending of the moratorium up to mid-1993, five of the states with the penalty (retentionist states) had not executed anyone, and four other states had executed only one each.

The extreme contrasts in death penalty practice rates raise baffling questions. Why should the state of Texas lead the country in executions, with fifty-six lethal injections carried out in the period cited, whereas a similarly populous state, Michigan, has had no executions since 1847? The answers to such questions are buried in the subtle political and cultural histories of the states; reasonably valid conjectural answers can be deduced, but not proven.

Also provocative is the question of why there should be such a difference between the country's readiness to sentence offenders to death and its reluctance actually to execute. The answers, if they can be found, reflect the complexity of the process of formulating public policy. It has been theorized, for instance, that legislators actually do not wish to encourage executions despite their campaign rhetoric as candidates for office. But they can give themselves a strict law and order image by keeping the death penalty in force, knowing that the extensive appellate process will hold actual executions to a minimum. As one of the noted proponents of the penalty comments, "Why do we sentence people to death but do not carry out the sentence? According to polls more than eighty percent of Americans favor the death penalty. Juries apparently do too; but, obviously, many judges and lawyers do not. More or less intentionally they sabotage executions, delaying them (the average wait of those actually executed is eight years) and enormously inflating the cost." (van den Haag 1990, 501)

Probably no aspect of the criminal justice system has been studied and debated so intensively as the death penalty. If considering only the minuscule numbers of offenders it affects, the subject could hardly justify such attention, but its importance derives from the sharply focused study it affords of the basic principles of retribution, deterrence, and punishment. These principles, if refined by better understanding of the death penalty, would have useful application well beyond to other aspects of punishing for crime.

Of the several justifications for punishment, capital punishment is mainly based on retribution and deterrence. Incapacitation may be cited to some extent, but when research projects address the issue of capital punishment, it is almost invariably to assess the effectiveness of the penalty as a deterrent. Experts from all branches of behavioral science have attempted ambitious research projects to ascertain the deterrent effect of the death penalty; collectively, it can be said only that the use of the penalty cannot be proved to have any effect on murder rates. The research will no doubt continue since the emotional quality of the debate makes it inevitable that every research report is attacked by critics of the research methods. No one's findings seem to be immune to allegations of flaws.

The Deterrence Controversy

The most dependable comment to be made about the deterrent value of the death penalty is that some studies show a slight deterrent effect under certain conditions and others show none, or even the reverse. Researchers, while admitting serious defects in the approach, have attempted to test deterrence by (1) studying the homicide rates of contiguous states, one of which has, and the other of which does not have, capital punishment; (2) studying homicide rates in the same state for comparable periods before and after a change in law either restoring or abolishing the death penalty; (3) comparing homicide rates in a state before and after a well-publicized execution; and (4) studying other variations of these comparative situations. Partisans on both sides of the issue agree that the findings are not conclusive, and that perhaps they never can be since there is no hope of ever conducting research that would permit manipulation of human lives to provide comparison of experimental and control groups.[15]

One research project reported in 1975 seemed to be an exception to the usual experience, catching the surprised attention of both camps for its assertion that the death penalty was indeed found to be a deterrent.[16] Isaac Ehrlich, an economist at the University of Chicago, conducted an econometric study of the subject and came to the conclusion that each execution probably deters as many as eight murders. The retentionists predictably seized on the report as proof that they had been right all along. The abolitionists predictably found flaws in the research design immediately. Typical of the many ensuing debates were such comments as these by van den Haag, retentionist: "I believe that it has been shown by Professor Ehrlich and others that 'the executioner can save more victims than the life sentence.' His conclusions—that each execution saves between seven and eight victims who would have been murdered by others if there were no execution—seems to me well proven." A rebuttal followed from Conrad, an abolitionist: "A considerable literature has followed on the publication of Professor Ehrlich's famous paper. . . . The upshot of the numerous studies [of it] that have been undertaken is that no one has been able to produce findings similar to Ehrlich's. . . . It is now as clear as a consensus of econometricians can make it that there is no reason to believe that executions have any effect in deterring murder." (van den Haag and Conrad 1983, 128, 140)

Several arguments favoring executions have dealt with the practical issue of costs. With the well-established high cost of operating prisons today (annual expenditures per prisoner ranging anywhere from $12,000 to double that amount), one could surmise that an execution will save the state a great amount in tax dollars. The costs involved in running a prison, however, are mostly fixed costs that remain constant through ordinary changes in the occupancy rate. One prisoner added to or subtracted from the institution, whether by execution or any other reason, has virtually no effect on the institution's operating costs. The exercise of the death penalty is of enormous cost, however. A 1982 study of the probable cost of resuming executions in New York state projected a probable figure of $1.9 million per case. One analyst observed that "where the death penalty is enacted, it uses up financial resources that could be put to far better uses which, unlike the death penalty, could help control violent crime. According to one estimate, the death penalty would cost New York taxpayers approximately $550 million over its first five years."[17]

Similar studies showed that in Kansas it would cost more than $11 million each year to restore the death penalty, and that in Florida, one of the most active execution states, the cost of prosecuting each case through to final execution was over $3 million.[18] One observer, in summarizing the issue of cost, comments, "Recognizing the growing concern over the availability of funding for the criminal justice system, the abolitionist movement has argued that capital punishment does not make economic sense. Instead of dedicating scarce resources to executing a relative handful of prisoners, it would be more worthwhile to sentence capital offenders to long prison terms and use the money saved to fully fund efforts such as victim-assistance programs." (Flanders 1991, 33)

It is natural to wonder why legislators, who must be aware of these costs, nevertheless uncomplainingly support death penalty statutes. A 1991 survey of New York state legislators revealed that more than 60 percent of those responded supported the death penalty. When asked if they would support the penalty even if the costs of the penalty much outweighed the costs of life imprisonment, 59 percent were still in favor of the penalty. Additionally, 49 percent still voiced support if convinced that the penalty were not a deterrent. "Taken together, these data suggest that New York lawmakers believe in the deterrent value of the death penalty, are troubled by the prospect of unfairness in its administration, but are not swayed by economic considerations."[19] The researchers might have added that whether the legislators themselves believe in the deterrent effect of the death penalty, they are well aware that their constituents believe in it.

The Risk of Wrongful Convictions

Among the arguments expressed by abolitionists is that execution is irrevocable, and as long as the possibility of a wrongful conviction exists—as it always does—this ultimate punishment should not be used. The response by retentionists is to point to the extensive system of appeals, presumably giving the defendant every advantage in his or her defense and all but eliminating the possibility of error. If a rare mistake does lead to a wrongful execution, retentionists often add, it is a justified risk for the system to take in the interest of accomplishing its purpose of deterrence.

In 1987, two noted students of this subject reported the results of a project to identify all the cases since 1900 in which a defendant had been convicted of a capital crime, with the conviction later being invalidated. The research located 350 such cases that had either received death penalties or that could have earned the defendant a death sentence if the judge or jury had so chosen and if it had been in a retentionist state. In seven cases, the innocence of the defendants became especially convincing when the presumed victims showed up alive. Of the 350 erroneously convicted persons, 23 had been executed.[20] Abolitionists argue that since such cases of wrongful convictions continue to surface with some frequency, any effort to streamline the appeals system would be unacceptable.

Whether called upon to sentence a misdemeanant to a fine or a few days in jail, or to sentence a murderer to death, the court system with its sentencing procedures is severely tested as an instrument for dealing with the infinitely varied human situations requiring just and appropriate dispositions. Taking a broad perspective on the system, continual tinkering with the laws is necessary for adapting concepts of justice to changing public moods and maturing concepts of fairness. Particularly difficult is the way that courts must identify various human values having very subtle distinctions, and force them into ill-fitting categorical definitions (guilt or innocence, first degree or second degree homicide, etc.). Human psychology is much too complex for the law to be sensitive to all its vagaries.

Progress is made in meeting such challenges, but seldom in a straightforward way; rather, it responds variously to society's wavering feelings and perceptions of how to achieve effective justice. Thus, courts have been required to use determinate sentences until new and supposedly progressive ideas prevailed and led to indeterminate sentencing, followed by a rediscovery of the determinate sentences. In the same way, capital punishment, used profusely in the first half of the century, experienced a precipitous decline until the 1960s, when it seemed likely to stop altogether. To the surprise and dismay of abolitionists, however, capital punishment was making a strong resurgence in the early 1990s.

Regarding these issues, it is apparent that although the public, through its legislators, continually tinkers with criminal justice policies in search of strategies to improve crime control, policy is often determined not so much by thoughtful legislative intent as by fluctuations in crime rates, limitations in resources, and sometimes in response to a specific publicized crime. When the numbers of incoming offenders exceed the capacity of the criminal justice system to handle them, policy must adapt. No matter how inspired a policy concept may be, its success depends upon having an apparatus, with interacting components, in place for its implementation, including prosecutorial and defense services, correctional institutions, and probation and parole services. Often interfering with successful operation of the criminal justice apparatus is the subjective, even irrational, reactions of the public to criminal incidents, crime trends, or issues of the moment.

Although the death penalty affects a minuscule portion of criminal cases, there is a strain between the high-volume demand for executions and the capacity or the willingness of the system to accommodate to it. This is a situation that any criminal justice student will watch with interest in future years to see how policies adjust. Similarly, with the criminal justice system as a whole proving to be a fluid, continually adapting instrument, and with this society rapidly changing in its demographics and technology, it is evident that in the years immediately ahead criminal justice philosophy and its applications will also make profound changes.

Notes

1. People v. Dominguez, 256 CA2d, 64 Cal. Rptr. 290 (1967).
2. Robert Martinson. "What Works?—Questions and Answers about Prison Reform." *Public Interest* 35 (Spring 1974), 22.
3. For the best compendium of the federal sentencing guidelines, with discussion of their history, the law, the Commission operation, and complete delineation of the guideline instrument, see United States Sentencing Commission, *Sentencing Guidelines and Policy Statements,* Washington, D.C.: GPO, 1987.
4. Robert Martinson. "New Findings, New Views: A Note of Caution Regarding Sentencing Reforms." *Hofstra Law Review* 7:2 (Winter 1979), 243.
5. Unless otherwise referenced, the factual data about the California sentencing laws and their revisions are taken from an unpublished doctoral dissertation, "From Discipline to Management: Strategies of Control in Parole Supervision 1890–1990," by Jonathan Steven Simon, University of California, Berkeley, 1990.
6. Richard Singer. "Sentencing." *National Institute of Justice, Crime File Study Guide,* NCJ-97233.
7. Information on Maine's elimination of parole, plus relevant examples in other states, is found in "Abolishing Parole: An Idea Whose Time Has Passed," by Kevin Krajick in *Corrections Magazine* 9:3 (June 1983), 32–40.
8. Barbara S. Meierhoefer. *The General Effect of Mandatory Minimum Prison Terms: A Longitudinal Study of Federal Sentences Imposed.* A research report from the Federal Judicial Center, Washington, D.C. (1992), 3, 5, 9, 24.
9. Elizabeth L. Beardsley. "The Ethics of Mandatory Sentencing." Chapter 12 in *Ethics, Public Policy, and Criminal Justice,* ed. Frederick Elliston and Norman Bowie. Cambridge, Mass.: Oelgeschlager, Gunn & Hain, 1982, 220–222, 224.
10. *Americans behind Bars.* New York: The Edna McConnell Clark Foundation, 1993, 9.
11. *Drugs, Crime, and the Justice System.* Washington, D.C.: Bureau of Justice Statistics, 1992, NCJ-133652, 181.

12. A particularly clear explanation of the dilemma characterized by false positives and false negatives is given in *The Future of Imprisonment*, by Norval Morris. Chicago: University of Chicago Press, 1974, 65–68.

13. An exhaustively detailed account of Gilmore's life, crime, trial, and execution is the subject of Norman Mailer's *Executioner's Song*. New York: Warner Books, 1979.

14. Death row and execution statistics are supplied by the Legal Defense and Education Fund of the NAACP, New York, in a periodic report, *Death Row, U.S.A.*, issued two to four times annually.

15. As useful sources of details on deterrence research, see Hans Zeisel, *The Deterrent Effect of the Death Penalty: Facts v. Faith;* chapter 3 in Bedau 1982 (below), and chapters 9 and 10 in Sellin 1980 (below).

16. Isaac Ehrlich. ''The Deterrent Effect of Capital Punishment: A Question of Life and Death.'' *American Ecomomic Review* 65 (June 1975), 397–417.

17. Ronald J. Tabak and J. Mark Lane. ''The Execution of Injustice: A Cost and Lack-of-Benefit Analysis of the Death Penalty.'' *Loyola of Los Angeles Law Review* 23:1 (Nov. 1989), 137.

18. For a general discussion of the issue see Barry Nakell, ''The Cost of the Death Penalty.'' *Criminal Law Bulletin* 14:1 (Jan./Feb. 1978), 69–80. Also, *Capital Losses: The Price of the Death Penalty for New York State*, a report by the New York State Defenders Association (1982).

19. Timothy J. Flanagan, Pauline Gasdow Brennan, and Debra Cohen. ''Conservatism and Capital Punishment in the State Capitol: Lawmakers and the Death Penalty.'' *The Prison Journal* 72:1 and 2 (1992), 44–46.

20. Hugo Adam Bedau and Michael L. Radelet. ''Miscarriages of Justice in Potentially Capital Cases.'' *Stanford Law Review* 40:1 (Nov. 1987), 21–179.

Bibliography

Purpose and Nature of the Sentencing Process

American Friends Service Committee. *Struggle for Justice.* New York: Hill & Wang, 1971.

As the collected product of a large committee of noted observers of the criminal justice system, this book gained wide attention for its contribution to criminal justice philosophy. In general it discusses the defects in public perceptions of what is or should be orthodox in trial procedures and punishments for crime. The authors are especially critical of the place of discretion in sentencing of offenders. It remains a provocative ''think piece,'' analyzing basic issues of fairness in the handling of criminal matters.

Champion, Dean J., ed. *The U.S. Sentencing Guidelines: Implications for Criminal Justice.* New York: Praeger, 1989.

A thorough and valuable resource on the sentencing reform subject; the authors are highly qualified criminal justice practitioners and professors.

They examine the issues related to the federal Sentencing Reform Act, particularly looking at judicial attitudes, police and prosecutorial functions, impact on probation services and prisons, and the apparent results regarding disparity and deterrence.

Coffee, John C., Jr. and Michael Tonry. "Hard Choices: Critical Trade-offs in the Implementation of Sentencing Reform through Guidelines." Chapter 6 in Tonry and Zimring 1983 (below).

A perceptive analysis of the pros and cons of sentencing reform; it covers many examples of either intended or unintended results of reform legislation.

Cullen, Francis T. and Paul Gendreau. "The Effectiveness of Correctional Rehabilitation: Reconsidering the 'Nothing Works' Debate." Chapter 3 in *The American Prison: Issues in Research and Policy,* ed. Lynne Goodstein and Doris Layton MacKenzie. New York: Plenum, 1989.

Federal Probation 55:4 (Dec 1991). Entire issue.

This issue deals entirely with the federal Sentencing Reform Act. Judges, defense and prosecuting attorneys, and prison and probation workers discuss the many aspects of experience with the new law. They present varied and opposing viewpoints on the value of the sentencing guidelines.

Fogel, David. *". . .We Are the Living Proof. . .": The Justice Model for Corrections.* Cincinnati: W. H. Anderson, 1975.

This book introduced the concept of a "justice model" for sentencing for crime; it was one of the first influential arguments for the adoption of sentencing guidelines that would create a system of prescribed determinate, or flat time, sentences.

Frankel, Marvin E. *Criminal Sentences: Law without Order.* New York: Hill & Wang, 1973.

Frankel has written here in readable style about the defects in criminal trial procedures which work against fairness. He examines the failure of courts to provide true justice when criminal sentences are seriously disparate and often reflect the bias of the judge rather than being judicially objective. Also discussed is the failure of correctional systems to deal openly and fairly with their prisoners. The author, who was a respected federal judge, gives substantial attention to various measures which could help to correct the sentencing problems he has identified. Although the book is somewhat dated, the basic problems and principles discussed are still fully pertinent.

Goodstein, Lynne and John Hepburn. *Determinate Sentencing and Imprisonment: A Failure of Reform.* Cincinnati: W. H. Anderson, 1985.

Presents a survey of the many examples of determinate sentencing, with a well-organized description of each, state by state. The readable material covers the legal, philosophical, and practical aspects of the various plans, making this valuable for basic information on the subject.

Gottfredson, Don M., Leslie T. Wilkins, and Peter B. Hoffman. *Guidelines for Parole and Sentencing.* Lexington, Mass.: Lexington Books, 1978.

Two competent social scientists provide a knowledgeable understanding of the issues in determinate sentencing; they include the relevant social context and the significant prospects for the revised laws. Somewhat dated but still pertinent.

Greenwood, Peter. *Selective Incapacitation.* Santa Monica, Calif.: Rand Corporation for the National Institute of Justice, 1982.

Griset, Pamala L. *Determinate Sentencing: The Promise and the Reality of Retributive Justice.* Albany: State University of New York Press, 1991.

Mainly a history of New York's approach to determinate sentencing, though it takes into account the parallel developments in other states. Its extensive detail about New York's experience in crafting a determinate sentencing law reveals the complex philosophical, political, and practical issues that are confronted in attempts to reform sentencing. A thorough, practical resource on the significant movement away from indeterminate sentencing.

Hatch, Orrin G. ''The Role of Congress in Sentencing: The United States Sentencing Commission, Mandatory Minimum Sentences, and the Search for a Certain and Effective Sentencing System.'' *Wake Forest Law Review* 28:2 (Summer 1993): 185–198.

Hawkins, Gordon and Franklin E. Zimring. *The Pursuit of Criminal Justice.* Chicago: University of Chicago Press, 1984. (For annotation, see bibliography, chapter 2.)

Kittrie, Nicholas N. and Elyce H. Zenoff. *Sanctions, Sentencing, and Corrections.* Mineola, N.Y.: Foundation Press, 1981.

A systematic summary of the most valuable data and arguments available in the whole of criminal justice literature. The work is well-organized, detailed, and well-documented. It covers the legal issues and the best concepts of practice in such areas as sentencing, incarceration, policy related to measures for deterrence, the death penalty, and efforts toward criminal justice reform.

Knapp, Kay A. and Denis J. Hauptly. ''U.S. Sentencing Guidelines in Perspective: A Theoretical Background and Overview.'' Chapter 1 in Champion 1989 (above).

Luttrell, Mark H. ''The Impact of the Sentencing Reform Act on Prison Management.'' *Federal Probation* 55:4 (Dec. 1991), 56.

Meierhoefer, Barbara S. *The General Effect of Mandatory Minimum Prison Terms.* Washington, D.C.: Federal Judicial Center, 1992.

A short monograph making a solid contribution to the literature about mandatory sentences; it is packed with concise, well-organized statistical data on all the pertinent trends and effects of this type of sentencing.

Schwartz, Louis B. *Options in Constructing a Sentencing System: Sentencing Guidelines under Legislative or Judicial Hegemony.* Chapter 3 in Tonry and Zimring 1983 (below).

This essay is a review of the many problems that must be considered in attempting to rewrite sentencing legislation.

Shane-DuBow, Sandra, Alice P. Brown, and Erik Olsen. *Sentencing Reform in the United States: History, Content and Effect.* Washington, D.C.: National Institute of Justice, 1985.

This government monograph gives a comprehensive and explicit discussion of the general issue of sentencing options. Following a well-prepared history of sentencing in the United States and Europe, it presents a specific account of sentencing revisions in the laws of every state in modern times.

Starr, Kenneth W. "The Impetus for Sentencing Reform in the Criminal Justice System." Chapter 17 in *Crime and Punishment in Modern America,* by Patrick B. McGuigan and John S. Pascale. Washington, D.C.: Free Congress Research and Education Foundation, 1986.

Steury, Ellen Hochstedler. *Prosecutorial and Judicial Discretion.* Chapter 5 in Champion 1989 (above).

Tonry, Michael and Franklin E. Zimring, eds. *Reform and Punishment: Essays on Criminal Sentencing.* Chicago: University of Chicago Press, 1983.

Presented here is a short list of essays by several astute scholars who analyze some aspects of the country's experience and difficulties with reform of sentencing practices. The chapters include substantial bibliographies.

Twentieth Century Fund Task Force on Criminal Sentencing. *Fair and Certain Punishment.* New York: McGraw-Hill, 1976.

The committee of authors commissioned to prepare this work produced a significant proposal for reform of sentencing, carefully defining and explaining a new legislative model, presumptive sentencing. Having described the design and its rationale, the authors go on to discuss the general historical context in which sentencing patterns have developed.

United States Sentencing Commission. *The Federal Sentencing Guidelines: A Report on the Operation of the Guidelines System and Short-Term Impacts on Disparity in Sentencing, Use of Incarceration, and Prosecutorial Discretion and Plea Bargaining.* Washington, D.C.: 1991.

United States Sentencing Commission. *Special Report to the Congress: Mandatory Minimum Penalties in the Federal Criminal Justice System.* Washington, D.C.: 1991.

von Hirsch, Andrew and Kathleen J. Hanrahan. *The Question of Parole: Retention, Reform or Abolition.* Cambridge, Mass.: Ballinger, 1979.

Two noted students of criminal justice issues present here an analysis of current arguments regarding the pros and cons of various possible modifications of traditional parole practice.

Wake Forest Law Review 28:2 (Summer 1993).

All articles in this issue deal with various aspects of the trend toward use of sentencing guidelines. In addition to thorough discussion of the federal sentencing guidelines, there are articles on those of Minnesota, North Carolina, and Washington. The authors are competent and reputable in this subject area and are responsible in looking objectively at the pros and cons.

Wallace, Henry Scott. "Mandatory Minimums and the Betrayal of Sentencing Reform: A Legislative Dr. Jekyll and Mr. Hyde." *Federal Bar News and Journal* 40:3 (March/April 1993), 159–164.

Expansion of Sentencing Options

Lerman, Paul. *Community Treatment and Social Control: A Critical Analysis of Juvenile Correctional Policy.* Chicago: University of Chicago Press, 1975.

An analysis of two highly touted California correctional programs, most notably the probation subsidy, which here is given a critical look that tends to discredit its presumed accomplishments. Lerman argues a negative point of view, but without finally resolving the controversy about the value of the subsidy program.

Smith, Robert L. *A Quiet Revolution.* U.S. Department of Health, Education and Welfare publication (SRS) 72-26011. Washington, D.C.: GPO, 1971.

This monograph was written by one of the California professionals who was involved in the design and operation of the probation subsidy program. It is a detailed description of the subsidy and its first years of operation.

Smith, Robert L. "The Quiet Revolution Revisited." *Crime and Delinquency* 32:1 (Jan. 1986), 97–133.

As implied by the title, this article updates the story of the California probation subsidy program, evaluating it with the advantage of the perspective of the full period of its operation.

The Sentence of Death

Bedau, Hugo Adam, ed. *The Death Penalty in America.* New York: Oxford University Press, 1982.

This is the third edition of this useful book, and the serious student may want to consult all three editions, as each has some items that do not appear in the others. Though he opposes the death penalty, Bedau is conscienciously objective; he chooses contributors who discuss many aspects of the controversy, including some who advocate retention of the penalty.

Berns, Walter. *For Capital Punishment: Crime and the Morality of the Death Penalty.* New York: Basic Books, 1979.

Berns is one of the most thorough and thoughtful of the advocates of the death penalty. His book includes some chapters that present and analyze the arguments usually given for abolition of the penalty, though of course the author gives his rebuttal to these. He gives an examination of much of the history of the issue and the many discussions of it, pro and con, in other literature.

Carrington, Frank G. *Neither Cruel Nor Unusual.* New Rochelle, N.Y.: Arlington House, 1978.

This energetic polemic is entirely devoted to presenting arguments in favor of capital punishment. It is not a report of any systematic study; the author writes plainly from his own subjective feeling, with much anecdotal material and emphasis upon the concern that the public should have for victims.

The Criminal Law Bulletin 14:1 (Jan./Feb. 1978).

This entire issue of this journal is devoted to discussion of the death penalty, with articles by five writers on various aspects of the issue, pro and con.

Flanders, Stephen A. *Capital Punishment.* New York: Facts on File, 1991.

A well-organized compilation of factual and legal information basic to the capital punishment history and functioning. It includes an unusually extensive bibliography.

Radelet, Michael L., ed. *Facing the Death Penalty: Essays on a Cruel and Unusual Punishment*. Philadelphia: Temple University Press, 1989.

The editor, an avid opponent of the penalty, presents here an unusual collection of essay authors who discuss the issue from somewhat off-beat but thoughtful and interesting viewpoints.

Radelet, Michael L., Hugo Adam Bedau, and Constance E. Putnam. *In Spite of Innocence: Erroneous Convictions in Capital Cases*. Boston: Northeastern University Press, 1992.

Sellin, Thorsten. *The Penalty of Death*. Beverly Hills, Calif.: Sage Publications, 1980.

A particularly useful source for review of statistical evidence or other research results regarding the death penalty experience in the United States. Though an opponent of the death penalty, Sellin is also a noted and respected sociologist, and as such is workmanlike and thorough in presenting pertinent evidence on the subject from the many studies that researchers have conducted.

van den Haag, Ernest. "Why Capital Punishment?" *Albany Law Review* 54: 3/4 (1990), 501–514.

A studious polemic by one of the most noted of the scholars advocating the death penalty.

van den Haag, Ernest and John P. Conrad. *The Death Penalty: A Debate*. New York: Plenum, 1983.

An unusual format, presenting a series of thoughtful, responsible arguments and rebuttals on opposing sides of the death penalty issue by two noted and scholarly criminologists.

White, Welsh S. *The Death Penalty in the Nineties*. Ann Arbor: University of Michigan Press, 1991.

This is a competent review of current issues in the death penalty controversy. Its particular usefulness is in its careful discussion of the complex and extensive legal processes and issues, implications for public policy, and the role of the Supreme Court. Well documented and supplied with legal case listings.

Zimring, Franklin E. and Gordon Hawkins. *Capital Punishment and the American Agenda*. New York: Cambridge University Press, 1986.

A review of death penalty issues by two noted criminologists who look at the research on the deterrent effects of capital punishment, the history of its application, and the experience with Supreme Court decisions. Includes a chapter on the political and other factors in decisions regarding methods of executing, particularly the recent trend favoring lethal injection.

CHAPTER 5

Defining Justice
for the Juvenile

I n presenting his dissent in a case before the Court in 1928, Supreme Court Justice Louis Brandeis made the cogent point that "experience should teach us to be most on our guard to protect liberty when the government's purposes are beneficent. . . . The greatest dangers to liberty lurk in insidious encroachments by men of zeal, well meaning but without understanding."[1] Though he probably did not realize it at the time, the justice was making a point profoundly relevant to the practice of juvenile justice, one echoed forty years later in a majority decision written by another justice who perceived the "insidious encroachments" which had tarnished the luster of the juvenile court.[2]

The Virtue of Separating Juveniles from Adults

Until the beginning of the twentieth century, the history of criminal justice is a history only of adult offenders. The present-day concept of the separately defined juvenile had not yet been invented. Historically, any child being tried for a crime had to be handled in the same courts with adults, under the same procedures, and if a child then were to be sent to some sort of confinement it would be, with rare exceptions, to the same facility that held adult criminals. (Mnookin 1978, 759–760) Although the nineteenth century saw gradual development of refuges and a few "reform schools" for confinement of wayward children, the present legal definition of the juvenile did not take form until the first juvenile court was created in Cook County (Chicago), Illinois, in 1899.

108

The Hopeful Turning Point: 1899

Seldom has a major new public policy been so quickly and widely adopted: thirteen years after the juvenile court's advent in Illinois, twenty-two states had created their own juvenile courts, and by 1925 all but two states had them.[3] With the new court's philosophy, misbehaving children were assumed redeemable and were to be protected from their own immaturity. Rather than being categorized as criminals, they were delinquents needing control and help. Their adjudication as such was not to be construed as a conviction for a crime. Regardless of the seriousness of the behavior, there would be no criminal conviction. The case records were to be kept confidential and not allowed to handicap the child's future adult life.[4] Juveniles (in most states defined as having not yet reached the eighteenth birthday), if confined at all, would be placed not in jails or prisons with adult offenders, but in separate facilities meant for children only.

The governing philosophy of juvenile court, both its greatest appeal and, as later revealed, its most serious flaw, was that children would receive the special quality of care provided by a wise and loving parent. (Platt 1977, 138) To justify and define this approach, the court reached back into English common law for the concept of *parens patriae,* which empowered the state to act in the capacity of the parents. Inherent in this concept was the assumption that the adversarial character of the criminal trial would be inappropriate in a court exclusively concerned with the child's welfare. Roscoe Pound, respected dean of the Harvard Law School, "regarded the establishment of the Juvenile Court as one of the most significant advances in the administration of justice since the Magna Charta." (Ketcham 1962, 39)

The Unnoticed Process of Corruption

Neither the juvenile court's founders, nor its next generation of leaders, recognized that when public policy bestows a mantle of such purity of purpose on a public institution, the opportunity for gross abuse also arises. State laws usually gave the juvenile courts jurisdiction over children for a wide range of conditions or behaviors, and imposed no effective checks on the discretion given judges in adjudicating and disposing of cases. Typically, a child could be found delinquent for any violations of criminal laws, but also for such undefined transgressions as being incorrigible, for growing up in idleness or crime, for immoral or indecent conduct, for begging, for wandering the street at night, and many more vaguely stated misbehaviors. (Johnson 1975, 32–33) Only much later would there be a more mature perspective on these courts "with their procedural informality, inquisitorial as distinct from adversary systems of justice, their surprising power to control the lives of children who have not committed a crime but who are neglected and in need of care and protection, as well as children who are incorrigible, who are truants, or who are thought to be in moral danger." (Morris and Hawkins 1970, 157)

Solid popular acceptance of the juvenile court idea essentially blinded a whole generation to the critical flaw in its parental approach. "This philosophy led to the vesting of sweeping discretionary powers in the juvenile court judge, and the establishment of few, if any, procedural protections for the child beyond the wisdom of the judge. Informal benevolence was thought to be clearly in the child's best interests."[5] In criminal courts handling adult offenders, any unfairness in the procedures ordinarily will be countered by defense attorneys and an easily triggered appeal process. But the benevolent climate of the juvenile court presumes that defense attorneys are unneeded and inappropriate; so the child is left defenseless. Keeping court hearings private and confidential also denies juveniles as a class the protection they might gain from public scrutiny of the process.

The special vocabulary adopted for use in the juvenile court is thought by some to have been a subtle negative factor. The child was not to be convicted of crime, but adjudicated delinquent. The child was not sentenced to serve time, but was placed in a reform school for an indefinite period until sufficiently corrected.[6] Other symbolisms such as the informal courtroom where the judge would not sit at a high bench and would not wear a robe, reinforced the implications of the softer vocabulary. But the irony has been that the juvenile court, conceived as civil rather than criminal, has withheld the constitutional protections of due process accorded to an adult criminal.

Gault Brings a New Perspective

The advent of the first juvenile court in 1899 signaled a relatively sudden change nationwide in the concepts and practices relevant to children in the criminal justice system. Discovery of the need for fundamental revision sixty-five years later brought an equally abrupt and sweeping reappraisal of the philosophy of services to children. Public policy regarding problem children changed substantially as the result of a provocative event in 1964; initially it seemed to be an ordinary delinquency matter when an Arizona boy named Gerald Gault was accused of making an obscene phone call.

Gerald had been arrested on the verbal complaint of a neighbor who accused him of being the caller. Without informing his parents, police put Gerald in detention; when the parents learned of this indirectly and made inquiries, they were told of a hearing scheduled for the next day. The juvenile court in Gila County, Arizona, handled Gerald Gault's case with procedures that were typical of many juvenile courts. At the hearing, no complaining witness was present, no sworn testimony was taken, no transcript of the hearing was made, and no written petition was filed. The only written material was a report to the court by the probation officer, but this was not shown to the parents. Gerald, then age 15, was committed to the State Industrial School for his minority.

Unlike the usual juvenile court matter, the Gault case was appealed, going first to the Arizona Supreme Court (which upheld the juvenile court) and subsequently to the U.S. Supreme Court, which rendered a decision giving notice to juvenile courts that the overarching aura of benevolent intent had introduced unfairness in juvenile court procedures.[7]

The Supreme Court noted that if Gerald had been an adult, his maximum punishment would have been a $50 fine or two months in jail instead of the possible six years of confinement (until his twenty-first birthday) he could have received from the juvenile court. In reversing the juvenile court's action, the Supreme Court did not interfere with the concept that juveniles should be accorded protective separation from adult offenders. Juveniles could still have this protection but must also have the basic fairness rights that are given adults, particularly: (1) the right to receive notice of the charges, (2) the right to counsel, (3) the right to confront and cross-examine witnesses, (4) the privilege against self-incrimination, (5) the right to have a transcript of the proceedings, and (6) the right to an appellate review.

The System Reappraised

Several other appellate court cases in the 1960s clarified and expanded upon the principles introduced by the Gault decision.[8] The Gault case gave legitimacy and a clear focus to a gathering mood of disillusionment with the juvenile court. One juvenile court judge, writing in extensive detail about the court's problems, noted that it had been founded upon the sense of a compact in which the state, in allowing the informal civil nature of this court, would in return promise to provide the child with the care and services needed. He blamed a lack of support from the state, rather than a flaw in its design, for the court's failure. "If the state fails to keep the promises upon which the mutual compact theory of the American juvenile court is based, there is no justification for juvenile courts to abrogate the constitutional protections of criminal due process or to intervene in the lives of children without a finding of criminal guilt." (Ketcham 1962, 38)

Not surprisingly, juvenile court loyalists were glum about the direction court decisions were taking in the 1960s. Some feared virtual emasculation of the court and its cherished emphasis upon parental treatment of the juvenile. The perspective since then, however, seems to prove that the juvenile court has been too solidly grounded to be seriously threatened. Without losing its basic concern for humane treatment of children, it has adapted to the demands of due process, incorporating a new dimension of fairness into its philosophy. Whereas the founders of the court were more concerned with protection of children than with punishment, current court workers are agreeing, without losing the humane ideals, that a juvenile, like an adult, must be held accountable for his or her behavior. A respected family court judge could observe without regret that "since the Gault case the criminalization of the juvenile courts has continued. The 'purpose' clauses of the juvenile court law of many states have been modified to add to the concepts of rehabilitation and family preservation the policies of accountability and punishment. Once unwanted and unnecessary in the juvenile court, the district attorney has now become an integral part of its operation." (Edwards 1992, 7)

The American Bar Association (ABA) expressed the mixture of regret and optimism that gradually emerged after Gault. "The development of the current juvenile justice system, often heralded as a courageous and innovative reform movement, is permeated with confused concepts, grandiose goals, and unrealized dreams. The system has failed in many ways. Yet it really is wonderful in many ways too—a social institution that cares, a separate court to deal exclusively with juvenile and family problems, a blending of public and voluntary programs, a body of law focused on the best interests of the child, and a correctional authority organized for the rehabilitation of offenders." (ABA 1977, 27)

Although public policy supports the juvenile court concept, there is a growing recognition that the convenient view of humans as neatly divisible into sharply defined juvenile and adult ages is too simplistic. Changing concepts of the boundaries of childhood, adolescence, and adulthood have led in some cases to suggestions by critics that the courts should be reconstituted to specialize in several separate levels of youth maturity, creating "a clear dividing line between younger and older children and offering a treatment model to the younger children and a due process model to the older." (Edwards 1992, 17)

A recently published and well-crafted polemic makes the case for ending the juvenile court's jurisdiction over children who commit criminal offenses, and sending these cases instead to adult criminal courts. "Today we are witnessing the breakdown of the binary opposition between child and adult, which provided the conceptual foundation of juvenile court jurisprudence. Conservatives and liberals may disagree on the policies that ought to be implemented to deal with youthful criminal offenders, but both ends of the political spectrum agree that the child-adult distinction is a false dichotomy that can no longer support disparate justice systems.'' (Ainsworth 1991, 1103–1104)

An opposite view by a noted spokesman on juvenile court issues is that the virtues supposedly sought in adult court processes are not in fact as assured there as in juvenile courts. ''The juvenile court can be improved but that improvement cannot come from emulation or substitution of the criminal justice system. Our system of criminal justice is too deeply and irrevocably flawed to serve as a model. One should realize that what defense lawyers call 'justice' and the rest of us call 'fairness' is in short supply in our criminal justice system. . . . But perhaps most importantly, the juvenile court has the dual mandate of protecting society and acting in the interest of children. The criminal court has no such mandate.'' (Hurst 1994, 621–622) Similarly, a former juvenile court judge believes that any reduction of juvenile court responsibility would transfer that much additional burden on other, busier courts. ''Reform of the juvenile court is needed, but abolition would create massive problems. The misdemeanor courts, which would absorb the bulk of delinquent offenders, are currently the largest blight on American judicial administration.'' (Rubin 1979, 281)

Such a commentary is part of the broader context of general public uncertainty about the many ways to define the threshold of adulthood. Policymakers produce confusing and often irrational answers in law to such questions as when is a young person old enough—to drink beer or liquor, to vote, to join military service, to be ineligible for child support, to buy contraceptives, or to be held accountable for crime. The confusion also reflects a perception that juveniles are becoming more sophisticated, and at an earlier age, than was true in previous generations. One student of the subject notes that compared to the time when the juvenile court was created, today's youth are more knowledgeable and educated, and much more urban, which of course affects their social adjustments. In 1900, just 26 percent of the country's population under age twenty lived in urban areas, while in 1970 this proportion had risen to 65 percent. (Zimring 1982, 17–19, 42)

Inadequate social services have perhaps most often been the reason for disappointment. ''At the root of much of the criticism is a woefully under-resourced juvenile delinquency system. The lack of resources occurs at every level, including the services available for the delinquent child and the family in the community, what legal assistance the child has during the legal process and what treatment and supervision is available after the court process.'' (Edwards 1992, 18)

Criticism of the court's social services has been frequent and usually valid. The needs of children vary. Many have suffered from child abuse or inept parenting in dysfunctional families; for any of a plethora of reasons, they may need special kinds of professional treatment. Local governments will likely be unable to fund even the basic probation services adequately; the additional clinical services that so many children need may have to be provided by private agencies, if at all. For this reason some state governments contribute to the costs of local services such as detention, probation, and specialized clinical programs in the belief that helping a locality to serve a delinquent child in the community should result in one less child being admitted to the expensive state institution.

The public's uncertain attitude about troublesome children contributes to irregular financing of the juvenile control and treatment programs. Legislators or other appropriating bodies must balance the public's natural wish to be generous toward children against its considerable fear of ungoverned teenagers: ". . . public policy toward youth is inherently ambivalent, at times almost schizophrenic. Ambivalence is built into the very marrow of the juvenile court, which is expected both to nurture and protect the young against older members of society, and to protect society against the misbehaving young." (Silberman 1978, 313)

While acknowledging its presence, some experts believe that the ambivalence has been overrated. A former administrator of the federal Office of Juvenile Justice and Delinquency Prevention (OJJDP), citing public opinion polls, states that "the public does not appear to be nearly as punitive and demanding of retribution toward juvenile offenders as many politicians and, in some instances, juvenile justice officials have made them out to be." (Schwartz 1992, 222)

Current discontent with the juvenile court seems at least partially to stem from disappointed awareness of an apparent increase in juvenile crime. The court should never have been expected to cure delinquency. This was clearly recognized by one key governmental document that observed, "Studies conducted by the Commission, legislative inquiries in various States, and reports by informed observers compel the conclusion that the great hopes originally held for the juvenile court have not been fulfilled. It has not succeeded significantly in rehabilitating delinquent youth, in reducing or even stemming the tide of delinquency, or in bringing justice and compassion to the child offender. To say that juvenile courts have failed to achieve their goal is to say no more than what is true of criminal courts in the United States. But failure is most striking when hopes are highest." (Department of Justice 1967, 80)

Adapting the Court to New Philosophies

The family court, which first appeared in Rhode Island in 1961, marked a significant departure from the basic juvenile court design.

Since then many other states have expanded the jurisdiction of their juvenile courts to include a range of other family issues. When the Department of Justice issued standards for juvenile justice in 1980 it specified that "Jurisdiction over matters relating to juveniles should be placed in a family court." Among other matters such a court should have exclusive original jurisdiction of child support, adoptions, termination of parental rights, assignment of legal guardians for children or family members with problems of alcohol or drug addiction, divorce and related decisions, and any intrafamily criminal offenses. (OJJDP, *Standards for the Administration of Juvenile Justice* 1980, 245)

During the 1970s, in most jurisdictions in the country, officials, whether or not they embraced the family court idea, recognized "status offenders" as a significantly different category of problem children. The term describes those children whose behaviors are problems only because of their *status* as juveniles. Charged with truancy, incorrigibility, or running away from home, these children have been among the more difficult for the court to serve satisfactorily and have often comprised as many as half of those committed to institutions for delinquents. Public policymakers decided that it was inappropriate, unfair, and contrary to their needs to include these children among more criminally inclined juveniles. By the mid-1970s there were insistent calls for separate treatment of status offenders. (Berkman 1980, 17–19)

In 1975 the board of the National Council on Crime and Delinquency (NCCD), a prominent standard-setting agency, announced its support for removing status offenders from court jurisdiction. The board asserted that "subjecting a child to judicial sanctions for a status offense—a juvenile victimless crime—helps neither the child nor society; instead it often does considerable harm to both." (NCCD 1975, 97) Not surprisingly, a substantial change such as this disrupted some well-entrenched practices and consequently provoked some sharp dissents. The NCCD board later gave equal space in its publication for two authors who took the opposite viewpoint, arguing that status offenses, if not criminal, are still unlawful. They pointed out that often such children are actually quite delinquent and are in the status offense category only because they were allowed to plea bargain to a lesser charge; they usually repeat their incorrigible behavior until after several court appearances they must be committed to some custodial facility. (Martin and Snyder 1976, 44–47)

Despite the calls for noncourt handling of these cases, status offenses generally remain within juvenile court jurisdiction, but there has been widespread acceptance of the principle that such children shall not be placed in facilities or programs for truly delinquent juveniles. This trend has been strong and countrywide, with states and communities developing alternate ways of meeting the needs of children who have not been criminal but have been rebelling against intolerable (to them) family situations. Innovations, as one expert observes, may include "crisis intervention techniques, hot-lines to keep runaway kids in some contact with their parents, and residential arrangements that kids might find less onerous. We can provide these services when we have to." (Zimring 1982, 73)

Policy adjustments of both conservative and liberal national administrations, with the expected differences, reflect general social trends. While the OJJDP, administered by Ira Schwartz under the Carter administration, initiated and strongly advocated such policies as removal of status offenders from facilities for delinquents, and deinstitutionalization of all but the most serious delinquents, the emphasis changed appreciably under Reagan's OJJDP administrator, Alfred Regnery. Taking a conservative view of the delinquency problem, Regnery reluctantly tolerated the juvenile court but with the admonition that it must become more punishment-oriented. He argued that 16-year-old boys commit crimes at a higher rate than any other age group and that juveniles commit 30 percent of all violent crimes; he consequently called for the courts to treat them as criminals, using the usual adult court procedures. "Rehabilitation has been the premise of the juvenile court system throughout the twentieth century, but it has failed miserably." He added that as a first step in correcting the problem "the deterrent approach should be the main focus of the justice system." (Regnery 1985, 65, 67, 68) In rebuttal, Schwartz asserted that Regnery's figures were grossly in error; that in 1984 persons under age 18 had committed only 8 percent of murders and manslaughter, and that Regnery had overstated the juvenile crime problem by 150 percent. (Schwartz 1989, 25)

Within this general ferment the lines dividing conventional conservative from liberal positions have become blurred. Many partisans from both sides seem able now to listen calmly to argument in favor of a view that heretofore has been heresy to juvenile court apologists—that juveniles should be granted jury trials in criminal cases. The point is made that dispositions made by juries tend to be somewhat more lenient than those rendered by the judge alone, and yet the juvenile is denied this advantage. (Ainsworth 1991, 1123) But the more drastic proposal for abolishment of the juvenile court (at least in respect to criminal offenses) is currently not the dominant view, even though there is increasing discontent with traditional juvenile court philosophy.

Lest policymakers look too favorably on arguments for abolishment of the juvenile court, experts usually insist that, with all the moves toward more rigorous due process protections, the juvenile court can and should continue. As one has stated, "It seems that the only institution that can reasonably exercise leadership on behalf of the society and the children is the juvenile court. The reason is simply that no other institution can claim to have an equally broad view of all the interests at stake, to have as wide a range of action, or to be able to make decisions that are designed to reflect the values of the society as expressed in its laws and constitution.'' (Moore 1987, 176)

Institutions and Other Resources

Institutions for delinquent juveniles have generally been of two basic types: (1) the local detention facility that is meant to hold a child temporarily while awaiting court disposition of the case, and (2) the training school (or whatever other label) as the long-term institutional resource to which a child may be committed.

Specialized resources for service to adjudicated children became essential with creation of the juvenile court. Separate institutions had begun to appear well before creation of the first juvenile court in 1899, but developed quite unevenly among the states. Massachusetts opened the first such institution in 1846, but nearly a century passed before most other states built theirs. Unfortunately, the institution managers, often political appointees, did not have the benefit of public policy to guide them in designing corrective approaches for helping their juvenile charges. Even as early as the 1920s, the noted Ben Lindsey, judge of the Denver juvenile court, was acutely disturbed by the repressive regime at the Colorado reform school. As his biographer explains about this and most other state schools, ''Inadequate appropriations, the lack of any theoretical framework for 'reforming' the inmates, and the usual deficiencies of the spoils system under which the schools were administered, combined to reduce them to a status little better than junior prisons.''[9]

Use—and Abuse—of Juvenile Detention

Orthodox public policy holds that a child awaiting a court hearing should be placed in detention only if he or she is considered likely either to abscond or to commit further delinquent acts if not confined. The accepted view (well supported by experience) has been that most juveniles may safely be left at home pending their dispositional hearings. The first national standards for detention specified that ''The number of children admitted to a detention facility should not exceed 10 per cent of the total number of juvenile offenders apprehended by law enforcement officers, excluding traffic cases and cases outside the court's jurisdiction such as out-of-county runaways and federal court cases.'' (NCCD 1961, 18) Nor should a child be put in detention for punishment purposes, according to the standards, although in practice a judge all too often will order a child into detention for a few days to "teach him a lesson."

Just as jails have been the more degenerate element in the adult correctional systems, detention homes have often been the facilities of least quality among juvenile resources. They have typically suffered from poor support, untrained staff, insensitive practices, and severe overcrowding. As one experienced juvenile court judge observed, "Outright cruelty is not unknown in some of the country's detention centers, to say nothing of dismal, crowded quarters and a staff calloused in spirit by overwork and inadequate facilities." (Ketcham 1962, 34)

Though presumably intended for the custody of only delinquent juveniles, detention homes also have been used for dependent and neglected children, who tend to stay longest in detention. The child who has committed a serious delinquent act can usually be adjudicated fairly quickly and moved on to a training school, but the dependent child needs a more individualized plan and is likely to endure a lengthy wait while a substitute home is found. A changed attitude toward status offenders has meant a substantial reduction in the use of detention for this group. A national survey of detention populations in 1983 found that status offenders made up just 11 percent of the populations, compared with 40 percent in 1975.[10] In 1989 a broader survey, the Children in Custody census, looked at children in *all* types of custodial facilities and found that 98 percent were charged with delinquent acts. The total count was 56,123 children, an increase of 14 percent since 1985, although the actual rate of commitments was higher because the number of juveniles in the general population had declined during those years. (OJJDP 1991, 2)

Economic factors severely affect detention quality in many locations. Until recently, an expensive detention facility has been feasible only in urban jurisdictions, where the volume of juvenile cases justifies investment in the building and its operation.[11] As a result, most rural jurisdictions are left without any juvenile detention facilities and must work out substitute arrangements. In some localities with innovative leadership, this has led to humane and constructive alternatives, but unfortunately, it has more commonly meant use of the county jail.

Although there has been an increasing repugnance for using county jails for juveniles, the practice has yielded very slowly; over many decades, about half of the children detained throughout the country have been held in adult jails. (Sarri 1974, 5) While this often happens in sparsely populated jurisdictions where the jail is the only detention resource, it also occurs in urban localities that have juvenile facilities. Many detention homes are overcrowded, with untrained staffs and insufficient programming; thus the older, more aggressive boys or girls often seem too threatening for the staff to handle and thus are transferred to jail.

Most courts, reluctantly using jails in the absence of any better resource, have conscientiously tried to keep jailed children from being held in company with adult prisoners. The catalyst for this movement was the 1974 Juvenile Justice and Delinquency Prevention Act, which stated significant new principles for handling juveniles and created the federal agency, the Office of Juvenile Justice and Delinquency Prevention, to plan and coordinate a national plan to improve the juvenile justice system. As a prerequisite for obtaining federal funds, the new policy required that juveniles "shall not be detained or confined in any institution in which they have regular contact with adult persons incarcerated because they have been convicted of a crime or are awaiting trial on criminal charges." (OJJDP, *Forum on Deinstitutionalization* 1980, 2) In response the states generally have specified that children may not be jailed except when they can be held "out of sight and sound" of adult prisoners.

Although isolating jailed juveniles from adult offenders is better than indiscriminately housing children and adults together, it also has the negative effect of making it easier for the court to order the jailing of any child. Whenever an approved arrangement exists for use of a jail, the county can delay the day when a truly proper facility—or other alternatives—will be provided. Often a perverse outcome of this sort will result from the most well-intentioned public policy. For instance, beginning in the mid-1940s, the NCCD campaigned for elimination of children from jails. Its efforts helped persuade many localities to invest in specialized juvenile detention facilities—presumably a desirable outcome. But when the NCCD looked at the results some years later, it became evident that the proliferation of juvenile detention facilities had made it easier for more children to be locked up for longer periods of time. As one writer expressed it, "the ease with which juveniles can be detained provides an enormous temptation to judges, policemen, and probation officers and parole agents to lock youngsters up for a few days, or longer, to 'teach them a lesson'—to 'put a little fear in them' as an incentive to 'shape up.' " (Silberman 1978, 321–322) Already realizing this tendency, the NCCD in 1975 resolved that status offenders had to be kept out of detention, a change of practice that might require the elimination of these children from juvenile court jurisdiction. (Murray 1983, 67–68)

In this respect the 1974 OJJDP Act, with its concern for separate treatment of status offenders, did not go far enough, but it started a trend that eventually did go farther. In 1980 the Act was reauthorized and amended to call for all jailing of juveniles to be abolished within another five years. After that many states tightened their laws on use of jails. "Most significantly, the state legislation enacted since 1974 has removed many of the ambiguities which plagued earlier statutes. In addition, states have moved increasingly to an outright prohibition on the jailing of juveniles, rather than the traditional response of mere separation within the facility.'' (OJJDP, *Forum on Deinstitutionaliza-tion* 1980, 4)

The great importance of banning juvenile jailing has become clear in recent years as new understanding is gained of jail's potential for harm to children. The child who repeatedly runs away from an unhappy home situation, though having committed no offense, is all too easily sent to jail by a frustrated judge who has no other resources at hand and who must do something with the case while awaiting some elusive solution to the social problem it presents. Ironically, the very policies meant for the protection of these children sometimes hurt these children. If juvenile jailing is kept to a minimum, and if the out-of-sight-and-sound policy is adhered to, a child often will be in jail alone, in isolated quarters, and without any activity program. The boredom, loneliness, and uncertainty of the situation is acutely depressing to an already disturbed child. (Schwartz 1989, 71) As a result, ''the suicide rate for juveniles placed in adult jails is nearly five times greater than the suicide rate for juveniles in the general population, and almost eight times greater than that of juveniles placed in separate juvenile detention centers.'' (OJJDP 1983, 3)

Detention Alternatives

Recent years have seen the gradual development of viable alternatives to detention. In the so-called home detention design, first used by the St. Louis juvenile court in 1973, juveniles who otherwise would have been in a locked detention facility instead were closely supervised at home and in school by workers who were strictly limited to caseloads of five boys or girls. The workers' flexible hours permitted them to respond to the needs of their five children at any time.[12] Many other courts have developed their own adaptations of this intensive program, which has proved capable of controlling the assigned children safely and at much less cost than institutional confinement.

Pennsylvania was the first state to legislate outright prohibition of juvenile jailing. In the mid-1970s, voluntary groups and some legislators publicized the state's record of jailing more than three thousand juveniles annually, typically in degrading conditions, while many status offenders were being held in secure detention facilities. An extensive and energetic campaign culminated in the passage of a law in 1977, and which became effective two years later, banning the jailing of juveniles. (Allinson 1983, 12–20)

Similar types of sweeping legislation have had limited success, typically because no matter how needed and commendable is the new policy prohibiting a discredited practice, the state must finance and plan the means of implementation. If public servants do not know how to do their job differently, or do not have the financial resources to make the change, the simple fact of a law being passed will not accomplish its intended results. The Pennsylvania law included financial incentives to counties to develop detention alternatives, and provided for training in more skilled handling of disruptive juveniles so that the staff in juvenile facilities could handle crises without transferring the problem elsewhere. A two-year grace period allowed the important planning in preparation for the change, resulting in a near complete removal of juveniles from Pennsylvania jails.

For status offenders in Pennsylvania, as well as for many of the delinquents, foster home programs have been effective. State funds that help pay for transportation among counties have made possible more sharing of detention homes among them. Pennsylvania also proved that the initiatives taken to provide alternatives to jailing had the effect of reducing the need for detention of any kind, resulting in the closing of at least one of the small detention homes.

The Long-Term Institutions

Over the century-and-a-half that state juvenile correctional institutions have been in use, their character has changed less than might be expected. They have tended to use a combination of work, usually farming and other jobs of institutional maintenance, simple academic school classes, and often military drill. Lacking any standards or guides to follow, or any funds for training of staffs, the institutions typically stagnated and lapsed into repressive conditions until adverse publicity occasionally caused temporary improvements. Rules have always tended to be repressive; disciplinary measures have been peremptory and surprisingly harsh, with generous use of the leather strap. In the 1940s, an investigative reporter visited a number of representative reform schools throughout the country, finding shocking physical conditions and often brutal treatment of the children. The resultant book attracted national attention, but since it did not offer the institutions any suggestions on how to do the job better, the publicity did not result in improvement. Twenty years later, another reporter, in a reprise of the previous inquiry and book, found and described the same dismal conditions.[13]

Since those studies and reports were published, corporal punishments have generally been discontinued and programs have improved, but critics still find much to lament about these institutions. One pronounced change in the last two decades has been that serious offenders make up a much higher proportion of the institution populations. Whereas at mid-century, status offenders represented from a third to a half of institutional populations, by 1987 their representation had dropped to only 2 percent of the populations. About 40 percent of the juveniles were charged with violent offenses, most of which were types of assaults; nearly 2 percent were charged with murder or manslaughter. To no one's surprise, studies have shown that many of those being held in state-operated juvenile institutions come from single-parent families (54 percent), with about half having other family members who have been in jail or prison. (Bureau of Justice Statistics 1987, 1–3)

This trend toward a higher percentage of more serious offenders in the juvenile institutions is not necessarily proof of increased violent juvenile crime, but it does reflect the system's success in handling status offenders in alternative ways. Treatment programs have been developed which, depending on the capability and motivation of the managers in each institution, now make possible a constructive, therapeutic environment for the inmates, rather than providing just basic storage for a period of time. (Keve 1967, chapter 5)

Decisive Approaches to Institutional Change

During the early 1970s two separate events, a lawsuit in Texas and an administrative action in Massachusetts, profoundly affected juvenile institutions. The Texas event was a reminder that, while adult prisoners frequently file civil suits to improve confinement conditions, juveniles rarely sue, and so juvenile institutions have seldom been subject to this corrective force. A significant exception was the Morales case, litigated over several years beginning in 1971, and brought on behalf of children in custody of the Texas Youth Council (TYC).[14] The essential elements of the complaint were that the youth institutions offered no rehabilitative programming, that they were repressive in nature, and their disciplinary procedures grossly violated basic civil rights. Untrained staffs supervised children in purposeless work programs, and as punishments used humiliating and often physically brutal measures. Unruly boys were arbitrarily transferred to the higher security institution at Gatesville where especially degrading punitive measures were common.

In its final decision the federal court closed two of the Texas youth institutions, due to the state having violated its own law requiring constructive rehabilitative training for the confined juveniles. Among many other positive changes, the court ordered the TYC to provide adequate casework or other treatment services, adequate diet, a right to privacy, freedom to communicate with outside persons and to talk in their native language without punishment, the right to free expression of feelings, and the right to housing in physical plants providing security, privacy, and dignity. The humanitarian principle of always using the "least restrictive'' measures, now axiomatic in the field, was given prominence and authority by the Morales decision when the court directed that "defendants must cease to institutionalize any juveniles except those who are found by a responsible professional assessment to be unsuited for any less restrictive, alternative form of rehabilitative treatment. . . . Those juveniles for whom close institutional confinement is necessary must actually be treated. They may not be abandoned as hopeless and simply warehoused until they grow too old for juvenile facilities." The decisive, comprehensive nature of the court's requirements had a salutary effect on institutional operations in many states. (Roberg and Webb 1981, 207–211)

The significant Massachusetts event was not a court decision but a drastic administrative action, taken in 1971 and 1972, to deinstitutionalize most juvenile cases. Massachusetts had ten different institutions for delinquents, including the oldest state training school in the country at Lyman. Conditions at all the institutions were much the same as in the insensitive, repressive Texas operations then under court scrutiny. The impetus for change in this case began with a series of investigations in the 1960s following complaints of brutal treatment of children in custody, particularly at the Bridgewater facility. (Ohlin, Coates, and Miller 1974, 76–78)

In 1969 Dr. Jerome Miller was hired as the Commissioner of Youth Services with the expectation that he would remedy the problems. At the time no one anticipated the degree of resistance that would meet any effort to change institutional operations. Coming from out-of-state, and able to look at the institutions with a fresh, detached view, Miller saw the stagnant and damaging character of the entire system; wholesale reform was clearly needed. But when he tried to phase in changes, the staff stubbornly resisted, bolstered by support from their sympathetic legislators.[15] Juvenile court judges, perturbed by the prospect of losing the usual places to send delinquents, also opposed the changes. When it proved virtually impossible to implement his new approaches, Miller, with the governor's backing, resorted to the unprecedented step of closing the institutions on short notice one after the other, moving the children to a variety of hastily organized, community-based programs. (Guarino-Ghezzi 1988, 3–5)

The obvious question remaining is concerned with results: what happened to suddenly deinstitutionalized juveniles, and was public protection compromised by their release to the communities? The Center for Criminal Justice at Harvard Law School conducted a ten-year evaluation of the effects of the closings, and found that compared with juveniles who had been in training schools, significantly fewer of the juveniles from the community-based programs later went on to adult prisons. In 1972, graduates of the juvenile system comprised 35 percent of the adults being admitted to adult prisons. In 1985 this figure had declined to 15 percent. (Schwartz 1989, 52–53) Among other encouraging findings, it was noted in 1985 that Massachusetts enjoyed a much lower juvenile crime rate than most other states, ranking forty-sixth among the fifty states and the District of Columbia. (NCCD 1991, 9)

Shortly after these events in Texas and Massachusetts, a new national commission on accreditation of correctional programs was created, and acceptance of the accreditation standards gradually spread, as will be discussed in chapter 9. Reflecting the Texas decision, the standards declared that a juvenile in an institution has a right to treatment; a companion standard, which represents a more daring policy innovation, specifies that the juvenile also has the right to refuse treatment. "While the juvenile should have the right to refuse services, the facility administration must provide those services required by the dispositional order of the court or those which are legally required of all juveniles, such as school attendance."[16]

Less dramatic but similarly significant institutional closings have occurred in some other states. Vermont and New Hampshire have discontinued their juvenile correctional facilities, and Utah closed its institution at Ogden, known as the Youth Development Center. The Ogden facility, which was old and in bad repair, had been severely criticized for its poor management before a task force appointed by the governor recommended its closure. Both Massachusetts and Utah replaced the institutions with a variety of intensive community programs (also described in chapter 9) to serve all but the most incorrigible boys or girls who could not be controlled except in custody. For these particularly recalcitrant children, Massachusetts developed twelve small high-security units of no more than twenty beds each, scattered in various areas of the state. Utah has two such units of thirty beds each, and one with ten beds.

The philosophical ferment involving juvenile correctional services has its parallel in the processes of change affecting adult institutions. Adults too are detained in short-term facilities (jails) and are committed to long-term custody in state institutions, all of which have undergone profound changes in operational philosophy in recent decades. New correctional approaches, after trial and acceptance in the juvenile field, will find their way into adult corrections, as will be seen in the next chapter.

Notes

1. Olmstead v. U.S. 438 (1928) 479.
2. Justice Abe Fortas. In re: Gault 387 U.S. 1 (1967).
3. Mennel, Robert M. *Thorns and Thistles: Juvenile Delinquents in the Unitea States 1825–1940*. Hanover, N.H.: University Press of New England, 1973, 132.
4. Although the popular view has been that the movement in Chicago that promoted the juvenile court was motivated by a purely beneficent interest

in all children, a later perspective has held that the court backers were of an elitest society, interested in protecting itself from the threat of what had been seen as the "dangerous classes." See Anthony Platt, *The Child Savers: The Invention of Delinquency.* Chicago: University of Chicago Press, 1977, 98–100.

5. Jeffrey S. Leonard. "Juvenile Justice in Arizona." *Arizona Law Review* 16:2 (1974), 236.
6. The use of the term *reform school* as a part of the euphemistic juvenile court vocabulary illustrates the continuing problem with the changing meaning of words. Though the term originally had a benevolent connotation, it gradually became degraded by usage and has been replaced by such terms as *industrial school*, or *training school*. In some jurisdictions these terms too are now considered stigmatic; one recently contrived replacement label is "learning center."
7. In re: Gault 387 U.S. 1 (1967).
8. See for example: Kent v. United States (1966), 383 U.S. 541, 86 S.Ct. 1045, 16 L.Ed. 2d 84; In re Winship (1970) 397 U.S. 358, 90 S.Ct. 1068, 25 L.Ed. 2d 368; McKeiver v. Pennsylvania (1971) 403 U.S. 528, 91 S.Ct. 1976, 29 L.Ed. 2d 647.
9. Charles Larsen. *The Good Fight: The Life and Times of Ben B. Lindsey.* Chicago: Quadrangle Books, 1972, 28.
10. U.S. Department of Justice. Bureau of Justice Statistics. *Report to the Nation on Crime and Justice,* 2nd ed., 1988, 78.
11. For useful detail on the economic costs see *It's Your Move: Juveniles in Adult Jails and Lockups.* [Washington, D.C.]: Office of Juvenile Justice and Delinquency Protection, 1983, 7.
12. Paul W. Keve. *Corrections.* New York: John Wiley, 1981, 416–417.
13. Albert Deutsch. *Our Rejected Children.* Boston: Little, Brown and Co., 1950; and Howard James. *Children in Trouble.* New York: David McKay, 1970.
14. Morales v. Turman, 383 F.Supp. 53, 75 (E.D. Tex. 1974).
15. The most complete and useful of the accounts of the Massachusetts institution closings is provided in a full-length book by the official who engineered the change. See *Last One over the Wall,* by Jerome G. Miller. Columbus: Ohio State University Press, 1991. A useful source for evaluative data is *Unlocking Juvenile Corrections: Evaluating the Massachusetts Department of Youth Services,* a monograph published by the National Council on Crime and Delinquency in 1991.
16. American Correctional Association. Commission on Accreditation for Corrections. *Manual of Standards for Juvenile Training Schools and Services.* Rockville, Md.: The Association, 1979, 80.

Bibliography

The Virtue of Separating Juveniles from Adults

Ainsworth, Janet E. "Re-imagining Childhood and Reconstructing the Legal Order: The Case for Abolishing the Juvenile Court." *The North Carolina Law Review* 69:5 (June 1991) 1082-1133.

A systematic examination of all possible arguments for abolishing the juvenile court, or at least removing from its jurisdiction the delinquency cases. Hurst 1994 (below) is a rebuttal.

American Bar Association. Institute of Judicial Administration. Juvenile Justice Standards Project. *Standards for Juvenile Justice: A Summary and Analysis.* Cambridge, Mass.: Ballinger, 1977.

This monograph, and the two below, are in a series produced by a highly professional group of juvenile justice experts, presenting the best recent concepts of both philosophical and operational principles in respect to courts and their social services.

American Bar Association. Institute of Judicial Administration. Juvenile Justice Standards. *Corrections Administration.* Cambridge, Mass.: Ballinger, 1980.

American Bar Association. Institute of Judicial Administration. Juvenile Justice Standards. *Youth Service Agencies.* Cambridge, Mass.: Ballinger, 1980.

This monograph includes an extensive bibliography.

Baker, Falcon. *Saving Our Kids from Delinquency, Drugs and Despair.* New York: HarperCollins, 1991.

A comprehensive overview of factors causing delinquency, and approaches to the problem as found in juvenile court philosophy and modern programs for alternative court dispositions.

Berkman, David J. *A Preliminary National Assessment of the Status Offender and the Juvenile Justice System.* Washington, D.C.: Office of Juvenile Justice and Delinquency Prevention, 1980.

Carter, Robert M. and G. Thomas Gitchoff. "An Alternative to Youthful Mass Disorder." *The Police Chief* 37:7 (July 1970), 52–56.

Chesney-Lind, Meda and Randall G. Shelden. *Girls, Delinquency and Juvenile Justice.* Pacific Grove, Calif.: Brooks/Cole, 1991.

A history of the conditions characterizing the delinquency patterns of girls. The text is thorough, sensitive, and readable, and discusses perceptively the court processes and the institutional experiences affecting female delinquents.

Department of Justice. *The Challenge of Crime in a Free Society: A Report by the President's Commission on Law Enforcement and Administration of Justice.* Washington D.C.: GPO, 1967.

Edwards, Leonard P. "The Juvenile Court and the Role of the Juvenile Court Judge." *Juvenile and Family Court Journal* 43:2 (1992), 1–2.

Gives a well-stated view of current juvenile court philosophy, including copious references to relevant source materials. The other articles in this single-topic issue address the same general subject.

Faust, Frederic L. and Paul J. Brantingham, eds. *Juvenile Justice Philosophy.* St. Paul, Minn.: West Publishing Co., 1974.

An anthology covering a wide range of juvenile justice policy issues, among them in-depth examinations of the history, the rationale, and the outcomes of the movement to humanize justice procedures for juveniles. A valuable research source is its presentation, with annotations, of the full text of the Supreme Court opinion in the Gault case.

Hurst, Hunter. "Imagining Legal Scholarship; The Case for the Juvenile Court and for Teaching Juvenile Law and Procedure." Chapter 34 in S. Randall

Humm et al., eds., *Child, Parent and State: Law and Policy Reader*. Philadelphia: Temple University Press, 1994.

The author, a particularly knowledgeable apologist for the juvenile court, gives the arguments for continuation of the court without undue modification. It is prepared as an answer to Ainsworth 1991 (above).

Hurst, Hunter and Louis W. McHardy. "Juvenile Justice and the Blind Lady." *Federal Probation* 55:2 (June 1991), 63–68.

Two outstanding authorities on juvenile court matters review the current state of philosophy and actual state operations of juvenile and family courts.

Johnson, Thomas A. *Introduction to the Juvenile Justice System*. St. Paul, Minn.: West Publishing Co., 1975.

A useful overall examination for the sudent beginning to study the general subject of the court processes and the social services likely to be found throughout the country.

Ketcham, Orman W. "The Unfulfilled Promise of the Juvenile Court." In *Justice for the Child: The Juvenile Court in Transition*, ed. Margaret K. Rosenheim. New York: Free Press of Glencoe, 1962.

Krisberg, Barry and James Austin, eds. *The Children of Ishmael: Critical Perspectives on Juvenile Justice*. Palo Alto, Calif.: Mayfield, 1978.

A comprehensive anthology looking at the pertinent issues in juvenile court operations and in the innovative social programs serving them.

Martin, Lawrence and Phyllis R. Snyder. "Jurisdiction over Status Offenses Should Not Be Removed from the Juvenile Court." *Crime and Delinquency* 22:1 (Jan. 1976), 44–47.

Mnookin, Robert H. *Child, Family and State: Problems and Materials on Children and the Law*. Boston: Little, Brown and Co., 1978.

A detailed, factual, and exhaustive information resource on the many legal issues affecting children. Thoroughly documented, and the dry data of laws and court decisions are enhanced by the inclusion throughout of life situations and the human psychology involved in the legal contests cited.

Moore, Mark Harrison. *From Children to Citizens: Vol I, The Mandate for Juvenile Justice*. New York: Springer-Verlag, 1987.

An anthology on the legal issues, the current trends, and the future prospects with respect to legal approaches to the range of children's problems.

Morris, Norval and Gordon Hawkins. *The Honest Politician's Guide to Crime Control*. Chicago: University of Chicago Press, 1970.

Two sophisticated experts in criminal law offer a refreshing review of the best concepts of criminal justice principles that include measures for community protection and fairness to the offenders, both adult and juvenile.

Murray, John P., ed. *Status Offenders: A Sourcebook*. Boys Town, Nebr.: The Boys Town Center, 1983.

This book provides a series of articles or brief observations by highly knowledgeable persons with varied viewpoints on status offender issues, pro and con. It includes an extensive bibliography of resource materials.

National Advisory Commission on Criminal Justice Standards and Goals. *Juvenile Justice and Delinquency Prevention: Report of the Task Force on Juvenile Justice and Delinquency Prevention*. Washington, D.C.: 1976.

National Council on Crime and Delinquency. "Jurisdiction over Status Offenses Should Be Removed from the Juvenile Court." *Crime and Delinquency* 21:2 (April 1975), 97–99.

National Council on Crime and Delinquency. *Unlocking Juvenile Corrections: Evaluating the Massachusetts Department of Youth Services.* San Francisco: 1991.

Office of Juvenile Justice and Delinquency Prevention (OJJDP). *Forum on Deinstitutionalization: Selected Readings on Children in Adult Jails and Lockups.* Urbana-Champaign: University of Illinois, 1980.

OJJDP. *It's Your Move: Juveniles in Adult Jails and Lockups.* Washington, D.C.: 1983.

OJJDP. *National Symposium on Children in Jails.* Washington, D.C.: 1980.

OJJDP. *Update on Statistics. Public Juvenile Facilities: Children in Custody 1989.* Washington, D.C.: 1991.

OJJDP. *Standards for the Administration of Juvenile Justice: Report of the National Advisory Committee for Juvenile Justice and Delinquency Prevention.* Washington, D.C.: 1980.

    A thorough, detailed compendium of recommended policy positions on every aspect of juvenile justice operations. It was produced by a large and prestigious committee and its staff, and it represents the best modern view of operational philosophy and its practical application in juvenile justice systems. It may well be used as a companion document to the 1976 Task Force Report by the National Advisory Committee on Criminal Justice Standards and Goals (above).

Platt, Anthony M. *The Child Savers: The Invention of Delinquency.* Chicago: University of Chicago Press, 1977.

Regnery, Alfred S. "Getting Away with Murder." *Policy Review* 34 (Fall 1985), 65–68.

Rubin, H. Ted. "Retain the Juvenile Court." *Crime and Delinquency* 25:3 (1979), 81–298.

Schwartz, Ira M. *(In) Justice for Juveniles: Rethinking the Best Interests of the Child.* Lexington, Mass.: Lexington Books, 1989.

    A perceptive, nontheoretical discussion of the modern concepts of juvenile justice reform, with good anecdotal material and discussions of the political elements that confuse policymaking in this subject area. The author is a former administrator of the OJJDP in the Carter administration.

Schwartz, Ira M., ed. *Juvenile Justice and Public Policy: Toward a National Agenda.* New York: Lexington Books, 1992.

    An anthology of current perspectives on reform of juvenile courts and services to delinquent children.

Silberman, Charles E. *Criminal Violence, Criminal Justice.* New York: Random House, 1978.

    Written for the popular market, this book covers criminal justice issues, adult and juvenile, of interest to the general reader. The author, an experienced reporter, writes in a fast-moving, readable style.

Standards and Guides for the Detention of Children and Youth. New York: National Council on Crime and Delinquency, 1961.

Weisheit, Ralph A. and Diane M. Alexander. "Juvenile Justice Philosophy and the Demise of Parens Patriae." *Federal Probation* 52:4 (Dec. 1988), 56–63.

Zimring, Franklin E. *The Changing Legal World of Adolescence.* New York: Free Press, 1982.

A learned and concerned study of issues relevant to law and policy regarding rights of children and youth, and the rationale for controls and restrictions on their privileges.

Zimring, Franklin E., ed. *Confronting Youth Crime: Report of the Twentieth Century Fund Task Force on Sentencing Policy toward Young Offenders.* New York: Holmes & Meier, 1978.

A rational, systematic review of juvenile justice policy by a knowledgeable group of experts, with policy recommendations.

Institutions and Other Resources

Allinson, Richard. "There Are No Juveniles in Pennsylvania Jails." *Corrections Magazine* 9:3 (June 1983), 12–20.

Bureau of Justice Statistics. *Special Report. Survey of Youth in Custody, 1987.* [Washington, D.C.]: 1988.

Guarino-Ghezzi, Susan. "Initiating Change in Massachusetts' Juvenile Correctional System: A Retrospective Analysis." *Criminal Justice Review* 13:1 (Spring 1988), 1–11.

A useful, concise description of the steps taken to close the juvenile institutions in Massachusetts in the 1970s, and an objective appraisal of the consequences.

Keve, Paul W. *Imaginative Programming in Probation and Parole.* Minneapolis: University of Minnesota Press, 1967.

Lerman, Paul. "Trends and Issues in the Deinstitutionalization of Youths in Trouble." *Crime and Delinquency* 26:3 (July 1980), 281–298.

Murray 1983 (above).

National Council on Crime and Delinquency. *Standards and Guides for the Detention of Children and Youth.* New York: 1961.

National Council on Crime and Delinquency. *Unlocking Juvenile Corrections: Evaluating the Massachusetts Department of Youth Services.* San Francisco: 1991.

Norman, Sherwood. *The Youth Service Bureau: A Key to Delinquency Prevention.* Paramus, N.J.: National Council on Crime and Delinquency, 1972.

Though dated, this book still serves as a well-organized, descriptive account of how youth service bureaus should be designed and operated. The author was a national consultant with the NCCD on specialized youth resources.

Office of Juvenile Justice and Delinquency Prevention (OJJDP). *Forum on Deinstitutionalization: Selected Readings on Children in Adult Jails and Lockups.* Urbana-Champaign: University of Illinois, 1980.

OJJDP. *It's Your Move: Juveniles in Adult Jails and Lockups.* Washington, D.C.: 1983.

OJJDP. *Update on Statistics. Public Juvenile Facilities: Children in Custody 1989.* Washington, D.C.: 1991.

Ohlin, Lloyd, Robert B. Coates, and Alden D. Miller. "Radical Correctional Reform: A Case Study of the Massachusetts Youth Correctional System." *Harvard Educational Review* 44:1 (Feb. 1974), 74–110.

A clear, scholarly account of the political context in which the Massachusetts institution closings developed, but because it was written early in the experience with the closings, it does not provide an appraisal of the effects. On that point, see Rutherford, below.

Platt 1977 (above).

Roberg, Roy R. and Vincent J. Webb, eds. *Critical Issues in Corrections*. St. Paul, Minn.: West Publishing Co., 1981.

An anthology of articles on arbitrarily selected, but important, correctional issues in both juvenile and adult services.

Rutherford, Andrew. "The Dissolution of the Training Schools in Massachusetts." In Krisberg and Austin 1978 (above), 515–534.

This is a thorough account of the experience with the Massachusetts institution closings, and with an evaluation of the effects.

Sarri, Rosemary C. *Under Lock and Key: Juveniles in Jails and Detention*. Ann Arbor: University of Michigan, 1974.

Schwartz 1989 (above).

Silberman 1978 (above).

CHAPTER 6

The Jails

C orrectional institutions are widely varied and designed differently
according to security level, the sex or age group to be housed,
or any of several special problem types of offenders to be contained.
They are also different according to the jurisdictions they serve—local,
state, or federal. Some are called penitentiaries, some prisons, and some
are reformatories. And then there are jails. Whatever the category, any
custodial institution is expensive to build and operate, and difficult to
manage, but in some ways the jail is an especially frustrating challenge,
operating in the context of local political and economic concerns that
are often inimical to the proper purposes of the jail. This chapter focuses
on the policies, principles, and practices that shape our jails, noting
also the compromises required by their interaction with other institutions
and other components of the criminal justice system.

Though jails differ from prisons in purpose, function, and operating
characteristics, they are very much a part of the same overall system
and subject to the same political factors that shape public policies on
crime and punishment. They are likely to be the first place of confinement for most adult offenders, and whereas a jail usually holds fewer
inmates at any given time than does a prison, high prisoner turnover
causes jails to affect the lives of an extremely large number of persons.
They are the most underrated and undersupported of the components
of the criminal justice system, while at the same time having perhaps
the greatest potential for either constructive, or destructive, effect on
their inmates.

The Correctional Pariah

Jails vary widely in their management, function, and most other characteristics; their character also varies from state to state according to state

131

laws, history, demographics, and many other factors. It is therefore
hardly surprising that public policy respecting county jails often seems
illogical. Historically, no governmental institution has had to be such
a "catchall" as the typical county jail. Supposedly, jails are to serve
as custodial holding facilities for persons awaiting trial for alleged
crimes, and for persons serving short sentences for misdemeanors. But
that is only the start.

Accommodating the Variety of People and Problems

The usual jail is located in and operated by the smallest unit of
government—the city or county—a fact essential to an understanding
of jail issues. The convenient county seat location of the jail, coupled
with the typical lack of other resources for people with problems, has
always meant that the county jail has had to admit people with many
types of misfortunes. Many of these misfortunes would not warrant
jailing if more suitable housing were available. Presumably, local control should be an asset, consisting of having the jail within the community
and easily available in situations demanding immediate and convenient
custodial housing. But because of poor financial support and, until relatively recently, a virtual absence of standards, local control has more
often resulted in notably poor management. Hans Mattick, a noted
expert on jails, asserted that local administration is the "central evil"
in the overall jail problem.[1]

Historically, jails have rarely been designed or managed with
humane sensitivity. Because of the general expectation that prisoners
in jails either are held awaiting trial (in which case they cannot be
required to work) or are serving short misdemeanant sentences (in
which case it is not cost-effective to have any sort of production
shop), jails have rarely had constructive work programs. The result
is a dead storage situation in which the least deleterious effects for
inmates are likely to be depression, loss of motivation, loss of normal
supportive relationships, and loss of work habits. More serious is
the likelihood of some inmates becoming vicious and predatory from
a need to relieve boredom or sexual tensions, or just to assert their
dominance. The result for their victims will be severe physical abuse
and humiliation. (Laite 1972, 36–60)

Estimates of the number of jails in the United States vary according
to how jail is defined. With the lack of uniformity from state to state,
a dependable definition is elusive, but in 1983 the Department of Justice
counted 3,338 U.S. jails.[2] A high percentage of these are in thinly
populated rural counties and are very small. In Virginia a study of jail
living conditions from 1929 to 1930 found that only 10 percent of the

state's jails had admitted more than five hundred prisoners during that two-year period. (Hoffer, Mann, and House 1933, 367) Whereas that seems like a substantial number, it amounted to an average of only one new admission every day-and-a-half, and, with the usual high turnover of jail populations, that left the average daily population for these jails extremely low. In that same two-year period, the study found that 37 percent of the jails had admitted less than one hundred prisoners. If the average length of stay in each case is estimated at fifteen days, and if all the cases had been evenly distributed over the two years, that would result in an average daily population of about two. Although this was a condition reported more than a half century ago, a low average daily population remains characteristic of many jails today. In Iowa, for example, the state jail inspector reported that in 1992, one of the county jails had a capacity of three, twenty-one had capacities of less than ten, and seventy-one of the state's ninety-five jails had capacities of less than twenty.[3]

In operating a jail with so few inmates there is little motivation for the sheriff or the county board to maintain decent conditions, and a jail with so few cells has none of the flexibility that any jail, large or small, needs. Properly operated, it should keep the men separate from the women, drunks separate from the sober, adults separate from the juveniles, felons separate from the misdemeanants, pretrial prisoners separate from the convicted, and the sexual predator separate from the smaller and easily intimidated prisoner. From time to time the police might bring in an additional two or more suspects who should be kept separate from each other so they cannot collaborate on their stories before being interrogated. There will be occasional transients, temporarily housed homeless, and perhaps a mentally disturbed person awaiting a hearing and transfer to a hospital.

Compounding this predicament are the immense swings in occupancy. If at midweek the prisoner count is low, the weekend will be the reverse as the incoming drunk and disorderly and simple assault cases fill the jail admission area to overflowing. By Sunday night prisoners may be sleeping on the floors. With such pressures the rural sheriff with a small jail will be unable to separate prisoners according to the requirements of legal and proper security considerations. Prisoners have to be put wherever there is space for them, even if this means men and women together when space is limited.

In recent years, pressure on local jails has increased as a result of civil suits brought against many state penitentiaries where inmates are challenging conditions of confinement, especially overcrowding. Courts have responded by ordering population limits for the state prisons, causing newly committed felons to be housed in the local jails while waiting for penitentiary space. The Bureau of Justice Statistics

(BJS) showed a count of 16,748 prisoners housed in jails in 1990 awaiting transfer to overcrowded state facilities.[4] Only a year later the BJS reported that the nation's jails were holding 39,917 prisoners for other authorities, and that 23,495 of these "were being held because of crowding elsewhere, principally in State prisons."[5] Many of those with short sentences of a year or two were likely to wait out their entire time in the idleness of the jail.

This problem had been particularly severe for a number of years in Texas, where as early as 1980 an unmanageable glut of felons was awaiting transfer after a federal court decision found the entire state prison system unconstitutional and put a cap on its population level.[6] By 1987 the excessive backlog led twelve Texas counties to join in a suit, demanding that the state either take their committed felons or else pay the counties for the expense of keeping them. Lacking the bed space to accommodate the waiting prisoners, the state finally agreed to pay the counties at a rate of $20 per day per prisoner. The size of the problem is suggested by the 1993 situation in the Dallas County jail where, with a capacity of 6,488, more than half of its prisoners were felons awaiting transfer.[7]

Also demonstrating the crucial interaction between local jails and state prisons was Tennessee, where a suit alleging that overcrowding caused dangerous prison conditions was filed against the state in 1975. At the time, a combination of stiffened sentences and restrictive parole practices raised prison populations by twelve hundred inmates annually. The result was a serious backlog in jails, where felons with prison sentences sometimes waited several years for transfer. Reductions in prison populations ordered by the court further increased the overcrowding in jails, leading in turn to another suit and a new court directive requiring the state to remove committed felons from the jails.

Of course, crowding in jails is just as deleterious as crowding in prisons, so the backlogs have invited suits from jails in several jurisdictions. An example was a 1976 court suit in Alabama, which revealed excessively crowded and severely deteriorated conditions in the state prisons. When the court ordered prison populations to be reduced, the subsequent backlog in jails resulted in court challenges of jail conditions. The resulting court order required the state to take prisoners from the affected jails. This type of situation creates a dilemma that can be solved only by reducing the numbers of prisoners committed in the first place, or, more likely, by expediting the construction of more prisons.[8]

In the Tennessee example, with both jails and prisons under court-ordered limits, the state responded by forming a coordinating committee of state officials representing the various components of the system. The committee intensively searched for measures to relieve inmate population pressures, developing "an array of suggestions as to how jail populations might be reduced. . . . The suggestions incorporated all of the ideas that are currently being advocated across America in terms of diversion, alternatives to incarceration, and accelerating decision-making at all levels of the criminal justice process. The uniqueness of the process was not the creation of new approaches but the involvement of police, district attorneys, judiciary, corrections, and the private sector in tailoring ideas to meet their local needs, and developing an 'ownership' of the program that resulted."[9] Slow and difficult as the process was, it did work, pointing up the fact that whereas the jail is organizationally an independent facility, it still is not an island. Every shifting current in the other components of the system impinges significantly on the function of the jail.

The Heritage of Politicized Management

When Hans Mattick spoke of local administration as the central evil in jail management, he was referring mainly to the problem of sheriffs acting as untrained jail managers, operating without professional guidance, and depending on county boards for financial support. The sheriff is an elected official, a constitutional officer responsible only to the electorate. He or she may come to the job without knowledge or experience in managing a correctional facility, for historically the sheriff has been anyone who could get the necessary votes. Any deputies hired by the sheriff were likely to be political patronage appointees, perhaps qualified only by their political support of the sheriff. Once in office, the sheriff could run the jail as independently as he or she wished, for the sheriff's only superior, other than the electorate, was the county board, and that body was the "boss" only to the extent of controlling the budget. Along with considerations of economy, the factor most influential in jail management has been the reality that no voting constituency is in support of jails.[10] Policy at that local level reflects the public's usual feeling that jail prisoners are not to be made comfortable at taxpayer expense, and if this leaves them meanly treated, it is only what they deserve. This feeling has led to management practices with sometimes vicious effect—the fee system, for example, which is, fortunately obsolete. But the lessons learned from the fee system are important to remember.

Until the mid-twentieth century, it was common throughout the country to support the sheriff and the jail operation by paying the sheriff a fee for each prisoner day. On the surface this seemed a sensible policy, but it meant that whatever the sheriff saved by reducing expenditures for food, sanitary supplies, and utilities left that much more for the sheriff's income. The inevitable result was that prisoners typically received only two meals per day, sanitary conditions often were appalling, and jail structures deteriorated from poor maintenance. Prisoners could expect little or no attention for health problems, or even basic physical protection. Economizing also required sheriffs to spend as little as possible for staff salaries, so the typical jail had many hours each day when no staff person at all was on duty.

Together, economic factors and the basic character of the sheriff's office has delayed amelioration of the management problems inherent in the political context of jail operations. Traditionally, sheriffs have cherished their independence, and resisted interference in the management of their jails. This was particularly evident when, as often happened, sheriffs even took their jail records with them when leaving office, something especially likely when a departing sheriff felt no obligation to a successor who had defeated him or her for the office. When state governments began to oversee and set standards for jails, they ran into stout resistance from two powerful sources—the state sheriffs' associations and the similar associations of county supervisors. The politically astute sheriffs effectively opposed state interference in their jail management practices, and the equally adept county boards resisted the prospect of state-dictated jail standards that would require increased county expenditures. In consequence, state legislatures often found it necessary to compromise with this political opposition to the point that standards and their enforcement were so diluted as to be essentially ineffective. "Kansas, for example, had mandatory inspection and then backed off when political pressure forced the legislature to relegate it to an advisory status." The same has happened in state after state, leaving too many without mandatory standards.[11]

Nevertheless, change had to come, and by the 1960s and 1970s state and county governments were seeking ways to upgrade their jails. Driving the trend were court suits against government units for mishandling of prisoners or for unacceptable conditions of confinement; the growing number of deteriorated jails; a new generation of sheriffs having more appreciation of both good business methods and modern concepts of correctional practice; and the initiative by state governments to bring sheriffs themselves into the process of designing jail standards. "By 1985, 32 states had adopted standards, and 25 of those states had incorporated enforcement legislation with these standards."[12] As a journal for jail administrators put it: "It used to be that a person from any walk of life could run for the office of sheriff. It is not that way any more. Competition for the office is so keen that some sort of background in the field of criminal justice is imperative if a candidate hopes to be elected. A few states have even set standards that a person must meet before he can seek the office.''[13]

Improved Management Formats

In the last two decades the move toward quality jail management has gained impressive strength, one reason being the advent of accreditation, which gives sheriffs a professionally approved goal to reach as a source of pride (see chapter 9). New architectural designs contribute to efficient jail operations; sheriffs benefit from the availability of computers and other technology that contribute importantly to law enforcement. Driven to improve government efficiency, many counties find it useful to combine jail operations with county or town police facilities, building new public safety centers that are models of attractive design and technical competence. Unproven, but no doubt present also, is the sense of competition among jurisdictions in the building of these symbols of community pride. One indicator of the increased pride is the tendency to drop the term ''jail'' in favor of a newly preferred term such as ''adult detention center'' or sometimes ''county law enforcement center.''

Public health concerns have also played a role in jail reform. As a group, jail prisoners are poor in health, exhibiting a high incidence of such problems as hernias, dental defects, malnutrition, and even frostbite (the badge of the derelict alcoholic in cold climates). As they appear at the admissions desk in a jail, new prisoners present an array of physical conditions that may be benign or life threatening. But any such case is potentially embarrassing to the county, and can expose it to legal liability if the admitting officer ignores or misconstrues the prisoner's symptoms. General improvement in the country's public health services, plus the effect of court suits resulting from failure to diagnose and treat prisoner ailments, has led to a great improvement in the medical staff and equipment in most jails. And still more recently, the threat of AIDS has had a profound effect in alerting jail staffs to health issues.

In the early 1970s the American Medical Association (AMA) took notice of the serious health problems presented by jails and developed jail health care standards and an accreditation system. In 1983, with the accreditation process well established, this function was split off from the AMA to be the National Commission on Correctional Health Care, whose focus is on health care in correctional facilities generally.

Jail reforms reflect to some degree the increasing public fear of crime and its consequent willingness to spend more on criminal justice services. Also, the trend toward governmental efficiency has in many instances resulted in the consolidating of services across political jurisdictions, since the country still has a large proportion of jails that are too small to be cost effective under today's more exacting standards. A national survey in 1983 revealed that 63 percent of the jails in the United States had capacities of less than fifty.[14] More recently, the American Jail Association has estimated that the country still has nearly one thousand jails with prisoner populations of less than ten, a condition that increasingly leads counties to seek a more cost-effective custodial resource.

Whereas half a century ago a typical county would have strongly resisted giving up its own jail to combine with a neighboring county, today this is becoming a frequent solution to the problem of affordably serving areas of low population. Counties need the economy gained by joining with adjacent counties in building a regional jail which, with its larger size, can afford to have the capacity, the equipment, and the services not feasible in a small jail. And with jails having become such complex management challenges, sheriffs today more readily reconcile themselves to losing, or sharing, that immediate responsibility. In some states, for example, in Kentucky, Delaware, Connecticut, Vermont, New Hampshire, Hawaii, and Alaska, sheriffs no longer operate jails. One typical administrative arrangement for a regional jail is to place it under a professionally qualified manager who is then responsible to a board whose members are the involved sheriffs and various citizens selected by the county boards.

A variation on the regional jail is the regional jail coalition, a device aimed at conserving and specializing jail space through the organization of several jails into a regional cooperative. For example, when four or five adjoining counties agree to this arrangement, they are likely to use a central control office with computer hookups to the participating jails, perhaps coordinating transportation among the jails, and distributing prisoners by type. This permits specialization of the facilities, for example, with one jail taking all the female prisoners, and the others taking various other classes of prisoners according to the jails' different capabilities. Additionally, the regional coalition reduces overcrowding by distributing prisoners among the jails according to space available.

Sometimes "de facto" regionalization occurs through an informal arrangement by one county to buy space on a case-by-case basis from another jail. The 1991 annual survey of jails by the Department of Justice found that 47 percent of the contacted jurisdictions were holding inmates for overcrowded jurisdictions elsewhere.[15] Sometimes state governments assume the responsibility of enforcing the regionalization that individual counties find difficult to accomplish. By combining jail services for several counties, savings are possible in respect to both capital costs and operating expenses. The state of Virginia has for many years substantially subsidized the operations of local jails, and in more

recent years has modified this plan to give strong financial encouragement to counties to join in building regional jails. Currently Virginia
has twelve regional jails serving twenty-four counties and eleven cities,
with more under construction or planned.[16] West Virginia is in the
process of regionalizing all of its jails, and hopes to complete this project
by the end of this century.

Nevertheless, overcrowding continues to be endemic in jail operations. Jails shared fully in the overall trend toward increased incarcera-
tions during the 1970s, and as jail populations rapidly grew there was,
of course, no time to respond so quickly with increased capacity. Severe
jail overcrowding was recorded as early as 1970 and continued into
the 1980s. The total U.S. jail population increased 76.9 percent from
1983 to 1989, with many of the large urban jails holding 85 percent
or more over their capacities.[17] Not surprisingly, the crowding causes
such potentially dangerous conditions that desperate officials in some
jurisdictions seek extreme solutions. In the District of Columbia, for
instance, the glut of prisoners had been so severe that two different
efforts, both unsuccessful, were made to place prisoners in rented space.
In 1988, finding that Spokane County, Washington, had jail beds available, the D.C. authorities sent fifty prisoners there by air transport.
The arrangement lasted only three months, however, for the D.C. inmates were so uncontrollable that Spokane County demanded their removal.[18] Previously, in March 1986, the D.C. officials had tried to
use a newly opened private prison in western Pennsylvania. But when
Pennsylvanian legislators heard that fifty-five D.C. prisoners had been
bused into their state, they reacted in alarm, and hastily enacted prohibi-
tive legislation. The D.C. inmates had to be bused back after only four
days.

As previously mentioned, a long-time problem in jail management
has been the pervasive idleness of the prisoners. The problem is still
far too common, but with the trend toward jails of larger populations,
work programs are now appearing, adding appreciably to the psychological health of the institution. In a few instances the inmates are hired
by a local industry, which has been allowed to set up a shop in the jail.
Inmates usually receive straight wages and no other advantages. At
other sites the assigned work may not pay wages but instead results in
"good time," which shortens the sentence to be served. Where wages
are paid, the inmates are usually charged room and board; in one program they also must contribute to a crime victims' assistance fund.[19]
With larger, modern jails, there is an encouraging trend toward programming that is in great contrast to the former "dead storage" character of the small county jails. Increasingly, sheriffs are taking pride in
having mental health and substance abuse programs, industries, and
other work plans.[20]

The extra cost of operating a jail with such programming concerns county officials, but some counties now are charging jail inmates for the services they receive. In one Michigan county jail with a population of nearly one thousand inmates, a fee of up to $30 per day is charged to all those who are able to pay. The payment schedule is agreed upon with the inmate while he or she is serving time and the inmate is then billed after release. The basic charges are for room and board, but charges may also be made for dental and medical care. Collecting the fees is not easy or cheap, but achieves an adequate gain. "An average of 700 accounts are billed monthly; more than 15 percent result in payment."[21]

The Fortunate Invention of "Direct Supervision"

The Federal Bureau of Prisons, through the example of its new urban jails, has had an important influence on detention facilities in respect to both architecture and styles of prisoner management. The first of the federal high-rise jails was opened in San Diego in 1974, followed by two more the following year in New York and Chicago. Not for reasons of coddling the prisoners, but to increase realistic measures for safe management, the Bureau adopted a new approach to custodial architecture with designs that would enhance privacy and bring more warmth and human feeling into the usually hard environment. The federal jails (called metropolitan correctional centers) made use of such softening features as warm colors, modular housing units, and sound-absorption materials. Because wood is a more friendly material than steel or concrete, it was used wherever possible in doors and stair railings.

The Bureau accompanied its new architecture with a new style of management that emphasized constant interaction between staff and prisoners. Now known as "direct supervision," this management style has become remarkably popular among jails. The concept is better understood when contrasted with the former tendency of jail managers to operate with little direct contact with inmates. With the use of the control center, remote control of locks, closed-circuit television, and the public address system, a very few staff members could control a large number of inmates—but rather poorly, as is now realized. The former approach was appealing for its economy, but in saving staff salaries it tended to treat inmates as units rather than people. Television cameras can monitor inmate activities down a corridor or in a dayroom, but the camera fails utterly in respect to the need for human interaction and feeling.

The direct supervision plan took staff members out of control rooms or their separated office areas and put them into the housing units in continuous and direct contact with inmates.[22] The advantage is that jail prisoners, with their endless questions and worries, can get answers to their questions or at least relieve tension by talking to someone who will listen. In one of the federal jails the Catholic chaplain got into the spirit of the plan so well that he set up an altar on wheels, which he moved from one housing unit to another.

The direct supervision concept when introduced to long-time jail staffs has usually been deeply unsettling for them at first; officers accustomed to the protection of their control rooms have predicted dire consequences in having to circulate among inmates directly all day. Nevertheless, wherever direct supervision has been tried, the staffs generally find to their surprise that it works, and works better than they would have believed. Managers find that it lowers tension, solves problems before they escalate, makes the jail a safer environment for both staff and inmates, and the gains seem adequately to justify any extra cost. This is evident in both the staffing patterns and the architecture of the new generation of jails. One prison expert asserts that with the new management style "everything from inmate-staff relations to rates of violence and cost-effectiveness seemed to improve."(DiIulio 1991, 17)

A review of the trend in California shows that the new jails with housing modules of manageable size are "designed to increase the amount of interaction with and supervision of inmates by staff." Cells are built more like rooms, and where dormitories are used, a modicum of privacy is provided by partial partitions around the individual beds.[23] The trend has been so significant that it has caught public attention. One detailed newspaper account enthusiastically reports that "because direct-supervision jails are safer places than traditional jails, the cost to build them is less. Almost all the fixtures and furnishings in a direct-supervision jail are less expensive to build and upkeep is also lower."[24] This assertion that such jails are less expensive is stated too confidently, but the experience of achieving much improved safety and control is warmly and consistently confirmed by the jail managers.

Jails in the General Social Service System

Jails are usually the crucial first custodial experience for the beginning law breaker, or for more or less accidental offenders. Jails may push them either in the direction of more crime, or else help deter them from repeating serious mistakes. So it would seem sensible that jails should be especially competent in handling neophyte offenders in a manner intended to be as corrective as possible, in the hopes of preventing their further involvement in the judicial system. Traditionally, however, jails have been the worst of correctional facilities in this respect, lacking any counseling or helping services.

Jails also receive high numbers of repeat offenders; many of them misdemeanants who sometimes are said to be serving life on the installment plan. Jails have a daily intake of people with a bewildering variety of personal problems that include threatening health conditions, emotional or mental health pathology, family dysfunction, economic distress, unsuspected criminal propensities, and varieties of legal complications. Among the most discouraging types of inmates are the chronic alcoholics, some of whom serve successive short sentences over a period of years. Judges dislike giving repetitive sentences but usually are not provided with constructive alternatives. Jailers too are well aware of the futility of giving one short jail term after another, without offering any medical or social services aimed at correcting the basic problem.

With all of the human needs represented in jail populations, and with all of the opportunity there is to bring help to people at a time when help could be most effective, the jail historically has been the most neglected and least competent of correctional facilities. The reasons are not at all mysterious. Partly it is due to the assumption that most jail prisoners are incarcerated only briefly, and that they are mainly misdemeanants who, being minor offenders, are not considered appropriate subjects of expensive social services. Added to this is the general public attitude that persons in jail deserve punishment rather than help. Legislative policymakers are well aware that their constituents see no need to be taxed for the costs of jail improvements. Also serving to dampen any interest in treatment services is the high volume of persons passing through jails, inducing a sense of futility about trying to serve so many who stay so briefly. To give a sample count, on an average day during the year ending June 30, 1991, the population of all U.S. jails was 422,609. But during that year, jails admitted more than 10 million prisoners and released almost as many.[25] Collectively, U.S. jails offer a massive challenge to social planners who seek better ways to serve both communities and prisoners. Some of the effective means to this end have been well demonstrated, but the jail system has a ponderous inertia that frustrates the hope of accomplishing reform rapidly.

Designs for Alternatives to Jail

In retrospect it seems surprising that generations of jail managers have given so little thought to how excessive jail populations might be reduced. The reason, however, is not difficult to surmise: the severity of jail overcrowding has become a matter of acute concern only in the last couple of decades, when it finally countered the heritage of the fee system that for so long had made it profitable to keep a jail population high. One simple example of how traditional thinking has changed involves the practice in regard to allowable telephone calls. For many years in most jails, it was almost a cliché that a newly admitted jail prisoner could make just one telephone call. The policy seemed to make sense; the limitation seemed a reasonable measure to hold down costs of telephone service and to save the time of jail staff who would have to escort the prisoner from the cell block and to the front office, wait until the telephone call was completed, and then escort the prisoner back to the cell block. But when jails became chronically clogged, often to double their capacities, managers finally realized that if a prisoner is allowed to make an unlimited number of telephone calls, this can appreciably increase the chance that the prisoner will find the necessary help for getting bailed. Consequently, in many urban jails, banks of pay telephones are now commonly installed where prisoners can easily use them to make as many calls as they wish to pay for. The arrangement can lead to a welcome relief of the population pressure, and, contrary to the former concern about cost to the jail, it actually serves as a profit center. One manager claims that his jail's telephones are earning several hundred dollars per day for the telephone company, with the profit being shared with the jail.[26]

The revised attitude toward telephone privileges points up the significant new focus on that group of jail inmates who are held pending indictment and trial. The practice of pretrial detention has been one of the most important targets of jail reformers, and with good reason. Collectively, pretrial prisoners represent a massive waste of human resources, requiring public support of their incarceration while they lose their jobs and suffer other serious disadvantages, even while still presumed innocent. They are jailed in significant numbers; a one-day count of jail populations in 1991 found 426,479 inmates in U.S. jails, and 51 percent of these were unconvicted persons.[27]

Pretrial Detention: A Well-Entrenched Handicap

Various research projects have shown that most pretrial jail prisoners could safely be released without danger while awaiting trial, and also that they are significantly disadvantaged by being held. One study of a large sample jail population showed that first offenders who were jailed before trial were three times as likely to be convicted as the ones on bail who came to trial from "the street." Being outside, at home, and at work while awaiting sentencing proved to be a significant advantage. Furthermore, of those convicted, the ones who had awaited trial in jail were twice as likely to be committed to prison. (Goldfarb 1975, 38)

In being detained before trial, a defendant is handicapped in conferring with his or her attorney or in otherwise preparing his or her defense. Such a defendant is likely to lose his or her job, as well as the motivation to work, and a jailed defendant comes to court from jail looking in every way much less promising than the one who comes in from outside—well groomed and showing the asset of having a job and a home situation.

The problem a jailed defendant has in conferring with his or her attorney is much more serious than it would ordinarily appear, especially with the current crowding of jail space, which results in jail prisoners being moved over distances as necessary to find beds. In New York City, for example, federal pretrial detainees presumably are held in the federal Metropolitan Correctional Center next door to the federal courthouse, but an excess volume of prisoners necessitates the housing of some detainees in a federal prison in Otisville, New York, while others are boarded in county jails as far away as Tennessee and Texas.[28]

But even when their clients are locally held, attorneys with many cases to handle are hard put to keep in frequent touch with each individual. The bitter frustration this can cause became evident when, on July 4, 1970, a disastrous riot broke out in Philadelphia's Holmesburg Prison, which served as the city's jail. The subsequent investigation made it clear that there were prolonged frustrations for pretrial prisoners, causing the bitter resentment which fueled the disturbance.

> Inmates, defense attorneys, prison authorities, social workers and impartial observers alike have concluded that the prime source of the frustrations which fed the violence at Holmesburg Prison is the prolonged, uninformed uncertainty which faces detentioners there. Many prisoners complain and many defense counsel frankly admit that on many occasions lawyers are too slow in making contact with their clients and too casual in keeping their clients informed as to the progress of their cases. Prisoners are often brought to City Hall for trial and returned to prison totally ignorant of the reason they were not tried. Apparently when defense attorneys obtain continuances for tactical or other reasons—or when the prosecutor must ask for a continuance or the court cannot hear the case—they often do not fully explain to their clients why they must spend another month in jail untried.[29]

Alternatives to Bail

Historically, the bail process has been based on the belief that a defendant posting a cash bond or its equivalent in property is reasonably certain to show up for trial, rather than forfeit the assets by absconding. Because a high percentage of defendants in criminal cases have little cash or property, the practice has relied on bail bondsmen who will put up the bail for a fee. A continuing tragedy is that so many defendants cannot afford such a fee, and so must remain in jail until disposition of their cases. The effect on the judicial system is to take much of the release decision away from the courts; "the defendant's release often rests in the hands of the professional bondsman, who may deny release for lack of a premium, lack of collateral security, or any other reason." The strong movement toward bail reform comes from a long delayed realization of the basic unfairness of conventional bail. "Probably the most serious indictment of the bail system is that it discriminates against the poor." (Ares, Rankin, and Sturz 1963, 70, 71)

Fortunately, there is a solution to the problem; unfortunately, it is used all too seldom. The major initiative for bail reform was introduced by the Vera Foundation, a private agency organized in New York City in 1961 and since renamed the Vera Institute of Justice. Although currently the Vera Institute conducts a variety of criminal justice programs, its first and most noted effort was the Manhattan Bail Project, which developed a successful process for effecting release of pretrial detainees without financial bail. Using New York University Law School students as part-time interviewers, the Project staff visited the jails early every morning to interview newly jailed persons to identify those who could safely be released on recognizance (ROR).

The genius in this process was a structured interview with a questionnaire asking about certain key conditions (prior record, employment, family ties, etc.) in the defendant's life that are reliable indicators of stability. The interview is simple and takes an average of only 15 minutes. Through telephone calls the information is verified and finally a resultant score is calculated. If the score is above a prescribed level, the case is considered safe for release and later that same morning the court receives the report and recommendation.

"The project achieved immediate success. Within a year over 250 defendants had been released and the project had begun to attract considerable interest." Adaptations of the program quickly appeared in widely separate parts of the country, and Congress passed the Bail Reform Act of 1966, which "created a presumption in favor of releasing defendants on their personal recognizance and also set forth a series of conditions that were to be used to structure pretrial release to the needs of the individual defendant. . . . The Act led to the revision of bail laws in at least a dozen states within five years of its passage." (Thomas 1976, 5, 7)

From the beginning the various ROR programs seemed to be succeeding beyond expectations in their low nonappearance rates, a record of the percentage of clients who fail to appear for trial. The nonappearance rate has always been the test of effectiveness of these programs, providing an objective basis for comparison with the conventional financial bail. In its first published report, the Vera Institute asserted that during its initial three years, before turning the Bail Project over to the New York City Office of Probation, it had gained release of 3,505 of the nearly 10,000 defendants the staff had interviewed. The nonappearance rate for these was only 1.6 percent, while the rate was 3 percent for those released on conventional bail during the same time.[30] This and similarly reported experiences of other such programs encouraged the rapid proliferation of ROR programs. Gradually, however, it has become apparent that the records of ROR programs are not quite so simple or clear.

Statistical accounting in this type of endeavor becomes complex and accordingly unreliable. A valid comparison of success rates among different release practices requires agreement on a standard definition of nonappearance, and this has proven to be stubbornly elusive. Success rates will also vary considerably according to the extent of the assistance given the defendants in adjusting to the requirements ordered by the court. Overall it seems safe to say that ROR programs can expect to have an appearance rate just as good as conventional financial bail, or better, depending on the degree and quality of supervision provided. (Thomas 1976, 93–102) "Willful failures to appear in court, where the defendant absconds or is returned only after being apprehended, typically do not exceed 4 percent of all released defendants. In addition, risk of nonappearance does not appear to increase with the seriousness of the original charge."[31]

The evaluation of pretrial programs is subject to the same distorting factor common to all programs for diverting offenders from incarceration: too easily a program can be rigged for success or failure simply by being either more, or less, cautiously conservative in the selection of cases in the first place. For this reason it is typical for managers of a radical new approach to start it in a conservative mode by picking the safest cases (often referred to as "creaming") for release. After obtaining public acceptance by establishing a good safety record in this way, it is then feasible to liberalize the process by gradually including riskier cases. By 1990 the Department of Justice could report that about three out of five defendants released pretrial were in ROR status, and these represented 26 percent of all felony defendants.[32]

In addition to the importance of the initial selection process, the type and extent of supervision of releasees is crucial to success. There is a natural reluctance to resort to aggressive supervision of these cases because these are persons who have not yet been found guilty of crime; however, a degree and type of supervision exists that is both reasonable and essential to success. It is a matter of recognizing that when defendants on release miss their trial dates, their action is usually not deliberate, and is more often a characteristic of their lifestyle. Of the people who typically make up the bulk of misdemeanants in jails, many have little experience in keeping appointments; they are not conditioned to its importance and are not practiced in providing themselves with reminders of important dates and times. Often they even have difficulty in getting around their city and finding unfamiliar places, especially the courthouse or a designated courtroom.

To Enhance Program Success

To be successful, the ROR program will need to include some friendly monitoring of the releasees, with phone call reminders of dates, and checking to be sure that the person knows when to report, has transportation, and knows exactly where to appear. The monitoring staff needs to be alert to such details as the insufficiency of the routine court notices; for instance, the futility of postcard reminders written in English and mailed out on the assumption that all defendants are able to read in that language. "Notification services are perhaps the most basic service the pretrial program can provide after release. There is much experience demonstrating that improving the notification process of defendants as to court dates will measurably decrease failures to appear in a jurisdiction."[33]

The impressive accomplishments of the original Vera program stimulated a large number of replications throughout the country, with many variations in design. Two of them are useful to mention as illustrations of innovative and effective local adaptations. In Des Moines, Iowa, where the ancient Polk County jail needed costly expansion, the municipal court judge and his chief of probation services contrived a pretrial program that was so successful that it postponed for several years the need for more jail beds; it also became the first LEAA-funded program to earn the status of an "exemplary" project.[34]

The Des Moines program used the basic Vera actuarial device to screen candidates for pretrial release, but then took the screening process one step further. The project staff took a second look at all the pretrial inmates who failed to attain a qualifying score, and on a more subjective basis evaluated them as candidates for release under enhanced supervision, a status they called "supervised release with services." Many additional men and women were accordingly released on condition that they accept intensive supervision designed to keep them law abiding and available to the court as scheduled for trial.

A somewhat different approach was taken by another ROR program, De Novo, organized in the early 1970s in Minneapolis. The De Novo staff routinely interviewed all newly arrived jail inmates to find those who were charged with nonviolent offenses, who had no prior felony convictions, and who were willing to waive their right to a speedy trial and agree to active involvement in the program's special activities. With the consent of the prosecutor, these candidates could then be released under the control and supervision of the De Novo staff, participating daily in a project aimed at restoring them to successful employment. Included in each case as appropriate was vocational counseling and training, payment of required restitution, group counseling, and substance abuse monitoring. A particularly attractive feature of this program has been the plan that each participant who becomes employed and otherwise performs well will be returned to court after a specified number of weeks with the recommendation that his or her case be dismissed. About three-quarters of the clients accomplish this goal, relieving that much institution bed space and bringing these misdemeanant cases to much more constructive conclusions than incarceration would achieve.

Even if nonappearance rates between bail and ROR defendants are not different, there is still a substantial gain with the ROR programs. As one advantage, they help relieve jail population pressures with consequent saving of tax money; the Vera Institute, speaking of the first three years of the Manhattan Bail Project, noted that "budget officials determined that the project, operating in only one of the city's five counties, had already saved over a million dollars in the Department of Correction's operating budget."[35] Less measurable, but undoubtedly more important, is the gain in human values, as men and women who would otherwise be stagnating in the destructive confines of jails are instead back in normal community life with the chance to work, to prepare their defense, and to improve their chances of continuing that course without further criminal record.

Altogether, it is heartening to look at the recent history of jails and to find that so much progress has been made lately in making them more humane in operation. At the same time, however, the reforms are hampered by the continued overcrowding, which frustrates many of the progressive measures that are attempted. In this respect, the jail experience is not materially different from conditions throughout the general field of corrections. As noted, jails and prisons, though usually in separate governmental jurisdictions, are highly interactive, affecting each other's operations directly and continually. As will be seen next, prisons too have made great progress toward better understanding of their effects upon their inmates, and toward better management, better architecture, and better rehabilitative programming. Prisons too have had to suffer overcrowding so severe as to cripple their modern improvements. As the next chapter will show, the current conflict between punitive public attitudes and the new and exacting standards for control and treatment of incarcerated persons provides a daunting challenge for policymakers who must balance these contradictory pressures.

Notes

1. Mattick 1974, 778 (below).
2. Charles B. DeWitt. "New Construction Methods for Correctional Facilities." *Construction Bulletin* (March 1986), 4.
3. Eugene J. Gardner. "Regional Jails." *American Jails* 6:1 (May/June 1992), 46.
4. Bureau of Justice Statistics. *Sourcebook of Criminal Justice Statistics—1991.* Washington, D.C.: GPO, 1992.
5. Bureau of Justice Statistics. *Bulletin. Jail Inmates, 1991* (June 1992), 1.
6. Ruiz v. Estelle, 503 F.Supp. 1265 (S.D. Tex. 1980).
7. David G. Gutierrez. "Texas Jails." *American Jails* 7:4 (Sept./Oct. 1993), 14.
8. For details on the Alabama court suits and the efforts to adjust to the resultant court orders, see Michael Haley, "Alabama Jail Assistance Project." *American Jails* 7:1 (March/April 1993), 36–39.
9. Allen F. Breed. "Prison Reform Leads to Jail Crisis." *The Prison Journal* 71:1 (Spring/Summer 1991), 27.
10. Mattick 1974, 787 (below).
11. Dick Ford and Ken Kerle. "Jail Standards—A Different Perspective." *The Prison Journal* 61:1 (Spring/Summer 1981), 24–25.
12. Michael T. Charles, Sesha Kethineni, and Jeffrey L. Thompson. "The State of Jails in America." *Federal Probation* 56:2 (June 1992), 57.
13. Francis R. Ford. "Politics and Jails." *American Jails* 6:6 (Jan./Feb. 1993), 18.
14. Charles B. DeWitt. "New Construction Methods for Correctional Facilities." *Construction Bulletin* (March 1986), 4.
15. Bureau of Justice Statistics. *Bulletin. Jail Inmates*, 1991 (June 1992), 1.
16. Morton J. Leibowitz. "Regionalization in Virginia Jails." *American Jails* 5:5 (Nov./Dec. 1991), 43.
17. Michael T. Charles, Sesha Kethineni, and Jeffrey L. Thompson, "The State of Jails in America." *Federal Probation* 56:2 (June 1992), 56.
18. Linda L. Zupan. "This Jail for Rent." *American Jails* 6:6 (Jan./Feb. 1993), 22–32.
19. Rod Miller, George E. Sexton, and Victor J. Jacobson. "Making Jails Productive." *Roll Call* (April 1992), 8. Or, *National Institute of Justice Reports* 223 (Jan./Feb. 1991), 2.
20. Tom L. Allison. "Making Offenders More Accountable and Offering Opportunity for Change." *Corrections Today* 55:6 (Oct. 1993), 92–95.
21. Donald J. Amboyer. "Michigan County Requires Inmates to Defray Cost of Incarceration." *Corrections Today* 55:6 (Oct. 1993), 88–90.

22. Linda L. Zupan. "Direct Inmate Supervision." *American Jails* 7:1 (March/April 1993), 7, 21.
23. Norma Phillips Lammers and Mark O. Morris. "Jail Construction in California." *Construction Bulletin* (Aug. 1990), 5.
24. *New York Times* (Jan. 8, 1992), A16.
25. Bureau of Justice Statistics. *Sourcebook of Criminal Justice Statistics—1991*. Washington, D.C.: GPO, 1992, 611, 617.
26. Arthur M. Wallenstein. "A Jail Warden Looks at Overcrowding and Alternatives." *The Prison Journal* 61:2 (Autumn/Winter 1981), 10.
27. Bureau of Justice Statistics. *National Update* 11:1 (July 1992), 1.
28. Broderick, Vincent L. "Pretrial Detention in the Criminal Justice Process." *Federal Probation* 57 (March 1993):1, 6.
29. From an unpublished report by James D. Crawford, Deputy District Attorney, Philadelphia, "Preliminary Report on the July 4, 1970 Riot at Holmesburg Prison," 62.
30. Vera Institute of Justice. *Programs in Criminal Justice Reform: Ten Year Report 1961–1971* (May 1972), 35.
31. National Coalition for Jail Reform. "Position Paper on Pretrial Release." *Prison Journal* (Fall 1981), 33. A Department of Justice statistical report for 1990 shows a higher rate of nonappearance for ROR releasees, but also points up the complexity of the national experience on this subject. See Bureau of Justice Statistics, *Bulletin*, "Pretrial Release of Felony Defendants, 1990" (Nov. 1992), 8–9.
32. Bureau of Justice Statistics. *Felony Defendants in Large Urban Counties, 1990*. Washington, D.C.: 1991, 8.
33. D. Alan Henry. "Pretrial Programs: Describing the Ideal." *Federal Probation* 57:1 (March 1993), 25.
34. The program is described in detail in an article, "Plaudits in Des Moines But Problems in Salt Lake," by Rob Wilson in *Corrections Magazine* 2: 5 (Sept. 1976), 13–24.
35. The Vera Institute of Justice. *Status Report* (July 1991), 2.

Bibliography

The Correctional Pariah

Design Guide for Secure Adult Correctional Facilities. College Park, Md.: American Correctional Association, 1983.
DiIulio, John J., Jr. *No Escape: The Future of American Corrections*. New York: Basic Books, 1991.
   A thoughtful examination of some of the important issues in management of correctional institutions. The author discusses the rationale for better management technique, the case for alternatives to jails, the hope for rehabilitative programs, and the pros and cons of privatized prisons.
Goldfarb, Ronald. *Jails: The Ultimate Ghetto*. New York: Anchor Press/Doubleday, 1975.

Hoffer, Frank W., Delbert M. Mann, and Floyd N. House. *The Jails of Virginia.* New York: D. Appleton-Century, 1933.

Though dated and confined to only one state, this report is useful for its perceptive depiction of the conditions which for so long were definitive of jail operations in most states.

Laite, W. E., Jr. *The United States vs William Laite.* Washington, D.C.: Acropolis Books, 1972.

The subjective account by one federal prisoner of his experience of being tried, jailed, and then incarcerated briefly in a prison. But since Laite's jail time was considerable and his experiences are told here so graphically, it is a particularly instructive picture of the destructive quality of life in a typical poorly supervised urban jail.

Mattick, Hans. "The Contemporary Jails of the United States: An Unknown and Neglected Area of Justice." Chapter 21 in *Handbook of Criminology,* ed. Daniel Glaser. Chicago: Rand McNally, 1974.

Mattick was a noted expert on the history and operational problems of jails, and this lengthy chapter is one of his solid contributions to the literature.

Designs for Alternatives to Jail

Ares, Charles E., Anne Rankin, and Herbert Sturz. "The Manhattan Bail Project: An Interim Report on the Use of Pre-Trial Parole." *New York University Law Review* 38 (1963), 67–95.

A useful discussion of the general background of bail practice in the United States, with description and explanation of the operation of the pioneering Manhattan Bail Project in its early days.

Federal Probation 57:1 (March 1993).

This entire issue deals with matters related to pretrial release and the various program approaches serving as alternatives to jail. Its 11 articles discuss types of pretrial programs and the viewpoints of judges, prosecutors, and others directly involved.

Gettinger, Stephen. "Has the Bail Reform Movement Stalled?" *Corrections Magazine* 6:1 (Feb. 1980), 26–35.

Thomas, Wayne H., Jr. *Bail Reform in America.* Berkeley: University of California Press, 1976.

CHAPTER 7

The Prisons

F or nearly two centuries, the U.S. public has thought of prisons mainly as the massive, walled penitentiaries that have been a fixture of each state's criminal justice system since the two early prototypes were built in Auburn, New York, and Philadelphia, Pennsylvania, in 1817 and 1827. Although the basic purpose of these institutions has remained essentially unchanged, the philosophical concepts shaping their operations today could hardly be more different than those of their origins. In the first half century of the penitentiary experience it was generally thought that the prison, to be an effective deterrent, would have to be seen as a particularly frightful place. Advocates for prisons often spoke of the "terrors" of imprisonment being an essential aspect of their utility, and to this end the prisoners were kept in solitude as much as possible, working in silence with no communication with persons outside the institution, and remarkably little inside. Prison architecture reflected this mood, with grim, fortress-like walls surrounding monotonous granite cell-block buildings.

Prison as the Basic Criminal Punishment

With the appearance of the "reformatory" soon after the Civil War, new concepts of how to handle prisoners began to take hold. The first one of the new type, at Elmira, New York, was designed to receive young adult "redeemable" offenders who were offered a rich educational program. Other states rapidly imitated the Elmira model, starting a trend that by the present century had substantially changed the philosophy of prison management. (McKelvey 1977, 85–87, 133–138) Rejecting the early practice of silence and noncommunication, prison managers embraced the idea that prison should be not just punitive, but rehabilitative. It was a strongly held view until the 1960s, when doubts about the effectiveness of rehabilitation sent prison managers back to thinking of punishment as the primary purpose. Nevertheless, a strong concern for basic decency has survived, reflecting new understanding of the deleterious effects of the old type of prison regime. As stated by an authoritative guidebook on prison architecture, "the institutional atmosphere should be as normal as possible for the welfare of both inmates and staff and, ultimately, for that of the public, as conditions during confinement will likely influence behavior after release." (*Design Guide* 1983, 6) The philosophical change affects both architecture and management style.

Current Trends: Architecture

Much of what has already been noted about jail architecture, old and new, is fully applicable to the evolution of prisons. The old traditional prisons (many of which are still in use) tend to be fortress-like heavy masonry, with a cold, monotonous quality. Housing units are large and impersonal, with cell blocks having anywhere from about two hundred to as many as five hundred men in identical cells stacked as high as five tiers. The stress of prison living is exacerbated by incessant noise, as all surfaces—walls, ceilings, and floors—are hard materials that bounce and echo the sounds, particularly the noise of clanging steel cell doors. One criminologist, a former prisoner, agrees that "cell blocks were harsh worlds of steel and concrete, of unbearable heat in the summer and chilling cold in the winter, of cramped quarters, and of constant droning, shouting and clanking noise."[1] With several hundred people living in constant sight and sound of each other, any disruptive incident is immediately known to everyone and has a contagious effect that can easily be dangerous.

In new prisons, as in new jails, humanizing the architecture is no longer a frill but a necessity. Softer, quieter environments (in contrast to what had been universal construction style), including acceptance of acoustical treatment, and an occasional concession to ideas of simple visual attractiveness, contrast sharply with earlier construction styles. This sometimes is seen in the use of wood for such items as doors and stair railings; wood is a warmer, more friendly construction material than masonry and steel. Where the traditional prison usually had only the monotonous bland colors of its basic stone and metal, more often now there is a mixture of colors, sometimes including graphics on walls. In some facilities, including certain federal jails and some minimum security institutions, carpeting is thought to be justified for its acoustical property and its help in reducing stress, but whatever its value, use of carpeting will remain limited as long as the public sees it as the ultimate in coddling prisoners. One architectural specialist observes, "Some people will make the case for a drab and spartan prison environment to remind the inmate where he is, what he has done, and how low he has fallen. . . . [but] I do not know of any evidence that a drab or ugly correctional environment is in anyone's interest—the inmate's, the staff's, or society's. Accounts of men who have spent time in strip cells show resentment rather than repentance, anger rather than reflection." (Sommer 1974, 46)

Whereas new prison management principles encourage the current architectural trends, the high cost of prison construction, often running more than $50,000 per bed, has forced states to compromise with the ideal. The inexorable growth of prison commitments causes severe overcrowding in nearly all prisons and a consequent heavy drain on tax dollars to provide new prison space. To keep construction costs down, planners are forced to compromise. Prison managers, for instance, usually firm in their preference for individual rooms rather than the less manageable, more dangerous dormitories, often must accept new institutions that house inmates in the more cheaply built dormitories.

One effective economy is to build separate types of institutions for different categories of prisoners. This avoids the waste of putting low-risk prisoners in facilities with high-cost security features needed only for more dangerous inmates. It is generally accepted that "maximum security institutions are required for no more than 5 percent to 15 percent of a correctional system's population. . . . [and] about one-third of a correctional system's population can be placed in minimum security facilities." (*Design Guide* 1983, 9) To reduce the tensions, stress, and monotony of long-term prison living, in high-security facilities, living units housing forty to sixty-five inmates in separate rooms are arranged around a control center and dayroom, while a facility for minimum-security inmates uses the much cheaper design of open dormitories, perhaps with moveable partial partitions around the beds.

Much has been learned too about economy in the construction process. Instead of following the traditional brick-by-brick, on-site type of construction, designing buildings with prefabricated walls that are trucked to the site and quickly hoisted into place has been found to result in substantial savings. Time saved is money saved, so when the job is superintended by a method termed "fast track construction," the work is expedited and expenditures are reduced accordingly.[2]

Only in recent years has the public been willing to tolerate the judgment of policymakers who authorize prisons designed with more humane living conditions. Although a prison with "comforts" is politically anathema to a conservative public, managers know that money spent on these features contributes importantly to a safer operation. At its best a prison is an exceedingly stressful place in which to live. Animosities are severe and life is cheap. Any prolonged, continuous irritant in a prison can potentially trigger a major disturbance, causing damage that may be far more costly than the proper design would have been in the first place.

Living conditions are just as important for the guard force (correctional officers, in proper modern terminology) as for inmates. These important staff members must deal in a cool, competent way with provocative situations every day; a correctional officer who is tired, nervous, or edgy may say the wrong thing just at the wrong time, and the whole institution may have to pay for the error. This is another reason why air conditioning is a valid feature today: "it can help minimize the normal tensions of confinement that inevitably escalate in a hot, humid environment, thus preventing violence and disturbances that too often occur during hot weather and exact high costs not only in repairs but in injuries and, sometimes, loss of life for both staff and inmates." (*Design Guide* 1983, 149)

Current Trends: Management

The concept of "direct supervision" management for jails, described in chapter 6, grew from a plan developed in the Federal Bureau of Prisons in the late 1960s and known as "unit management" when used in prisons. Generally considered the most significant single improvement made in prison management in recent decades, unit management divides a prison into small living units, each with several relevant staff members working together as a multidisciplinary administrative group. In a large prison, for example, one floor or a section of a cell block may be designated a unit, and the corrections officers and counselors, the psychologist, chaplain, and any other person regularly having some responsibility for that group of prisoners will function together as a group of cooperating equals in managing the daily conduct of that part of the institution.[3]

Usually one of the staff group acts as chairperson, with the duty rotated occasionally to involve both custodial and treatment staff in this responsibility. One of the impressive assets of the plan is that it solves the long-standing prison management problem of the intransigent competition between these two staff types. The treatment personnel, including counselors, psychologists, medical personnel, recreation supervisors, chaplains, and teachers, have long felt frustrated by the custodial staff that "holds the keys." Any activity that a treatment person would want to plan might be vetoed as incompatible with security. In this context the treatment personnel would often resent the uniformed staff as insensitive to programming, whereas those in uniform viewed the counselors as naive and unrealistic. The experience has been, however, that when the two types must work together daily in small units with joint responsibility for both security and quality of living, the bifurcation of attitudes and interests is resolved.

In many prisons the concept of direct supervision has counteracted the popularity of monitoring inmate movement by use of closed-circuit television. Hoping to save costs by reducing staff positions, many institutions in the 1950s and 1960s adopted television surveillance to enable a central command post to keep watch on activity areas. Only a relatively short time was needed to realize that what serves best in stabilizing a prison is constant interaction among people. A television camera can see what is happening in a hallway, but it provides no human interaction and can even increase inmate resentment of the officers. Accordingly, the use of the television has dwindled appreciably.

Along with the importance of direct supervision is the equally important concern for the quality of the top management of a prison, and for the management of a whole state system. The position of the state director of corrections (or commissioner), the director's qualifications, the process of his or her selection, and the director's relationship to the governor are all crucial to the quality of the state's correctional services. Some states attempt to stabilize the corrections service and insulate it from politics by having the director of corrections selected by and responsible to a bipartisan board. That goal is elusive, however. Most often the state corrections administrator is appointed by and serves at the pleasure of the incoming governor without any assurance that he or she can expect to stay after the next change of political party control. In some instances, a state director has managed to stay through several political changes, but this is by no means assured. Some states have experienced a change in the top position every two or three years, seriously disrupting departmental management.

Any corrections system director is painfully aware that the corrections department and the director's own work in it has little or no chance of being an asset to the governor, for it ordinarily will be noticed in the public press only when troubles occur. The best to be hoped is that the department can be operated quietly with no unfavorable events. An experienced corrections administrator commented that, ''One basic lesson not often clear to the uninitiated is that cabinet officers and heads of departments appointed by the political executive are expendable. These appointees serve at the pleasure of the elected chief executive or, at best, for short, specified terms. In this position, one is in constant danger of becoming a political liability to his chief, whether by his own fault or that of others.'' (McGee 1981, 11)

Although the distinction is somewhat too simple, it is useful to note the choice a governor has in selecting as a department head either a political appointee or a "professional." The former is obviously a person who has experience and proven effectiveness in politics as such, or who has been helpful enough to the governor or the governor's political party to deserve a reward. The professional is one who has prepared for the work with education in a relevant academic area such as public administration or one of the behavioral sciences. He or she usually works up through levels of increasing responsibility in the field and is eventually selected on the basis of proven corrections experience rather than any political activity.

It would seem logical to hope that a governor would seek to appoint to the executive post an experienced and progressive corrections professional rather than a political favorite, especially after some of the embarrassing experiences that have occurred with political appointees who had no expertise in this exacting field. Unfortunately, however, professional knowledge and skill in managing correctional institutions or programs is not the same as skill in forging effective relationships with politicians in the legislature. For this reason, it sometimes works best for the governor to appoint as the top executive someone primarily qualified with political skill and influence, and who will then rely on second-level careerists to guide the specialized departmental operations.

Overcrowding: A Dilemma for Everyone

Overloaded prisons are a natural and inevitable result of legislative concern to spend public money frugally. Expensive new prison space will not be built until the need is urgent. Consequently, during the entire history of prisons the problem of crowding has been endemic. And it is indeed a problem. Although architects have designed prison cells for one person each, prison managers have invariably been forced to double the occupancy by fastening an extra bunk to the wall above the first bunk, and then in some cases place a third prisoner in the cell with a mattress on the floor. Whereas it would seem prudent for a state to build extra prison space in anticipation of future demand, experience teaches that if prison beds are available they will be filled. It seems impossible to have a reserve of beds.

The national prison system experienced a surge in overcrowding conditions during the 1970s when rising prison commitments caught the states unprepared for the influx of prisoners. A 1981 news report spoke of the Texas situation, though it was not different from many other states. "Last spring, Texas was bunking about 3000 inmates on the floors of small cells already occupied by two other men. Almost all the cells are smaller than the minimum space recommended for one inmate, measuring nine feet by five feet. Thousands more prisoners are double-celled in Texas. Some of its prison dorms pack double bunks so tightly that one witness said they resemble 'one gigantic bed.' "[4]

The glut of prisoners has resulted in civil suits against individual prisons or entire prison systems in most states during the last two decades. In 1992 some of the extreme examples of overcrowding included Pennsylvania, with 21,400 prisoners in a system having a rated capacity of 14,338, indicating a 49 percent overload. Wisconsin was overloaded by 42 percent, California by 78 percent, and Massachusetts by 84 percent. As a result of civil suits, the entire prison systems in nine states were under court orders or consent decrees that in various ways attempted to control the population levels. In thirty-one other states one or more individual prisons were subject to court orders.[5]

When New York built its first penitentiary (in Auburn in 1817), it held its prisoners in individual cells of only about 28 square feet each. Costly as it is to build larger cells, experience has shown that a much larger allocation of space is essential both for the mental health of the prisoner and for the safe operation of the prison. In recent years the accepted view has been that each inmate should have at least 60 square feet of space.[6] While courts have found it useful to have a standard like this to guide them in deciding class action suits, they have also found that allocation of space is more complex than making simple measurements of a cell. One court decision stands out in addressing this matter. In Ohio a court suit was brought in an effort to enforce a single occupancy rule, making the point that if one person should have 60 square feet of his own living space, that would mean that in a cell of that size there should not be more than the one inmate. The case made its way to the U.S. Supreme Court where it was decided that double celling of itself did not constitute impermissible crowding. Instead, all aspects of the situation must be considered; double celling can be tolerated if the inmates are in the cell only during sleeping time, and if during most other hours they are in work, education, or recreation programs.[7] The case had an extensive effect in allowing other states to go ahead with double celling on this basis.

At the same time, some of the research on prison overcrowding has supported the court's view in finding that "social space" is more important than simple physical space. Social space is a concept of the importance of privacy, security, independence, and some choice of activity. To live in a dormitory with an adequate number of square feet per prisoner, but with no privacy and no opportunity to keep private possessions secure or to indulge in personal activity, is more oppressive that having less space, but with space of one's own and with some sense of social distance from one's immediate neighbors.

When overcrowding becomes severe, and under conditions that cause loss of privacy or social space, tensions increase, leading to more stressful incidents, more disciplinary actions, and more suicides. Part of the problem is that in the usual prison when all normal bed space is used and more is needed, then mattresses appear on floors in gymnasiums, in hallways, in dayrooms, and even in chapels. Just when more staff and more activity space is needed there is relatively less of both.[8]

A principle seldom fully appreciated is that even when a prison has just barely filled all its beds, it is at that point overcrowded. To properly manage a prison, the warden needs to have a few vacant beds to have the flexibility for the daily adjustments that are necessary. For many possible reasons an inmate may need to be moved from one cell block to another, or may need to be moved to, or out of, disciplinary segregation. But if the prison is full this cannot be done without moving someone else to make room, which will sometimes be most difficult to do without raising anger. For this reason court decisions limiting prison populations have in an occasional case set the mandated limit, not at the institution's rated capacity, but at a rate such as 97 percent of capacity.

Corrections administrators appreciate these problems, and generally are doing what they can to keep up with the need, using predictive tools to determine future prison bed space requirements and asking for it promptly. But the lead required time to select a prison site, design the building plan, and complete the construction usually means that by the time the facility is ready for occupancy, it is already too small for the swollen population awaiting it. Despite ongoing prison construction projects in most states, it is unlikely that they will ever build their way out of prison overcrowding.

The Prisons for Females

For most of correctional institution history it has been a singular irony that women were fortunate in having so few of their number in prison, while at the same time this was the central handicap for those going to prison. A state penitentiary with a volatile population of several hundred or one thousand men demands constant administrative attention, whereas a small prison beside it for a few relatively quiet female prisoners seems comparatively unimportant, and may be ignored. If this is an exaggeration, the point is nevertheless valid. Whereas it is cost effective for a large prison to install various work and treatment programs, with all the needed equipment for shops, recreation, and academic and vocational education, it is usually thought too costly to provide equivalent programs and equipment for the minuscule female population. Women also have been handicapped by the traditional view that skills training for them need not go beyond the conventional roles of homemaking, secretarial, and beautician work.

In the last two decades this has changed, though not for the best of reasons. In large degree the change has been due to the pronounced rise in female prison populations. The trend has been so strong that even the states that had always had a negligible number of female prisoners have now had to build sizable institutions for females. As noted in a federal statistical report, "The number of women under the jurisdiction of State and Federal prison authorities at year end 1989 reached a record 40,556." This represented a 200 percent increase, with 27,000 more women in prison since 1980.[9] As another agency observes, "simply put, the criminal justice system now seems more willing to incarcerate women. In 1970, 45 percent of women charged with murder were imprisoned. By 1975, this figure surged to 73 percent." To compare with male imprisonment rates, in the period from 1980 to 1989, the country's male prisoner population increased by 120 percent, while the number of female prisoners increased by 230 percent.[10]

Programming for female prisoners has been affected by the increased concern throughout society for fairness toward women. One specific outcome of this trend appeared in Kentucky in 1980 when female prisoners sued the Kentucky Correctional Institution for Women, alleging that their educational and vocational training fell far short of the programs offered in the male institutions. The court directed the corrections agency to develop and propose a plan for achieving parity in programs between male and female prisoners. Among proposals considered was the creation of a co-correctional institution for male and female inmates; another was that female inmates could be bused daily to a men's prison to participate in educational programs there.

When the corrections officials moved too slowly in presenting an acceptable plan, the court ordered the agency to add two more vocational courses and one more industry in the women's facility, commenting that "the inferiority of programs, and discrimination in the area of privileges . . . are not always the result of conscious sex discrimination. They are often attributable to oversight, omission, and traditional views of female offenders which have not kept pace with the changing inmate population. The discriminatory treatment which has resulted must be remedied."[11] With the impetus of such legal challenges, but perhaps more because of the growing sensitivity to sexist issues, prison systems are gradually adopting more liberal vocational training programs for women as well as providing a wider range of industrial production jobs.

Since there are always a few pregnant women among those arriving in prisons, another challenging issue has been the care of their babies.

Throughout the nineteenth century and until well into this century, babies usually stayed with their mothers in prisons, partly because there were insufficient social services to make alternative arrangements, and it was often impractical to send an infant back to the mother's home at a distance without having a wet nurse to accompany it. Additionally, in the great majority of cases the mother and child would be released well before the child would reach the age of school attendance. Until the last two decades the average amount of time served by female inmates in most prisons was from two to three years, so babies born to inmate mothers would leave prison before being affected by the prison environment.

Today in nearly all corrections systems imprisoned mothers are not allowed to keep their babies with them. An exception is the prison for women at Bedford Hills, New York, where, backed by state law and with a nursery caring for up to twenty babies at a time, the administration supports a mother's decision to keep her baby with her. The institution allows the babies to stay up to a year, and with a high percentage of the mothers serving no more time than that anyway, this means that many if not most babies may stay until they leave with their mothers.

Those advocating a return to the practice of allowing prisoner mothers to keep their babies cite the importance of mother-child bonding in the healthy development of the child, while discounting any effect of prison stigma on a child who is too young to be aware of it. Although a few prisoner mothers have brought suit to keep their babies with them, the complexity of the issue has kept these suits from producing definitive decisions applicable to such cases generally.[12] Consequently, the ban on babies in residence is sustained in virtually all women's prisons, although the managers usually maintain liberal visiting privileges for families so that prisoners can see their children as often as family members will bring them. For the newborns, the nearly universal practice is that immediately after its birth the infant is sent to a prearranged placement, either to the mother's family, to foster care, or to adoption, as the mother may decide.

It can well be argued that architecturally most prisons are not able to accommodate babies appropriately, but it is also argued that with minor physical changes prisons could acceptably permit mothers in certain cases to keep their babies, and this would be safe and psychologically beneficial. One psychiatrist who made a careful study of the issue commented that

> For humanitarian and moral reasons, more can be done for inmates' children and their families. Which options are selected depend upon the characteristics of the particular case and the availability of funds.
>
> As far as I have been able to determine, the reasons for discontinuing prison nurseries have been administrative, organizational, or political ones. I have not found any scientific evaluation or research that shows that having children in correctional institutions is either good or bad for the children, inmates or the institution.[13]

A Radical Innovation: Co-correctional Institutions

In one sense, the co-correctional prison has been around for nearly two centuries. From their beginnings penitentiaries housed all adult offenders, male and female, with the female prisoners in one small cell block, a dormitory wing, or perhaps a separate building on the grounds of the men's prison. This economically expeditious way of serving both sexes was not truly a co-correctional plan, for the men and women were kept entirely apart to the extent that administrative diligence could thwart inmate resourcefulness. Being subject to management by men who were oriented mainly to the larger male prisoner population, the women's units too often received inadequate and insensitive attention. By early in this century, under pressure from women's organizations, most states had built separate institutions for women, and this is now standard. In the 1970s, however, some of the correctional systems discovered the possibility of having a true co-correctional facility, meaning a prison in which male and female prisoners, though housed in separate quarters on the same grounds, mix freely in program activities.

Like many if not most new developments in corrections, the movement originated not as an inspired idea for improved institutions, but as a response to an immediate problem, in this case the aftermath of a prison riot. Not quite the first, but easily the most significant, early experience with mixing of male and female prisoners occurred in 1971 in Fort Worth, Texas, when the Federal Bureau of Prisons was converting a U.S. Public Health Service hospital to a prison. There had been some thought of making it co-correctional, but what actually precipitated the plan was a riot at the Bureau's institution for women at Alderson, West Virginia, in September 1971. Following the disturbance many of the women were so emotionally charged and disruptive that some removal was necessary; forty-five of the most disturbed women were bused out of Alderson, placed temporarily at another federal facility, then taken to the new prison at Fort Worth where they arrived still in a mood of intense hostility. Here was a challenging test of any prison's capacity to calm and control such a group, but a particularly touchy situation for an untried co-correctional situation. The warden who greeted the bus that day tells what it was like:

> It was a compelling learning experience for all of us. It provided a dramatic illustration of how much people are inclined to respond according to the way they are treated, as well as a compelling demonstration of the powerful influence of expectations. We had no reasonable choice but to tell these women we needed their help, that a large share of responsibility for the co-correctional experiment would be resting on their shoulders. Apprehensive though we were, we behaved toward them as if we couldn't be more delighted to have them. Forty-five rowdy, foulmouthed women responded to this treatment magnificently. We had some tense and difficult times then

and during the months thereafter, but to observe the growth of these women in dignity and self-respect was a tremendously gratifying experience.[14]

A significant variation on the co-correctional mode was a prison that opened in 1975 in Ringe, Denmark, attracting critical interest on both sides of the Atlantic. A small prison for young adult offenders, Ringe went further than any modern prisons in its efforts to replicate normal outside living within a secure perimeter. Inmates have individual rooms arranged in separated sections of sixteen rooms each. Unlike co-correctional prisons in the United States, the men and women inmates at Ringe may be mixed in these living units and allowed to form close relationships. Each unit has its own kitchen where the residents prepare their own meals from groceries bought at an institution grocery store, paying from a weekly food allowance. Men and women work together in the various job assignments, including the principal industry, a furniture factory.[15]

For all the fascinated attention Ringe has attracted among U.S. correctional managers, it is not likely to be imitated here. Even the many admirers of the Ringe program realize that its replication would be quite difficult, suitable for only a small fraction of prisoners, and politically risky. In fact, the U.S. correctional systems have abandoned the co-correctional institutions that they did have. The co-correctional mode was typically utilized as expedient for dealing with various management problems, often to take advantage of empty beds in prisons for females when prisons for men were overcrowded. Although the federal prison system has had as many as five co-correctional institutions, and as many as fourteen states operated such facilities, the overall experience was mixed, with some administrators liking the plan, and others finding it less than satisfactory. It became apparent that some physical plants were not suitable for this arrangement, and it also became a less attractive expedient when female commitments rose substantially during the 1980s, making a demand for larger all-female institutions. Although experience proved that, if skillfully administered, the co-correctional prison was quite feasible, by the early 1990s all the institutions had reverted to single sex status.

Modern Management Issues

From the earliest operation of prisons the public has held the strongly conflicting attitudes that prisoners should be made to work and help defray the costs of their imprisonment, but should do so somehow without competing with free labor. Both concerns are natural and reasonable, but most difficult to reconcile. After more than a century of contention between prisons, manufacturers, and unions, and after experimenting with different approaches to the problem, most prison systems have developed policies that preserve a fragile peace regarding this issue.

Prison Industries: An Issue for Public Ambivalence

State laws typically provide that prison-made products will be sold only for "state use," usually meaning that the products may be sold only to governmental agencies within the state. Often these laws also provide that state government agencies must turn first to the prison-made goods before buying elsewhere. The federal prison system, which contains numerous industrial shops in the more than sixty federal institutions and is operated by a separate corporation known as Unicor, also enjoys this guaranteed market. Its products are sold only to federal agencies, though Unicor makes sure that it will not produce and sell more than a modest percentage of the supplies available on the general market. This keeps the competition with private industry at a minimum, while the protected federal market ensures full operation of the prison shops. Even so, prison industries remain vulnerable. In 1993, for instance, Vice President Al Gore's National Performance Review, seeking ways to make the federal government more efficient, recommended that Congress should "take away the Federal Prison Industries' status as a mandatory source of federal supplies and require it to compete commercially for federal agencies' business."[16]

Half a century ago the description of a usual prison would have given prominent attention to the prison farm as a healthy work placement for many of the prisoners, as well as being an economic mainstay, supplying much of the institution's food. Today, however, farming has virtually disappeared as a prison activity. Most prisoners are from urban settings, with no expertise or interest in farm work. States have been finding that the institution farm can no longer be operated economically; it is cheaper to buy the foodstuffs than to raise them with prisoner labor. Those prisons which have adjoining farmland usually lease it to privately operating farmers.

Custodial Extremes: The Camps and the Prisons of Last Resort

One of the public's favorite criticisms of prisons is that they are too "soft"—too comfortable and not enough like the grueling punishment they ought to be. Particularly subject to such complaints are the so-called "country club" prisons, the minimum-security camps operating without walls or fences. They are found in a variety of formats and often they are operated in connection with some steady source of labor. Such a camp, as an example, may be located near a state forest, with the inmates employed in forest fire protection or in raising and transplanting seedlings for reforestation. Others have been operated in connection with fish hatcheries, road maintenance, or farming. Obviously, the inmates assigned to such facilities must be stable, preferably nonviolent persons who are judged unlikely to escape.

It is a natural reaction for people to be irritated on hearing of some prominent offender going to such an open, "easy" prison camp, but in the interests of governmental efficiency as well as other penological considerations it is sensible to maintain this type of institution.

The white collar, nonviolent offender who is stable enough to do his or her time without threatening others or attempting to escape should not be housed with violent prisoners. But also it is in the taxpayers' interest not to waste costly resources. The construction of a high-security prison is exceedingly expensive, so to use that type of facility for a prisoner who does not require it is simply irresponsible. Not only is the minimum-security camp much cheaper to build than the conventional prison but also it is much cheaper to operate. In 1987 the minimum-security camps operated by the federal prison system were costing an average of less than $8,000 annually per inmate, compared with an annual cost of about $12,000 annually per inmate in the maximum-security institutions.

At the other extreme is the special maximum-security institution, a type known as the prison of last resort. The most noted prototype was the high-profile prison on Alcatraz Island in San Francisco Bay, which the Federal Bureau of Prisons operated from 1934 to 1963. More than any other prison in the country it caught public attention, gaining a mystique that still endures thirty years after its closing. Alcatraz had its effect on every correctional system that finds itself contending with a few violent prisoners who skillfully and ruthlessly disrupt order, attempt escapes, and viciously attack staff or other inmates. After closing Alcatraz the Bureau of Prisons opened its new high-security prison at Marion, Illinois, and by then several states were also developing "maxie" institutions. By 1992 the Bureau of Prisons had begun construction of a new prison complex at Florence, Colorado, with several interconnected institutions, one of which was to be another institution of last resort, incorporating the latest and best techniques of extra-tight security and control.

The management of this type of prison has proved to be complex and difficult, but, after trial and error, a reasonably successful approach has emerged. Some of the efforts initially included intensive treatment programs, though these have usually been modified, if not outright eliminated, by court decisions. Despite good intentions on the part of prison managers who want to rehabilitate in addition to locking up, courts have declared the compulsory special confinement arrangements to have the characteristics of punishment rather than treatment, and have required that placement in such programs must be protected by the usual due process procedures. (Keve 1974, 160–161)

Evidence exists that an intensive treatment program can succeed in a maximum-security facility for violent inmates, but this kind of program requires so much skill, administrative energy, and motivation that it can seldom be accomplished or sustained.[17] In view of such difficulties, and a current general attitude that favors punishment more than rehabilitation, managers of the special last resort prisons are inclined to operate without pretense of treatment, concentrating instead on what might be termed as humane secure storage.

Administrators contend that the presence of a high-security facility has a salutary effect on the whole system. By separating out disruptive prisoners, it enables other institutions to operate more safely, without spending so much time and energy dealing with the violent few.

A prisoner in the usual last resort type of facility is likely to be confined alone in a cell as much as 23 hours per day; food is brought to the cell, as are most other services. When he is let out of the cell for a shower or for some solitary recreation, his hands are cuffed behind his back before he leaves the cell; then he is escorted by two officers who remove the handcuffs only after the prisoner is in the next locked area. In some instances, to relieve the boredom of long hours in the cell, the inmate may be provided with a black-and-white television set.[18]

The maximum-security units operate continually at the edge of legal acceptability. Violent prisoners are highly provocative and correctional officers can eventually reach the point at which they lose their self-control and objectivity in dealing with the threatening behavior. Civil suits may result from overreactions of staff, or because the physical conditions of the close confinement may be cited as too repressive for the psychological health of the prisoner. The federal institution at Marion, as other institutions have had to do, has had to refine its confinement conditions to comply with court orders, without compromising security.

A similar court challenge has affected a large new maximum-security prison that opened in Pelican Bay, California, in 1989. Its designed capacity was 2,080 prisoners, but within three years its population had reached more than 3,000, a situation virtually guaranteed to produce litigation. Within the prison is a separate twelve-hundred-bed "security housing unit" for last resort prisoners, which at present writing is under attack in federal court for alleged brutality and failure to provide needed medical care.[19] This is an almost inevitable type of court challenge, for staff will indeed sometimes have to use heavy-handed means to control violent prisoners, and in doing so they may use excessive force. The court eventually has to determine whether there is truly a pattern of staff violence in reaction to prisoner violence, or whether the control measures have been necessary and sufficiently restrained. These occasional legal challenges serve the useful function of forcing a review of policies and procedures as needed and appropriate in maintaining a defensible balance between necessary control and the basic requirements of humane care.

Although many prisoners apparently dread transfer to rigorous prisons such as Marion or Pelican Bay, they may also find this type of institution a preferred place to serve time. The disruptive, hostile prisoner, who usually has no interest in rehabilitative programs, finds this type of prison a no-nonsense place where the prisoner can do time without being bothered by counselors or others who would try to "treat" him. One noted student of the prison culture reported on his comparison of two prisons, one of them a psychiatrically oriented institution with attractive and comfortable modern architecture, and the other "a traditional fortress-type prison with walls that were five feet thick." He found that "by a heavy margin, the inmates preferred the traditional fortresslike prison. They preferred it because its climate featured the vital ingredient of predictability. Particularly for the long-term inmate, predictability is a commodity that is heavily prized. For the inmates, the effort and confusion of trying to second-guess the mysterious psychiatrists . . . was infinitely more important than the physical amenities."[20]

For many prisoners the related element of firm control is the most welcome feature. Prison is a dangerous place and this type of prisoner knows this better than any other. While cell confinement is depressingly tedious to a person who has always been action-oriented, many prisoners find comfort in seeing that the prison is under firm control and that they are comparatively safe from assault. This became evident when Alcatraz closed and many of its inmates were transferred to the federal penitentiary at Atlanta. "The Alcatraz inmates regarded Atlanta as a very dangerous place—full of violence and unpredictable people. . . . In their opinion, Atlanta would be better off if it were managed in the manner that Alcatraz was managed; at least under that regimen, men did not worry about whether they would live through the day."[21]

Another experience with this type of institution points up a nagging problem typical of the usual prison. Prisoner resourcefulness ordinarily is able to defeat the most determined institutional controls in acquiring drugs; it is rare that any prison is actually drug free, and with drugs circulating, prison is more dangerous. Gang leaders competing for the traffic in drugs tend to be ruthless. It is accordingly an impressive contribution to prisoner safety when a prison like Marion, through its rigorous control of all contacts with outsiders, is actually able to run routine tests on the prison population and find everyone negative for drugs.

Protective Custody

Perhaps the most easily visible evidence of the dangers inherent in prison life is in the protective custody (PC) units that are necessary in all prison systems. A tragic aspect of prison life for all the easily victimized inmates is that if the prison management is not capable of protecting them they are virtually helpless. Certain categories of offenders, such as child molesters or former police officers, are likely to be in danger. In a men's prison anyone who is physically slight, unaggressive, and especially one who is physically "pretty," may be a natural victim. Sexually predatory prisoners will waste no time in approaching and victimizing this type of prisoner. Others who are physically rugged may also be victimized, however, if suspected of having "snitched" on anyone else. For the sexually attractive inmate the ordeal will be anal rape, sometimes with successive attacks by different prisoners, sometimes as the exclusive and continuing partner of one dominant inmate. For the "snitch" the likely fate will be a single vicious attack, usually with a prison-made knife and usually with fatal intent.

The prison's correctional officers, no matter how conscientious about wanting to protect the victim, cannot ensure the victim's safety in the general population; the only recourse is to maintain a separate housing unit for such potential victims where their adversaries cannot get to them. Over the last two decades the need for PC has substantially increased, as seen in a 1980 report of an informal study of the problem, which indicated that most states could not meet the demand for protective custody space. In California 4 percent of the prison population was in protective custody, in Illinois 17 percent, while various major prisons in Washington, Michigan, and Massachusetts had 12 percent or more being protected, with these figures representing a significant recent growth of the problem.[22]

Increased use of PC is presumably an outgrowth of the many other changes in the criminal justice field, such as the greater use of informers by prosecutors, the growth of prison gangs, and the growth of the drug culture. Easier access to the courts by prisoners becomes another factor because it encourages prison managers to give the inmate the benefit of the doubt if the inmate claims to be in danger and wants protection. Though the staff may be skeptical, there is an anxious awareness that if a prisoner is denied the special protection he or she requests and then suffers a serious attack, prison management will probably be vulnerable if sued.[23]

Whereas such factors may help explain the growth of the problem in general, they do not help to account for the substantial differences sometimes to be seen when different prisons have quite different levels of PC populations. Some speculate that the PC cases will be fewer in a prison with overall good management, adequate and well-trained staff, and a variety of work, education, and recreation programs. Architecture may also play an important part; massive cell blocks, for instance, make the living situation more impersonal and increase the vulnerability of an inmate by exposing him constantly to several hundred other inmates. More specifically, it may offer too many opportunities for hidden activity, especially in the older prisons with various building additions that are placed without regard to the need for line-of-sight supervision. A frequent site for inmate attacks is any congregate shower room placed where it is not readily observable, and where the victim, nude, is caught at a serious disadvantage.

Architectural design is an important element in making a separate, protected unit for PC inmates successful. Older prisons with no housing space designed for the purpose have had serious difficulty in handling this special class of inmates efficiently. Too often, one cell block has had to be used entirely for PC men, keeping it locked and off limits to other inmates. But that also means that the PC unit has no recreation area outside, for there usually is not enough space available for duplicate recreation areas. Likewise, there is no duplicate space or staff for any of the other program elements. With no separate dining room, meals for PC inmates have to be taken to their cell areas, with the food perhaps being cold when it arrives. Although many institutions are now trying to set up work, study, and recreation opportunities in PC units, a high proportion of these inmates have simply been stored in locked cell blocks with no activity of any kind, a condition that closely approximates being in disciplinary segregation. A further irony and unfairness is that the predator inmate, from whom a potential victim has to be protected, remains in the general population, able to use any of the program elements, while the potential victim must be deprived of the program opportunities he is supposed to have. Nevertheless, current standards demand that as far as possible the PC units must have recreational space commensurate with that used by the general prison population, or else should use at a separate time the same facilities serving the other prisoners.[24]

Although counselors on a prison staff occasionally succeed in finding a way to protect a prisoner without placement in PC, it is a difficult and most uncertain process. Often the inmate fears to name the prisoner who is a threat to him or her. This places the staff in the untenable position of making a PC placement on an unverified basis, with the worrisome possibility that the requesting inmate is not in danger, but is instead a "hit man," seeking access to an intended victim in PC.[25] This point underscores the enduring savagery of the prison culture in relation to any prisoner who is even suspected of "informing." Once a prisoner has entered the PC unit, even briefly, other inmates are likely to assume that the prisoner has been informing, and that is enough to put the prisoner in serious jeopardy. The resultant problem of getting inmates out of PC was expressed by prisoners who were queried in the course of a study of such units. "Inmates were then asked what would have to change before they would request to return to general population. By far the most common answer was that they would not return, period! The next most frequent answer was that certain inmate(s) must be out of the general population before they would return."[26]

To a limited extent this type of threat can be countered by transferring a potential victim to another institution, and separating the inmate from the enemy. Sometimes it will work, but more often than not the transfer is not a solution; the prisoner "grapevine" is efficient and word of the transfer quickly gets to the receiving institution, where usually some inmate is willing to carry out the reprisal.

The Conjugal Visit

An idea often discussed but seldom implemented is the conjugal visit. This is an issue that puts a rational concern about family values and sexuality in direct conflict with fundamental political concerns, and the political factor usually prevails. Advocates of a conjugal visit policy argue that sexual activity always exists in a prison, but that, in the absence of heterosexual opportunity, it becomes predatory homosexual activity. Opponents argue that the conjugal visit does little to solve the problem because it serves only the married inmates, leaving out the greater number who have no viable marriage at the time, and thus giving the privilege to only a fortunate few. A more telling argument against conjugal visiting is the political reality that the public is likely to oppose the practice as contrary to the punitive intent of prisons.

In the United States three states—Mississippi, California, and New York—currently allow conjugal visits, with some significant differences among them in the factors that shaped the practice and enabled it to be adopted. Mississippi has the oldest program and it serves as as good example of how public policy sometimes emerges as a fait accompli resulting from an unchallenged informal practice. The Mississippi penitentiary at Parchman is an enormous plantation with a number of separate prison camps scattered about on its more than twenty thousand acres.

Until the 1960s the prisoners were racially segregated and the captains in charge of the separate camps had wide latitude in what they might decide to do in managing their prisoners. They began, apparently about 1915, to allow any well-behaved prisoner to seek a secluded corner for brief intimacy with his visiting wife or girlfriend. For its first many years this practice was followed only in the camps for black prisoners; gradually, without written policy or any official notice taken by government officials, it settled into a regularly accepted status. (Hopper 1969, 52–53) The development was so low key and informal that the general corrections field was mostly unaware of it.

Eventually the conjugal visit privilege was extended to white men and by 1970 it had been granted also to women. It finally achieved the status of official policy, in effect, when the state appropriated funds for the construction of buildings for the private visits; until then, the private visits took place in small shacks built by the prisoners from salvaged materials.

Using a different approach, California instituted a "family visiting" program on a trial basis in one prison in 1968 and later let it spread to the other prisons in the system. Using former bachelor officers' quarters, or even trailers brought to the grounds, inmates are granted weekend visits with their families. The policy allows the inmate's spouse and children to come for the two days and two nights of the visit, having complete privacy, preparing their own food, and spending their time together as they wish. Nor is it just the spouse who may visit; a prisoner may have the weekend visit with parents, brothers, sisters, or others in the family, and the visits may be scheduled with a frequency related mainly to the availability of the visiting quarters. Security is not a problem as the facilities used for the visits are apart from the areas in use by other inmates, but on the grounds within the security perimeter. Since an inmate must be free of any recent disciplinary actions to be eligible, the visits serve as an effective incentive to good behavior. The California policy was closely copied in 1976 by the New York State correctional system when it inaugurated its Family Reunion Program, now operating in eleven of its prisons.

In both California and New York, the correctional systems protect the political acceptability of the programs by downplaying the sexual aspect of the visits, and directing attention instead toward the importance of strengthening family ties. The distinction seems to have forestalled the public opposition that is likely to thwart initiation of such a policy. Other states and the federal prison system have not attempted the conjugal visit plan, however, sometimes arguing in favor of granting furloughs to qualified prisoners as a less obvious way to permit sexual satisfaction. Others note that furloughs are not enough, as they are available to an almost negligible number of inmates. Whatever the best approach, it is apparent that for the great majority of prisoners, satisfaction of sexual needs remains incompatible with prison management in the context of present social and political mores.

The Origins and Character of Riots

A conservative public viewpoint of the management of prisoners favors minimal privileges, tight controls, and the expectation that prisoners are to do as ordered without argument or the right of protest. A more practical view from experienced prison managers usually shows awareness that such an intransigent attitude may be a prescription for riot, or at least for chronic and dangerous unrest. The safety of a prison depends on a fragile equilibrium between the conflicting interests of the two groups, staff and inmates, and the protection of that equilibrium requires skilled management with keen understanding of the limited capacity of the custodians to achieve control just by blunt force.

In any prison the inmates heavily outnumber the correctional officers, and many long-term prisoners know the prison routines so well that they are even in a position to give instruction to new officers. Except in the few heavily staffed and specialized last resort prisons, some degree of cooperation from the prisoners is essential. Forceful physical controls alone are not effective, or even safe. As one observer has expressed it, "the use of force is actually grossly inefficient as a means for securing obedience, particularly when those who are to be controlled are called on to perform a task of any complexity. A blow with a club may check an immediate revolt, it is true, but it cannot assure effective performance on a punch-press. A 'come-along,' a straitjacket or a pair of handcuffs may serve to curb one rebellious prisoner in a crisis, but they will be of little aid in moving more than 1200 inmates through the mess hall in a routine and orderly fashion." (Sykes 1958, 49)

Whereas legislators prescribe prison sentences for crime, and prison managers maintain security in their prisons with the necessary surveillance and enforcement of rules, both legislators and wardens must know the peril of forgetting that even prisoners are human in their need for a degree of self-esteem and in their resentment of humiliating or unfair treatment. This is not a matter of coddling prisoners; this is a matter of recognizing the practical necessity of treating people with consideration and fairness. Nor is it a matter of being lenient in application of control and disciplinary measures. Prisoners appreciate a prison under firmly safe control. One of the relevant conclusions reached in one study of riots was that, "where administrators and guards are powerful, unified and competent, the conditions of imprisonment themselves seem more legitimate; the captors are seen as authoritative rather than merely powerful.'' (Useem and Kimball 1989, 219)

The qualities of consideration and fairness are not incompatible with administration by a strong, resolute, and unified staff. If considerate treatment cannot be given out of simple concern for basic principles of decency, it can certainly be justified as a matter of self-serving public economy. A riot can cost the taxpayers millions of dollars for repair or replacement of prison buildings, and for settlement of resultant civil suits. The major riot at the Jackson, Michigan, prison in 1952 caused a death, many injuries, and $3 million worth of damage. Among many more examples, a 1974 riot at the Oklahoma State Prison caused three deaths and $20 million worth of damage. Extremes in damage can be accomplished in only minutes of rioting, whereas a previous minor improvement in staff attitudes or a small increase in the budget for reasonable amenities might have been all the preventive action needed.[27]

Preventive Measures

Various researchers have studied the conditions leading to prison riots, and the conditions that seem to prevent them; their findings tend to be consistent and clear. Competent management is essential to safe prison operations, whereas uncommunicative, arbitrary, and indecisive management will have a dangerous, destabilizing effect. ''There are potentially three basic power groups within a correctional institution: administrative personnel, line personnel, and the inmate population. Discord between administrative and line personnel within a correctional institution . . . will diminish the effectiveness of treatment programs as well as increase the level of emotional stress and discontentment among the inmate population.'' (*Riots and Disturbances* 1970, 4) The obvious antidote is a crisp, consistent, and communicative style of management. In this case, the communicative efforts must be reciprocal. Top management must give clearly enunciated policy directives, along with rationale, to both staff and inmates, but management must also listen to the concerns of the rank and file. In addition, management must also listen to the concerns of inmates, taking care not to give staff reason to think that inmate feelings are given more weight than staff feelings.

Addressing the problem of inept management, one study notes that in the recent major riots ''the key factor has not been organization of the inmates but the disorganization of the state. The riot-prone system is characterized by certain ailments which, on the one hand, sap the ability of the state to contain disturbances and, on the other hand, convince the inmates that the imprisoning conditions are unjust.'' (Useem and Kimball 1989, 218)

The point is echoed in the official report of the Attica riot of 1971 in which more than eighty persons were injured, while thirty-two inmates and eleven staff members were killed. "Examined separately, many of the inadequacies and frustrations of inmate life may appear insignificant. But their cumulative impact created a dehumanizing environment. . . . In most ways life at Attica in 1971 was still based on . . . discarded theories of penology described. . . . But inmates reacted to the dated prison methods as contemporary men, and the resulting gulf between them and the imposed life style produced a setting in which frustrations and tensions flourished." (*Attica* 1972, 21)

A significant point in this connection is that no matter how much a person dislikes being in prison, typically he or she will not resent being in prison as much as the treatment in prison. This is a crucial distinction. Journalist Tom Wicker heard this point made by an Attica prisoner: "You take my case. In for armed robbery. All right, I did it. My lawyer tells me that as these things go, I got a fair trial and a fair sentence. . . . So we're even, right? I did it, I'm in here for doing it. Fair and square, no complaint. Paying my debt to The Man. But, brother, you got to understand that's just the way it *ought* to be, that's not the way it *is*. That Man is committing crimes against *me* every day I'm here." The prisoner described the constant atmosphere of intimidation, the unfairness, thefts, unnecessary deprivations, and the administrative indifference to it. All these gratuitous indignities went well beyond the punishment ordered by the court. Therein was the real cause of resentment and the lurking readiness to rebel. (Wicker 1975, 112–113)

With all that is known about how to forestall riots, and with all the improved management principles now practiced in prisons, the reality is that no prison can avoid and eliminate all of the aggravations that cumulatively lead prisoners to a rebellious mood. While there will always be some prisons that are more safely and competently managed than others, even in the best-managed prisons provocative and demeaning conditions or episodes will always exist. These need not provoke a disturbance, however, if managers regularly listen honestly to prisoners' questions and gripes, and respond promptly to them according to their merits.

Listening to and acting decisively on legitimate prisoner grievances is one of the most important measures for prevention of riots. Reinforcing this view is the finding that riots are much less likely to occur in prisons where the warden and other top management officials "circulate about the institution maintaining as much contact as possible with inmates and employees. This contact will serve to answer questions and relieve the anxieties and tensions of both the inmates and line employees." (*Riots and Disturbances* 1970, 7, 19) One warden's technique is to carry a pocket-sized tape recorder; when stopped and questioned by an inmate as he walks about the institution, he promises to check for the requested information upon returning to his office. In the inmate's presence, he uses the tape recorder to quickly dictate a reminder to himself of the question and the name of the inmate concerned. It should go without saying that promptly following through with the promised note to the inmate is essential. Even if the answer is not the one wanted, the inmate's receipt of an honest follow-up answer fosters a climate that contributes potently to institution stability, and the warden's responsiveness to staff inquiries is equally important. If this approach seems obvious, it should be noted that it is in remarkable contrast to what was common practice until recent years. American prisons had more than a century of experience with wardens who seldom went into the shops, yards, or cell blocks of their prisons and rarely allowed prisoners to speak to them directly.

How well do riots accomplish the goals of rioting prisoners who list their demands and finally release their hostages in return for promises from the government? The usual experience has not favored the inmates. A careful study of this question would show a wide variation in results, with the only semblance of a pattern being a tendency for the officials afterward to interpret the post-riot agreements to their own advantage. In fairness to the managers, however, it must be observed that a prison is a ponderous operation that is highly resistive to any quick-fix solutions, no matter how honest the intent of its warden. Even the most honorable and conscientious administrator will find that when the riot is over and the inmates are safely locked in their cells, the concessions made to get hostages released may be extremely difficult to implement. If the concessions depend on general staff cooperation, the warden may find this difficult to marshal when the officers are seething with resentment toward their prisoners. If the concessions depend on obtaining additional funding, the warden may find that the necessary public and legislative support is negated by lack of sympathy toward the rioters.

Examples are legion; a fairly typical one is found in the West Virginia experience following a state prison riot in 1986, when thirteen hostages were released and order was restored after inmates and the administration concurred on a several-point agreement. Days after the surrender, eighty-six of the inmates were punished with placement in segregation, despite the fact that one of the points agreed to in the negotiation was that "there will be no retaliation as a result of resident takeover of the institution." But the specific meaning of that phrase had been left undefined. "Furious, inmates saw the state's actions as a blatant and dishonorable violation of the 'no retaliation' pledge. The governor saw it differently; in his view, the promise meant only that the inmates 'would be secure in their body and person.' " (Useem and Kimball 1989, 191, 196)

Formalizing the Grievance Procedure

A growing number of civil suits against prison managements, punctuated by prison riots in the early 1970s, heightened interest in designing ways to deal with prisoner complaints before they lead to rebellions. One result was the development of formal prisoner grievance procedures. In the past, prison inmates were virtually without rights, and managers held arbitrary powers to punish. But this began to change slowly after a landmark federal court ruling in 1944 stated the then radical principle that "a prisoner retains all the rights of an ordinary citizen except those expressly, or by necessary implication taken from him by law."[28] When the Attica riot erupted in 1971 it generated new interest throughout the corrections field in possible remedial measures. In New York State, "one positive result of the devastating violence at that institution was state legislative budgetary approval of a departmental investigative staff to seek out inmate complaints and try to resolve them prior to their reaching crisis proportions."[29] That was a first step in developing a way of listening to prisoners.

With fresh and painful experiences of riot suppression, and with the hope of addressing complaints *before* they become critical, corrections experts by the mid-1970s had fashioned designs for formal and responsive disciplinary and grievance procedures. Grievance hearings are not the same as disciplinary hearings, but a close similarity exists in the principles involved. When courts gave attention to prison disciplinary matters and began to define principles to be followed, many prison managers, as well as line staff, protested that courts were siding with inmates and weakening the authority of prison management. The court-prescribed rules, however, defined only basic principles of fairness. In a key legal case in Virginia, a class action suit charged a list of management failures in the prison and particularly complained of prisoners receiving arbitrary punishments for vaguely defined offenses while having no adequate privilege of defense. The court specified that an inmate may be charged with misbehavior only if it was a violation of a written rule of which the inmate had been informed. Also, the prisoner must be informed of the charges against him or her, must have a reasonable time to prepare his or her defense, must be allowed a formal hearing, and the punishment must be limited to the penalties previously defined and published.[30]

This case addressed a problem that was prevalent throughout the correctional systems; subsequently, correctional agencies have formulated grievance procedures that permit prisoners a guaranteed way to protest any act or situation that they consider improper or unfair. The details vary from state to state, but the basic principles are common to all. To take one typical example, the prison designates one staff person as a "special counselor," and the inmate with a complaint first talks with this counselor to see if the problem can be resolved informally. If not, the next step is to present a written complaint to an institutional inquiry board, which holds a hearing and is required to respond with a written reply within ten days. The board's finding is considered by the warden, who renders a decision; if the inmate is still dissatisfied a final appeal can be made to a review board of three members, one of whom must be a layperson from the general community.[31]

The Prison as Punishment: A Blunt Instrument

Playwright George Bernard Shaw, who once took a close look at the prison problem, commented that "our prison system is a horrible accidental growth and not a deliberate human invention, and its worst features have been produced with the intention, not of making it worse, but of making it better."[32]

Shaw can be accused of being too sweeping in his criticism of prisons, but his statement is thoughtful and accurate in noting that often society's hopeful strategy for making punishment more corrective and more protective of public safety has instead proved to be counterproductive. The problem started with the original prisons, which were conceived as a means to sequester wayward persons in prolonged isolation where they could meditate on their sins and become penitent. Instead, isolation produced anger, resentment, and often mental unbalance. Still today, the unnatural world of prison life corrupts many of the people whom it was meant to reform; the exigencies of institutional operation often frustrate and even reverse the well-intended strategies of prisoner control.

In considering what the prospects may be for remediation of imprisonment practices, there is good news and bad news. The good news is that we know how to correct criminal behavior in many cases, and how to run safe and more constructive penal institutions. The bad news is that we have not yet found effective ways of using this knowledge within the political context that necessarily supports and shapes the correctional systems. The continuing quest for improvement of the penal systems is confused and often diverted by the emotional, rather than rational, demands from the public. And yet, a broad perspective on the historic trends in this field of public concern shows a gradual and persistent progress that encourages hope for the future. In the two subsequent chapters some indicators of this progress should become apparent.

Notes

1. John Irwin. *Prisons in Turmoil.* Boston: Little, Brown and Co., 1980, 4.
2. Charles B. DeWitt. "New Construction Methods for Correctional Facilities." *Construction Bulletin* (March 1986), 5.

178 *The Prisons*

3. For a detailed discussion of the concept and functioning of the method, see "Unit Management: Implementing a Different Correctional Approach," by Douglas Lansing, Joseph B. Bogan, and Loren Karacki in *Federal Probation* 41:1 (March 1977), 43–49.
4. *Wall Street Journal* (Aug. 18, 1981), 21.
5. *Washington Post National Weekly Edition* (March 9–15, 1982), 21.
6. *Design Guide for Secure Adult Correctional Facilities*. College Park, Md.: American Correctional Association, 1983, 51.
7. Chapman v. Rhodes, 434 F.Supp. 1007 (S.D. Ohio 1977).
8. Among the many articles on the effects of prison overcrowding, one useful government publication is an undated monograph from the Department of Justice, National Institute of Justice, *The Effect of Prison Crowding on Inmate Behavior*. Another that is thorough in its coverage of the subject and in supplying an excellent bibliography is "Prison Overcrowding: The Case of New Jersey," by Edward W. Sieh, *Federal Probation* 53:3 (Sept. 1989), 41–51.
9. Bureau of Justice Statistics. *Special Report. Women in Prison* (1994), 1.
10. National Council on Crime and Delinquency. *Women's Prisons: Overcrowded and Overused*. San Francisco: 1992, 3, 4.
11. Canterino v. Wilson, 562 F.Supp. 106, W.D. Ky. 1983; and 644 F.Supp., W.D. Ky. 1986.
12. For a discussion of the various legal cases and arguments, see a law review article, "Babies behind Bars: Should Incarcerated Mothers Be Allowed to Keep Their Newborns with Them in Prison?" by Donna L. Brodie. *University of Richmond Law Review* 16:3 (Spring 1982), 677–692.
13. From an unpublished monograph, "Prisons and Kids," by James Boudouris, Iowa Department of Social Services (1983), i.
14. Charles F. Campbell. "Co-corrections: FCI Fort Worth after Three Years." Chapter 3 in Smykla 1980 (below), 88.
15. In addition to updated information supplied by a letter dated May 9, 1994, to the author from the Denmark Ministry of Justice, the information on Ringe comes from an article, "The State Prison at Ringe: Europe's Most Radical Corrections Experiment," by Michael Serrill. *Corrections Magazine* 3:1 (March 1977), 30–35.
16. Al Gore. *From Red Tape to Results: Creating a Government That Works Better and Costs Less*. Report of the National Performance Review (Sept. 7, 1993), Appendix C, 165.
17. For a thorough description of the experience with a particularly competent program of the sort, see Cormier 1975 (below).
18. For an in-depth discussion of the regimes at both Alcatraz and Marion, see chapter 9 in Keve 1991 (below).
19. Madrid v. Gomez, U.S. District Court, No. Dist. Calif., C-90-3094 TEH.
20. Hans Toch. "Classification for Programming and Survival." Chapter 4 in Ward and Schoen 1981, 41 (below).
21. David A. Ward and Annesley K. Schmidt. "Last Resort Prisons for Habitual and Dangerous Offenders: Some Second Thoughts about Alcatraz." Chapter 6 in Ward and Schoen 1981, 67 (below).

22. David C. Anderson. "The Price of Safety: I Can't Go Back Out There." *Corrections Magazine* 6:4 (Aug. 1980), 8.
23. *Protective Custody in Adult Correctional Facilities: A Discussion of Causes, Conditions, Attitudes and Alternatives.* College Park, Md.: American Correctional Association, 1983, 9.
24. Ibid., 47.
25. James D. Henderson. *Protective Custody Management in Adult Correctional Facilities: A Discussion of Causes, Conditions, Attitudes, and Alternatives.* Laurel, Md.: American Correctional Association, 1991, 22.
26. *Protective Custody in Adult Correctional Facilities: A Discussion of Causes, Conditions, Attitudes and Alternatives.* College Park, Md.: American Correctional Association, 1983, 29.
27. For detailed accounts of specific prison riots and their causes, see the reports below on Attica, 1972, and New Mexico, 1980. For an instructive discussion of a North Carolina riot, see Paul W. Keve, *Prison Life and Human Worth,* Minneapolis: University of Minnesota Press, 1974, 70–72. For a detailed listing of prison riots between 1900 and 1971, see *Collective Violence in Correctional Institutions: A Search for Causes.* Columbia: South Carolina Department of Corrections, 1973.
28. Coffin v. Reichard, 143 F2d, 443.
29. *Inmate Grievance Procedures.* Columbia: South Carolina Department of Corrections, Collective Violence Research Project, 1973, 8.
30. Landman v. Royster, 333 F.Supp. 621 (E.D. Va. 1971).
31. U.S. Department of Justice. Law Enforcement Assistance Administration. *Prescriptive Package: Grievance Mechanisms in Correctional Institutions.* Washington, D.C.: 1975, 39.
32. George Bernard Shaw. *The Crime of Punishment.* New York: Greenwood, 1946 (reprint), 104.

Bibliography

Prison as the Basic Criminal Punishment

Bowker, Lee H. *Prison Victimization.* New York: Elsevier, 1980.
Design Guide for Secure Adult Correctional Facilities. College Park, Md.: American Correctional Association, 1983.
Goffman, Erving. *Asylums.* New York: Anchor Books, 1961.
 An outstanding contribution to an understanding of the special characteristics of any institution, including prisons and mental hospitals. Goffman usefully reveals the ways that institutions become blind to the human feelings of their inmates and consequently defeat their own remedial purposes.
Jacobs, James B. *New Perspectives on Prisons and Imprisonment.* Ithaca, N.Y.: Cornell University Press, 1983.
Jacobs, James B. *Stateville: The Penitentiary in Mass Society.* Chicago: University of Chicago Press, 1977.

Johnson, Robert. *Hard Time: Understanding and Reforming the Prison.* Monterey, Calif.: Brooks/Cole, 1987.

An analytical discussion of the prison culture, as affecting both inmates and staff. It is presented mainly from the personal views of affected individuals.
Keve, Paul W. *Prison Life and Human Worth.* Minneapolis: University of Minnesota Press, 1974.
Lockwood, Daniel. *Prison Sexual Violence.* New York: Elsevier, 1980.

A report of interviews with many sexual aggressors and victims in New York prisons. It presents useful insights on prisoner attitudes about aggression, told mainly through specific case histories and quoted prisoner comments.
McGee, Richard A. *Prisons and Politics.* Lexington, Mass.: Lexington Books, 1981.

A well-known and respected former corrections administrator (in New York and California) discusses the many aspects of operating a prison system within the challenges and constraints of the usual political context. It is a practical, realistic, and rational review of how to deal effectively with legislators and the public.
McKelvey, Blake. *American Prisons: A History of Good Intentions.* Montclair, N.J.: Patterson Smith, 1977.

A noted historian's overview of corrections history; generally recognized as the most authoritative and comprehensive work on the subject.
Nagel, William G. *The New Red Barn.* New York: Walker & Co. for American Institute of Corrections, 1973.

A roundup of information on historical and contemporary prisons in the United States, focusing on their architecture as it affects operations. It also covers many aspects of prison management, including educational and treatment programs. Well-illustrated, and a useful supplement to a companion book by Norman Johnston, *The Human Cage: A Brief History of Prison Architecture.* New York: Walker & Co. for the American Foundation, 1973.
Smykla, John Ortiz, ed. *Coed Prison.* New York: Human Sciences Press, 1980.

A series of competent articles that examine the experience with co-correctional prisons, including opposing viewpoints.
Sommer, Robert. *The End of Imprisonment.* New York: Oxford University Press, 1976.
Sommer, Robert. *Tight Spaces: Hard Architecture and How to Humanize It.* Englewood Cliffs, N.J.: Prentice-Hall, 1974.

A skilled assessment of the psychological effects of the immediate environment on confined people, exploring the ways in which the prison setting in general, and its architecture in particular, affect behavior. More broadly, the book also looks at the same architectural effects in zoos, airports, and mental hospitals.

Modern Management Issues

Attica: The Official Report of the New York State Special Commission on Attica. New York: Bantam Books, 1972.

Cormier, Bruno M. *The Watcher and the Watched.* Montreal: Tundra Books, 1975.

A psychiatrist's readable and instructive account of one impressive experience with the introduction into a maximum-security prison of a therapeutic treatment program for high-risk prisoners.

Garsons, G. David. "The Disruption of Prison Administration: An Investigation of Alternative Theories of the Relationship among Administrators, Reformers, and Involuntary Social Service Clients." *Law and Society Review* 6:4 (May 1972), 531–562.

A resource for any study of the history of prison riots, this article reviews a selected but considerable number of riots that have occurred over more than a century, and discusses their causes and effects.

Hopper, Columbus B. *Sex in Prison: The Mississippi Experiment with Conjugal Visiting.* Baton Rouge: Louisiana State University Press, 1969.

Though dated, this book remains the most useful source of information about the unique conjugal visit practice in the Mississippi prison at Parchman. It discusses the general problem of prison sexual practices, and recounts the history of the Parchman conjugal visiting, its operational character, its racist origins, and the viewpoints of inmates, their families, and others regarding the value of conjugal visits.

Keve, Paul W. *Prisons and the American Conscience, a History of U.S. Federal Corrections.* Carbondale: Southern Illinois University Press, 1991.

Morris, Norval. *The Future of Imprisonment.* Chicago: University of Chicago Press, 1974.

A particularly astute discussion of the rationale for imprisonment as punishment for crime. It includes a detailed concept of how a prison for seriously difficult prisoners should be designed and operated, a plan that was adapted in designing one new federal prison, Butner, for special problem prisoners.

New Mexico. Office of the Attorney General. *Report of the Attorney General on the February 2 and 3, 1980 Riot at the Penitentiary of New Mexico.* Santa Fe: 1980.

Riots and Disturbances in Correctional Institutions. Washington, D.C.: American Correctional Association, 1970.

Sherman, Michael and Gordon Hawkins. *Imprisonment in America: Choosing the Future.* Chicago: University of Chicago Press, 1981.

Sykes, Gresham M. *The Society of Captives: A Study of a Maximum Security Prison.* Princeton, N.J.: Princeton University Press, 1958.

A classic that retains its value as an insightful picture of prison life and the ways that prisoners and staffs must compromise with each other. Much of the book is concerned with analysis of a riot at the New Jersey prison at Trenton, but its perspective is much more broad and is relevant to prisons generally.

Useem, Bert and Peter Kimball. *States of Siege: U.S. Prison Riots, 1971–1986.* New York: Oxford University Press, 1989.

A perceptive discussion and analysis of several prison riots and their significance in revealing the problems in operating prisons.

Ward, David A. and Kenneth F. Schoen. *Confinement in Maximum Custody.* Lexington, Mass.: Lexington Books, 1981.

A series of conference papers on the subject of last resort prisons. Topics covered include legal issues, social and psychological effects of close confinement, classification and identification of disruptive prisoners, and research techniques in this subject area.

Wicker, Tom. *A Time to Die.* New York: Quadrangle/The New York Times Book Co., 1975.

A journalist's account of his experience at the 1971 riot at the Attica Correctional Facility, New York.

CHAPTER 8

Probation and Parole

T he figures make clear the importance of the probation and parole systems in this country; during 1990 "State and Federal agencies reported that 2,670,234 adult offenders were on probation and 531,407 were on parole—an estimated 1.7% of all adults in the United States. The number of men on probation or parole was about 3% of all adult males."[1] This means that offenders on probation or parole outnumber those in prisons or jails. This chapter, after defining the two terms, will discuss the techniques involved in probation and parole, the variations in methods, and the strengths and weaknesses of these community-based corrections strategies.

The definitions will show minor variations as specified in the many federal and state laws, sometimes even in county or city jurisdictions. But as generally understood, probation is the legal status of an offender who, after being convicted of a crime, has been directed by the sentencing court to remain in the community under supervision of a probation service for a designated period of time and subject to certain conditions imposed by the court or by law. The most usual legal procedure is for the court to sentence the offender to a period of incarceration, with this sentence then suspended on condition that the offender complies with the rules of probation. As one variation, sometimes the court leaves the sentence unstated, reserving the right to pronounce and impose a sentence if future misconduct makes revocation of probation necessary. In either case the possibility that the probation status can be revoked and the sentence to incarceration imposed is the leverage backing up the probation service in its supervision of the probationer.

Parole is similar in that it too consists of an offender living in the community under supervision. By contrast with the probationer who remains in the community in lieu of prison, the parolee has been to prison and served some part of the sentence, then is released by the paroling authority on condition that he or she comply with parole rules, which will usually be almost the same as those for probationers. For failure to remain law-abiding, the parolee can be returned to serve the remainder of his or her prison time by action of the authority which released the parolee.

Administration of Probation

The practice of probation first appeared and was gradually developed through the latter half of the 1800s in Massachusetts. By the first decade of the twentieth century, probation was being defined and authorized in the statutes of many states, though it was mid-century before it had permeated all criminal justice jurisdictions.

Unlike many of the smaller countries where probation and parole services are provided under a single federal agency (the Home Office in Great Britain, for example), probation and parole services in the United States are fragmented, and serve separate federal, state, and local jurisdictions. Sometimes probation is a statewide service delivered by a state agency. In other states (e.g., Minnesota) one or more populous cities or counties early in the century may have created their own probation services, whereas outlying areas were served by a state agency that was established later. This leaves a mix of state and local services that may be awkward, and no longer appropriate, but difficult to change. (Cromwell et al. 1985, 97–100) Where state systems exist, they are varied in the way the different services are combined, and across the country state legislatures reorganize their criminal justice services as they seek improved efficiency.

An Array of Combinations

Historically, most juvenile services were first organized under the juvenile courts, with the probation officers being responsible to the judge or judges. This has meant that the judiciary, though intended to be separate from the executive branch of government, is forced to assume an executive function. Often state or local social service agencies, particularly in densely populated jurisdictions, administer the probation services. In some states juvenile correctional services, including probation, have been combined within the departments administering welfare, and sometimes even with the mental health services. The variety of administrative arrangements is shown in a compendium of such services released in 1987. It listed the District of Columbia and twenty-two states as having juvenile probation services under either state or local judicial administration. In another fourteen states they were under state or local executive agencies, and the remaining fourteen states used various combinations of these.[2]

Juvenile correctional institutions release their inmates to "aftercare" rather than "parole," and in a high percentage of states the release decision is not made by a separate board, as in adult parole, but by designated members of the institution staffs. In a marked change from the informal approach that typified this function for many decades, modern standards call for a structured procedure with a concern for due process; for example, "The criteria which are employed by the releasing authority in its decision-making are available in written form and are specific enough to permit consistent application to individual cases."[3] On being released to aftercare status, juveniles may return to supervision by the probation offices, but in more than forty states this supervision is given by state agencies.

Although not the most common arrangement, sometimes the same agency serves both adult and juvenile cases. Some states, and the federal government, handle both adult probation and parole in the same agency; some states administer them separately. Some probation services, in such places as New York, Los Angeles, Chicago, or Philadelphia, are organized at the county or city level, and yet are larger than the usual state level agencies elsewhere. Parole, however, is almost always a state responsibility.

Some municipal courts have probation services, although at this level the work is likely to be less than full service (larger caseloads and perhaps no presentence investigations) due to the high volume of cases and the general notion that misdemeanants are less in need of service than felons. For many years, at several governmental levels the quality of probation services suffered from the jobs being subject to political patronage. In many jurisdictions, appointments and tenure of probation officers depended on the favor of the political party in power, which invariably meant that political activity weighed more heavily than professional qualifications in getting and holding the job. (Rothman 1980, 85) Fortunately, a general move toward professional quality during the last two decades has taken most probation departments out of the patronage practice.

Probation Functions: The Presentence Investigation

From early in its history the probation concept has included the view that since the sentencing court has the option of committing a defendant to prison or placing him or her on probation, it is important, if not essential, for that decision to be based on detailed knowledge about him or her as an individual. This diagnostic aspect of the probation officer's function was given major impetus early in this century by the writings of William Healy, a noted Chicago psychiatrist.[4] His detailed studies of the pathology of criminal types influenced the development of the probation officers' standard diagnostic instrument, the presentence investigation (PSI), and its product, the presentence report.

Although the diagnostic (investigative) function has long been a standard feature of probation work, practice has always varied widely among agencies in the format, focus, purpose, and general quality of the reports. In all probation offices, for instance, the investigating probation officer seeks information about the defendant's present offense and prior criminal record, but different courts or probation offices will have different ideas on how to present it. One style will be simply to copy a police or FBI report verbatim into the presentence report, letting the judge read and assess it without evaluative comment from the probation oficer. Another practice will be for the probation officer to prepare his or her own narrative about the offense and prior arrests, along with evaluative comment, pointing up significant aspects of the record. These practices reflect philosophical differences that are considered important by many practitioners, and similar differences may appear in other sections of the report.

In conducting a typical presentence investigation, the probation officer will interview the defendant to obtain his or her version of the offense and important data about the defendant's personal history. The probation officer also will contact law enforcement agencies, and subject to individual case differences, is likely to contact many others such as the defendant's family members, neighbors, employers, complainants, teachers, and friends. The resulting report will be a typewritten account containing case information on topical areas such as current offense, prior record, family history, education, employment history, psychological or psychiatric information, physical and mental health, residence, and financial condition.

Adapting the PSI to Current Demands

The last two decades have seen a trend toward brevity and a somewhat more mechanistic, less evaluative style of report. The increasing volume of cases and the new tendency to favor punishment as a key factor in sentencing have pressured probation managers to prepare reports quickly, even to the extent of just checking boxes on a form, rather than preparing extensive narrative material.[5] The shift toward more emphasis on punishment has raised the question of how much information a judge needs to impose an appropriate punishment sentence. ''The consequence of this question was that a number of jurisdictions embarked on a road of developing 'short form' PSIs. That is, probation officers, according to guidelines, completed reports that were shorter than usual, especially for designated kinds of cases, based on the instant offense."[6] Although it is risky to generalize, it seems safe to say that presentence reports now tend to give less attention to the personal, social history of the defendant, and put more emphasis on the factual elements of the offense and prior criminal record.

Those who must write these reports and those who read and use them tend to regret the trend toward brevity and the obviously reduced value of the product. The report is important not only to the sentencing judge, but also to the probation officer who must plan the handling of the probation case, or to the staff at the penal institution that receives the otherwise unknown new prisoner.

Not all, but many of the probation agencies will conclude the presentence report with a section presenting a recommended sentence for the court to consider. How this section is used becomes an individual matter, as some judges resist having anyone seem to be telling them what to do. Other judges, however, expect to receive these recommendations and consider them seriously. A new aspect of this issue has emerged in recent years as sentencing guidelines have taken hold. In the federal court system the disposition of a criminal case is derived from a specified set of factors defined in the guidelines and related to the individual offender's personal situation as well as his or her criminal record and current offense, as noted in chapter 4. The calculation of the proper sentence can be somewhat intricate, and this is the responsibility of the probation officer. Accordingly, the federal probation officer does not just recommend a sentence, but actually provides the judge with the sentence that is to be imposed.[7]

All courts recognize the basic principle that it is unacceptable to start the presentence investigation until the defendant has been convicted. Sometimes it is tempting to expedite the process by having the work done during the long wait for the case to come to trial, and in a few situations this happens. However, legal propriety demands that the defendant's privacy be protected from this investigative process until and unless he or she has been tried and convicted. This is not just a philosophical concept. The probation officer's inquiries into the defendant's offense and details of the defendant's personal life will compromise his or her rights if the defendant has not yet been convicted. (McCarthy and McCarthy 1991, 109) It also will prevent the officer from obtaining all facts about the offense, as the defendant must not be required to incriminate himself or herself before being tried. (Cromwell et al. 1985, 53)

Those probation offices serving the juvenile courts also prepare investigative reports in cases before the court, but, with the special terminology characteristic of juvenile courts, these reports are likely to have other titles such as social histories or prehearing reports. A troubling aspect of confidentiality policy, and an issue on which some ambivalence exists in the corrections field, concerns the question of whether to allow these reports in juvenile cases to be made available later to adult probation offices. As a practical matter it makes sense for the juvenile record to be known and considered if and when the subject person comes to court as a young adult, especially if the juvenile record is extensive and recent. Countering this view is the juvenile court philosophy holding that the misbehavior of a child should not be allowed to handicap the offender when he or she becomes an adult. Accordingly, the policy in most juvenile courts is that the juvenile record is held confidential and not shared with adult probation agencies. Actual practice tends to be spotty. For instance, where a local probation office combines both adult and juvenile services in the same agency it is likely that probation officer colleagues will share case information with each other freely. Where the services are separate the juvenile agencies are likely to stick to orthodox policy on confidentiality of the juvenile records, but the adult probation officers will likely find that they can learn about the juvenile record simply by questioning the defendant. One researcher who studied the practices countrywide found that "information sharing practices are so varied between juvenile and adult courts that few generalizations can be made. . . . information sharing is primarily the result of local policy, subject to the whims of the police, prosecutor, and probation officer."[8]

Another controversial aspect of confidentiality is the question of whether the defendant (adult or juvenile) should be allowed to see the report. For more than half a century it had been the unchallenged policy countrywide for presentence reports, before the trial, to be available only to the sentencing judge. After disposition of the case, the reports were usually supplied—in case of institutional commitment—to the receiving correctional institution, but still not to the offender. By the 1960s, with new attention being given to the rights of offenders, a radical revision of this position took hold as probation services began to recognize that there were reasonable arguments in favor of disclosing the report to the defendant.

Probation workers had always feared that a policy of sharing the report with the defendant would cut off sources of the needed information, for persons being interviewed would decline to discuss the case if it were known that the subject person could learn who had talked about him. But spurred by some court cases dealing with the principle, a new appreciation of the value of honesty in dealing with all criminal justice clients developed and led some probation offices to alter the policy. Contrary to the fears, the disclosure practice has not dried up information sources to any serious extent. Consequently, the field has made a general shift to disclosure policies, which at their most conservative, may allow the prosecuting and defense attorneys to read the report, and at their most liberal, will give a copy of the report to the defendant to keep and may even place the report in the public record. (Cromwell et al. 1985, 53–55) Most jurisdictions have learned to live comfortably with the disclosure practice; many agree that the defendant after all should have the right to see and challenge a report that may substantially affect the defendant's freedom. A fortunate side effect is that because the probation officer knows the report will be shared, the officer is encouraged to be more careful and responsible in its preparation.

The Supervisory Function: The Search for Its Proper Mission

The second of the two main functions of the probation officer is the responsibility of supervising those offenders placed on probation. As a public service, this presents the challenge of deciding what is the goal or mission of this work? For much of its history the probation field has not had a clear concept of its mission, and indeed for much of the time its practitioners have not shown much awareness that they needed a guiding philosophy. Worse, the judges to whom the probation officers are responsible for the supervision of probationers have themselves been so divided in their views on this question that the effect has been to leave the field without any definitive standard.

For many decades probation services generally saw their task as being somehow to make over the probationer into a person who not only would obey the law, but also would accord with standard middle-class habits and attitudes. With varying approaches from one jurisdiction to another, judges and probation officers together decreed conditions of probation that sometimes had little to do with illegal behavior. Probationers were required to attend church, to change their style of clothing, to get permission before making any change such as getting married, getting divorced, going on a trip, moving to a new address, and so on. Even probationers who had never had any problem with drinking were forbidden to have so much as a bottle of beer. Especially with juvenile probationers, rules often required attendance at Sunday school, writing essays on patriotic duty, memorizing the Ten Commandments, and in some cases keeping to a prescribed style of haircut.[9]

The enforcement of these behaviors would be attempted with whatever measures came most naturally to the individual officer: counseling, blustery warnings, scolding, or big brotherlike assistance with any or all kinds of personal problems. Virtually everywhere in the probation field the standard means of reaching the client has been to require him or her to "report" regularly. That is, the probationer has been ordered to come to the probation office for a brief contact with the officer periodically—perhaps once a month, sometimes as often as weekly. Unfortunately, this practice, when conducted by officers with little or no professional training, has all too often been only empty ceremony, a fact that probationers quickly perceive, whether or not the probation officers do. Here then is the most salient evidence of the lack of a clearly conceived, legally sound philosophy or mission. After half a century or more of operating without a concept of mission, there has been in recent years an encouraging discovery of the philosophical principles that are properly basic to community correctional programs. In formulating such principles it has been necessary to resolve the question of whether the probation officer is a policeman or a rehabilitation counselor, and the question of how to deal with the field's greatest handicap, gross overloads of cases.

The Supervisory Function: Control or Treatment

Courts and their probation offices long persisted in believing that supervision of probationers, however it may be approached, should protect public safety by somehow promoting an improvement in general attitudes and living skills of the probationer. Whereas the probation officer might often function as a sort of specialized police officer who keeps surveillance on the probationer, this was only part of a broader rehabilitative effort. For a long time it was not fully realized that although improvement in the client's general social functioning is a worthy goal, there is good reason to argue against forcing any therapeutic counseling. An influential discussion of this issue was published in 1960 by a criminal justice professor who disturbed many in probation work with the flat statement that "the function of the probation officer is to help the offender comply with the order of the court. Period."[10] The author fully supported any rehabilitative assistance given to an interested and receptive probationer; he objected only to the forced imposition of treatment measures on an unwilling client. With his persuasive criticism of coercion to remold clients into the prevailing middle-class image, the author hastened the trend toward the new and more honest concept that as long as a probationer obeys the law he or she has a right to his or her own lifestyle.

This idea did not find easy acceptance in the probation field, where rehabilitative assistance to clients had for so long been an unquestioned point of pride. Soon, however, a still more influential report was published, which undercut the support for treatment programming in corrections. This came in the 1974 article by Robert Martinson, as mentioned in chapter 4, which reported on a study that he and his colleagues had made of the outcomes of more than two hundred correctional treatment programs. Their discouraging finding was that whereas there were occasional apparent successes, "these instances have been isolated, producing no clear pattern to indicate the efficacy of any particular method of treatment." (Martinson 1974, 22)

Overreacting, the criminal justice field in general ignored Martinson's cautious allowance of possible exceptions and construed the message to be that "nothing works." This resulted in a widespread redefinition of both probation and parole in favor of their law-enforcing function, and in a downgrading of rehabilitative efforts. A single published article usually does not produce such a general reaction unless it appears, as this one did, during a period of social ferment, which at that time "profoundly affected many Americans, including criminologists and criminal justice policymakers. . . . Protest seemed ubiquitous, first over issues of civil rights and then over Vietnam. Riots and bombings rocked cities and campuses; crime rose at an alarming rate. . . . names such as Kent State, Attica, and Watergate became etched in the public mind."[11] The general cynical mood was infectious, and the criminal justice systems caught their full share of it. Legislative policymakers found in the "nothing works" argument the justification to reduce or terminate correctional treatment programs, thereby serving two political interests at the same time. This not only saved money, but also, the shift to a more punishment-oriented mode of sentencing appealed to the public's need to get tough on crime. Regarding the issue of the proper mission of probation services, the result seemed to be a redefinition of probation officers as mainly law enforcement specialists. However, despite the highly publicized Martinson findings, at the rank-and-file level of corrections counselors or probation and parole officers, the conviction that their counseling assistance to clients can make a difference has stubbornly persisted.

Martinson himself modified his position appreciably, though his second series of findings did not get anywhere near the notice that his first findings achieved. Five years after his initial publication on the subject, Martinson reported on his follow-up research. Referring to his earlier finding that treatment programs had been found ineffective, he said, "On the basis of the evidence in our current study, I withdraw this conclusion. . . . The most interesting general conclusion is that no treatment program now used in criminal justice is inherently either substantially helpful or harmful. The critical fact seems to be the *conditions* under which the program is delivered."[12]

A substantial percentage of probation officers find this view quite creditable, as they have daily experience in seeing what they believe to be positive results of their counseling efforts in certain cases, notwithstanding the notable failures in others. But defining the mission of the probation field remains elusive, complicated considerably by the exigencies of bureaucratic job requirements. One study that appraised probation officer attitudes at the beginning of the turbulent 1970s found that they "tend to be client-related, but at the same time they are burdened with too many court-oriented and administrative duties to work steadily at the job of reformation and rehabilitation. . . . The probation officer thinks he should be working more closely with and for his clients, but he does not have time to do so adequately."[13]

A later study in 1989 of the same issue found that probation officers had shifted with the general mood of the times to accept a more authoritative role. "Several findings in this study support a conclusion that concern for authority has grown among probation officers. . . . Concern for authority has become a more meaningful philosophy than either assistance or treatment."[14] But that has not been the final word. One year later a criminologist reported on his survey of the professional literature on this subject, noting that "much about probation has changed over the last 10 years, but there appears to be a core element which has resisted change and continues to focus its energies in the direction of rehabilitation."[15] Another observer went further, saying that "the public never abandoned completely rehabilitation as a major goal nor lost belief in its ability to reform offenders, and does not oppose rehabilitation-oriented correction programs. . . . There is also growing recognition and evidence that the 'nothing works' claim of Martinson was overstated, and there are rehabilitative programs that do show various degrees of success in changing the attitudes and behavior of offenders."[16]

Philosophical trends such as these, combined with an inexorable increase in the volume of criminal cases, leave the current practice of probation in a spotty condition nationwide, varying widely in quality from one locale to another. However, this is a matter that has so much in common with parole practice that probation and parole supervision practices will be addressed together in the next section, after discussion of the concept and structure of parole in the criminal justice apparatus.

Administration of Parole

Of the major components of the criminal justice system, parole is likely to be the most politically volatile. Ironically, whereas it is an urgently needed element in the system, if only to relieve prison overcrowding, it is also the subject of frequent political attack. Periodic alarms about rising crime rates lead to demands for less use of parole, and sometimes for its outright abolition. A nation in a punitive mood from a chronic fear of crime wants to have criminal offenders locked up and incarcerated to the very end of their prison sentences, an attitude continually reinforced by news accounts of brutal crimes committed, as the media is likely to note, by parolees. One notorious crime by a parolee easily offsets any awareness the public might have that thousands of parolees live quietly and peaceably. State legislatures, pledged to get tough on crime, continually tinker with the parole laws. (Rothman 1980, 159)

The United States had nearly a century of experience in the use of penitentiaries before the parole idea became common. In most states during that time a person sent to prison received a determinate sentence and in normal course simply served that time to expiration. From the beginning, however, it always was evident that in some cases incarceration was unnecessary and even contrary to the best interests of everyone involved. For this reason state laws have invariably provided their governors with pardoning power, a privilege that governors were continually called upon to exercise in "deserving" cases. Many governors spoke of their frustration with this duty, which occupied an inordinate portion of their time and required difficult decisions without any system for assembling the needed background information. Far too often prisoners whose "merit" was only in their financial or political standing pressured the governors for pardons. Not all governors were disturbed by this part of their responsibility, but enough were so that by the late 1800s parole laws were proliferating. Ohio took the lead with a state parole law in 1885, and by 1900 twenty states had enacted parole laws. By 1944 the remaining states and the federal government had authorized parole.

With all the variations to be expected among states, the parole laws define that point in the course of a criminal sentence at which the prisoner is eligible to be released on parole. Parole boards, in their most visible duty, then make the decision in each case of whether the prisoner shall be released, on what date, and subject to what conditions. Many secondary decisions are also necessary in the determination of parole revocations and in the review and revision of policy.

Board Structure, Operating Patterns, and Decision Making

Philosophically, the concept of the parole board arose from the reasonable view that if a prisoner were to be released from a portion of his or her prison sentence to return to community living, then representatives of that community should participate in the process of deciding for or against release. For this reason the earliest parole boards usually consisted of part-time, nonprofessional people of repute (and political attractiveness) in the general population. (Rothman 1980, 163) Also, as an economy measure, some states avoided the expense of parole board positions by designating certain officials to serve as ex-officio board members. This was especially common in low-population states where such officials as the secretary of state, the attorney general, or even the governor would double as parole board members. (Hussey and Duffee 1980, 80)

As the volume of work increased and board memberships became full time, most states began to seek persons with professional qualifications for these appointments, gradually getting away from the use of these jobs as political patronage. Experts studying the state of parole in 1973 noted that "emerging concepts of administration, new directions in correctional programming, prisoner protests against what are seen as inequities and arbitrariness, and significant shifts in court views about the legal rights of offenders have all contributed to a demand for revisions in parole decision-making practices." The same observers reported that the use of ex-officio members had finally ceased. "No adult authority now includes among its membership the operating staffs of penal institutions."[17]

With a heavy volume of cases to study and dispose of, particularly in populous states, the relentless growth in work loads calls for adding more and more members to each board. But beyond a certain size a parole board becomes too unwieldly to be an efficient administrative body. The likely answer to this problem is to limit board membership to a suitable size, while gaining the necessary additional manpower by creating a subsidiary position typically titled "examiner" or perhaps "hearing officer." Federal and state laws vary in their definition of the examiner's role and authority. As a typical approach, the examiner holds hearings on parole applications just as a parole board member would, but his or her decision requires parole board approval to be effective. In ordinary cases the examiner's recommendation is likely to be routinely confirmed.

The move toward professionalism of parole boards led to an interest in ways to make the decision-making process more objective, and less a matter of guesswork and hunches. As one authority describes the former practice, "parole board members review a file on an inmate, interview him, and then apply some theory of human behavior or intuitive judgements to the information they have gathered. While such techniques are useful and, for a number of reasons probably necessary in parole decision-making, the evidence is quite strong that over a large number of cases for the narrow purpose of predicting the likelihood that a specific offender will succeed or fail on parole, they are prone to a fair amount of error."[18]

Many parole board members find it difficult to trust the objective, actuarial (usually called statistical) approach to decision making whenever its findings are at odds with their personal, subjective appraisal of a case. For such reason, wherever parole boards have adopted statistical prediction instruments, they have reserved the right to override the objective final score with their own intuitive opinions. However, ample experience has shown that the statistical instrument will be more reliable in most cases. "Thus, when empirically derived statistical prediction devices are pitted against clinical judgement and the accuracy of prediction compared, the statistical prediction instrument generally has fared better in the comparison." (Gottfredson and Gottfredson 1988, 178) Objective risk prediction measures are increasingly employed in any or all of the criminal justice settings. "This kind of information is useful to administrators of community service agencies. It allows them to rank order their clients as to potential risk to the community, thus permitting closer supervision of those who are most likely to offend again."[19]

The first notable effort to develop a statistical prediction process for use in parole decisions was in Illinois where a sociologist, Lloyd Ohlin, at the Stateville penitentiary undertook a monumental study to identify case characteristics with predictive value. The resulting instrument used twelve factors charted for each case to produce a predictive score as an objective basis for the release decision. In presenting his findings and design for the procedure, Ohlin noted that it was "based on a great mass of data on more than 17,000 prisoners paroled from the Joliet-Stateville and Menard Division of the Illinois State Penitentiary System from 1925 to 1945."[20] This suggests the size of the effort needed in developing this type of instrument, and the reason why some agencies, lacking the necessary staff and budget, are tempted to adopt an instrument already designed by some other agency. Experts generally insist, however, that no matter how excellent the process used in one jurisdiction, it cannot be considered valid in another. Each state or locale must develop an instrument tailored to the particular factors affecting its own population and criminal justice system.

The Federal Parole Board, which had been the target of criticism for its obsolete practices, finally joined the march to objective decision-making in the early 1970s. In April 1974, after its own substantial developmental project, it put into effect a process of "salient factor scoring," a structured way of combining two categories of data to arrive at a prediction of level of risk. In one category, seven items indicative of behavioral risk were compiled for each case; these were then combined in a grid format with seven possible levels of offense severity. The intersection of these factors on the grid produced for each case a range in terms of months within which the board could select the time to be served.[21]

Various other jurisdictions have since constructed their own decision-making guides. Virginia, for instance, started developing a parole guidelines instrument in 1985, studying over one thousand parole cases to ascertain reliable predictive factors. With factors identified and guidelines tentatively written, their validity was tested by checking the guidelines against the known outcomes of over four thousand cases. The end result, after six years of development, was a complex predictive instrument requiring extensive, detailed case data, and designed for computerized processing.

The Parole Decision and Prisoner Morale

Prison managers have long been aware of the prisoner management problems caused by insensitive parole practices, noting that a nagging irritation for prisoners has been the inscrutable uncertainty of the parole decision process. Parole boards generally have operated without clear guiding concepts of their philosophy and purpose, and prisoners usually have even less understanding on this point. The prisoner, needing to make a favorable impression on the board, is eager to know all he or she can about what the board will see as evidence of the prisoner's suitability for release. Constantly frustrated in trying to anticipate parole board viewpoints, prisoner populations may show raised levels of stress, which can contribute materially to prison unrest.

The 1971 Attica prison riot, as one example, revealed this kind of resentment. The so-called McKay Commission, which investigated the riot, was impressed with the festering anger toward parole board practices. Evidently prisoners perceive, whether officials do, that "the grant of parole often depends largely on factors over which the inmate no longer has control once he is in prison—his prior criminal record, the nature of the crime for which he was sentenced, his opportunities for employment." The negative effect of this is exacerbated by the inability of prisoners to get helpful feedback. The board "engenders hostility because of the inconsistency of its rationale. Some inmates who have had good behavior records in prison are 'hit' (denied parole), while others with many infractions are granted parole. Some inmates with a long record of prior offenses may receive parole, while others, including first offenders, may be denied it. Nobody gives the inmate an explanation for these obviously inconsistent decisions or describes in anything more than meaningless generalities the criteria used by the board in arriving at its decisions." The investigators of the Attica riot perceived the damage caused by this and all the other humiliations of prison life; the prisoner becomes a greater danger when "his sense of injustice has been sharpened by his Parole Board experience."[22]

The Attica riot occurred at the right time to give extra urgency to issues of prisoners' rights, a time when parole board practices everywhere were beginning to be reexamined and challenged after decades of uncritical acceptance. The principal defects in parole procedures, especially as perceived by prisoners, were that: boards tended to retry the prisoners for their crimes; parole decisions appeared to be inconsistent, subjective, and without ascertainable rationale; and decisions were delayed and, when eventually communicated to the prisoner, were without any explanation in case of a denial. A former corrections administrator described the typical process in which a board member, sometimes known as a parole "judge," would hold summary hearings on as many as fifty or sixty prisoners per day:

> One at a time, the inmates were admitted to the room, and they stood stiffly before the desk. The "judge" asked each a question or two, and the hearing was concluded. If the inmate had more to say, he was cut off, and if necessary, a guard led him out. The inmate had to remain in ignorance of his parole decision for weeks—often months. And when he got it, if it was a denial, there were no reasons of any kind given. All he got was a slip of paper with his name on it, and a terse "Parole denied." And there was nothing he could do to appeal the decision.[23]

In many cases parole boards would have rejected the allegation that they gave no explanations; some boards could in fact say that prisoners were given the decisions in writing, and with comments. However, all too typically parole boards couched their "reasons" in contrived phrases that were only vague generalities, or even polite, insipid evasions of the truth. This was particularly true for prisoners convicted of publicized crimes that had incurred public anger, cases that would bring severe public reproach to the board if a release were seen as too early to leave the offender adequately punished. A prisoner who has been well behaved inside is likely to resent denial of parole for this "political" type of reason, and is able to see through the dishonest, evasive reasons that parole boards long resorted to in such cases. Finally recognizing this, boards are accepting the principle that reasons must be written in ruggedly honest terms, telling explicitly the rationale, what the prisoner must do to earn more favorable consideration, and, when appropriate, informing the prisoner bluntly that he or she is being held for more time in order to satisfy the public need for his or her punishment. No prisoner likes that reason, but at least the prisoner will likely be less troubled than when the news of an adverse decision is delivered along with the insult of an evasive explanation.

With its newfound concern for these principles, and with adoption of its scoring instrument, the federal board (renamed the Federal Parole Commission) has provided that any prisoner denied parole should receive "in writing the panel's severity rating, salient factor items and score, the guideline range specified, and for a decision outside the guidelines, the factors considered."[24]

The Linkage with Sentencing

Obviously, reforms in parole decision making closely parallel reforms in sentencing. Parole decision guidelines follow the same principles involved in the design of objective sentencing guidelines for use by trial courts, as discussed in chapter 4. Furthermore, objective parole guidelines must be made compatible with the sentencing structure in that jurisdiction. Indeterminate sentences, for example, have the effect of requiring the parole authority to take over from the sentencing court the responsibility for setting the actual time to be served by each offender. Some critics accuse public policymakers of posturing as "tough on crime" by authorizing more severe prison sentences, while shifting to parole boards the onus of setting release dates as needed to keep the prison systems from being overloaded.

In its original development, parole practice reflected an optimistic belief in the corrective effect of imprisonment. Parole boards were given wide latitude to adjust prison time on the assumption that they could ascertain the most likely moment for safe release of the prisoner. Advocates assumed that the consideration of any inmate for parole would be deferred until the inmate had been in prison long enough to allow observation and review of his or her progress. "After several decades of research, however, empirical evidence generally fails to demonstrate that institutional rehabilitative programs are effective or that the 'optimum time' for release can be ascertained. Behavior in prison does not appear to be a good predictor of future criminal conduct."[25] As one expert opinion has it, "parole's assumption of the responsibility for rehabilitation was then, and may well be now, one of its most presumptuous and ultimately ill- advised moves." (Hussey and Duffee 1980, 78)

If rehabilitation through imprisonment is uncertain at best, then no defensible basis exists for extending an inmate's time in prison to engage him or her in "treatment," and no reason remains for deferring the parole *decision*, even though the release date decided upon may be years in the future. Rather than leaving the inmate in suspense for all the interim time, there is good reason for giving what is called an "early fix." Experts now insist that whatever information about the prisoner may be needed for making a parole decision, it is available at the time of admission to the prison. "Recently, deferral has become a much criticized feature of parole. It is said to rest on outdated assumptions, and to subject prisoners to the needless cruelty of waiting for a decision. A number of penologists and study commissions have proposed moving toward an early decision on the duration of confinement."[26]

Influential trendsetters on this point emphasize the problem of prisoner morale and the requirements of basic fairness, both long unappreciated. "It has been customary for the parole board to wait until the inmate has served a substantial period in confinement before considering him for parole. . . . Parole release thus is typically a deferred decision: the inmate will not know when he can expect to be released until well into his prison sentence." After carefully developing a rational response to this defect in parole practice, these authors go on to argue that a prisoner, if inclined to plan his or her life sensibly, deserves to have dependable information about what to expect. "Ought the prisoner be subject to *any* uncertainty about his release in the absence of affirmative justifying grounds for deferring the fix? Our answer is that he should not." (von Hirsch and Hanrahan 1979, 2, 36, 37) In general, this viewpoint has been gaining wide acceptance among penologists even though only a few states have so far acted on it.

The glacial rate at which the early fix (presumptive parole decision) is being implemented seems due more to the inertia of bureaucratic procedures than to rejection of the concept. One prominent convert to the new procedure, the U.S. Parole Commission, adopted the early decision policy along with its salient factor scoring instrument. In the federal system, "the first stage of the decisionmaking process takes place within 120 days after incarceration when almost all Federal prisoners are eligible for an initial parole hearing. At this hearing, the case is assessed against these guidelines, and the prisoner is notified of a presumptive date of release."[27] Of course, the release date will be revised if unsatisfactory behavior occurs. To ensure fairness, "there should be a specification by rule of which kinds of infractions lead to how much added time. The amount of time extensions should bear a reasonable relationship to the gravity of the conduct." (von Hirsch and Hanrahan 1979, 42)

Prior to the introduction of the presumptive parole decision, and in accord with the punishment-as-rehabilitation concept, in a state such as California (which had used completely indeterminate sentences) the parole board would be likely to make its own rules about the proportion of a sentence to be served before a parole hearing would be granted. States providing sentences with a stated minimum time to serve before parole eligibility typically wait until shortly before the prisoner's eligibility date to give the prisoner a parole hearing. But with the discovery of the ineffectiveness of treatment efforts, loyalty to the longtime practice of deferred decisions began to change. A few states in recent years have adapted their parole laws to the shift away from a rehabilitation mode toward the newly respectable "just deserts" philosophy. The concept was spurred by the work of a prestigious committee that labored during the early 1970s to formulate more rational sentencing principles.

Its report, later published as a book, gained wide attention (von Hirsch 1976) by arguing that sentences for crime should be designed to give the offender the punishment he or she *deserves,* regardless of whether any rehabilitative effect is sought or gained. "The offender may justly be subjected to certain deprivations because he deserves it; and he deserves it because he has engaged in wrongful conduct—conduct that does or threatens injury and that is prohibited by law." The committee was not seeking to increase severity of punishments; its chairman was explicit in hoping otherwise. "We can mitigate severities of punishment to levels more consistent with our pretenses of being a civilized society. . . . We can, I am convinced, mitigate the harshness and caprice of the penal system without losing whatever usefulness in crime prevention it now has." (von Hirsch 1976, 51, xix)

One of the first states to adopt the "just deserts" philosophy was Oregon, which in 1977 enacted a new sentencing and parole law that established an advisory commission to write standards or guidelines governing sentence lengths. These standards, "based on a primarily desert-oriented rationale," provided guidance for parole decisions. The new law made especially clear the linkage between sentencing and parole, as the advisory commission was to be composed of the five members of the parole board, five circuit court judges, and the governor's legal counsel, who could vote only to break a deadlock. The Oregon law also provided for early parole decisions.[28]

As previously mentioned in chapter 4, California rewrote its sentencing laws primarily to accomplish determinate sentencing, which also affected parole. "In 1977 California adopted a new sentencing law which completely dismantled the structure of the [indeterminate sentencing law] and fundamentally reordered the way prison and parole terms had been set since 1917. In place of broad sentences such as five years to life for robbery, the statute establishes two, three, or five year terms, with the middle term presumptive unless the judge finds aggravating or mitigating factors present."[29]

Determinate sentencing, when carried to its ultimate consequence, was certain eventually to suggest the abolition of parole altogether. The state of Maine was the first to take this step with a revised sentencing act in 1976. Under that law the trial court gives an offender a determinate sentence which he or she must serve entirely except for the reduction allowed for good behavior. Not only is there no provision for parole release, but also there is no parole supervision; the only provision is for completion of the sentence and outright release. (Hussey and Duffee 1980, 95–96) This act represents the farthest reach of the new belief that imprisonment is neither able nor intended to rehabilitate, but only to punish. As with any radical change in public policy, the Maine law attracts both praise and dissent, and as elsewhere in the criminal justice system, those officials who find it objectionable can find ways to circumvent it. One way is through the "split sentence" in which the court places the offender on probation with the condition that he or she first spend a portion of it in prison. With the demise of parole in Maine, courts substantially increased their use of split sentences.[30]

After the Maine experience has had more time to demonstrate what type of effects can be expected from a radical revision of this kind, other state sentencing laws are likely to be redesigned in ways not yet apparent. Meanwhile, during the last two decades, all the states have reappraised their parole procedures, and at least twenty-five of them to date have developed and adopted some form of objective decision making. For some, the outright abolishment of parole is a tempting idea, but so far the states have been cautious and reluctant to abandon parole. Meanwhile, however, the most prominent revision of parole policy has been the move to abolish federal parole as authorized by the Sentencing Reform Act of 1984.

The Sentencing Reform Act provides a useful demonstration of the complexity of any such change, and the impossibility of its immediate accomplishment. Though the law was enacted in 1984, its actual effective date was November 1, 1987. All federal prisoners who were convicted of crimes that occurred prior to that date are still to be subject to the parole process. This could mean that offenders who avoided apprehension for some years could be tried and sentenced long after the 1987 date, but still be covered by the prior parole law. In early 1994, six years after the official abolition of parole, the federal prisons still had a residue of about twelve thousand prisoners, from a total of nearly eighty-two thousand, who were subject to parole. Because this makes it likely that some inmates will still be subject to the old parole law until the end of the century or beyond, the Federal Parole Commission will remain active for many years.

Notwithstanding the increasingly dismissive attitude toward parole, the national standard-setting agency in corrections clearly supports continuation of parole practice. "For more than 100 years, the American Correctional Association has recognized parole as an important method of protecting the public safety. Parole is a proven method for the reentry of incarcerated offenders into society and a proven method for providing supervision of the released offender in the community. Experience has demonstrated that an effective system of parole is essential to any corrections system."[31]

Supervising Parolees: A Mechanistic Trend

A full understanding of the conditions of probation and parole today requires an awareness of the effects of the general increase in correction populations. Probation and parole services have long been the most burdened and crippled when the criminal justice system becomes overloaded. The reason is as understandable as it is lamentable. An overcrowded jail or prison has an immediate, measurable, and substantive effect on its inmates. Overcrowding is more of a threat to public safety than the public realizes. A seriously crowded institution is less manageable and more dangerous; it also causes acute disadvantages for the inmates, such as reduction of privacy, less access to recreation, work, and educational programs, and more stress in the general living situation. As a natural result, prisoners are motivated to bring suit for relief, and courts find ample reason to be responsive.

But no matter how overcrowded probation or parole caseloads become, the usual client, as long as he or she is not incarcerated, feels no disadvantage from being on an over-large caseload. The infrequency of contact with the supervising agent is an effect that the client on probation or parole is more than likely to welcome. From the earliest beginnings of probation or parole practice, there never has been an effective, widely accepted definition of the desirable limit to each probation agent's caseload. In a prison the desirable limit is self-evident: quite simply, when all the beds are full the next admission is in excess. But in probation work, it has always been possible to add one more case to the probation office's responsibility, and another, ad infinitum. Consequently, even in the best of times caseloads in some jurisdictions have reached as high as four hundred per officer. Caseloads in juvenile court probation offices usually have been lower, but here too the numbers have still been extremely high in many locales.

In recent years, as the general crime rate has increased, the public's response has focused almost entirely on the most visible sanction, prisons. Substantial appropriations for new prisons have been forthcoming, whereas less visible resources have often been cut back. Legislative bodies contending with limited public funds find it politically feasible to reduce their support of community programs in favor of institutions. In fact, it is nearly impossible to reduce the budgets for institutions if they are to continue to exist and operate. In the mid-1980s the Rand Corporation studied this issue and noted in its report that:

> Whereas prison crowding is a matter of common knowledge and concern, relatively few people are aware that other sanctions—particularly probation and parole—are equally overburdened. Over the past decade, the national prison population increased by 48%, but the probation population grew by 63%. And probation's pace continues to outdistance both prisons and parole. In 1983, growth in the number of prisoners slowed down from 12% to 6% whereas the probation population continued to ascend at a record-breaking increase of 11%.[32]

In many parts of the country the rise in probation and parole caseloads, combined with a concurrent reduction of appropriations for community services, has had disastrous effects. California presents a graphic example of how general economic problems can affect the quality of correctional services at the community level. "The seven-year drought in the Central Valley cost farmers roughly $1.7 billion. The three days of rioting in 1992 cost 57 lives and $1 billion in destroyed property. Last summer brush fires devoured nearly 1,000 homes in some of the richest enclaves in America. All the while the re-engineering of America's post-cold war economy drained California of 202,000 aerospace jobs."[33] All this was a prelude to the monumental costs of recovery from the January 1994 earthquake. But financial resources had been reduced since 1978, when Proposition 13 was approved in a taxpayer revolt, causing a drastic decrease in county revenues. Although the state managed to keep law enforcement agencies supported, "almost all other county and city agencies were forced to begin cutting. And in some counties the programs and funds of local corrections agencies were considered the most expendable." Hardest hit was the Los Angeles County Probation Department, which soon had to eliminate enough programs and personnel to decrease its budget by more than $5 million.[34] The cumulative effect of all these events was to drastically reduce the state's ability to support probation and parole services. Twenty years earlier Los Angeles County had been hoping to find a way to cut adult probation caseloads down from their average of 250 per officer; by 1992, however, the levels were still higher. With cases differentiated by degree of risk, and with low-risk cases grouped on larger caseloads, "the chief probation officer of Los Angeles County reported that two-member teams supervise as many as 2000 cases."[35]

Reporting on this trend, one researcher notes that "most probation and parole agencies have generally had their budgets cut at the same time that their caseloads have grown. For instance, in California the probation population has risen by 15% since 1975, while the number of probation officers has fallen by 20%. In the same period, California spent 30% more on criminal justice in general, but 10% less on probation."[36]

When a probation or parole service is subjected to rising caseloads and falling budgetary support, it will inevitably result in the use of less personal, more mechanistic, practices to keep some degree of contact with clients. One observer of the California parole system sees evidence of this in the language of employees who no longer use a vocabulary that reflects a helping process. "Increasingly the job does not require much language since checklists and boilerplate language suffice. Interpretive validity does not reside in a powerful charismatic boss, but in a complex set of procedures and routines." The same writer finds the roots of this condition both in the discouraging case overloads and in the determinate sentencing law which California passed in 1977. "The new law was seen by all observers as deeply hostile to the philosophy which had guided parole in California for a quarter century or more. It explicitly rejected the relevance of rehabilitation and declared the purpose of imprisonment to be punishment." (Simon 1993, 112, 115)

Although the problem has been less severe in most other states, excessive caseloads are nevertheless endemic in the system. Even in Minnesota, where criminal justice services had always been well supported and imprisonment rates kept low, a task force studying probation services issued a report in 1993 under the title, *Minnesota Probation: A System in Crisis.* The report described the same problem that was common elsewhere, increased workloads with no increase in resources. "Caseloads across the state range from 55 to 400 clients per probation officer; group supervision caseloads have ratios of up to one agent per 1,200 offenders! While caseloads have more than doubled in the past nine years, there has been no accompanying increase in probation staff or resources. An estimated 12% of these offenders are serious public risk cases. They are more violent and dangerous than ever before."[37]

A common result of case overloads has been the deliberate neglect of large blocks of cases. Some courts have become resigned to the necessity of placing offenders on unsupervised probation. One probation chief in California explained in late 1993 that "presently there are some 400,000 probationers in California, including some 70,000 juveniles. It's my best guess that most of the offenders never see a probation officer. Here in Sacramento County, where the number of probationers increases some 10.2% annually, we now have almost 20,000 such persons, and our projections are that, in less than five years, we'll have 30,200." He added that California counties commonly supervised as few as 6 to 30 percent of their probationers.[38]

One ominous aspect of these numbers is that the probation system is getting a higher proportion of serious felony cases as a direct result of limited prison space. Courts are using probation at an increasing rate for many felons for whom the presentence reports had recommended imprisonment.[39] The rate of probation violations inevitably rises with these conditions; again, quoting a Rand Corporation study, "In our opinion, felons granted probation present a serious threat to public safety. During the 40-month follow-up period of our study 65% of the probationers in our subsample were rearrested, 51% were reconvicted, 18% were reconvicted of serious violent crime, and 34% were reincarcerated."[40]

Similarly, a sampling of statistics from elsewhere in the country showed the effects of placing more serious offenders on probation.

"State courts in 32 counties across 17 States sentenced 79,000 felons to probation in 1986. Within three years of sentencing, while still on probation, 43% were rearrested for a felony. An estimated 18% of the arrests were for a violent crime (murder, rape, robbery, or aggravated assault); 33% were for a drug offense (drug trafficking or drug possession)." The same report noted the effect of courts having to use probation even when probation officers had recommended against it. "The probationers who were not recommended for probation were nearly twice as likely to have their sentence revoked and to be sent to prison (37%) as those recommended for probation (22%)."[41]

The Supervisory Function: Adapting Methods to Demands

Job satisfaction for most probation and parole officers has been highest when they could conduct their work as a helping service—when the client's root problems could be diagnosed, and constructive, individualized help could be given. The process would involve a relationship of trust developed through frequent discussions with the client in the parole officer's office or in the client's home. At its best, the process functions as a casework process in which the client sometimes is given direct practical help in such essentials as job finding and interpersonal relations. Though this ideal approach is seldom realized, every probation or parole agent has had a few cases that were reachable in this way, usually because the client himself wanted and responded to such help. For probation agents the occasional experience with such cases keeps the job satisfying despite its otherwise discouraging aspects.

The reality of the probation agent's job, reflecting both the increased work volume and the philosophical shift to the "just deserts" orientation of the field, has been that supervision has become more routine and superficial. The law enforcement function is favored over counseling. Community services have always operated under some uncertainty about how to reconcile the presumably incompatible functions of assistance and surveillance. Theoreticians have debated the question of how a probation or parole officer can gain the trust and cooperation of a client when the officer is also seen as an enforcer who is ready to detect violations and rearrest. To a considerable extent the issue has been academic, and probation agents have ably made adjustments to the needs of each case. A relatively recent survey of the attitudes of probation officers on this point produced a return of questionnaires from over 500 agents and showed that "probation professionals clearly view probation goals as equally focused on both enforcement and rehabilitation."[42]

Significantly, this attitude also persists with legislators despite the pressures to "get tough on crime." When the California legislature enacted its determinate sentencing law in 1977, it called for surveillance, but gave at least equal weight to rehabilitative efforts. "It is in the interest of public safety for the state to provide for the supervision of and surveillance of parolees and to provide educational, vocational, family and personal counseling necessary to assist parolees in the transition between imprisonment and discharge."[43]

Under pressure of case volume, enforcement has been adjusted to fit different levels of perceived risk in both probation and parole cases. This is part of a general approach referred to as caseload management, an approach which, among other things, calls for application of risk measurement instruments much like those being used by parole boards. After clients are classified by level of risk, they are assigned to relevant caseloads and given attention accordingly. Typically an agency will establish three or more levels of cases, consisting of low-, medium-, or high-risk. The low-risk cases are likely to be given virtually no supervision except for infrequent contacts to verify the client's current status. Obviously the high-risk cases should be handled on caseloads small enough to permit frequent and meaningful contacts with the client, but under present circumstances the number of high-risk "intensive" caseloads, which should be kept down to fifteen cases or less, are likely in time to creep upward to as high as forty.

Probation and parole professionals are well aware that a caseload of forty is too large to be truly intensive; furthermore, research has shown that virtually nothing is gained by reducing caseloads unless agents are trained to use special techniques and resources. But the reality is that an agency must do what it can do with the budget it is given; for the sake of public support, an agency must at least maintain the appearance of making intensive efforts. There are ways to make intensive caseloads effective, as will be discussed in chapter 9, but this is not done just by reducing numbers of cases. A cynical but valid observation has been that if an officer's caseload is substantially reduced without giving the officer new training in relevant techniques to help exploit this advantage, nothing is accomplished except giving the officer more time to do paperwork. True intensity can be claimed only when specialized techniques are used with a caseload size that permits a level of assistance and control commensurate with need.

Formulating and Enforcing Conditions

Probation or parole clients are ordinarily given a list of rules or conditions, and are usually required to sign an agreement to abide by them. In the past, all the states have been too inclusive in formulating these rules by including requirements that reflect a desire to impose middle-class values rather than just to prevent criminal conduct. Unfortunately, imposing strict conduct rules tends to give the criminal justice system a "quicksand quality," pulling the probation client more deeply into the system instead of helping him or her to leave it. Demanding unreasonably strict conduct requirements of a nonserious offender, for example (especially requirements that are contrary to his or her usual lifestyle), may only set the client up for failure. Great numbers of probationers and parolees have suffered revocation and incarceration for behaviors that are not illegal, but are "technical violations," or failure to cooperate fully with the probation office in respect to the imposed conditions.

Because the probation and parole field has become more aware of the unfairness of these extensive lists of conditions, they are gradually being modified to focus on fewer and more basic requirements. Some argue that the only requirement should be that the client violate no laws. This is an ideal, however, that is difficult to defend because in so many cases the client needs to be forbidden certain activities which, though legal in themselves, tend in the client's case to lead to something worse. One authority suggests that there may properly be three types of conditions: (1) *operational*—those that would apply to all offenders, such as to obey all laws, (2) *punitive*—fines, community service, and so on, and (3) *preventive*—any activity required or prohibited as necessary to help keep the client from being arrested. "The conditions of supervision should be restricted to those that are meant to be enforced and are necessary to the maintenance of the supervision relationship."[44]

That is a statement with important implications not fully appreciated by the judges or probation officers who write detailed and extensive conditions. Rules, if obeyed, can help an offender keep from reoffending. But rules also lead to rule-breaking. The more rules or conditions, the more likely it is that violations will occur, making a disciplinary response necessary. The challenge is to find a sensible point of balance.

The same issues of rules and conditions apply to parole supervision. By keeping the parolee's requirements to a minimum, the supervising agency will help keep disciplinary actions within modern legal principles. A significant factor in shaping the practice of parole has been the generally held philosophy that parole is a privilege extended by the state, not a right. Presuming this to be true, it was long supposed that rules and conditions could be decreed and disciplinary actions taken summarily. In 1972, however, the U.S. Supreme Court recognized that the relative freedom of parole status had become deserving of protection. An Iowa parolee, Morrissey, challenged his parole revocation after he was returned to prison on the arbitrarily accepted word of his parole officer that he had violated the parole rules. The Supreme Court commented:

> We turn to an examination of the nature of the interest of the parolee in his continued liberty. The liberty of a parolee enables him to do a wide range of things open to persons who have never been convicted of any crime. We see, therefore, that the liberty of a parolee, although indeterminate, includes many of the core values of unqualified liberty and its termination inflicts a "grievous loss" on the parolee and often on others. By whatever name, the liberty is valuable and must be seen as within the protection of the Fourteenth Amendment. Its termination calls for some orderly process, however informal.[45]

The Morrissey decision mandated the application of due process principles to parole revocation decisions, including a preliminary hearing before an independent official. With the hearing the parolee is to receive notice of the charges against him or her and to have the opportunity to present evidence and confront witnesses.

Probation and parole practitioners, contemplating the many recent economic and philosophical changes that are affecting their methodology, may wonder at times whether the present course of their work is effective, and whether the results are justified. For some, however, an unconventional view takes comfort from the same findings that have previously brought dismay. The research of Martinson and others has shown that in most cases subjecting prisoners and other corrections clients to treatment programs, or supervising them on smaller caseloads, are not provably more successful methods. On the other hand, neither are they worse methods; this implies that if agents lower their sights, resort to large caseloads for low-risk cases, and handle some cases by surveillance only, they are still accomplishing just as much as before, and they are perhaps being more efficient. As one authority has thoughtfully expressed it:

> Any combination of visits and reports keeps pressure on the parolee to be law abiding and to stay in touch with the parole office. It is very hard to say whether such supervision really prevents relapses into crime. A parolee determined to make it does not need surveillance, a parolee determined to con his parole officer, evade him, or engage in illicit activities can find ways to do so. A parolee who is not committed either way may be induced to accept guidance and help. (Kittrie and Zenoff 1981, 505)

The point is well taken, but nevertheless the corrections field is gradually developing innovative alternative programs and specialized treatment techniques that show promise of being effective if they are expertly administered. Evaluating these techniques or predicting their success is difficult; special treatment programs, particularly if operated in a community setting, are highly dependent upon the constant availability of skilled staff, and sometimes just good luck. This is why massive, expensive prisons are so politically popular. A prison has a visible, reassuring durability, and as long as it can avoid escapes and riots, its public acceptance is impervious to whatever inept management it contains within. A community-based program, on the other hand, is vulnerable to almost any publicized defect or threatening event. Many a community program has been closed because of just one crime by one parolee.

To counter this perspective with a more encouraging observation, the public apparently continues to be eager for a correctional panacea, and is willing to support new and promising approaches again and again. Admittedly the public's zeal in this respect is shallow and easily disillusioned, but it offers the opportunity for persistent attempts by professionals to develop better corrective programs or methods. Indeed, the general effort to improve is alive and well, and various significant innovations are underway, many of which will be discussed in chapter 9.

Notes

1. Bureau of Justice Statistics. *Bulletin. Probation and Parole 1990* (Nov. 1991), 1.
2. *Organization and Administration of Juvenile Services,* July 1987, revised November 1990, 27. An unpublished report supplied by the National Center for Juvenile Justice, Pittsburgh, Pa.
3. American Correctional Association. Commission on Accreditation for Corrections. *Manual of Standards for Juvenile Training Schools and Services.* Rockville, Md.: 1979, 95.
4. See, for example, William Healy. *The Individual Delinquent.* Montclair, N.J.: Patterson Smith, 1969. (reprint of 1915 edition)
5. Alvin W. Cohn and Michael M. Ferriter. "The Presentence Investigation: An Old Saw with New Teeth." *Federal Probation* 54:3 (Sept. 1990), 18.
6. Ibid., 17.
7. Harry Joe Jaffe. "The Presentence Report: Probation Officer Accountability and Recruitment Practices." *Federal Probation* 53:3 (Sept. 1989), 12.
8. Joan Petersilia. "Juvenile Record Use in Adult Court Proceedings: A Survey of Prosecutors." *The Journal of Criminal Law and Criminology* 72:4 (Winter 1981), 1769.
9. Paul W. Keve. *Imaginative Programming in Probation and Parole.* Minneapolis: University of Minnesota Press, 1967, Preface, 3–4.
10. Dale Hardman. "The Function of the Probation Officer." *Federal Probation* 24:3 (Sept. 1960), 4.

11. Francis T. Cullen and Paul Gendreau. "The Effectiveness of Correctional Rehabilitation: Reconsidering the 'Nothing Works' Debate." Chapter 3 in *The American Prison: Issues in Research and Policy,* ed. Lynne Goodstein and Doris Layton MacKenzie, 27. New York: Plenum, 1989.

12. Robert Martinson. "New Findings, New Views: A Note of Caution Regarding Sentencing Reform." *Hofstra Law Review* 7:2 (Winter 1979), 254.

13. Jay A. Sigler and Thomas E. Bezanson. "Role Perception among New Jersey Probation Officers." *Rutgers Camden Law Journal* 2:2 (Fall 1970), 263.

14. Patricia M. Harris, Todd R. Clear, and S. Christopher Baird. "Have Community Supervision Officers Changed Their Attitudes toward Their Work?" *Justice Quarterly* 6:2 (June 1989), 242–243.

15. Thomas Ellsworth. "Identifying the Actual and Preferred Goals of Adult Probation." *Federal Probation* 54:2 (June 1990), 15.

16. David Shichor. "Following the Penological Pendulum: The Survival of Rehabilitation." *Federal Probation* 56:2 (June 1992), 20.

17. Vincent J. O'Leary and Joan Nuffield. "A National Survey of Parole Decision-making." *Crime and Delinquency* 19:3 (July 1973), 378, 380.

18. Vincent O'Leary. "Parole Administration." Chapter 25 in *Handbook of Criminology,* ed. Daniel Glaser, 917. Chicago: Rand McNally College Publishing Co., 1974.

19. Kevin N. Wright, Todd R. Clear, and Paul Dickson. "Universal Applicability of Probation Risk-Assessment Instruments." *Criminology* 22:1 (Feb. 1984), 113–114.

20. Lloyd E. Ohlin. *Selection for Parole: A Manual of Parole Prediction.* New York: Russell Sage Foundation, 1951, 12.

21. For a discussion and a full reproduction of this significant instrument, see Peter B. Hoffman and Lucille K. DeGostin, "Parole Decision-Making: Structuring Discretion." *Federal Probation* 38:4 (Dec. 1974), 9, 12–15.

22. Robert B. McKay. *Attica: The Official Report of the New York State Special Commission on Attica.* New York: Bantam Books, 1972, 95, 97, 101.

23. Maurice H. Sigler. "Abolish Parole?" *Federal Probation* 39:2 (June 1975), 43.

24. Peter B. Hoffman and Lucille K. DeGostin. "Parole Decision-Making: Structuring Discretion." *Federal Probation* 38:4 (Dec. 1974), 9.

25. Peter B. Hoffman and Michael A. Stover. "Reform in the Determination of Prison Terms: Equity, Determinacy, and the Parole Release Function." *Hofstra Law Review* 7:1 (Fall 1979), 91.

26. Page 9 in Andrew von Hirsch and Kathleen J. Hanrahan, *Abolish Parole?,* a monograph published in 1978 by the National Institute of Law Enforcement and Criminal Justice, U.S. Department of Justice. It also is reprinted in part in Cromwell et al. 1985, 193–197 (below).

27. Barbara Stone-Meierhoefer and Peter B. Hoffman. "Presumptive Parole Dates: The Federal Approach." *Federal Probation* 46:2 (June 1982), 41.

28. von Hirsch and Hanrahan 1979 (below), 93, 123–124. The book gives the full Oregon statute in its Appendix IV.

29. Page 168 in "From Discipline to Management: Strategies of Control in Parole Supervision 1890-1990," an unpublished doctoral dissertation by Jonathan Steven Simon, University of California at Berkeley, 1990.
30. Kevin Krajick. "Abolishing Parole: An Idea Whose Time Has Passed." *Corrections Magazine* 9:3 (June 1983), 35.
31. *Public Policy for Corrections: A Handbook for Decision-Makers.* Laurel, Md.: American Corrrectional Association, 1986, 48.
32. Joan Petersilia. "Community Supervision: Trends and Critical Issues." *Crime and Delinquency* 31:3 (July 1985), 339.
33. *Time* 143:5 (Jan. 31, 1994), 34–35.
34. Dan Bernstein. "Proposition 13: Probation Feels the Squeeze in California." *Corrections Magazine* 5:1 (March 1979), 47, 48.
35. Charles Lindner. "The Refocused Probation Home Visit: A Subtle But Revolutionary Change." *Federal Probation* 56:1 (March 1992), 16.
36. Joan Petersilia. "Community Supervision: Trends and Critical Issues." *Crime and Delinquency* 31:3 (July 1985), 339.
37. *Minnesota Probation: A System in Crisis.* Report of the Probation Standards Task Force, Minnesota Department of Corrections, St. Paul, 1993, ii.
38. Letter to the author, December 22, 1993, from Robert E. Keldgord, Chief Probation Officer, Sacramento.
39. Charles Lindner. "The Refocused Probation Home Visit: A Subtle But Revolutionary Change." *Federal Probation* 56:1 (March 1992), 17.
40. Joan Petersilia et al. "Granting Felons Probation: Public Risks and Alternatives." *Crime and Delinquency* 31:3 (July 1985), 381.
41. Bureau of Justice Statistics. *National Update* 1:4 (April 1992), 10.
42. Thomas Ellsworth. "Identifying the Actual and Preferred Goals of Adult Probation." *Federal Probation* 54:2 (June 1980), 12.
43. California Penal Code, Sect. 3000.
44. Vincent O'Leary. "Reshaping Community Corrections." *Crime and Delinquency* 31:3 (July 1985), 360.
45. Morrissey v. Brewer, 408 U.S. 471 (1972).

Bibliography

Administration of Probation

Champion, Dean J. *Probation and Parole in the United States.* Columbus, Ohio: Merrill, 1990.

A college textbook on the operation and character of probation and parole. It discusses the many variations among states in both the administrative formats and the programming approaches. Readable, well-organized, with an extensive bibliography.

Cromwell, Paul F., Jr., George C. Killinger, Hazel B. Kerper, and Charles Walker. *Probation and Parole in the Criminal Justice System.* St. Paul, Minn.: West Publishing Co., 1985.

A competent and thorough textbook, giving an explanatory discussion of all aspects of probation and parole organization, philosophy, and practices in the United States.

McAnany, Patrick D., Doug Thomson, and David Fogel, eds. *Probation and Justice; Reconsideration of Mission.* Cambridge, Mass.: Oelgeschlager, Gunn & Hain, 1984.

This anthology presents chapters dealing with various aspects of probation under the major headings, "The Justice Model and Probation," "Probation Ideology and Structure," and "Prospects for Probation Reform."

McCarthy, Belinda Rogers and Bernard J. McCarthy, Jr. *Community-Based Corrections.* Pacific Grove, Calif.: Brooks/Cole, 1991.

Covers the distinctions between adult and juvenile corrections, the wide variety of programmatic approaches for special problem types of clients, and the probation and parole practices.

Martinson, Robert. "What Works?—Questions and Answers about Prison Reform." *Public Interest* 35 (1974), 22–54.

Morris, Norval and Michael Tonry. *Between Prison and Probation: Intermediate Punishments in a Rational Sentencing System.* New York: Oxford University Press, 1990.

These astute authors present an erudite, philosophical examination of the principles affecting the design and practice of treatment or punishment options for offenders.

Rothman, David J. *Conscience and Convenience: The Asylum and Its Alternatives in Progressive America.* Boston: Little, Brown, 1980.

A noted authority on corrections history contributes useful understanding of the antecedents of probation and parole, and perceptively analyzes the less known problems with these services.

Smykla, John Ortiz. *Community-based Corrections: Principles and Practices.* New York: Macmillan, 1981.

Smykla, John Ortiz. *Probation and Parole: Crime Control in the Community.* New York: Macmillan, 1984.

Trester, Harold B. *Supervision of the Offender.* Englewood Cliffs, N.J.: Prentice-Hall, 1981.

Administration of Parole

Gottfredson, Don M. and Michael Tonry. *Prediction and Classification: Criminal Justice Decision Making.* Vol. 9. Chicago: University of Chicago Press, 1987.

This anthology, part of a series on criminal justice research issues, discusses many aspects of the systems and purposes for classification of offenders, and of predictive instruments. Penetrating, scholarly viewpoints from two outstanding experts.

Gottfredson, Michael R. and Don M. Gottfredson. *Decision Making in Criminal Justice: Toward the Rational Exercise of Discretion.* New York: Plenum, 1988.

A thorough examination of the levels and types of situations in which criminal justice officials make decisions regarding offenders. It discusses the influencing factors and the decision processes in matters ranging from the victim's decision to report a crime in the first place, to the decisions by parole boards.

Hussey, Frederick A. and David E. Duffee. *Probation, Parole and Community Field Services.* New York: Harper & Row, 1980.

A well-organized overview of the theory and practice of the fields of probation and parole.

Kittrie, Nicholas N. and Elyce H. Zenoff. *Sanctions, Sentencing, and Corrections: Law, Policy, and Practice.* Mineola, N.Y.: Foundation Press, 1981.

A competent compendium of laws and court decisions affecting the conduct of correctional services. It includes useful discussions of the legal concepts and arguments, and of their applications to correctional practice.

O'Leary, Vincent. "Parole Administration." Chapter 25 in *Handbook of Criminology*, ed. Daniel Glaser. Chicago: Rand McNally College Publishing Co., 1974.

Simon, Jonathan. *Poor Discipline: Parole and the Social Control of the Underclass, 1890–1990.* Chicago: University of Chicago Press, 1993.

A significant study of the development and present functioning of parole systems. It reviews parole history in the United States and abroad, but its discussion of current parole practices mainly targets California, particularly in the context of the labor market and the drug culture.

von Hirsch, Andrew. *Doing Justice: The Choice of Punishments.* New York: Hill & Wang, 1976.

A rational, intellectual polemic that discusses the philosophy of punishment, analyzes the problems with sentencing practices, and presents concepts that should guide sentencing policy. The author is noted for the significant contribution made here to the development of objective standards for sentencing. The book is not anecdotal, nor is it as easily readable as other books on parole, but it is significant as a prime influence behind some legislative changes in sentencing laws.

von Hirsch, Andrew and Kathleen J. Hanrahan. *The Question of Parole: Retention, Reform, or Abolition?* Cambridge, Mass.: Ballinger, 1979.

Astute analysis amd observations of operational problems in parole administration, with concepts of possible reform measures. The authors examine the legal, philosophical, and practical approaches to parole reform as they perceive them.

CHAPTER 9

Current Adaptations, Future Prospects

Although the figures are sometimes deceptive, and are always subject to differing interpretations, criminal justice statistical reports each year show that the United States has a worsening problem with crime and seems to be losing ground in applying measures for its control. To some extent the problem is one of perception rather than substance. People tend to think of crime in terms of stranger-to-stranger violence, which in fact is the lesser portion of the overall problem, and, by some accounts, this category is currently showing no increase in rate. Another factor distorting the apparent size of the problem is the country's increase in the general population, and the increase in the proportion of young adults. This will appreciably increase the number of crimes, even without a rise in the crime rate.

Whether or not crime rates are increasing, the public response to crime is to demand tougher treatment of criminals, not realizing that the United States already is among the most punitive countries in the world. European countries generally impose much shorter criminal sentences than are common in the United States (Stenson and Cowell 1991, 37–38) Imprisonment rates in 1990 showed that England and other major countries in Europe were incarcerating at a rate less than 100 people per 100,000 persons in the general population. Canada was more severe with a rate of 109 per 100,000, but the count for the United States was 426 per 100,000! Additionally, "prison and jail populations, Federal and state, have doubled over the past decade; well over 1 million of our adult fellow citizens are now in prison or jail, and 4 million are under the control of the criminal justice systems of this country."[1]

At the same time, Department of Justice statistical reports showed that the increases in U.S. prison and jail populations were recent and precipitous. For example, whereas the number of sentenced prisoners in state and federal prisons had doubled (from 100,000 up to 200,000) in the forty-five years from 1925 to 1970, over the following twenty years, this number jumped by an additional 500,000 prisoners. Jail populations too were up, having more than doubled in the last decade.[2]

The *New York Times* noted an interesting tangential trend in the way that the drive to build more prison space was draining available funds away from a public service that should be utilized more in prevention of crime—schools. "In fact, 70 percent of all the prison space in use today has been built since 1985, at a cost of $32.9 billion. But only 11 percent of the nation's classrooms were constructed during the 1980s."[3] This observation was later augmented by a report in the *Washington Post* that graphically depicted the crisis in the public schools in Harlem where "there are almost twice as many children under 12 in this upper Manhattan neighborhood today as there were 20 years ago." Classroom space has not kept up with the influx of students, causing overly large class sizes, with teaching done in shifts. "There are only two school playgrounds for 25,000 children because all the rest have been swallowed up by portable classrooms and makeshift additions." On the basis of births already recorded, the near-future prospects appear still worse. "The consequences for the criminal justice system are profound."[4]

With similar problems in varying degrees elsewhere throughout the country, the demand for prison space will most likely continue to grow. Whereas social conditions such as those described earlier will sustain the *crime* rate, two other factors will affect the *imprisonment* rate. One factor is the increased number of persons given prison sentences; the other factor is the increased average length of sentences given. The latter factor has been particularly pronounced in recent years, reflecting increasingly punitive public attitudes.

At the same time that public fear of crime leads to longer prison sentences and crowded prisons, the high cost of long sentences and overcrowding eventually forces governments to explore designs for noninstitutional "corrective" measures. With prison construction dollars limited, legislators have to find politically acceptable alternative strategies for preventing crime and accomplishing a corrective or rehabilitative punishment for at least some nonviolent offenders.

Some examples of improved criminal justice methods will be discussed here in respect to both their intrinsic value and to the policymaking strategies involved. To this end it is necessary to review and build upon topics presented in preceding chapters regarding the conventional functioning of police, courts, correctional institutions, and probation and parole services. Subsequently, this chapter will examine: (a) some of the trends in redesigning administrative patterns to accommodate new anticrime approaches, and (b) trends in programmatic strategies that may offer more effective correction of offenders.

In speaking of corrective programs, it is important to caution anyone who is searching for effectiveness in a treatment program. Whereas some program designs are of course more effective than others, planners of any types of remedial social programs must remember the following principle: programs don't help people, *people* help people. The program serves as a vehicle, focus, and frame for social interaction, which brings people together in a way that fosters interaction of a potentially therapeutic quality. Nevertheless, the successful utilization of people for curative services requires appropriate and efficient organizational contexts in which they can be employed and their efforts supported.

Organizational Directions and Public Policy Initiatives

Many criminal justice professionals have felt that since corrective efforts for adult offenders are implemented too late in the lives of offenders, remedial help should be concentrated more on juveniles. But this raises questions about the suitability of the juvenile court to meet this need, because the juvenile world has changed substantially during the near century of the court's existence. Today the juvenile court must adapt to a social milieu in which children of the middle classes grow up with much more sophisticated knowledge of the adult world compared with previous generations, and with much less of what once was cherished as "childhood innocence." At the same time, the children of chronically failed families, for all the disadvantages they still endure, have much improved access to social opportunity. If the extent of the gains of disadvantaged children is easily forgotten, graphic reminders exist in the literature of the desperate plight of the thousands of children who were part of the raw savagery of street life at the time the juvenile court was created.

Modern-Day Threats to the Welfare of Children

Novelists such as Charles Dickens, Victor Hugo, and Horatio Alger have pictured graphically the lives in the past of the "throw-away" children of the great cities. In the United States the problem of abandoned children festered in the big cities through the nineteenth century, during the latter part of which an unusual social worker contended with and wrote about those in New York City. Charles Loring Brace, founder of the New York Children's Aid Society, spoke frankly of them as the "dangerous classes" and was deeply concerned about the great numbers of children who were abandoned and living by their wits on the streets. "Of the number of the distinctively homeless and vagrant youth in New York, it is difficult to speak with precision. We should be inclined to estimate it, after long observation, as fluctuating each year between 20,000 and 30,000."[5]

At the same time that urban homeless children lived so roughly, middle-class children were usually more protected than they are today; middle-class parents tended to keep their children ignorant of the behaviors of socially disapproved persons, and even of sexual matters. The literature contains much evidence of young people of middle-class families growing up "innocent," and of young ladies entering marriage with no preparation for its intimacies. During the present century, however, the two extremes have moved closer. Though poverty is still prevalent, the presence of various social agencies and governmental support programs have made the lower socioeconomic classes less disadvantaged in a material sense, and their lives are less primitive than they were a century earlier. With changes in general social attitudes, aided by exposure to candid movie and television programs, children of all classes now have easy access to any and all kinds of information, much of which would have been shocking, if not unheard of, to their grandparents' generation. Along with the gains made, however, there has been a breakdown in the family's ability to ensure the child's normal development.

A significant report by the Carnegie Corporation in 1994 noted the extent and depth of the problem in the United States. More than one million adolescent girls become pregnant each year. "Most adolescent mothers are neither financially nor emotionally prepared for parenthood." Compounding this problem is the high percentage of unmarried parents. "No change in American families should concern this nation more than the skyrocketing number of single-parent families. Since 1950 the percentage of children living in one-parent families has nearly tripled." Whereas a single parent may be capable of giving a child a loving and normal quality of life, the family suffers from more pressure because of the necessity of the single parent to work. "In the 1970s, few mothers of infants worked outside of the home; today more than half do. The large number of working mothers is a matter of concern because the American workplace is, by and large, not family-friendly, and arrangements for child care for children under three are often hard to find and of poor quality." (Carnegie Corporation of New York 1994, 12–16)

By the 1990s, the alarmed public was seeing children of all social levels vulnerable to the drug culture, even in grammar school. Deeply worrisome too was the alarming number of children carrying guns, and all too often using them. The U.S. Centers for Disease Control and

Prevention revealed that in 1991, deaths from firearms were second only to auto accidents as the leading types of injury deaths in the country. That trend, if continued, would lead to firearm deaths being the leading type of injury death by the mid-1990s. In 1991, among persons ranging in age from 15 to 34, the ratio of deaths per 100,000 of general population was 24.4 from firearms and 27.3 from vehicle accidents. A breakdown by race showed that for this age group in the black population, the rate for firearm deaths was 70.7 per 100,000![6]

Today the juvenile court, as it hears the cases of children from all social classes, assumes that whatever the child's socioeconomic level, and level of sophistication regarding life experience, every child is unaware of vulnerability to the effects of his or her adventuring. Arrest statistics reflect the growing problem. During the 1980s the population of juveniles age 15 through 17 had declined; this age group was producing two-thirds of all juvenile arrests. This decline brought a temporary moderate drop in juvenile crime, but in adapting the raw count of arrests to show instead the arrests per 100,000 juveniles in the general population, it was found that by 1989 the *rate* of arrests for this age group for violent crimes had risen to its highest level in twenty-five years.[7]

Rethinking the Proper Focus of the Juvenile Court

The upsurge in juvenile crimes has produced demands for tougher measures than the juvenile court, according to popular perception, could provide. There is general agreement that a few particularly egregious cases of young toughs merit transfer to the trial courts for handling as adult criminal cases. But court and correctional experts usually resist expansion of this practice, partly because teenagers in prison are so likely to be cruelly victimized by older prisoners. A prison term is a much more punishing, and damaging, experience for a juvenile. A more practical reason for not transferring these cases to adult trial courts is that, contrary to public perception, the prosecution and disposition of a case can be more certain in juvenile court. A juvenile remanded to an adult trial court is often found not guilty because of the more stringent proof of guilt required in that court. Or, if found guilty, he or she may be released on probation as a first-time adult offender. This effect was studied in New York after a state law enacted in 1978 required any child age 13 or over to be tried as an adult if charged with a serious (Class A or B) felony. Subsequently, three different evaluative studies found that this practice "did not improve the protection of the public, did not improve the efficiency of government, and did not systematically punish serious offenders for their behavior. Only 4 percent of all those arrested and charged as juvenile offenders under the statute were sentenced to terms longer than they may have received from the Family Court.'' (Humm et al. 1994, 9.)

As a result of profound social changes, the juvenile court, which started with a paternalistic concern for helping (controlling) the children of the ''dangerous'' classes, has faced a bewildering challenge to adapt to new demands in a changed social milieu. Thoughtful suggestions in this respect are frequently voiced by corrections professionals, and from these it is possible to glimpse some ways in which the juvenile court will be modified in the future. But first the court must resolve its philosophical adjustment to an increasingly punitive society. In accord with the ''just deserts'' concept that is so popular in adult criminal justice, juvenile court critics tend to call for a more formalized approach that stresses holding the juvenile accountable. As mentioned in chapter 5, there has even been a strong call for outright abolition of the juvenile court.[8]

Predictably, any call for abolition of the court produces eager rebuttals from juvenile court loyalists who point out, as they have for decades, that the juvenile court should be retained and, before any other reform measures are carried out, should have its authority enhanced in order to be more effective. Echoing what many experts have said over many years' time, one current authority, himself a juvenile court judge, observes that ''one of the greatest challenges facing the juvenile court is attracting competent jurists to serve as juvenile court judges.'' He points out that too often the juvenile jurisdiction is in an inferior court, and the judges come to the court without special training and with little or no juvenile court experience in their previous law practice. In addition, there is little money to be made in juvenile court cases, and ''the juvenile court is perceived of as a social and not a legal court in which the lawyer's legal tools are useless. . . . Until there is sufficient attractiveness to the juvenile court judge's position, the court will be unable to fill that position with adequate numbers of qualified personnel.'' As an effective step toward solution of this problem, the author points to the wisdom of expanding the juvenile court to become a true family court. Such a court, in addition to having the conventional concern for dependent and delinquent children, ''has integrated jurisdiction over all legal problems that involve members of a family.'' As this advocate for juvenile court retention sees it, ''the critical component of the unified family court is its ability to attract and maintain a team of judges who have chosen to work in that court for a substantial period of their judicial life.''[9]

The family court concept has been well regarded for many years, and actively considered by many states, but the concept has seldom been employed. At present, versions of it exist in about twelve states. The family court is an idea that must be taken even further, in the prescient opinion of another juvenile court judge who has noted the increasing need for all varieties of social services to coordinate assistance to children. These services would include schools and public health services which, in conjunction with the courts, are increasingly needed to deal with the challenge of "the sexually abused child, the cocaine baby and the other abused and neglected children." This judge's view reflects that of many professionals who argue that dividing children into categories with simplistic labels such as educationally impaired, delinquent, neglected, dependent, incorrigible, or emotionally disturbed is too artificial in view of the complexity of the factors contributing to children's emotional and physical health. Accordingly, "in the cards is a complete fusion of the three major systems: juvenile court, public school, social services. It will be one single operation, housed in one location, with one communication network and one counselor to see the child from arrest through all three systems."[10]

This view accords with the belief of many professionals that whatever changes may be in store for the juvenile *court*, juvenile *services* must learn to rely less on institutional resources and instead develop more dynamic and comprehensive family support in the community. The large state training schools have an inherent tendency to focus on operational issues such as property maintenance and security measures to prevent abscondings or the more overt forms of inmate behavior. Their capacity to assist children in respect to personal adjustment and growth is meager at best. It is this tendency toward sterile rigidity that leads some critics to advocate sharply reduced dependence on the conventional institutions. A former administrator of the federal Office of Juvenile Justice and Delinquency Prevention was blunt in saying that "all large training schools should be closed. These institutions are expensive to operate and difficult to manage, and they simply don't work."[11]

Such a viewpoint is, of course, regarded with skepticism if not dismay by most juvenile justice careerists who have not had experience with dynamic alternatives to the custodial institution. But the numerous and varied alternative programs that have been tried in many locations support the contention that noninstitutional services can be safe and effective with perhaps all but 10 percent of the juveniles who now typically are sent to institutions. The St. Louis Home Detention program noted in chapter 5, for example, returned high-risk juveniles to their homes to await their court hearings; the program proved able to keep the juveniles from new offenses or abscondings, and did so at about one-third the cost of holding them in conventional detention. In Massachusetts, when Jerome Miller, Commissioner of Youth Services, closed the state training schools in 1971 and 1972, he successfully substituted a wide variety of small, intensive community programs that offered almost daily involvement with the young clients, using many different techniques to accommodate the many different kinds of problems they presented. (Miller 1991, 185–198)

In the area of public policy, courts, probation services, and detention and correctional institutions, similar to other bureaucracies, almost instinctively resist change. Nevertheless, new philosophical concepts regarding adjudication of children and delivery of services to them and their families have emerged during the last two decades. These new insights affect all the components of juvenile justice, and careerists now at work will be continually challenged to launch new initiatives in constructive defiance of traditional, but defective, orthodoxy.

As one example of refocused attention to juvenile court jurisdiction, the state of Montana entered the 1990s determined to remedy the problem of fractionated services to children. Assuming responsibility for guidance of the effort, the Montana Board of Crime Control, with the help of a conference of leaders from many different juvenile and family service agencies, sensibly recognized that "today's extreme pressure in the adult corrections system is not an anomaly—it is a direct result of a social system that has failed at previous stages." Analyzing the problem, the Montana planners criticized their juvenile services in terms that could apply to most other states. A major defect is that "the system has focused upon the individual and has not included approaches which focus on the family, the community and the educational system." This is a natural result of the gradual accretion of bureaucratic service units. "One of the problems which occurs as a result of the uncoordinated nature of our system is a lack of accountability of any single part of that system. . . . When problems are identified within the system, it is difficult to pin down the particular cause or solution. 'Passing the buck' is easily accomplished when there are so many different agencies and levels of government involved."[12]

Montana's resulting plan, which is being implemented during the mid-1990s, includes development of a computerized database uniting all caregivers, monitoring of performance quality of involved agencies, developing alternative programs intended to promote whole family involvement, and teaching accountability to juveniles. One perceptive part of the plan is to augment staff training with emphasis on whole family services, which promote uniform quality statewide. All components, including judges, will be cross-trained.

Montana and other states that are reappraising their correctional services are showing a welcome new interest in giving clients a sense of accountability as an important element in their rehabilitation. Also encouraging is a new interest in having the service agencies themselves practice a level of accountability that historically has not been required of them. Today, in the provision of services to both juvenile and adult offenders, the need for ensured quality has been increasingly felt and has led to a strong new initiative for definition and enforcement of uniform standards. The instrument for this purpose is accreditation.

Accreditation of Criminal Justice Services

The accreditation process as such is by no means recent; the general public has long known and endorsed accreditation of hospitals and educational institutions. But there is, of course, an obvious reason why such facilities would be subject to accreditation. Degrees conferred by an unaccredited college would be of little value to its graduates, and the college simply would not survive. Prisons, on the other hand, have never needed any certification of quality in order to receive inmates. When accreditation for correctional services was finally initiated, the impetus came from the same increasing interest in professionalism that also generated the new staff training programs in the 1970s. More specifically, it was spurred by the proliferation of civil suits against correctional institutions. The managers' efforts to defend themselves often made them realize the handicap of not having any uniform and recognized standards by which a facility could be judged. Some would also suggest that the shock from the Attica prison riot in 1971 considerably stimulated the interest in accreditation.

Actually, most of the correctional components of the judicial system have had standards for many years; the American Bar Association and the National Council on Crime and Delinquency, among others, have produced well-known and reputable sets of standards. But these have remained separate and to an extent competitive, without unified recognition by the corrections field. The American Correctional Association (ACA) has also been writing standards. In 1974, with a broad base of support from corrections workers throughout the United States, and with the help of federal funds, the ACA launched the Commission on Accreditation for Corrections, which then became the recognized accrediting agency.[13]

The Commission, under its twenty-person board, operated as a branch of ACA from 1974 to 1981, and then as a separate corporation until 1986, when it again became a part of ACA. Whatever its affiliation, the Commission needs to have sufficient independence to be free of bias and to resist intimidation when judging agency performance. This principle, though important, is not always easy to sustain. In its first few years, the Commission suffered sharp criticism for alleged favoritism, with some prominent observers charging that several substandard prisons were being accredited only because their wardens were influential among the "old timers" in corrections. As one example, the Florida State Prison was the subject of highly critical investigations in 1979 and 1980, but despite the findings of gross overcrowding and brutal treatment of inmates, the institution was approved for accreditation in 1981. Though this was not the only example of questionable accreditation, this action was stoutly defended: "Supporters of accreditation say they are not embarrassed by the fact that a few huge, aged prisons have won approval. They say that at least at the beginning, it is necessary to set the standards within reach of every facility."[14]

A point that invites dispute is that despite agreement that accreditation standards must be rigorous, the reality is that an old prison might be well managed, but unable to meet standards for physical improvements. Old prisons typically have cells about 40 square feet in size, sometimes less. If modern standards call for cells to be at least 60 square feet in size, the substandard prison cannot enlarge its cells, which were built for extreme durability, without sustaining exorbitant costs. Nonetheless, gradually over a period of years, many of the old prisons have been substantially upgraded under the influence of the accreditation movement.

Charges of favoritism are a natural hazard of the accreditation process. To ensure that the standards are credible, it is essential to use input from professionals in the field in designing the standards. But the accreditation process must also be consistently objective and resolute in judging some of those same professionals or their colleagues when they apply for accreditation. This may not be easy, as the Commission has discovered, but in recent years, after recovering from earlier bouts of criticism, the integrity of the process is generally accepted.

The Commission on Accreditation now utilizes nineteen sets of standards for as many services, including adult and juvenile institutions, probation and parole agencies, and food, health, and administrative services. To become accredited, an agency or institution must initially apply, pay a fee, and conduct a self-evaluation with respect to all the points that will be covered by the applicable standards, usually numbering four hundred or more. With continuing assistance from the Commission on Accreditation staff, the agency works over a period of time to bring its operation into accord with the required standards. The process culminates in a visit by a team of auditors who make a detailed check of agency performance regarding each standard, then make a recommendation to the Commission. If accreditation is granted, it is subject to annual review, and possibly to revocation if performance quality is not sustained.[15]

Since the process began in 1978, the corrections field has responded to accreditation with steadily growing involvement until in late 1993 the ACA could report that over one thousand agencies in the United States and Canada were accredited or working toward accreditation.[16] A major advantage of the accreditation status is found to be a result of the process of acquiring it. It is a long and involved process in which the staff of the institution or agency must develop a high quality of managerial system and orderly, reliable accountability. A pronounced benefit is a substantially improved staff morale derived from a sense of order and safety. The accreditation status may also be of help in backing up budget requests for the needed staff and equipment.

The field of law enforcement has also created an accreditation process, which evolved in much the same manner as did the corrections process. The Commission on Accreditation for Law Enforcement Agencies was organized in 1979 through the joint efforts of the International Association of Chiefs of Police, the National Sheriffs Association, the Police Executive Research Forum, and the National Organization of Black Law Enforcement Executives. The new Commission, governed by a board with eleven members from law enforcement and ten members from the general public, hired as its first executive a longtime careerist who had been head of the FBI's National Academy.[17]

Agencies subject to this accreditation include city, county, and state police departments, sheriffs' departments, and also more narrowly focused agencies such as park police or university campus police departments. By late 1993, the Commission had granted accreditation to 288 agencies in the United States and Canada and was undergoing a substantial expansion of this service.

Privatization of Law Enforcement and Correctional Services

Having private contractors supplement or assist with governmental services is a long-established practice, and in respect to some types of services, is not only well accepted but virtually indispensable. Until recently, however, law enforcement or corrections agencies have been less likely to invite the help of private entrepreneurs. Recently these agencies have shown increasing interest in the potential of the private sector to augment public services, as a result of the combined pressures of public fear of crime and the limitations on public financing. In recent years private corporations have provided many police services, often with little or no controversy or public attention. Most citizens hardly notice an obvious example of private contractors employed by the government, the privately contracted security guard who controls their entry into a government building and submits them to a routine identity check.

Security services comprise an important growth industry. A report from 1985 noted that "in the past 15 years the private security industry has leapfrogged public law enforcement in number of personnel. An estimated total private security employment in 1969 of less than 300,000 persons has grown to 1.1 million, more than double the number of sworn law enforcement officers at the state and local levels."[18]

Notwithstanding that high dollar figure, much of this growth results from limitations on public funds for police services. Often, for example, a residential neighborhood or development will contract for private patrol services, but, "it does not appear that citizens who employ private police are dissatisfied with their local police agency; rather they are pragmatists who recognize that there are limitations on what the police can do."[19] The same view prompts businesses to protect valuable property with their own or contracted guards. "These private security officers perform many of the same functions as public law officers; controlling entrances and exits to facilities; preventing or reporting fires; promoting safety; safeguarding equipment, valuables, and confidential material; and patrolling restricted areas."[20]

Although private police agencies are common, there are concerns about the quality control of these businesses. "States are finding that such firms must be carefully regulated and their employees screened and trained. About one half of the states have passed licensing laws aimed at accomplishing these goals. . . . Faced with mounting cost-containment problems, the police in future years may find that they must turn to private security providers to concentrate on crime-prevention efforts while the police turn their attention to violent crimes and crime response."[21]

In respect to the field of corrections, the recent privatization controversy has focused most visibly on the operation of prisons, inciting intense debate corresponding to the high visibility of those institutions. Here again, interest in the subject has come principally from financial problems combined with the problems governments have in financing and expeditiously building custodial facilities. Often the argument is made—and often refuted—that private entrepreneurs, free of some of the restrictions that apply to governmental agencies, can build institutions more quickly and operate them more efficiently. Sometimes there is a need to resort to the private sector, not so much to save money, but to solve an impasse, such as occurs when a county board wants to build a new jail even though the electorate has defeated a bond issue for it. In this case "the most significant advantage is the ability to evade debt limits by insisting on an annually renewable lease subject to non-appropriation."[22] Variations on this situation have led to a modest growth of privately operated correctional facilities; in 1985 it was reported that "about two dozen major correction facilities are owned or operated by private groups. . . . These are in addition to several hundred halfway houses and juvenile centers that private groups began operating in the 1970s." The same reporter, looking for factors favoring this trend, commented that "supporters see a new efficiency, greater vitality, flexibility and a reduction in costs."[23]

In rejecting private prisons, critics raise legal, ethical, and practical issues that present some basic and complex philosophical questions for public policymakers. Financial principles are perhaps the most immediate concern, prompting such protests as these: "The most disturbing aspect of such endeavors is that they represent camouflaged campaigns to short-circuit long established procedures for public financing of state facilities." (Geis 1987, 87) That comment by a criminologist was echoed by a former corrections administrator who observed that "private operators claim they can build prisons faster. True. Entrepreneurs can erect facilities without the encumbrance of plodding bureaucracies. They also avoid the lengthy process of going to the voters with a bond issue. Thus the public is denied a voice in deciding whether new prisons are to be built."[24]

Ordinarily, in obtaining services or products from private suppliers, government agencies are expected to put contracts out for a competitive bidding process each year, and to renew contracts on an annual basis. But such a process is not a practical possibility when a private contractor operates an institution in which the contractor has a substantial investment. If periodic competition and contract renewal were required, no contractor could afford this kind of venture. Consequently, once a private corporation has been engaged to operate an institution, the corporation virtually cannot be removed even though its quality of service may fail. Another aspect of the same problem is the virtual impossibility for the government to escape quickly from a situation involving a deteriorated contracted service. If a privately operated institution becomes badly managed, with possible dangerous conditions or mistreatment of its inmates, it is of little or no help for the terms of the contract to allow its cancellation. If the contract is canceled, and the government has no alternative space to which it can quickly shift several hundred inmates (and this would almost certainly be the case), or has no reserve staff to take over the operation, it is effectively deprived of an immediate remedy.

Another issue, the constitutional rights of prisoners, raises questions about the propriety of allowing private operators and their employees to make decisions of a quasi-judicial nature affecting prisoners. Staff decisions about disciplinary actions or about granting of "good time" have a direct bearing on the inmate's eventual release date. For some critics this raises the disturbing prospect that the profit motive will influence such decisions in the direction of sustaining a high prison population.[25] They are understandably perturbed by the prospect of lobbyists, on behalf of profit-making prison operators, urging legislative measures that will help to keep prison populations high. One criminologist fears that "private corporations, once in the field, will generate great political and public pressures to feather their own correctional nests, primarily by pushing for more incarceration and harsher senten- ces." (Geis 1987, 94)

Whereas fundamental questions such as these will probably continue to retard the spread of private prison operations, there seems to be a growing role in adult corrections for many privatized services that do not involve ownership or administration of facilities. Health services, for instance, are being offered by private providers to prisons that have had difficulty in attracting and holding their own medical professionals. Some smaller institutions such as jails have successfully used outside caterers to prepare and furnish all meals. A few institutions have con- tracted with private corporations to conduct therapeutic treatment pro- grams. During the 1980s, for example, the Kansas State Industrial Re- formatory at Hutchinson developed an intensive treatment program for drug addicts, using a separate building adapted for this purpose. The building had dormitory space for assigned inmates so they could live, work, and participate in the treatment process, but quite apart from the general prison population. The privately owned professional agency engaged to operate the program was free to use its own expertise in conducting the daily life in that building according to the best treatment principles.

One thoughtful author argued that this sort of private service in prisons might help overcome the insidious conditions typical of prison programs wherein the regular government personnel are under no com- pulsion to prove results. As long as they show up to work every day and go through their expected program routines, their function is sus- tained. For privately contracted service providers, however, "since their profit and livelihood would be contingent on program performance, they could not afford to allow the integrity of their programs to suffer corruption." It is also suggested that "the infusion of private interests into the prison environment creates the potential that new ideas and approaches to offender therapy will be forthcoming. With profits on the line, vendors will have clear incentives to develop more effective modalities."[26]

Another aspect of privatization is that the incursion of private indus- try into prisons is seen as a welcome trend in normalizing prison life. Typically, production shops in prisons have operated with obsolete equipment, little regard for efficiency, and without pretense of giving the inmate workers experience in the real-life demands of the workplace. In recent years, however, a few prisons have invited private industries to set up and operate realistic production shops in which inmates are hired and paid standard wages. The specific business arrangements vary from state to state, with the general concept being known as "free venture'' industries. One noted and unusual variation is in Kansas, where the State Correctional Institution at Lansing every day sends a number of its inmates out to a metalworking shop where they function as regular employees, along with civilian workers. The Lansing program is probably the country's most experienced and well-evaluated example of cooperation between correctional management and private manufacturing.[27]

An important prison industry project on the federal level was initiated in 1984 with the authorization by Congress of the Prison Industry Enhancement Program (PIE). The program funded twenty demonstration projects in federal prisons in which outside manufacturers could set up regular production shops, recruit and hire inmate workers, and pay full market wages. Unlike the usual prison work assignment, this work requires the inmate to be fully productive, subject to exacting supervision by a foreman, and subject to firing for poor performance. One requirement of this program is that deductions are made from the prisoner's wages to pay the prison for ''board and room,'' to put a specified amount in savings to be used on the prisoner's future release, and, as appropriate, to pay restitution to the victim, support to his or her family, and meet any other financial obligations.[28]

Juvenile corrections has a more extensive history of using private providers, and this practice, though changing in some ways, is generally unabated and usually uncontroversial. In addition to operating their own training schools for committed delinquents, many states have long made use of specialized schools operated by religious orders or other private agencies. When Massachusetts closed its juvenile institutions in the early 1970s, it turned for help to the community-based services of several private organizations. Other states too have found that the wide variety of services needed for the treatment of difficult juveniles can best be met by purchasing them from private specialists; altogether it appears likely that the juvenile corrections field will continue to exist as a useful mix of public and private services.[29]

New Attention to Victims of Crime

''Victimology'' is one of the newer words in the criminal justice vocabulary. It covers the general body of knowledge about factors contributing to victimization, the psychological effects of being a victim, the philosophy that should guide public policy in respect to crime victims, and the wide-ranging measures that may be taken for restoration or healing of victims. The first crime victim compensation program was legislated in New Zealand in 1963. In 1964, Britain enacted its victim compensation plan. The nationwide publicity about the Kitty Genovese murder in 1964 spurred interest in the idea of victim compensation in the United States. "California enacted the first State compensation program in 1965."[30] After that the concept spread steadily until currently the District of Columbia and all fifty states have victim compensation programs.

As one of the particularly healthy new developments in criminal justice, the compensation programs represent a long overdue sensitivity to both the feelings and the practical needs of crime victims. The most egregious of the callous attitudes has usually been toward victims of rape. Although inexcusable, it is understandable that police, with no special training in the psychology of victimization, and contending constantly with human deviousness, would become cynical and treat allegations of rape with skepticism. Rape likely involves one person's word against another, and the police know that the alleged activity in some cases may represent infinitely varied degrees of guilt on the part of either party. But police, prosecutors, and legislators have lately been made aware of the inhumanity of the customary practices of the law enforcement system, which ignored the rape victim's emotional trauma and physical stress, and which may have left the victim feeling that she was treated more like an offender than a victim. (Austern 1987, xi–xiv) Historically, law enforcement and criminal justice officials too often have not realized the excruciating effect of their routine procedures. "Sexual assault victims and battered women often experienced the criminal justice process as a secondary victimization. The victim was not kept informed of the case progress; not notified of proceedings; kept waiting at the court for long periods of time in order to testify; and not involved in the charging decision, the plea bargaining, or the sentencing."[31]

The highly personal needs of rape victims have engendered the rapid spread of "rape crisis centers," which customarily provide immediate response to calls for help at any hour. These centers may be operated by local governmental agencies, but often are organized by private care providers, typically with financial subsidies from county or city governments. One of the earlier and best of these was the Polk County (Iowa) Rape/Sexual Assault Care Center, organized in 1974. Typical of such agencies, the center was designed to respond immediately to a new rape case, with one of its counselors accompanying the victim to a hospital to ensure a private and considerate medical examination, then staying with the victim through interrogations by police and prosecutors. The counselor would give factual explanations of the processes to the victim, and provide emotional protection and support throughout the entire process. Also typical of such services, after proving its vital function, the Iowa agency was later reorganized with the new title of Polk County Victim Services, and was given an expanded function to serve victims in general.

Not only does sensitive, specialized assistance contribute greatly to the rape victim's emotional recovery, but also it helps with prosecutions. Faced by the intimidating ordeal of reporting and prosecuting the crime, many rape victims have preferred to keep silent. But with assurance of sympathetic treatment, the victims come forward more readily, and offenders are more often convicted. The Polk County agency reported that after its first two years "police clearance rates for rape cases have risen from 50 percent to 69 percent. Even more significant changes have been seen in the special prosecutor's office, where victims show an increasing willingness to press charges. Before the program began charges were filed in only a third of cases where the offender was identified; that figure has now jumped to three fourths of those cases."[32]

Various state laws serve victims of all types of crimes, but philosophical approaches vary and differences exist in the details of rules governing eligibility for compensation. Most commonly, compensation is allowed within an arbitrary limit to pay for medical expenses not covered by insurance, loss of wages or support, cost of temporary shelter, court transportation costs, funeral expenses, and in appropriate cases, psychological counseling, or moving expenses when a victim feels it necessary to move away from the home where the crime occurred. Claims are likely to be denied when the victim, as frequently happens, was partially to blame in the instigation of the crime, or when there was a lengthy delay in reporting the crime, or if there was a lack of cooperation with law enforcement.

In 1982 the federal government established the President's Task Force on Victims of Crime. Two years later, the task force's extensive report recommended a range of measures to compensate victims and to accord them more considerate treatment in the justice process. One targeted issue was the standard practice of keeping parole board hearings confidential. "Although this was done to protect the parolee, the result has been to insulate parole boards from accountability." Similarly, the task force urged that at the point of sentencing the presentence investigation reports should always include a victim impact statement. For police, the task force recommended that sensitivity to the needs and feelings of victims should be a part of their training, while their investigative procedures should be conducted with more concern for victims' immediate practical and psychological problems.[33]

The task force report led to the passage of the Victims of Crime Act of 1984 (VOCA) which, with several later amendments, encourages state programs in various ways on behalf of victims. VOCA provides for federal grants to states generally for *assistance* to victims as distinguished from *compensation* for loss or injury. The Act has influenced development of many victim service agencies on state and local levels, with an increasing variety of initiatives, and has revealed a substantial area of need, as is evident from the number of claims being filed. In 1985 the country's state compensation programs received 45,108 claims; by 1989 the number was 107,295.[34] The general vigor of the movement is also suggested by New York's experience with its Crime Victims Board, which is that state's general advocate for victims' rights, needs, and interests. This board receives and distributes funds from both state and federal (VOCA) sources. During the fiscal year 1991 to 1992, it made available nearly $7 million to eighty-three local victim assistance programs throughout New York State.[35]

The organization of programs to help victims of crime varies throughout the country, with many of the service agencies being governmental and others being privately organized. Minnesota, for example, illustrates the new trend of correctional agencies, which traditionally had been concerned only with the custody and treatment of offenders, and now serve victims as well. A principal victim service agency in Minnesota is the nonprofit, private Citizens Council on Crime and Justice. The council operates comfortably despite the irony that although it was founded primarily to serve offenders, it now is also operating an active victim service with a hotline that brings immediate practical help to a victim at any hour. Also unusual is the arrangement that about half of the support for this service comes from state and federal funds paid through the Department of Corrections.[36]

As experience with these services grows, additional types of service needs become apparent, and gradually states move to meet them. This discussion can be concluded with one example. In 1992 the Pennsylvania legislature enacted its "Crime Victims Bill of Rights" and gave responsibility for its implementation to the Department of Corrections. Accordingly, the Department now has a Director of Victim Services who oversees the various duties the new legislation requires. This includes counseling of victims as needed in relation to sources of compensation; it also promotes a communication system on behalf of victims, monitoring presentence report preparations to ensure input from victims. Victims also are informed of such events as the escape of the imprisoned offender, or of impending hearings where decisions will be made on a furlough, parole release, or transfer to or from a mental hospital.

There is a cheering quality in the fact that not only are victim services flourishing, but correctional agencies, after a history of having responsibility only for offenders, are also responding to the needs of victims. A much less cheering fact is that the proliferation of handguns among the general population is contributing disturbingly to the increasing numbers of victims, and that especially among teens, the young person with a gun may suddenly become an offender, a victim, or both.

The Divisive Issue of Gun Control

In 1981 the town of Morton Grove, Illinois, population 24,000, enacted an ordinance banning the sale or possession (except by law enforcement personnel) of firearms within the town. The following year the town of Kennesaw, Georgia, population 8,500, enacted an ordinance requiring every resident (with certain exceptions) to keep in the home a working firearm and ammunition.[37] The contrasting laws of the two towns prompted widespread debate and some court challenges, and seemed to symbolize the polarization of the country's population in general on this emotional issue. The gun control controversy has important relevance to strategies for crime reduction, while also highlighting the frustrations experienced by designers of public policy when dealing with a subject that few of its opposing partisans are able to approach objectively.

Although their concepts of how to control firearms differ sharply, both sides of the issue recognize that some strategy is needed to reduce the contribution made by guns, especially handguns, to a high proportion of the nation's crime. "In 1984 firearms were used in the United States in 59 percent of homicides, 36 percent of robberies, and 21 percent of aggravated assaults. In each category the predominance of the handgun is striking." (Zimring and Hawkins 1987, 38) To discourage this kind of weapon use the gun owners organizations, the most visible of which is the National Rifle Association (NRA), urge aggressive prosecution and severe penalties for offenders using guns in crimes. Those holding the opposing view maintain that the threat of prosecution and punishment has never been a deterrent and that the only effective measure will be to deprive potential offenders of handgun possession.

The conceptual aspect of the debate starts with interpretation of the Second Amendment of the Constitution. "A well regulated militia being necessary to the security of a free state, the right of the people to keep and bear arms shall not be infringed." The amendment has been endlessly analyzed word for word without a final authoritative consensus ever being reached. "Debate has been sharply polarized between those who claim that the amendment guarantees nothing to individuals, protects only the state's right to maintain organized military units, and thus poses no obstacle to gun control, and those who claim that the amendment guarantees some sort of individual right to arms." This comment comes from a researcher who notes that more than twenty thousand gun control laws exist at local, state, and federal levels, and that such laws survive and proliferate probably because, as written, they are not unduly intrusive and their enforcement is usually cautious. It is likely that if such laws would ever go as far as a serious effort at confiscation, the needed constitutional interpretation would be pursued and resolved. (Kates 1983, 206, 273)

Legislators are frequently importuned to enact new restrictions on guns, particularly after a publicized killing has occurred with a type of gun that is seen as "bad," such as a cheap handgun or an automatic assault rifle. Their dilemma is that some indignant constituents demand initiatives to outlaw weapons considered useless for any purpose except to kill people, whereas others, backed by well-funded gun owners organizations, protest that citizens have the right to self-protection. It proves virtually impossible to write a law that differentiates nicely between "useful" and "useless" guns. Even a cheap, unreliable, inaccurate pistol can dissuade an attacker. As one analyst points out, "any gun that can be used in self-defense has a legitimate purpose."[38]

Throughout the continuing debates in legislative halls, the opponents of gun control usually prevail even though polls usually show that a majority of the population favors controls of some kind. The public ambivalence reflects a confused wish for protection from irresponsible or degenerate users of guns, while at the same time wanting to allow the law-abiding person unrestricted gun possession. Well-organized lobbyists represent both sides of the issue, although gun control opponents have the greater share of the funding. By one count, in 1987, the National Rifle Association spent $668,058 for lobbying, the Gun Owners of America spent $608,672, the Citizens' Committee for the Right to Keep and Bear Arms spent $271,435, for a total of $1,548,165. This contrasted with an expenditure of $900,343 spent on the other side of the issue by Handgun Control, Inc.[39]

The NRA argues that any small move toward gun control, however innocuous, will lead inexorably to further restrictions and a gradual erosion of citizens' rights. With such intransigent opposition by the NRA to any curbs on the use of guns, even the slightest gains by gun control advocates are considered impressive. As one example, a very modest new federal restriction on gun sales was touted as a significant victory when Congress passed the so-called Brady bill, which did no more than require a five-day waiting period before any gun purchase.[40]

While gun owner organizations stridently assert that gun control does not work, researchers have found evidence that it can make an impact, although the nature of the subject is so complex that the findings tend to be mixed. One example often cited is the strict gun control law enacted in Boston in 1975; subsequent studies seem to agree that it has been effective. A police publication notes that "in Boston, researchers say that 28 people are alive today because of the Massachusetts gun law."[41]

Official police attitudes tend to be ambivalent on this subject, and vary from one setting to another; urban police officials tend to lean toward gun control, whereas police in small town or rural areas are more likely to oppose it. The official position on the subject by the International Association of Chiefs of Police makes three points: (1) there should be tighter restrictions on firearm purchases, with more use of waiting periods and exacting identification and record checks; (2) there should be limitations on manufacture of automatic and semiautomatic assault-type guns, with sale of these to the general public prohibited; and (3) legislation should require severe sentences for gun law violators, with the additional provision that confiscated guns are to be destroyed, not resold.[42]

The U.S. Conference of Mayors commissioned a study and report in the 1970s intended to provide guidance for city officials on the gun issue. The report findings emphasized the dangers of guns to their owners, and cast doubt on their value for self-protection. "Ownership of handguns by private citizens for self-protection against crime appears to provide more of a psychological belief in safety than actual deterrence to criminal behavior. . . . The use of a weapon in resistance to a criminal attack usually results in a greater probability of bodily injury or death to the victim." The study noted the danger to family members who are supposedly being protected. "A gun kept in the home for self-protection is far more likely to cause serious injury or death to family and friends than to an intruder. Children and young adults are most vulnerable to firearm misuse."[43]

This report, in referring to family and friends, spoke mainly of accidental injuries. But statistics on crimes committed with guns also show a preponderance of friends and family members among the victims. Noted researcher Franklin Zimring, after completing a study of homicides in Chicago in the 1960s, reported that 74 percent of the persons killed were friends, neighbors, business associates, or family members of the attackers. The latter category was by far the largest. Zimring reasoned that if homicides resulted from deliberate, planned intention to kill, then a prohibition on guns would have little effect on the murder rate, for the determined attacker would easily find substitute means. But in fact, murder is much more likely to result from an unplanned attack, which, in the absence of a gun, would require a substitute weapon. Studies show that attacks by alternative weapons, including knives, are considerably less likely to be fatal. "And if the probable substitute for firearms in these situations is less likely to lead to death, then the elimination of guns would reduce the number of homicides." (Zimring 1968, 722)

Over the years many research projects and astute analyses have produced similar observations, supplying ammunition for gun control advocates, and justifying their faith that fatal assaults would be reduced if handguns could be taken out of general circulation. But gun control opponents are equally compelling in pointing to the overwhelming reality that more than 120 million guns are in possession in the United States now, with the number increasing every year; that restrictions enacted in one state are hardly effective when guns can be obtained from the neighboring state; and that despite public acceptance of some form of gun control, confiscation of guns would simply not have the political support ever to be authorized, and, without confiscation, the present pool of guns will remain in the public's hands for many decades to come even if further manufacture were to be prohibited.

One author's thoughtful perspective on the controversy deserves quoting:

> Each side faces a delicate dilemma in their propaganda efforts, one familiar to fund raisers everywhere—they must convey the enormity of the problem, yet also instill confidence in their own effectiveness by pointing to their victories and the progress they have achieved. Thus the NRA must simultaneously convince its current and potential members and contributors that it is facing a powerful gun control movement that is a serious threat to gun owners' rights if not checked, but also convince them that the NRA has beaten the enemy in the past and can do so again in the future, if they are just given the support they need. Likewise Handgun Control, Incorporated (HCI) and the Coalition to Stop Gun Violence (CSGV) overstate the connection between guns and violence, and speak darkly of the NRA's vast political power, seemingly unlimited funds, . . . while also boasting of their own organization's growing membership and recent legislative victories. To believe both sides, one would have to believe that both parties to the conflict are simultaneously weak and strong, triumphantly victorious and headed toward ignominious defeat. (Kleck 1991, 16)

With motivated and committed forces deployed so resolutely against each other, the gun control issue will certainly continue to generate political heat for some years to come, while policymakers will wish only for relief from such a no-win issue. Zimring's view of the prospects is probably accurate: "Whatever happens will probably happen gradually. Thus, the condition for what might be viewed as a revolutionary shift in public policy is an evolutionary change in public attitude." (Zimring and Hawkins 1987, 185)

Evolving Concepts of Corrective Measures

"Hope springs eternal," it is said, and this includes the hope of finding a way to cure people of criminal tendencies cheaply, quickly, and in a manner that will be emotionally satisfying to the public. In this regard the correctional systems are periodically susceptible to fadism as successive panaceas come and go. In recent years two such magic bullets were the "boot camp" and the "Scared Straight" program.

Rough Discipline as a Treatment Tool: Boot Camps

It probably was inevitable that the boot camp idea would occur to legislators, many of whom themselves had gone through basic military training, and may have remembered boot camp as the ingredient that "made men" out of raw recruits. If boot camp could do that for soldiers, why not for undisciplined young delinquents who might be handled this way instead of being packed into expensive and crowded prisons? "Between 1980 and 1991 prison populations grew about 150 percent, reaching a total of 823,414 inmates. To handle this growth, corrections systems increased their capacities and looked for less costly alternatives to traditional forms of incarceration. One such alternative is the prison boot camp."[44]

The usual boot camp (also called "shock incarceration") accepts young adults, most of them convicted of nonviolent substance abuse offenses. As a last chance alternative to a prison sentence, it attempts in a relatively short period of time, typically from ninety days to six months, to give the participants a new sense of pride and self-discipline. The daily schedule includes rugged physical exercise conducted by drill instructors who use an intimidating, high-pressure approach as they demand unquestioning, immediate obedience to orders. The days also are filled with manual work assignments, drug counseling, and perhaps educational studies. Politically, the boot camps approach the status of an enthusiastically supported panacea. A federal government inquiry in 1993 found that twenty-six states were operating fifty-seven boot camps with a capacity of 8,880 inmates, and more were being planned. Despite the public's irrepressible belief in the technique, however, the finding was that "there is no clear indication that boot camps have measurably reduced recidivism. . . recidivism must be measured over time, and most boot camps are still relatively new."[45]

The persistent popularity of this program has demonstrated the potency of an idea that captures the public's hopeful wish for a quick and easy solution to a complex problem. General support for the program has been undimmed by adverse findings about its value or the unenthusiastic reception it receives from many corrections managers. One of the earliest of the knowledgeable critics commented that "corrections officials do not appear to be as delighted with shock incarceration programs as are judges, law enforcement officers, legislators, and prosecutors." He further observed that "the boot camp programs are often underfunded, sometimes underused or poorly implemented, clearly untested, and mostly incomplete efforts to provide full correctional programs for young offenders." (Sechrest 1989, 18, 19)

In the mid-1990s, with public interest surging in anticrime legislation, federal and state governments were funding or proposing still more of the boot camp programs at the same time that this technique was increasingly disparaged. A typical observation came from an economist-turned-columnist who declared that "ten years of experience have provided us with clear evidence the camps . . . don't reduce crime and don't reduce the prison population." He went on to discuss an especially troubling phenomenon known as "net widening," one way in which a diversionary program tends to defeat itself. Instead of being used for offenders who otherwise would have been sent to prison, it too often is used for those who would probably have been left in the community on probation. As a consequent effect, "the use of boot camps has increased, not decreased, the prison population. Young criminals whom judges would normally free on parole are instead sentenced to a few months in boot camp, where the high dropout rate guarantees that many of them will end up serving regular prison terms."[46]

News accounts have often reported the negative findings. *Newsweek,* for instance, noted the opposition arguments being expressed by criminologists: "Yet politicians are reluctant to relinquish the idea. Why? For elected officials scrambling to appear tough on crime, boot camps are a cheap and easy way of placating angry constituents. News footage of panting, shaven-headed young men in khaki jumpsuits, doing push-ups at the foot of a snarling drill instructor, satisfies the deep public appetite for seeing some civility pounded into thugs who terrorize their neighborhoods."[47]

A federal government study of a boot camp program in the Louisiana corrections system reflects certain concerns that have been expressed by many critics about this type of program, one being the potential for abuse by overly zealous and unrestrained staff. "The hard labor, physical exercise, summary punishments, boot camp atmosphere, and strict discipline of the Louisiana shock incarceration program combine to present a potential for both accidents and staff abuse of authority." The other point of concern has important significance. "Although offenders experience some positive changes while in the program, these changes are not enough to enable them to successfully overcome the difficulties they face when they return to their home environment."[48]

This is the same problem that defeats so many rehabilitative programs—the lack of follow-through. Typically, the same legislative bodies that are willing to fund boot camps are much less interested in committing funds for the kind of intensive follow-up supervision needed to protect the original investment. The young offender who sticks with the program and gets a new sense of purpose and resolve still needs close support and constant reinforcement of any gains achieved if he or she is to withstand the intense contrary pressures that will appear upon return to the youth's former environment, particularly when that environment involves a drug culture. But intensive follow-through supervision is expensive and does not have the politically appealing visibility needed to assure its financial support.

The "Scared Straight" type of program is quite different from the boot camp in that it is not residential and is only a one-time experience; the program involves jarring juveniles into a realization of the danger they face as delinquents. The Scared Straight program is similar to boot camps in the political appeal the program has in being seen as quick, cheap, and dramatic. (The idea originated with a prisoner group known as "The Lifers" at the Rahway State Prison in New Jersey in 1976.) With the cooperation of interested juvenile courts, selected "at-risk" juvenile boys and girls are conveyed in groups of a dozen or so to a prison, where they are confronted by several life-term inmates and told in the most graphic and threatening terms about what would await them should they ever become prison inmates. In a session lasting perhaps an hour, the young people are verbally assaulted by intimidating descriptions of the most brutal aspects of prison life, delivered with a bitter flavoring of vulgar and profane prison argot.

When the program started it was quickly reported in the press, and just as quickly gained local popularity. About two years later, a nationally distributed television program showed a typical encounter of juveniles with the Lifers, and touted the technique as practically an instant cure for delinquency. The narrators' comments during the television program included such unqualified assertions as: "The results of this unique program are astounding. Participating communities report that 80 to 90 percent of the kids that they sent to Rahway go straight after leaving this stage. That's an amazing success story, and it's unequalled by traditional rehabilitation methods." At its conclusion the program quoted a juvenile court judge who called the program "the most effective, inexpensive deterrent in the entire correctional process in America." (Finckenauer 1982, 96–97)

When the Scared Straight program was fresh and promising, a reporter for *Corrections Magazine* saw it as "among the most successful and widely publicized inmate efforts in the country." But he also noted its limited capacity to make a helpful impact. The least serious among the delinquents he found sometimes to be too disturbed by the experience, while the more committed delinquents seemed to be little affected. "The children they are most effective with are on the borderline between accepting criminal activity as a way of life, or rejecting it."[49]

Under the impetus of the extensive publicity, the Scared Straight idea was soon imitated in a number of prisons, but over time it has not survived as strongly as the boot camps. This may largely be due to research that showed that the florid optimism about the program's effectiveness was unfounded. Included in the principal research project on the program was a comparison of a group of juveniles who had attended Scared Straight sessions (the experimental group) with a similar group who did not attend (the control group). During the six-month period after attending the sessions, the experimental group actually showed a higher delinquency rate than the control group (i.e., the ones who had not attended). The researcher concluded that "in sum, my research strongly suggests that the Lifer's Project is not scaring kids straight. If nothing else, the findings challenge, and in my judgement, debunk any thoughts that this approach could be a panacea." (Finckenauer 1982, 135–136, 170)

The disappointing experience with programs such as these should not discourage further attempts to find approaches that will be effective, for some techniques that are currently being tried can be considered quite promising. The remainder of this chapter will examine several of these experimental techniques.

The Character and Use of the "Therapeutic Community"

Two characteristics of traditional prisons need to be mentioned as background for the therapeutic community (TC) idea and to highlight just how radical an idea it is. Traditional prisons have a long history of managment with a contrived distance between prisoners and their custodians. Early prisons prohibited talking among inmates, and even when that rule was eventually relaxed, it remained standard for the guard force to allow no expression of discontent or even to forbid prisoners to speak to staff unless necessary, and then only in the most respectful terms. The other characteristic of traditional prisons is well expressed by an old prisoner motto, "You do your time and let me do my time." It reflects the prisoner's adaptation to the volatile, dangerous prison world by minding his own business and taking no responsibility for any other prisoner's troubles.

The TC idea seeks to reverse both of these characteristics, with the aim of fostering a maturing, rehabilitative effect for individual inmates, or at least of making a safer prison environment. As originally developed by a British psychiatrist, Maxwell Jones, the TC was first used in a mental hospital to bring together the patients and the staff in a merged social group in which they all, as equals with common concerns, could discuss the daily problems of either the group or any individuals, and together seek solutions. (Jones as quoted in Toch 1980, 34–35)

As applied in a correctional institution, the TC design is a remarkable reversal of the usual inmate culture, which ordinarily is very at odds with the custodians. With the TC, staff and inmates have to learn a new kind of relationship as they sit together in daily meetings with a small group of ten to twenty inmates and one or two staff, talking about group or individual problems with unreserved candor. Inmates are allowed to express anger and criticism freely in their street language as long as it is in honest search of improvement in self and others, and on condition of absolutely no physical attacks. To make this feasible in the typical prison where this idea is so contrary to the usual pattern of relationships, the group meeting is held in a closed room with the understanding that during the meeting and in the privacy of that room the language can be uninhibited, but after the meeting no grudges will be held, no confidences violated, and staff and inmates will again relate to each other on conventional, respectful terms.

In the daily group meetings, the critical comments of group members, even though sometimes hostile and angry, may be directed at staff members as well as at other inmates. As might be expected, custodial staff will instinctively oppose such a process. When the TC program was initiated at California's prison at Chino, it was difficult to get the correctional officers to attend the meetings. As the therapist noted, "In this they were supported by their superiors who did not want them to be confronted openly by the inmates. They were reluctant to become involved in the discussions as they believed that open confrontation would jeopardize their authority." (Whiteley, Briggs, and Turner 1973, 122) Nevertheless, the success of the process requires that all staff come to understand and accept the principle that honest sharing of viewpoints, even though angrily outspoken, can take place in a prison and can in fact make a dramatic change for the better in an institutional climate.

Usually when the TC program has been initiated in a prison, it has been confined to only a portion of the population, incorporating just one cell block, one dormitory, or another definable unit. This has proved feasible and has even been able to affect the climate of the uninvolved population. Such experience "has repeatedly demonstrated that this organizational structure results in a more smoothly functioning, safer, more humane, and (there is reason to believe) more rehabilitative institution." (Levinson as quoted in Toch 1980, 51)

Under skillful leadership the process develops a group culture, which sets a high value on the importance of taking responsibility for oneself and each other. Unlike the conventional helping process in which a professional therapist on the staff counsels an inmate, the treatment effect in a TC is mainly accomplished by the inmates themselves in their critical appraisals of each other. "Contrary to established notions, one need not conquer all of one's own problems before being able to help solve the problems of others. . . . Rather, the very act of helping others becomes the first decisive step in overcoming one's personal problems. In reaching out to help another, a person creates his own proof of worthiness; he is now of value to someone.'' (Vorrath and Brendtro 1974, 11)

The basic principle underlying the TC concept is capable of many adaptations and can be recognized in a number of established programs. An early trendsetter was the Highfields program, developed in the 1950s by the state of New Jersey to serve young adult offenders. (Keve 1967, chapter 5) In each of the program's several sites the state operated small, open institutions of only twenty inmates each, with all twenty involved in an intensive, short-term, group therapy process. The wide visibility and high respect gained by the Highfields program led various other agencies to develop adaptations, for example, the Start Centers in New York State. Variations on the program's basic design can be seen in the most successful substance abuse treatment programs developed under private auspices, such as Synanon, Delancy Street, and Daytop Foundation. This use of the technique for drug addicts has also been applied by several state prisons. New York, for example, operates a TC called "Stay'n Out" for a portion of the population at the Arthur Kill Correctional Institution, whereas Alabama operates its entire prison at Ventress as a TC for drug addicts.

Still another variation is found in the so-called adventure or survival programs in use for delinquent juveniles. These typically take boys and girls referred from courts or schools and put them in a camping type of facility, where the usual daily group discussions build the TC. Added to this is the use of wilderness living and frequent trips. These elements give excitement to the daily life, capturing the interest of the adolescent clients and helping to develop self-esteem. Perhaps the earliest and best conceived of these was Camp Woodland Springs, sponsored by a Dallas, Texas, civic club to serve at-risk boys from that area. More recently, the camp takes boys and girls in equal numbers. The creator of the program decreed that no housing would be supplied for the boys; instead, they should plan and build their own. The boy "must learn elementary principles of construction; what timbers to select and why; how to use the saw and the ax. He must compute space requirements and design the shelter to his needs, learn to lash his timbers securely, and put the canvas on the frame he has built in such a way that he will be comfortable even in the heart of winter. These things call for creative planning and thorough workmanship.'' (Loughmiller 1965, 1)

Whatever its specific format, the TC has a fragile quality; it can easily go sour in case of poor judgment by staff leaders. It will not function at all in an institution unless everyone from the superintendent on down understands the technique and gives it unequivocal support.

When well-handled, the TC has shown more positive results than most other attempts at therapy in correctional settings. The many evaluative studies of such programs show different degrees of success, proving once again that there is no magic cure for social deviance. What can be said with confidence about the results of the well-run TC in a correctional setting is that: (1) it has a powerful effect in humanizing the general atmosphere of the institution, making it safer and more manageable; and (2) as with any other institutional treatment program, genuine progress can be made by the program participants, but for it to result in permanently improved social adjustment after return to the community, the released client must be given continuing and intensive follow-through supervision to protect the gains the inmate has made. It is the typical lack of this follow-through reinforcement that so often causes disappointing recidivism records for institutional treatment programs.

Caseload Management: Intensive Supervision

The follow-through supervision after release of a client from a TC program is the responsibility of the probation and parole service, and with the present level of pressures from high case volumes, this area of corrections is in the process of self-appraisal.

As mentioned in chapter 8, both probation and parole services have suffered a loss in effectiveness and public confidence as a direct consequence of being heavily overloaded. Among the attempts to remedy this handicap, one of the significant and most welcome is known as the "intensive supervision program" (ISP). The ISP design was developed in the early 1980s as a way to provide truly adequate probation or parole supervision for clients who were likely not to be controlled without especially close supervision, or offenders who might, with this kind of help, be safely kept in the community instead of going to prison. In fact, the effective incentive for development of the ISP came from the acute need to counter the rapidly growing cost of prison expansion.

The ISP concept has been adopted throughout the country, although in infinitely varied forms: "their diversity is such that the term has almost ceased to have useful meaning." (Morris and Tonry 1990, 180) The most basic and common characteristic among them is in having the caseload for each officer limited to the point that frequent and effective contact can be made with each client, instead of the barely token contacts allowed by the excessively large caseloads that have become common. Caseload sizes with the ISPs vary; perhaps the most common load would be twenty-five cases, though many would argue that this still is too high. Many of the programs use a team, such as in Georgia, where the probation officer in charge of a caseload will have from one to three "surveillance officers" working with the officer and doing most of the daily routine checking of the clients.

More important than simple reduction of caseload size is the extra quality of attention each case is expected to get. The frequent contacts with clients can be used to give practical advice on job finding and job handling, monitoring of job performance, and the handling of financial responsibilities. Frequently the clients are under orders to perform community services of specified kinds and amounts. Since drug abuse is particularly common in this clientele, the ISPs may require clients to use drug counseling services, and in virtually all instances will utilize urine testing.

These programs are used for either probation or parole cases, and in either type of case the primary goal may be to reduce the pressure on prison beds by offering extra stringent supervision for those who otherwise would have to be incarcerated. One problem this raises is the political difficulty of reassuring the public about a program that the public perceives to be a way of turning loose criminals who should be locked up. To meet this criticism, ISP managers emphasize the tight, no-nonsense aspect of the program. This is the logic behind the name picked by the state of Florida for its ISP, the Community Control Program. One of the earliest and best-managed of the ISPs, operated by the state of Georgia, is consistently described publicly with emphasis on its strict surveillance of clients and its demands for their accountability. In both Florida and Georgia, the ISP managers find that this grim approach serves the political necessity of giving the programs public acceptability, but does not impede their capacity to develop a truly helping relationship with the clientele.

Another problem that tends to defeat the advertised intent of diverting offenders from prison terms is a particularly frustrating effect known as "net widening." The ISP can reduce prison populations only if the clients assigned to it are those who otherwise would have been incarcerated. But judges, being human, will tend to exercise caution about taking such a risk, and will at the same time be pleased to use the ISP with an offender who would have been a candidate for probation but would be a better risk if put under intensive probation. And so the ISP, despite good intentions to the contrary, becomes a substitute for regular probation instead of a substitute for prison.

Planners of ISPs have addressed this problem in different ways, but with little success. In one of the most determined efforts to avoid net widening, the state of New Jersey designed its program with the proviso that placement in an ISP would not be made by the sentencing court. Instead, only nonviolent offenders already sentenced to and received in correctional institutions would be eligible. A new prisoner may on his or her own initiative apply for release to an ISP and be granted release by an institutional panel. This is a logical device for selecting exclusively prison diversion cases, "but the idea presupposes that the judiciary take no notice of this possible resentencing procedure when they sentence to prison one who qualifies for a resentencing application—and this is disingenuous." (Morris and Tonry 1990, 182)

The ISPs have been operating long enough for evaluations to be made. As with all other types of correctional programming, the findings are mixed. Research on the Florida Community Control Program (FCCP) brought the cautious conclusion that "overall, the impact of FCCP on prison crowding, offender behavior, and State correctional costs has been positive. . . . Furthermore, the new offense rate for community control offenders is lower than for similar offenders sentenced to prison and released without supervision."[50] Reviewing a recent major research project, the National Institute of Justice reports that "the programs were more successful in achieving some goals than others. The most singular success lay in the area of control—ISPs include more surveillance and other restrictions that curtail the freedom of the offender. . . . In meeting other goals, the programs were either not as successful or the results were inconclusive." The same report notes that the recidivism rates for ISP clients did not essentially differ from those on conventional supervision, but also points up the characteristic way that any intensive approach gains a deceptive appearance of failure. "The ISP offender, whose behavior is more closely monitored, may be caught in the enforcement net, while the offender on routine probation or parole may escape it."[51]

Another aspect of any correctional treatment program that challenges the practitioner's claim to honesty is the tendency toward "creaming" in the assignment of clients. Whereas the real purpose of such programs is to take the more serious cases, and divert them from prison or enhance their safety while under community supervision, there is, however, an understandable tendency to ensure the success of the effort by taking mainly the cream of the crop, that is, the clients who are the lesser risks. It requires some courage to select the more volatile cases and then have to defend a recidivism rate that subjects management to criticism. But if the diversionary programs are to serve their purpose, that will be necessary. John Conrad, one of the respected analysts of correctional methods, correctly observed: "So far, administrators have been commendably cautious in the formulation of policy for intensive supervision. . . . As the courts, the police, and the media gain confidence in the program, though, I hope that some risks will be taken. It makes no sense, really, to exclude violent offenders from intensive parole supervision; these are the fellows who need it the most."[52]

Electronic Assistance in Community Supervision

The fastest growing innovation in community supervision has been electronic monitoring (EM), first used in New Mexico and Florida in the early 1980s. Helped, no doubt, by the American liking for gadgetry, the technology was rapidly extended and refined until, by 1989, about sixty-five hundred persons were being monitored daily in thirty-nine states.[53]

There is no pretense that EM can substitute for human supervision, but it is proving to be a useful supplement in its ability to detect the client's coming and going from his or her home base. It generally is seen as useful for offenders who otherwise would not be candidates for probation, or who can be safely released on parole with this extra control. EM is being used for either felons or misdemeanants (more often the latter), although it is usually limited to offenders who are nonviolent. All types of corrections agencies are utilizing the technique, at federal, state, or local levels. In Virginia, for example, the state correctional system supports a number of local EM programs operated by its probation or parole services, while in a separate initiative about a dozen county sheriffs have undertaken their own EM programs as a badly needed instrument for relieving overcrowding in jails.

The technical equipment involved in EM has been quite varied, selected after experimenting with different types of devices to find the most dependable and cost-effective. There is still some variety of EM equipment in use, but a widely favored type is an anklet transmitter worn at all times by the client. The anklet communicates continuously with a receiver attached to the client's home telephone; by way of a leased telephone line the signal is fed to the company that holds the contract for the monitoring, and which may be located at some distance or even in another state. If the client leaves home, which breaks off contact, this is automatically registered on the monitoring computer, which is programmed to know which times the client is authorized to leave home to go to work. In the case of any deviation from authorized movements, the responsible probation officer is immediately called and informed.[54]

Any agency starting an EM program faces an initial investment of perhaps $40,000 to $60,000, depending on how many individual units (anklet transmitters) are purchased. To keep costs down, usually a minimum number of units are purchased, then each client is kept on EM for only a few weeks, which allows the anklet to be reassigned to another client. In this way an agency that equips itself with enough units to have only a dozen clients on EM at the same time can extend the process to as many as seventy-five or more clients over a year's time. The majority of EM programs are able to recoup part of the initial cost by charging the client a fee, which may be a one-time initial charge, or a weekly or daily charge.

Evaluative research on the EM experience so far has not produced precise data on the capacity of this technique to control criminal behavior, reduce jail or prison usage, or function in a cost-effective way.

Evaluations have tended to show generally satisfactory results in these respects, but satisfactory mostly in a "feel good" kind of sense. That is, agencies tend to have a good feeling about the value of the technique, both in regard to the practical case-handling aspect and also in its important public relations quality.[55] The current state of appraisals seems no different than the overview in 1988 of one researcher who reported that "both recidivism and escape rates for house arrest participants are quite low. Generally less than 25 percent of participants fail to complete the programs successfully. But the low rates result, in part, from such programs' selection of good risks. . . . As house arrest sentencing becomes more widespread and is extended to other types of offenders, the public safety question will undoubtedly resurface."[56]

Caseload Management: Varied, Innovative Approaches

Current programmatic variations in correctional services are legion, to say the least. In recent years, though corrections leaders have been grievously overloaded with a continually growing volume of criminal cases, they have at the same time addressed the task with energy and imagination. The result is an impressive potpourri of programs deserving discussion here; however, limited space permits only a few to be mentioned. Accordingly, several types of programs will be discussed, which will serve to illustrate fundamental principles commonly adapted in other approaches.

At the risk of being too simplistic, it might be said that corrections during the nineteenth century consisted solely of imprisonment; during the first half of the twentieth century, corrections consisted solely of imprisonment or its alternatives—probation or parole. Since mid-century, however, there has been a proliferation of imaginative variations on those conventional resources. The trend has been driven both by the discovery of new treatment concepts (such as the TC and its spin-offs) and by the need to relieve the extreme overloads on the conventional services, regarding both excessive probation and parole caseloads and overcrowded prisons.

The 1950s saw the development of a new resource for assisting the transition from prison to community—the halfway house—which offered a short-term residence to offenders needing practical help with job and living arrangements. More recently, the halfway house idea has evolved into the more dynamic concept of the "day reporting center" (DRC). Usually this is not a residence, but a physical facility that can serve as a center where either probationers or parolees can come in daily for individual or group counseling, drug use testing, and any monitoring of adjustment as needed. Attempting to encourage more sense of order and purpose in their clients' lives, the program may include a requirement for each person to plan his or her daily and weekly activities and prepare an "itinerary" in writing. "The weekly schedules are intended to help offenders structure and organize their lives by engaging in short-term planning. The daily itineraries are an important control device for the DRC staff. The itineraries show where the offenders will be (and give a phone number where they can be contacted) each hour of each day, and indicate how (and by what route) the offender will arrive at each location." (Parent 1990, 21)

Residential facilities such as halfway houses often are difficult to establish because neighbors are likely to resist them, sometimes aggressively. (Smykla 1981, 165) But the DRC, being nonresidential, has an advantage in this respect. "Using DRCs, diversionary and early release capacity can be expanded relatively quickly and cheaply. Unlike residential programs, DRCs are not as likely to become entangled in protracted siting problems. Typically, on a per client per day basis, DRCs cost about one third to one fourth as much as a halfway house. DRCs can provide such intensive levels of contact that they can be viewed as a control almost equivalent to total confinement." (Parent 1990, 5) Ownership of these centers is mixed, with some being an integral part of a state or county governmental agency, whereas others are operated by private charitable agencies under contract to a sheriff's office or a corrections department for the services rendered.

The DRC does not replace conventional probation or parole services; when properly used, it will be a tightly coordinated supplement, facilitating drug testing, and gradually leading the client to regular, longer-term supervision.

Community service is another relatively recent strategy that sometimes is used in conjunction with a DRC, but just as easily may be the sole penalty in the disposition of a relatively minor case. The idea of requiring the offender to make restitution to his or her victim has been prominent in criminal law from its beginning, and still is regularly favored by criminal courts. But often an offender cannot make restitution, either because the amount involved vastly exceeds the offender's means, or, as often happens, there may be no victim except the general public. So the idea has developed that a sort of symbolic restitution is in order and may have a therapeutic effect. This restitution becomes a matter of requiring the defendant in a criminal case, especially as a condition of probation, to make restitution to the community by doing a service that helps to offset the destructive effects of the crime.

The practice, which began as an adjunct to probation in England during the 1970s, has become common in the United States, with courts ordering specified numbers of days or hours of community service to be done by defendants who are not appropriate candidates for prison, but need more punishment than probation. Often there is a public relations aspect to community service, such as when it is used with a high-profile defendant for whom a fine would serve as little or no penalty. The program is being used for either adult or juvenile offenders.

Judges sometimes let their punitive feelings lead them to impose requirements of several weeks or even many months of community service, but this is contrary to the best view of how this technique should be designed. The original British design specified a relatively modest community service time of anywhere between 40 and 240 hours. This reflects a principle that is basic in helping people with problems; that is, the process should always be rigged for success. The correctional systems are prone to take people who are failures and then give them still further experience in failing by setting tasks for them that they are unlikely to accomplish. The therapeutic processes instead must first of all give the client experience in successfully accomplishing a task. If the task given a client exceeds the client's capacity for sticking with the job, this is only a formula for one more failure, thus defeating the value of the program.

In any well-managed community service program, the sentencing judge will order the community service, but the probation office will arrange the details. The client is interviewed to learn what hours he or she has available without interfering with the client's employment, and to learn what talents and skills he or she has that can be applied to the service assignment. The client should then be sent to a community service task that as far as possible is truly meaningful work (no "busy work" jobs), and which produces an impact, the value of which can be seen and appreciated.[57] The work assignments may be with cooperating governmental agencies or with churches or various charitable organizations. The probation officer must monitor the progress of the service and give recognition and credit when the service is successfully completed. One variation on the plan is to have restitution made directly to the victim of the offender's crime. This is more difficult as many victims have no wish to deal directly with the person who has wronged them. If the victim accepts the plan, the process calls for a meeting between victim and offender, with a mediator who helps them negotiate a written contract for the restitutional services or cash payments. The hope is that there is potential therapy for the offender in personally meeting his victim and making amends. One well-experienced application of this approach, organized as the Victim Offender Reconciliation Project, has spread to many juvenile court settings around the country.[58]

There can be no expectation that 200 or so hours of unpaid work in, for example, repainting walls at a YMCA, will turn around a life that is well set in a criminalistic pattern. But the agencies and courts using this approach are satisfied that it works usefully for appropriately selected cases. If nothing else, when used as an alternative to a jail sentence, community service avoids the mostly negative effect of a period of idleness in a county jail and helps, to a limited but useful extent, reduce jail populations.

Political acceptability tends to be one of the dependable assets of community service or other kinds of restitution. "A survey of citizens' views regarding creative restitution, which includes the use of monetary payments, service to victims, and service to the community as alternative dispositions, indicated that program support is overwhelmingly strong." (McCarthy and McCarthy 1984, 145) As with all other corrective efforts, evaluative research on restitutional programs shows mixed results, but courts and communities are generally happy with the idea and this in itself helps to foster good results. For those minor offenders who can be influenced for good or ill by the type of handling they receive, it is reasonable to believe that a well-planned stint at community service can leave the client feeling that he or she has been treated fairly and consequently receptive to further guidance. In any event, this program has achieved general popularity and seems likely to spread and endure.

Adapting Community Supervision to Modern Pressures

A probation or parole agency today, in facing a volume of cases that overwhelms the available staff, has to accept the possibility that even the minimum demands of these cases may not be met. Nevertheless, the agency can marshal some strategies that help to stretch the staff's reach. Several strategies that are fairly common and well-tested include the use of differentiated caseloads, brokerage, volunteers, and team supervision. The first strategy, differentiated caseloads, resembles the concept of triage as practiced in medical emergencies to sort injured persons into categories based on severity of injury: those who are going to die regardless of treatment, those who will recover in any event, and those whose fate depends on prompt treatment. Probation officers who once presumed that they would give attention to all their clients have had to revise their practice to resemble the triage approach, classifying clients according to risk levels, putting those of minimum risk "on the shelf" without any supervision, while a few riskier clients get the available assistance.

More explicitly, the grouping by risk levels often becomes grouping by problem types. Various probation or parole offices have established specialized caseloads for offender types such as sex offenders, bad check writers, or drunk drivers. In some cases, particularly in urban departments, some caseloads are reserved for clients who are committed to a criminal lifestyle and so are provided only strict surveillance. There have even been caseloads of mentally retarded and mentally gifted clients.[59] Currently, however, the drug addict is by far the most common of the special problem offenders and is most often the subject of treatment efforts. In one study of the problem, it was noted that in New York City drug addicts comprised 80 percent of all persons arrested for robbery, with similar findings in other urban centers. Contrary to a popular assumption, however, for most of these offenders it was not the drug usage that induced their criminal careers. "Numerous studies have found that the majority of addicts are involved in crime prior to addiction, so it may be argued that the post addiction criminality is simply a continuation of this behavior . . . the elimination of addiction among current users would not necessarily reduce the amount of crime committed."[60]

Notwithstanding this bleak outlook, probation and parole agencies are usually seeing it as imperative to target the substance abusers on their caseloads, using urine testing in combination with some type of counseling. The effort is encouraged by findings that whereas drug abuse treatment is of uncertain effect, when it is authoritatively required and enforced, it is clearly more successful than when voluntarily undertaken.[61]

With substance abuse counseling being a rather specialized skill, it is likely that in many localities the probation and parole services will use private providers of this service instead of their own staffs. A probation office that cultivates this brokering approach will have active arrangements with various community agencies that might provide, as needed, not only drug abuse treatment, but also family counseling, financial planning, and various kinds of health services. To be dependable and effective, the brokering, if possible, should include budgeted funds to pay for the purchased services, and the correctional agency must be organized to monitor each brokered case to ensure that the service is affirmatively sustained. Otherwise, the private agencies, accustomed to a voluntary clientele, may not follow through aggressively with the "drop out" client.

By dividing up the responsibility for a case among several workers, the team method takes away from the probation officer the sense of exclusive responsibility, a factor that is unsettling to many professionals and has kept the plan from spreading as generally as it otherwise might. In those offices that have given it a fair trial, the brokerage and team supervision design has usually taken hold strongly. Prospects are that it is likely to persist as a viable, highly regarded technique, but only in limited locations.[62]

The use of volunteers in probation or parole has been spotty. Not many agencies have used this resource, but those which have tried and have gained expert volunteers have been found to be a highly useful adjunct to regular staff.[63] Volunteers constitute a resource that fits in well with team supervision, a plan in which one probation officer may have a caseload of perhaps 250 or more cases. The probation officer will be the head of a team of four to six other workers, all with joint responsibility for the caseload. The other team members may be less experienced officers or trainees, they could include fieldwork students from professional graduate level studies, or they could include one or two part-time volunteers. Among the advantages of team supervision is that when a case emergency occurs at an inconvenient hour (as is all too usual), it is likely that at least one member of the team will be in the office and able to respond. In addition, when assigning cases the probation officer in charge of the team has a choice of whom to assign the case, enabling the case to be given to the officer who can best develop rapport with that client. When it becomes necessary to consider revoking a client's probation or parole, a conference of the full team often produces yet another plan to try in lieu of revocation.

Corrections workers, accustomed to working in an authoritative milieu, tend to suppose that a volunteer will not have the needed skill or status to do the job adequately. But a few administrators have found that by selecting volunteers carefully, giving them appropriate training, good supervision, and tasks suitable to their status, they prove to be a welcome asset.

The Outlook

As crime rates continue to soar, as all of the criminal justice components face increasing work loads, and as public protests about the threat of crime become more strident, public policymakers will be further pressured to do something—anything—to prevent crime. Legislators will face, as they do now, the frustrating problem of appeasing constituencies that are in no mood to consider the issue dispassionately. The public finds it hard to accept the view that a prison system has little or no capacity to reduce crime, or that a long-term preventive approach to the causes of crime offers more promise than any immediate favorites such as mandatory sentences.

Formulating public policy in the context of emotional demands is inherently dangerous as it becomes easy to discount basic principles of civil rights and to ignore the logic in proposals that are rational but unpopular. For example, the fear of crime leads to repeated increases in prison sentences; however, the public does not realize that tougher sentences will cause some persons to serve more time at the expense of having fewer offenders serve any time at all. Even with all of the new prison construction, prison beds are still a limited resource; they can either be allocated to many offenders with moderate time sentences or to fewer offenders with longer sentences.

The demand for crime control measures reached a crescendo in the early 1990s; this sharply affected political campaigns at both state and federal levels. The Clinton administration came into office with an anticrime plan that was essentially a continuation of the one pending from the previous administration. The plan well illustrated the persistence of the public's demand for get-tough measures that sound good even though previously proven ineffective. One proposal, popular with both federal and state legislatures, was the so-called three-strikes-and-you're-out type of sentencing law: a provision that anyone convicted for the third time of a crime of violence would categorically be committed to prison for life with no privilege of parole. As such proposals made their way through legislatures, widely published protests frequently appeared, attacking the logic of the proposed measures, but without noticable impact. As just one among many examples, reputable columnist David Broder noted the defects in the mandatory life term idea. He pointed out that violent crimes are committed mainly by young men who usually grow out of that type of activity after reaching their forties, or perhaps earlier. Life sentences without parole will mean that such persons will become aging prisoners of low risk taking up expensive prison space, bringing "the prospect of senescent former muggers spending their declining years in prison hospitals, while their grandsons' generation causes mayhem on the streets."[64] This and other criticisms of the public rush to punish were voiced by numerous commentators, but without noticable effect.

A more rational, but politically unacceptable, plan would be to reduce, not increase, prison sentences. Several arguments favor the idea; there would be no loss in crime control as research has consistently shown that long prison terms are neither deterrent nor corrective; a general reduction of prison sentences would save public money in significant amounts; prosecution costs also would be reduced as defendants facing short sentences fight the prosecution less vigorously; more offenders who should go to prison would in fact do so; and prisons with short-term inmates are less dangerous and less expensive to operate.[65] Although the citizenry is likely to reject the idea instinctively, corrections managers can appreciate the logic of shorter sentences. A retired director of the Federal Bureau of Prisons has argued for a new direction in prison operations in which a "tough," more rigorous regime of work, training, and education would be imposed on each inmate, but for less time. "Tough time is a sentencing strategy that imposes a more stringent, Spartan correctional regime on a criminal offender than now is the case in most prisons, while imposing those conditions for a significantly shorter time than now might be the case for the same crime."[66]

The high-pitched public fear of crime not only causes demands for more drastic punishment, but also tends to reduce public sensitivity to the protections guaranteed by the Bill of Rights. It is certainly understandable that people react with anger toward an offender who in some way captures the public's widespread disgust or resentment. In such instances many people are inclined to make summary judgments without considering the otherwise revered policies of due process or "innocent until proven guilty." But if the country is to remain strong and safe for all citizenry, basic civil rights must be rigorously protected for every criminal defendant, no matter how unpopular he or she may be at the time. Each person must understand that his or her own interests are best protected by the country's unprejudiced determination to observe the civil rights of all citizens, including the least deserving.

In a memorable speech to the British Parliament, Winston Churchill made this point in his characteristic way. "The mood and temper of the public in regard to the treatment of crime and criminals is one of the most unfailing tests of the civilisation of any country."[67]

Notes

1. Norval Morris. "The Case for Intermediate Punishments." *Federal Prison Journal* 2:2 (Spring 1991), 11.
2. *Sourcebook of Criminal Justice Statistics—1991.* Washington, D.C.: Bureau of Justice Statistics, 1992, 613, 634.
3. "America's Best Buildings." *New York Times Magazine* (Feb. 20, 1994), 38.
4. Malcolm Gladwell. "The Crime Bill May Not Be the Cure." *Washington Post National Weekly Edition* (June 6-12, 1994).
5. Charles Loring Brace. *The Dangerous Classes of New York and Twenty Years Work among Them.* New York: National Association of Social Workers, 1973, 31. (Reprint of 1872 edition)
6. National Center for Health Statistics. *Firearm and Motor Vehicle Injury Mortality—Variations by State, Race, and Ethnicity: United States, 1990–91.* Hyattsville, Md.: 1994, 1, 7, 8.
7. U.S. Department of Justice. Office of Justice Programs. "Juvenile Justice Bulletin, OJJDP Update on Statistics" (Jan. 1992), 7.
8. Janet E. Ainsworth. "Re-Imagining Childhood and Reconstructing the Legal Order: The Case for Abolishing the Juvenile Court." *North Carolina Law Review* 69:5 (June 1991), 1082–1133.
9. Judge Leonard P. Edwards. "Fulfilling the Expectations for the Juvenile Court Judge." *Juvenile and Family Court Journal* 43:2 (1992), 34, 35.
10. Seymour Gelber. "The Juvenile Justice System: Vision for the Future." *Juvenile and Family Court Journal* 41:2 (1990), 15, 16.

11. Ira Schwartz. *(In)Justice for Juveniles.* Lexington, Mass.: Lexington Books, 1989, 169.

12. Quoted material on the Montana developments comes from a 12-page unpublished, undated planning paper, *Assisting Montana's Youth into the 21st Century,* from the Montana Board of Crime Control in Helena. The comments are augmented by the author's personal discussion with Montana officials.

13. For a useful source of information on the efforts to develop the accreditation process, see Richard S. Allinson, "The Politics of Prison Standards." *Corrections Magazine* 5:1 (March 1979), 54–62.

14. Stephen Gettinger. "Accreditation on Trial." *Corrections Magazine* 8:1 (Feb. 1982), 9. See also "The Accreditation Debate: Two Views." *Corrections Magazine* 8:6 (Dec. 1982), and Lynn S. Branham, "Accreditation: Making a Good Process Better." *Federal Probation* 57:2 (June 1993), 11.

15. For detailed information on the accreditation process, see the official journal of the ACA, *Corrections Today* 54:3 (May 1992). This issue is devoted mainly to this subject, with most of the articles discussing various aspects of accreditation.

16. *Accreditation Guidelines: Blueprint for Corrections.* Laurel, Md.: American Correctional Association (undated), 1.

17. Information derived from a brochure, *Accreditation Program Overview,* 1993, and other materials supplied to the author from the Commission on Accreditation for Law Enforcement Agencies, Fairfax, Va.

18. Michael G. Shanahan. "Private Enterprise and the Public Police: The Professionalizing Effects of a New Partnership." Chapter 40 in *Police Leadership in America: Crisis and Opportunity,* by William A. Geller. New York: Praeger, 1985, 449.

19. Louis A. Radelet and David L. Carter. *The Police and the Community.* New York: Macmillan College Publishing Co., 1990, 452.

20. Henry M. Wrobleski and Karen M. Hess. *Introduction to Law Enforcement and Criminal Justice.* St. Paul, Minn.: West Publishing Co., 1993, 605.

21. Robert D. Pursley. *Introduction to Criminal Justice.* New York: Macmillan, 1991, 259.

22. "The Privatization of Corrections." *Issues and Practices in Criminal Justice* (Feb. 1985), 4.

23. Martin Tolchin. "As Privately Owned Prisons Increase, So Do Their Critics." *New York Times* (Feb. 11, 1985), A1.

24. Kenneth F. Schoen. "Private Prison Operators." *New York Times* (March 28, 1985), A31.

25. "The Privatization of Corrections." *Issues and Practices in Criminal Justice* (Feb. 1985), 72. For further discussion of the constitutional issue, see Harold J. Sullivan, "Privatization of Corrections and the Constitutional Rights of Prisoners." *Federal Probation* 53:2 (June 1989), 36–42.

26. Francis T. Cullen. "The Privatization of Treatment: Prison Reform in the 1980s." *Federal Probation* 50:1 (March 1986), 13.

27. The program is described in detail in a monograph published by the American Correctional Association: Herbert G. Callison. *Zephyr Products: The Story of an Inmate-staffed Business.* Laurel Lakes, Md., 1989.

28. A useful source of information on the PIE programs is a VCR tape, *Prison Industry Enhancement Certification Program: A Decade of Progress: Prospects for the Future,* produced by the American Correctional Association, Laurel Lakes, Md.

29. National Institute of Justice. "The Privatization of Corrections." *Issues and Practices in Criminal Justice* (Feb. 1985), 62–63.

30. Office for Victims of Crime. Office of Justice Programs. U.S. Department of Justice. "Report to Congress 1988–1990," 1992, 1.

31. Ibid.

32. U.S. Department of Justice. Office of Technology Transfer. Law Enforcement Assistance Administration. *An Exemplary Project: A Community Response to Rape: Polk County Rape/Sexual Assault Care Center.* Washington, D.C.: 1976, 8–10.

33. U.S. President's Task Force on Victims of Crime. *Final Report.* Washington, D.C.: 1982, 29, 33, 57.

34. Office for Victims of Crime. Office of Justice Programs. U.S. Department of Justice. "Report to Congress 1988–1990," 1992, 17.

35. New York State Crime Victims Board. "1991–1992 Annual Report," 9.

36. Minnesota Citizens Council on Crime and Justice. "1981–1982 Report," 4.

37. *New York Times* (April 11, 1987), A10.

38. Philip Cook. "The 'Saturday Night Special': An Assessment of Alternative Definitions from a Policy Perspective." *Journal of Criminal Law and Criminology* 72:4 (Winter 1981), 1737.

39. *New York Times* (Aug. 23, 1988), A18.

40. *New York Times* (Nov. 25, 1993), A1.

41. Stephen Gettinger, "Police and Gun Control: Can the Law Reduce Bloodshed?" *Police Magazine* 3:6 (Nov. 1980), 8.

42. International Association of Chiefs of Police. *Violent Crime in America.* April 27, 1993, 4–5. (An unpublished report available from the IACP, Arlington, Va.)

43. Matthew G. Yeager. *How Well Does the Handgun Protect You and Your Family?* United States Conference of Mayors (1976), 35, 1.

44. *Prison Boot Camps: Short Term Prison Costs Reduced, But Long Term Impact Uncertain.* Washington, D.C.: U.S. General Accounting Office, 1993, 2.

45. Ibid., 4.

46. "Boot Camps Are Degrading, Don't Work," by Martin Anderson, a columnist for Scripps Howard News Service and a Senior Fellow at the Hoover Institute of Stanford University. It appeared in the Richmond (Va.) *Times Dispatch* on Feb. 10, 1994.

47. "The Bust in Boot Camps." *Newsweek* (Feb. 21, 1994), 26.

48. "An Evaluation of Shock Incarceration in Louisiana." *National Institute of Justice Research in Brief* (June 1993), 6.

49. Kevin Krajick. "Lifers Try to Scare the Crime out of Juveniles." *Corrections Magazine* 3:4 (Dec. 1977), 17, 22.

50. Dennis Wagner and Christopher Baird. "Evaluation of the Florida Community Control Program." *National Institute of Justice Research in Brief* (Jan. 1993), 5.

51. Joan Petersilia and Susan Turner. "Evaluating Intensive Supervision Probation/Parole: Results of a Nationwide Experiment." *National Institute of Justice Research in Brief* (May 1993), 1, 5.
52. John P. Conrad. "Research and Development in Corrections." *Federal Probation* 51:2 (June 1987), 64.
53. Mark Renzema and David T. Skelton. "Use of Electronic Monitoring in the United States: 1989 Update." Reprinted from *NIJ Reports* No. 222 (Nov./Dec. 1990), 1.
54. James L. Beck, Jody Klein-Saffran, and Harold B. Wooten. "Home Confinement and the Use of Electronic Monitoring with Federal Parolees." *Federal Probation* 54:4 (Dec. 1990), 26.
55. For typical evaluative accounts, see Beck, Klein-Saffran, and Wooten, 1990, 22–31 (above); Renzema and Skelton, 1990, 1–5 (above); Lilly et al., 1992, 42–47 (below); and Keith W. Cooprider and Judith Kerby, "A Practical Application of Electronic Monitoring at the Pretrial Stage." *Federal Probation* 54:11 (March 1990), 28–35.
56. Joan Petersilia. "House Arrest." National Institute of Justice, *Crime File Study Guide* (1988), 4.
57. Joe Hudson amd Burt Galaway. "Community Service: Toward Program Definition." *Federal Probation* 54:2 (June 1990), 6–7.
58. This approach is well-discussed in an article by Sudipto Roy, "Two Types of Juvenile Restitution Programs in Two Midwestern Counties: A Comparative Study." *Federal Probation* 57:4 (Dec. 1993), 48–53.
59. See Keve 1967 (below), 10, 20. Also, chapter 2 of the same source provides a general discussion of varieties of caseload differentiation.
60. William H. McGlothin, M. Douglas Anglin, and Bruce D. Wilson. "Narcotic Addiction and Crime." *Criminology* 16:3 (Nov. 1978), 294.
61. David N. Nurco, et al. "The Criminality of Narcotic Addicts." *Journal of Nervous and Mental Disease* 173:22 (Feb. 1985), 99–100.
62. For a discussion of the team and brokerage approach as it appeared early in its development, see Rob Wilson, "Probation/Parole Officers as 'Resource Brokers.' " *Corrections Magazine* 4:2 (June 1978), 48–54.
63. Keve 1967 (below), 260–271.
64. David Broder. "All Locked Up." *Washington Post* (April 17, 1994), C7.
65. Paul W. Keve. *Prison Life and Human Worth*. Minneapolis: University of Minnesota Press, 1974, 169–170.
66. J. Michael Quinlan. "News of the Future." *Federal Probation* 57:4 (Dec. 1993), 61.
67. Robert Rhodes Ames, ed. *Winston S. Churchill: His Complete Speeches*, Vol. 2. New York: Chelsea House, 1974, 1598.

Bibliography

Organizational Directions and Public Policy Initiatives

Austern, David. *The Crime Victim's Handbook*. New York: Viking Penguin, 1987.

The rapid development of victims' services in recent years has left this book somewhat outdated in its factual statements about existing services. Nevertheless, much of its content is still valid for the victim seeking information about pertinent laws and practices, as well as their underlying philosophy.

Block, Richard. *Violent Crime: Environment, Interaction, and Death.* Lexington, Mass.: Lexington Books, 1977.

Clotfelter, Charles T. "Crime, Disorder, and the Demand for Handguns." *Law and Policy Quarterly* 3:4 (Oct. 1981), 425–441.

Finckenauer, James O. *Scared Straight and the Panacea Phenomenon.* Englewood Cliffs, N.J.: Prentice-Hall, 1982.

A thorough and explicit report of a comprehensive study made of a popular tactic for delinquency prevention. In addition to evaluating the outcome of the "Scared Straight" programs, the author discusses the larger subject of the eager response to "quick-fix" methods that appear to cure social problems cheaply and in ways that are emotionally satisfying to the public.

Geis, Gilbert. "The Privatization of Prisons." Chapter 6 in *Private Means Public Ends,* ed. Barry J. Carroll, Ralph W. Conant, and Thomas A. Easton. New York: Praeger, 1987.

Humm, S. Randall, et al., eds. *Child, Parent and State: Law and Policy Reader.* Philadelphia: Temple University Press, 1994.

Kates, Don B., Jr. "Handgun Prohibition and the Original Meaning of the Second Amendment." *Michigan Law Review* 82:2 (Nov. 1983), 209–273.

Kleck, Gary. *Point Blank: Guns and Violence in America.* New York: Aldine De Gruyter, 1991.

A thorough, scholarly, and balanced discussion of the place of guns in American society, historically and currently. It addresses the issue of gun control in depth, examining all the opposing arguments objectively, and includes a comprehensive bibliography.

Miller, Jerome G. *Last One over the Wall: The Massachusetts Experiment in Closing Reform Schools.* Columbus, Ohio: State University Press, 1991.

A personal memoir of the author's celebrated dismantling of his state's juvenile institution system. Though less objective than an academic report and evaluation, its personal and anecdotal style evokes the emotionally charged atmosphere of the event. A most useful contribution to an understanding of some of the political and logistical realities encountered in any such attempt at public policy surgery.

Sechrest, Dale K. "Prison 'Boot Camps' Do Not Measure Up." *Federal Probation* 53:3 (Sept. 1989), 15-20.

Stenson, Kevin and David Cowell. "The Politics of Crime Control." In *The Politics of Crime Control,* ed. Kevin Stenson and David Cowell. London: Sage Publications, 1991.

Zimring, Frank. "Is Gun Control Likely to Reduce Violent Killings?" *University of Chicago Law Review* 35:3 (Spring 1968), 721-737.

Zimring, Franklin E. and Gordon Hawkins. *The Citizen's Guide to Gun Control.* New York: Macmillan, 1987.

Two noted criminologists review the gun control controversy in an inclusive, perceptive, and responsible manner.

Evolving Concepts of Corrective Measures

Cormier, Bruno M. *The Watcher and the Watched*. Montreal: Tundra Books, 1975. A psychiatrist who introduced and conducted a therapeutic community program for a group of particularly difficult prisoners in the New York state corrections system gives a detailed account of the progress of the program and its outcome.

Finckenauer 1982 (above).

Galaway, Burt and Joe Hudson, eds. *Offender Restitution in Theory and Action*. Lexington, Mass.: Lexington Books, 1978.

Keve, Paul W. *Imaginative Programming in Probation and Parole*. Minneapolis: University of Minnesota Press, 1967.

Keve, Paul W. *Prison Life and Human Worth*. Minneapolis: University of Minnesota Press, 1974.

Lilly, J. Robert, et al. "The Pride, Inc., Program: An Evaluation of Five Years of Electronic Monitoring." *Federal Probation* 56:4 (Dec. 1992).

Loughmiller, Campbell. *Wilderness Road*. Austin, Tex.: Hogg Foundation for Mental Health, 1965.

A valuable, inspiring addition to the literature on therapeutic communities. It details one adaptation of the TC idea, the use of an open camp setting for a program to help delinquent boys in a format designed as one variation on the adventure or survival type of program.

McCarthy, Belinda Rodgers and Bernard J. McCarthy. *Community-Based Corrections*. Pacific Grove, Calif.: Brooks/Cole, 1984.

Morris, Norval and Michael Tonry. *Between Prison and Probation*. New York: Oxford University Press, 1990.

These astute authors present an erudite, philosophical examination of the principles affecting the design and practice of treatment or punishment options for offenders.

Parent, Dale G. "Day Reporting Centers for Criminal Offenders—a Descriptive Analysis of Existing Programs." *Issues and Practices in Criminal Justice* (Sept. 1990).

An extensive and thorough discussion of every aspect of this significant type of correctional program.

Petersilia, Joan and Susan Turner. "Intensive Probation and Parole." In *Crime and Justice,* Vol. 17, *A Review of Research,* ed. Michael Tonry. Chicago: University of Chicago Press, 1993.

Among the most valuable of recent source materials on the intensive supervision programs, this chapter analyzes the rationale and motivations behind their development, presents statistics on their characteristics and participants, and competently discusses the complex findings relevant to their effects.

Schmidt, Annesley K. "Electronic Monitors—Realistically, What Can Be Expected?" *Federal Probation* 55:2 (June 1991), 47–53.

Presents a concise and practical listing and description of electronic devices used for monitoring offenders. It also is useful in discussing some of the advantages and disadvantages of the technology.

Smykla, John Ortiz. *Community-based Corrections: Principles and Practices.* New York: Macmillan, 1981.

Starting Points: Meeting the Needs of Our Youngest Children. New York: Carnegie Corp., 1994.

Toch, Hans, ed. *Therapeutic Communities in Corrections.* New York: Praeger, 1980.

An experienced researcher of prison cultures has edited here articles by some of the most reputable therapeutic community practitioners, including Maxwell Jones, who originated the technique. The writers mainly tell about their own experiences with this technique in several different institutional settings. See particularly chapter 5, *TC or Not TC? That Is the Question,* by Robert B. Levinson.

U.S. Department of Justice. Office of Justice Programs. *A Survey of Intermediate Sanctions.* Washington, D.C.: 1990.

A comprehensive listing, description, and analysis of the various non-incarcerative correctional innovations.

Vorrath, Harry H. and Larry K. Brendtro. *Positive Peer Culture.* Chicago: Aldine, 1974.

An experienced practitioner of the group therapy process as applied to correctional settings with juveniles or young adults discusses his particular adaptation of the therapeutic community concept.

Whiteley, Stuart, Dennie Briggs, and Merfin Turner. *Dealing with Deviants: The Treatment of Antisocial Behavior.* New York: Schocken Books, 1973.

Three experienced practitioners describe the development and use of therapeutic communities and their adaptation in prisons, an example of which was a notable program operated at the Southern California Institution for Men in Chino.

Selected Sources for Research on Crime, Crime Control, and Justice

by Louveller M. Luster

T his section provides an overview of the available information sources that will assist your research on the topic of crime. A wealth of information is available in both traditional and nontraditional sources. Traditional sources include encyclopedias, dictionaries, periodical literature, reference books, government publications, directories, statistical materials, and subject bibliographies. Usually in paper or microform format, they can be found in most libraries and are basic for any type of research. Nontraditional or electronic sources offer the convenience of immediate access and currency. These include CD-ROMs (compact disk-read only memory), online computer database systems, computer diskettes, automated library card catalogs, and electronic bulletin boards and discussion groups (listservers) available on the computer network, the Internet. Some of the traditional sources mentioned are also available in electronic format.

Encyclopedias and dictionaries are most helpful in providing background information and an introduction to a subject. General encyclopedias such as *World Book* or *Encyclopaedia Britannica* provide a basic foundation on a subject that can be helpful before moving on to more detailed research. Subject or specialized encyclopedias provide comprehensive articles written by specialists or authorities in that subject field. Articles usually include a bibliography to help the reader in finding additional information. Subject dictionaries provide a lengthy explanation or detailed definition of terms or phrases and help the researcher become familiar with the terminology useful in designing search strategies.

Most academic libraries will have *Library of Congress Subject Headings*, a source that provides a listing of appropriate subject headings or vocabulary used to search by subject for books in a library card catalog and for government publications in the *Monthly Catalog* . Using subject headings such as CRIME, CRIME AND CRIMINALS, and CRIMINAL BEHAVIOR will identify books on those subjects. To find an encyclopedia on crime you would use the subject heading CRIME-DICTIONARIES AND ENCYCLOPEDIAS. *Library of Congress Subject Headings (LCSH)* also provides cross-references to appropriate related headings, narrower headings, and broader headings for a topic.

Searching the subject heading CRIME-BIBLIOGRAPHIES will lead you to sources, most often compiled by experts, that list books and articles on crime. Usually these publications are subdivided into smaller subject areas that will allow you to focus on selected topics. Armed with titles of interesting books, you can conduct a title search in the library's catalog. By combining the information gathered from encyclopedias, dictionaries, and bibliographies, you can conduct author, title, and subject searches effectively and efficiently.

In most academic and larger public libraries, the library card catalog is automated. This offers the option of conducting a search using keywords, those terms used in the title or other bibliographic information that are not found in *LCSH*. Keyword searching in automated catalogs also allows the user to link search terms together to help sharpen the focus of the search and narrow the range of titles meeting the user's requirements.

Magazine articles and periodical literature provide the most current information on a topic, but are less comprehensive than the treatment offered in books. The time lag between completion of a manuscript and its eventual publication and distribution as a book can be as long as a year, and as a consequence some of the information the book contains can become outdated. Journals and magazines, published weekly, monthly, and quarterly, usually will have more current data and be more narrowly focused. Periodical indexes and abstracts establish access to this kind of literature. Information is organized by subject and by author, with the index providing basic bibliographic information, and the abstract providing a summary of the article. Indexes can be general, such as *Readers' Guide to Periodical Literature*, or limited to a broad discipline, such as *Social Sciences Index*, or confined to a subject, such as *Criminology Abstracts*. A growing number of indexes are available as databases, and as is true with automated library catalogs, the user can conduct author, title, subject, and keyword searches, with the added advantage of linking terms for more search specificity.

Each year the U.S. government issues more publications than all other publishers combined. Federal output covers virtually all subject areas, but is particularly strong in science and the social sciences. This information is made available in print, microform, and electronic formats. The best source for locating government publications on a particular subject is the *Monthly Catalog of United States Government Publications*, available in both print and CD-ROM. The *Monthly Catalog* indexes documents by author (agency), title, and Library of Congress subject headings. The CD-ROM version of the *Monthly Catalog* also permits searching by keyword and by Superintendent of Documents classification number. Many government publications are classified as periodicals and the *U.S. Government Periodicals Index* and the *Public Affairs Information Service Bulletin*, both available in print and CD-ROM, provide access to articles. The government also publishes bibliographies, including *Subject Bibliographies to U.S. Publications* and the *Publication Reference File*, which lists government publications available for sale. Government collected statistical data can be found by using the *Statistical Abstract of the United States* and the *American Statistics Index*, the latter produced by a commercial vendor.

Electronic sources, which include compact disks, online database systems, and electronic bulletin boards, are available from commercial sources and the federal government. Most academic and larger public libraries provide access at no cost, or at a minimum charge, to these important types of sources. Several government agencies provide electronic bulletin boards over the computer network, the Internet, that offer current information covering a wide range of subject areas.

Encyclopedias and Dictionaries

Subject encyclopedias and dictionaries are useful resources when you begin your research. The subject encyclopedia provides an overview of a topic or contains articles written by recognized scholars. Most subject encyclopedias also provide extensive bibliographies that identify other sources of information. The subject dictionary provides an explanation of the specialized language you may encounter in your research.

Balay, Robert. *Guide to Reference Books Covering Materials from 1985–1990.* Chicago: American Library Association, 1992.
> Provides an annotated list of reference sources arranged by subject, author, and title. This version of the *Guide to Reference Books* bridges the period between the 10th and anticipated 11th editions of this title.

Burek, Deborah M. *Encyclopedia of Associations.* 29th ed. Detroit: Gale Research, 1995.
> An encyclopedia-directory that lists national and international organizations in a wide range of subject areas or fields of discipline with description of the organizations and addresses with the names of contact persons.

Fay, John. *The Police Dictionary and Encyclopedia*. Springfield, Ill.: C. C. Thomas, 1988.

    Provides definitions for a wide range of terms used in law enforcement. Appendixes include felony definitions and sentence limits by state, capital offenses, and method of execution by state, and a bibliography.

Kadish, Sanford. *Encyclopedia of Crime and Justice*. New York: Free Press, 1983.

    Provides an integrated account of the nature and causes of criminal behavior, the prevention of crime, the punishment and treatment of offenders, the functions of the institutions of criminal justice, and the bodies of law that apply.

Nash, Jay Robert. *Encyclopedia of World Crime*. Wilmette, Ill.: Crimebooks, 1989.

    Provides comprehensive information in the international fields of crime, criminal justice, criminology, and law enforcement. It presents a complete historical perspective of crime, from ancient times to the present.

Bibliographies

Bibliographies are listings of titles of books and other sources on a subject and usually concentrate around a specific or common theme. Often compiled by experts in the field, bibliographies offer a quick way to identify the more important works on a subject.

Brantley, James R. and Marjorie Kravitz. *Alternatives to Institutionalization: A Definitive Bibliography*. Rockville, Md.: Dept. of Justice, Law Enforcement Assistance Administration, 1979.

    Contains entries on topics such as alternatives to institutionalization, juvenile training centers, pre-release centers, halfway houses, and work-release programs.

Crime and Punishment in America: A Historical Bibliography. Santa Barbara, Calif.: ABC-CLIO, 1984.

    Abstracts of periodical articles published between 1973 and 1982 on crime, criminals, and criminal justice in the United States, from Colonial times to the present day.

Davies, B. L. *Criminological Bibliographies: Uniform Citations to Bibliographies, Indexes and Review Articles of the Literature of Crime Study in the United States*. Westport, Conn.: Greenwood Press, 1978.

    Over 1,400 references in seven subject sections. Indexed by subject, compiler, and issuing body.

Felkenes, George T. and Harold K. Becker. *Law Enforcement: A Selected Bibliography*. 2nd ed. New York: Scarecrow Press, 1977.

    Contains books and periodical articles on police personnel administration, police functions and practices, criminal law and evidence, and administration of justice.

Suvak, Daniel. *Memoirs of American Prisons: An Annotated Bibliography.* Metuchen, N.J.: Scarecrow Press, 1979.

Provides an annotated bibliography of writings of prisoners and ex-prisoners and includes the following sections: (1) civil prisoners, both criminals and prisoners of conscience; (2) voluntary prisoners committed for the purpose of studying and reporting on the institutions and prisoners; and (3) military prisoners, from the Revolution to World War II international camps.

Abstracts and Indexes

Subject indexes and abstracts are the most commonly used resources to identify periodicals and journal literature on a particular subject. Indexes and abstracts range from the general to the specific. They provide citations to hearings, reports, magazine articles, documents, and other specialized publications. The abstracts include a summary with the citation. It is always best to consult several indexes to locate materials with a wide range of viewpoints and perspectives on a topic.

Abstracts on Criminology and Penology (formerly *Excerpta Criminologica*). Amstelveen, Netherlands: Kugler, 1961–.

An international abstracting service covering the etiology of crime and criminal delinquency, the control and treatment of offenders, criminal procedure, and administration of justice.

Congressional Information Service (CIS) Index. Washington, D.C.: Congressional Information Service, 1970–.

Used to identify, evaluate, and obtain information contained in the working papers of the U.S. Congress. It covers hearings, prints, documents, reports, and special publications.

Criminal Justice Abstracts (formerly *Crime and Delinquency Literature*). Hackensack, N.J.: National Council on Crime and Delinquency, 1968–1977.

Contains lengthy abstracts of selected literature of international scope. Each issue has a comprehensive review of a pertinent topic: victimless crime, marijuana, and so on. There are about 175 abstracts per issue.

Criminal Justice Periodical Index. Ann Arbor, Mich.: University Microfilm International, 1990–.

Indexes leading criminal justice journals in the areas of criminology, criminal law, family law, security systems, corrections, and police.

Criminology, Penology and Police Science Abstracts. Amsterdam; New York: Kugler, 1992–.

Formed by the union of *Criminology and Penology Abstracts* and *Police Science Abstracts* and continues their numbering. Contains information on the etiology of crime and juvenile delinquency, the control and treatment of offenders, criminal procedure, the administration of justice and forensic and police sciences, including forensic medicine.

Index to Current Urban Documents. Westport, Conn.: Greenwood Publishing, 1972–.

Provides citations of local government publications on varying topics or subjects. Has geographic and subject indexes.

Index to Legal Periodicals. New York: H. W. Wilson, 1908–.

An index to legal periodicals published in the United States and foreign countries. Subject and author access is provided to specific cases and law review articles in legal periodicals, yearbooks, and annual reviews. Provides significant information on recent court decisions, new legislation, precedents, tax law, estate planning, and so on. This is also available on CD-ROM.

Public Affairs Information Service Bulletin. New York: Public Affairs Information Service, 1915–.

Includes material relating to criminal justice topics such as juvenile delinquency, capital punishment, and so on. Also available on CD-ROM.

Psychological Abstracts. Washington, D.C.: American Psychological Association, 1927–.

Contains citations with abstracts to journals in psychology and behavioral sciences. Topics include all aspects of psychology, as well as the behavioral aspects of education, medicine, sociology, law, and management. Also available on CD-ROM.

Social Sciences Index. New York: H. W. Wilson, 1974/75–.

Provides subject access to citations on varying topics such as crime and criminal justice. Contains over 240,000 citations to articles and book reviews in about 350 English-language periodicals in the social sciences. Covers anthropology, economics, environmental sciences, law and criminology, and so on. Also available on CD-ROM.

Sociological Abstracts. San Diego: Sociological Abstracts, 1952–.

Primarily abstracts and articles from journals, although includes conference papers and some monographs. Concentrates on the core journals in sociology with selective coverage of journals in other disciplines when the articles were written by sociologists or pertain to sociology.

U.S. Government Periodicals Index. Bethesda, Md.: Congressional Information Service, 1993–.

An index to government periodicals published in the United States and some foreign countries. It provides subject and author access to criminology topics. Also available on CD-ROM.

Periodicals

Periodicals and journals offer the best means of keeping up-to-date on current information on various subjects. Articles written by scholars or professionals provide insight into the issues, problems, viewpoints, background, research, and other sources of information on a subject.

CJSA Forum. Washington, D.C.: Criminal Justice Statistics Association, 1983–.

A newsletter focusing on criminal justice research at the state and national levels. Features book reviews, calendar of events, research reports, and statistical research.

Corrections Today. Laurel, Md.: American Correctional Association, 1979–.

Provides a forum for the presentation and discussion of issues related to the advancement of corrections. Includes topics from community programs, minorities, history and philosophy, probation and parole, correctional industries, and volunteer and service organizations.

Crime and Delinquency. Newbury Park, Calif.: Sage Publications, 1960–.

A policy-oriented journal for the professional with direct involvement in the criminal justice field. Subjects fall in the following broad categories of criminal justice: the social, political, and economic context; the victim and the offender; the criminal justice response; and the setting and implementation of sanctions.

Criminal Justice and Behavior. Newbury Park, Calif.: Sage Publications, 1974–.

Contains contributions examining psychological and behavioral aspects of the juvenile and criminal justice systems. The journal includes analyses of both clientele and employees in the criminal justice systems.

Criminal Justice Ethics. New York: John Jay College of Criminal Justice, Institute for Criminal Justice Ethics, 1982–.

Designed to focus greater attention on ethical issues in criminal justice by philosophers, criminal justice professionals, lawyers and judges, and the general public. Its editorial scope includes topics relating to the police, the courts, corrections, and issues in legal philosophy.

Criminal Justice Journal. San Diego: Western State University, College of Law, 1976–1992?

Features articles of current interest to those involved in criminal justice. A law review published by the students of Western State University, San Diego.

Criminal Justice Review. Atlanta: Georgia State University, 1976–.

Presents a broad range of perspectives on criminal justice issues, institutions, and processes. Focuses on any aspect of crime and the justice system and features local, state, or national concerns.

Criminal Law Bulletin. Boston: Warren, Gotham & Lamont, 1965–.

Covers criminal law fields, including enforcement, litigation, court administration, and rehabilitation.

Criminal Law Review. New York: Clark Boardman, 1979–.

A wide range of articles by experts in criminal law for everyone involved in the practical problems of the criminal process.

Criminology. Columbus, Ohio: American Society of Criminology, 1970–.

Devoted to the study of crime, deviant behavior, and related phenomena, as found in the social and behavioral sciences and the fields of law, criminal justice, and history. The major emphases are theory, research, historical issues, policy evaluation, and current controversies concerning crime, law, and justice.

FBI Law Enforcement Bulletin. Washington, D.C.: U.S. Dept. of Justice, Federal Bureau of Investigation, 1935–.

Presents five to seven concise articles on current police techniques, crime problems, and personnel and management techniques and problems, equipment, and training.

Federal Probation. Washington, D.C.: Administrative Office of the United States Courts, 1937–.

Includes articles, news notes, and book reviews on preventive and corrective activities in delinquency and crime. Articles, reviews (of books and journals), and columns on topics concerning preventive and correctional activities in delinquency and crime.

Journal of Criminal Justice. Tarrytown, N.Y.: Elsevier Science, 1973–.

An international journal intended to fill the need for dissemination of new information, ideas, and methods to both practitioners and academicians in the criminal justice area. The journal is concerned with all aspects of the criminal justice system in terms of their relationship to each other.

Journal of Criminal Law and Criminology. Baltimore, Md.: Williams & Wilkins, 1973–.

Articles often deal with issues on civil liberties and civil rights. Covered are basic legal issues that are central to the concerns of civil liberties. Materials are organized by constitutional amendment.

Journal of Research in Crime and Delinquency. Newbury Park, Calif.: Sage Publications, 1964–.

Devoted to reports of original research in crime and delinquency, new theory, and the critical analysis of theories and concepts especially pertinent to research development in this field.

Justice Quarterly. Highland Heights, Ky.: Academy of Criminal Justice Sciences, 1971–.

Features scholarly articles on issues of criminal justice, criminology, and justice studies.

Juvenile and Family Court Journal. Reno, Nev.: National Council of Juvenile and Family Court Judges, 1978–.

Contains articles on juvenile justice and family and includes statistics.

National Institute of Justice Journal (previously known as *NIJ Reports*). Washington, D.C.: U.S. Department of Justice, National Institute of Justice, 1992–.

Announces the Institute's policy-relevant research results and initiatives.

National Prison Project Journal. Washington, D.C.: National Prison Project, 1994–.

Features reports, legal analyses, legislative news, and other information about the corrections and criminal justice fields. Includes semiannual articles index and summaries of the National Prison Project.

Police Chief. Arlington, Va.: International Association of Chiefs of Police, 1953–.

Provides information to help professional law enforcement. Law enforcement practitioners share their years of education and experiences. Spans the full spectrum of law enforcement duties, from high-risk liability issues to counterterrorism efforts, from use of force to drug enforcement.

Police Studies. New York: John Jay Press, 1978–.

    Places special emphasis on comparative and international law enforcement. Approximately 50 percent of the articles deal with countries other than the United States. Includes police crime prevention programs, community relations, personnel policies and procedures, police techniques and methods, comparative police systems, and historical studies.

Prison Journal. Thousand Oaks, Calif.: Sage Publications, 1921–.

    Considered a focal point and the forum of choice for studies, ideas, and discussion of adult and juvenile confinement, treatment interventions, and alternative sanctions. Contributions in the form of articles, research notes, review essays, and book reviews explore broad themes of punishment and correctional intervention.

Social Justice. San Francisco: Social Justice, 1988–.

    Provides progressive or radical views on topics such as civil liberties, crime, prisons, the criminal justice system, racial and sexual discrimination, community strategies against crime, human rights, state terrorism, and international relations.

Women and Criminal Justice. Binghamton, N.Y.: Haworth Press, 1989–.

    Provides a forum in which the academic world, governmental agencies, and private institutions throughout the world can explore and exchange information on subjects such as women in the criminal justice profession, women as criminals, women as victims, and so on. Many articles are written from a feminist perspective.

Government Publications

    Government documents are printed at the expense of the federal government or are published by the authority of a governmental body. They provide a wealth of information in a variety of formats on crime and justice. Documents include books, pamphlets, magazines, reports, statistics, and electronic sources. The following list of resources provides access to some of these materials.

American Statistics Index (ASI). Washington, D.C.: Congressional Information Service, 1973–.

    Abstracts and indexes statistical publications of more than 500 sources within the federal government.

Bureau of Justice Statistics Bulletin. Washington, D.C.: U.S. Dept. of Justice, 1981–.

    Covers statistical information on crime, criminal victimization, capital punishment, prisons, prisoners, probation and parole, and sentences.

Compendium of Federal Justice Statistics. Washington, D.C.: U.S. Dept. of Justice, 1984–.

    Covers the number of suspects by offense, disposition of suspects, processing time, pretrial release or detention, disposition of cases, length and type of sentences, probation and parole, incarceration rate, and average time served.

Crime Victimization in the United States. Washington, D.C.: U.S. Dept. of Justice, 1973–.

Provides data on types of crime, victim characteristics, offender characteristics, crime characteristics, and reporting of crimes to police.

Directory of Criminal Justice Information Sources. Washington, D.C.: U.S. Dept. of Justice, National Institute of Justice, 1976–.

Includes a list of organizations that provide criminal justice–related information on national, regional, or statewide bases.

Index to International Statistics (IIS). Washington, D.C.: Congressional Information Services, 1983–.

A guide to statistical publications of international intergovernmental organizations. Includes basic information on population, crime, foreign trade, education, health, and so on.

Monthly Catalog of United States Government Publications. Washington, D.C.: Government Printing Office, 1951–.

Provides a listing of federal publications, including depository and non-depository documents from all federal agencies. The most comprehensive bibliography of federal publications, it is also available in print and CD-ROM.

National Institute of Justice Catalog. Washington, D.C.: U.S. Dept. of Justice, 1991–.

Provides information on new criminal justice publications.

Report to the Nation on Crime and Justice. Washington, D.C.: U.S. Dept. of Justice, Bureau of Justice, 1988.

Includes data concerning various aspects of crime from the Bureau of Justice Statistics, the FBI Uniform Crime Reports, the Bureau of Census, the National Institute of Juvenile Justice, and others. Topics covered include criminal events, victims, offenders, response to crime, and the cost of justice.

Sourcebook of Criminal Justice Statistics. Washington, D.C.: U.S. Dept. of Justice, Bureau of Justice, 1973–.

Provides a wide range of figures on the criminal justice system, public attitudes toward crime, nature and distribution of known offenses, characteristics of persons arrested, judicial processing of defendants, and persons under correctional supervision.

Statistical Abstract of the United States. Washington, D.C.: Government Printing Office, 1879–.

Provides the standard summary of statistics on social, political, and economic organization of the United States. Data is from both government and private sources. Also available in CD-ROM format.

Statistical Reference Index (SRI) . Washington, D.C.: Congressional Information Service, 1980–.

Used to identify, evaluate, and obtain significant statistical information published by U.S. associations, institutes, businesses, commercial publishers, independent research organizations, university research centers, and state governments.

Subject Bibliographies. Washington, D.C.: Government Printing Office, 1975–.

Provides a listing of government document publications on more than 300 topics. Has bibliographic information and some annotations. Subject bibliographies are free; the titles they list must be purchased.

Uniform Crime Reports for the United States. Washington, D.C.: U.S. Dept. of Justice, Federal Bureau of Investigation, 1930–.

Includes police department statistics collected by the FBI, charts and tables on murder, aggravated assault, forcible rape, burglary, larceny-theft, motor theft, and so on.

Electronic Sources

Electronic products include compact disks and online computer database systems available from commercial publishers or the federal government. Several reference resources, journals, indexes and abstracts, and other printed materials are now available in electronic format.

Congressional Masterfile: 1789-1969. Bethesda, Md.: Congressional Information Service, 1993–.

A set of databases containing bibliographic records for five major bodies of congressional publications (congressional reports, published and unpublished hearings, documents, committee prints, and Senate executive reports and documents) issued from 1789 to 1969.

Congressional Masterfile 2. Bethesda, Md.: Congressional Information Service, 1988–.

An index available on CD-ROM which contains bibliographic records for congressional publications issued from 1970 to the present.

LEXIS Federal Sentencing Library. Dayton, Ohio: Mead Data Central, 1973–.

Contains sentencing-related decisions from the Supreme Court since 1970, the Court of Appeals since 1789, and the District Courts since 1789. Also includes notices, rules, and decisions from the Federal Sentencing Commission, the Parole Commission, the DEA, and the FBI. This library file is available through the online system LEXIS/NEXIS.

National Criminal Justice Reference Service (NCJRS) Document Database on CD-ROM. Fort Collins, Colo.: Optical Publishing, 1991–.

Provides citations and abstracts of more than 118,000 criminal justice books, research reports, journal articles, grants, government documents, program descriptions, and evaluations.

NESE (National Economic Social and Environmental Data Bank) on CD-ROM. Washington, D.C.: U.S. Dept. of Commerce, 1992–.

Includes information from more than fifteen federal organizations that is fundamental to the study of economic growth, education, health issues, criminal justice, and the environment.

Newspaper Abstracts ONDISC. Louisville, Ky.: University Microfilms, 1987–.

   Provides indexing and concise abstracts for most material in the nation's leading newspapers: *Atlanta Constitution, Boston Globe, Chicago Tribune, Christian Science Monitor, Los Angeles Times, New York Times, Wall Street Journal,* and the *Washington Post.*

Statistical Masterfile. Bethesda, Md.: Congressional Information Service, 1990–.

   Contains bibliographic records for statistical publications issued by the federal government, state governments, international intergovernmental organizations, professional and trade associations, and business organizations.

Westlaw Criminal Justice Library. Eagan, Minn.: West Publishing Co., 1974–.

   Provides the complete text of articles and documents selected from a variety of law-related monographs and periodicals relating to federal criminal justice. It also includes federal sentencing guidelines from the U.S. Code, the Code of Federal Regulations, and the Federal Register. This library file is available through the online system of WESTLAW.

Electronic Bulletin Boards and Reference Referral Services

   Electronic bulletin boards are online services that enable users to enter information for others to read and that can store and retrieve files, often by a computer network called the Internet. The Internet consists of a series of interconnected networks that span the globe. Electronic bulletin boards provide the user with immediate access to current information from government agencies and private organizations. The reference referral services are information clearinghouses that enable the user to obtain current information about publications, projects, and products and services on a subject.

National Criminal Justice Reference Service (NCJRS)
   P.O. Box 6000
   Rockville, MD 20850
   (800) 851-3420
   Voice: (301) 251-5269
   Data: (301) 738-8895
   Contains current news, announcements, and online publications about justice and crime. Helps individuals and organizations involved in criminal justice policy and research obtain and share information, experiences, and views.

Bureau of Prisons Bulletin Board System
U.S. Bureau of Prisons
320 First St. NW
Washington, DC 20534
Voice: (202) 307-3104
Data: (202) 514-6102/6103
Provides an overview of Federal Bureau of Prison programs and access to Shareware and Freeware software.

Drugs and Crime Data Center & Clearinghouse
1600 Research Blvd.
Rockville, MD 20850
(800) 666-3332
Provides information on drugs and crime.

Bureau of Justice Statistics Clearinghouse
P.O. Box 6000
Rockville, MD 20850
(800) 732-3277
Provides general criminal and justice data. Responds to statistics requests by offering document database searches, statistics information packages, referrals, and other related products and services.

Juvenile Justice Clearinghouse
P.O. Box 6000
Rockville, MD 20850
(800) 638-8736
Provides a link to juvenile practitioners and policymakers. It produces and disseminates the agency's publications and prepares customized responses to information requests.

Bureau of Justice Assistance Clearinghouse
P.O. Box 6000
Rockville, MD 20850
(800) 851-3420
Informs state and local criminal justice practitioners about Bureau of Justice Assistance (BJA) products and programs. It disseminates BJA program briefs and reports to help criminal justice practitioners in their daily work.

National Victims Resource Center
P.O. Box 6000
Rockville, MD 20850
(800) 627-6872
Provides information on victims, physical and sexual abuse, victim services, domestic violence, victim/witness programs, and violent crime. Sponsored by the Office of Victims of Crime, the National Victims Resource Center responds to requests from researchers, practitioners, and individual victims for victim-related information.

National Archive of Criminal Justice Data
  University of Michigan
  P.O. Box 1248
  Ann Arbor, MI 48106
  (800) 999-0960
    Provides information on surveys on crime in machine-readable formats.

LISTSERV Lists (Discussion Groups)

  LISTSERVs are programs that act as message switches for electronic
mail on specific subjects. You can subscribe to any list on a topic of interest to you and receive all messages that are sent to the list. You have the
option to reply to those messages, and all other list subscribers will see
your message. On the Internet, the following LISTSERV is available.

National Crime Survey Discussion NCS-L
    An electronic conference devoted to discussing the design and use of
    the National Crime Survey. It covers criminology, victims of crime, and
    legal education.

Associations, Institutes, and Research Centers

Associations, institutes, and research centers provide information to the
public and private sectors on varying subjects such as new technologies,
medical developments, social and political issues, and public policy
and practices. For the researcher, they provide an excellent method for
locating relevant persons or organizations.

American Correctional Association
  8025 Laurel Lakes Ct.
  Laurel, MD 20707
    A major membership organization for corrections professionals. Studies
    causes of crime and juvenile delinquency and methods of crime control
    and prevention.

American Jail Association
  1000 Day Rd.
  Hagerstown, MD 21740
    Provides information on jail construction and operation. Works to raise
    the standards of local adult detention facilities, exchanges information on
    jail management techniques, and assures professionalization of jail per-
    sonnel.

American Justice Institute (AJI)
    705 Merchant St.
    Sacramento, CA 95814
    (916) 442-0707
    Seeks to help institutions and individuals become more willing and able to reduce the occurrence of crime, delinquency, and related social problems. Conducts research; disseminates information. Provides public and private justice agencies with statistics, demonstrations, and assistance in training and evaluation.

American Society of Criminology (ASC)
    1314 Kinnear Rd., Ste. 212
    Columbus, OH 43212
    (614) 292-9207
    Aims to develop criminology as a science and academic discipline, and to aid in the construction of criminological curricula in accredited universities.

CEGA Services (formerly Contact Center)
    P.O. Box 81826
    Lincoln, NE 68501
    Provides information in the fields of criminal justice, corrections, human services, and adult functional illiteracy. Issues a monthly publication entitled *Corrections Compendium: The National Journal for Corrections*.

Crime Stoppers International (CSI)
    3736 Eubank NE, Ste. B4
    Albuquerque, NM 87111
    (505) 294-2300
    Offers anonymity and rewards for information leading to the resolution of serious crimes and provides training, guidance, and services to improve the effectiveness of existing crime-stopper or crime-solver programs.

Criminal Justice Statistics Association (CJSA)
    444 N. Capitol St. NW, Ste. 606
    Washington, DC 20001
    Furthers the collection, analysis, dissemination, and use of data concerning crime and criminal justice at the federal and state levels, and assists in the identification and transfer of techniques for analyzing criminal justice data.

Edna McConnell Clark Foundation
    250 Park Ave.
    New York, NY 10017
    A large foundation, which, in addition to several other areas of interest, pursues an interest in the support of improved corrections services in a number of states.

Institute for Civil Justice
   1700 Main St.
   P.O. Box 2138
   Santa Monica, CA 90407-2138
   Conducts policy analysis of the American civil justice system. Seeks to
help the civil justice system become more efficient and more equitable by
supplying policymakers with research results and policy implications.

Institute for Law and Justice
   1018 Duke St.
   Alexandria, VA 22314
   Provides law and crime, management, resource allocation, training, less-
than-lethal weapons, and intermediate correctional options.

Justice Alternatives
   915 N. Wolcott Ave.
   Chicago, IL 60622
   Studies the criminal justice system, from crime prevention through prosecution and sentencing. Projects include research on young people accused
of serious crimes from 1974 to the present, alternative sentencing and case
management programs, death penalty mitigation, domestic violence, gang
violence, and related social policy issues.

NAACP Legal Defense and Educational Fund
   99 Hudson St., Ste. 1600
   New York, NY 10013
   An especially good resource on the operation of the death penalty. It
prepares periodic reports on all prisoners on death row and all executions.
Compiles statistics on capital punishment. Publishes annual report and quarterly newsletter, *Equal Justice.*

National Center for Juvenile Justice
   701 Forbes Ave.
   Pittsburgh, PA 15219
   Collects juvenile court statistics, conducts comparative analyses of juvenile and family codes and program evaluations, assesses juvenile justice
services, provides consulting on automated information and reporting systems, maintains research files and library of 1000 volumes on juvenile
justice, and operates applied technical assistance resource center.

National Center for State Courts
   300 Newport Ave.
   Williamsburg, VA 23187
   Provides information on how courts operate and function, and on how
judges and courts approach decision-making on certain issues of inquiry
in the criminal justice field.

National Center on Institutions and Alternatives
635 Slaters Ln., Ste. G-100
Alexandria, VA 22314
   Studies criminal justice, violent offenders, juvenile justice, developmental disabilities, mental health, psychological roots of violent behavior, mitigative studies in capital cases, and diagnosis and treatment of coercive sex offenders. Designs individualized alternative supervision and treatment programs for adolescents and adults, and prepares alternative sentencing proposals for presentations in court.

National Council of Juvenile and Family Court Judges
P.O. Box 8970
Reno, NV 89507
   Mainly training center for juvenile justice court judges. Compiles and disseminates research data. Provides continuing education programs.

National Council on Crime and Delinquency
685 Market St., Ste. 620
San Francisco, CA 94105
   Conducts research and initiates programs and policies to reduce crime and delinquency. This is a private agency doing contractual work in corrections nationwide and publishing monographs on current criminal justice issues.

National Criminal Justice Association (NCJA)
444 N. Capitol St. NW, Ste. 608
Washington, DC 20001
(202) 347-4900
   Seeks to focus attention on national issues and developments related to the control of crime.

National Institute of Justice
633 Indiana Ave. NW
Washington, DC 20531
   Research and development agency of the U.S. Department of Justice. The National Institute of Justice seeks to prevent and reduce crime and improve the criminal justice system.

National League of Cities
1301 Pennsylvania Ave. NW
Washington, DC 20004
   Develops and pursues a national municipal policy which can meet the future needs of cities and help cities solve critical problems they have in common. Offers training, technical assistance, and information to municipal officials to help them improve the quality of local government.

National Prison Project
1875 Connecticut Ave. NW, Ste. 410
Washington, DC 20009

Separately funded arm of the ACLU serving to take legal action against prison systems with substandard conditions. This is a prime source for information about legal cases involving prisons nationwide.

National Sentencing Project
918 F St. NW
Washington, DC 20004
A small private agency which gathers data on trends in criminal justice sentencing and issues monographs in support of what it sees as the best policies.

National Sheriffs' Association
1450 Duke St.
Alexandria, VA 22314
Provides comprehensive information on new techniques used by sheriff departments and training of personnel.

Police Executive Research Forum (PERF)
2300 M St. NW, Ste. 910
Washington, DC 20037
Studies community problem-solving policing, operational and administrative procedures, police response strategies, burglary investigations, criminal investigations, civil disorders, drug abuse and enforcement, problem-oriented policing, and spouse abuse and wife beating. Operates Police Information and Research Service to answer questions about policing and to act as a clearinghouse for information on police and management.

Police Foundation
1001 22nd St. NW, Ste. 200
Washington, DC 20037
Includes studies on reducing citizens' fear of crime, police use of force, shoplifting, child abuse, domestic disputes, women in policing, community-oriented policing, inner-city crime, and violence reduction. Seeks to increase law enforcement effectiveness through research and experimentation.

SEARCH, Inc.
7311 Greenhaven Dr., Ste. 145
Sacramento, CA 95831
Provides criminal justice information and statistics, especially their application to the interstate exchange of criminal justice histories. Studies technologies involved and the law and policy governing management of criminal justice information.

Southern Poverty Law Center
400 Washington Ave.
P.O. Box 548
Montgomery, AL 36101
Emphasis on civil rights litigation. Concerned with the prosecution of civil rights offenders.

United States Conference of Mayors
  1620 Eye St. NW
  Washington, DC 20006
    Promotes improved municipal government cooperation between cities and the federal government. Provides educational information, technical assistance, and legislative services to cities. Conducts research programs, compiles statistics, and bestows awards.

Author-Title Index

279

Subject Index

With a master's degree in social work, Paul Keve has worked in probation and parole programs and in both adult and juvenile correctional institutions. He has administered agencies in the states of Virginia, Delaware, and Minnesota, in the latter two of which he served as director of the state correctional systems. Keve has written eight other books on correctional topics, and served on the faculty of Virginia Commonwealth University. He is now retired as professor emeritus.

Louveller Luster is the team leader for the Government Documents Office, University Library Services, Virginia Commonwealth University.